Cultures reveal themselves in how they react to death: how they ritualize it, tell its story, heal themselves. Before the modern period, death and dying seemed definitive, public, and appropriate. The industrial revolution, the Great War, and the radical reenvisioning of inner and outer reality after Marx, Darwin, Nietzsche, Einstein, van Gennep, and Freud, destabilized cultural norms and transformed the protocols of death and dying. In *Fictional death and the modernist enterprise* Alan Friedman traces the semiotics of death and dying in twentieth-century fiction, history, and culture. He describes how modernist writers either, like Forster and Woolf, elided rituals of dying and death; or, rediscovering the body as Lawrence and Hemingway did, transformed Victorian "aesthetic death" into modern "dirty death." And he goes on to show how, through postmodern fiction and AIDS narratives, death has once again become cultural currency.

FICTIONAL DEATH AND THE MODERNIST ENTERPRISE

FICTIONAL DEATH AND THE MODERNIST ENTERPRISE

ALAN WARREN FRIEDMAN
University of Texas at Austin

Published by the Press Syndicate of the University of Cambridge
The Pitt Building, Trumpington Street, Cambridge CB2 1RP
40 West 20th Street, New York, NY 10011-4211, USA
10 Stamford Road, Oakleigh, Victoria 3166, Australia

First published 1995

Printed in Great Britain at the University Press, Cambridge

A catalogue record for this book is available from the British Library

Library of Congress cataloguing in publication data applied for

ISBN 0 521 44261 3 hardback

CE

For Liz and Daniel
with Love

"So here it is at last, the distinguished thing."

Henry James, on his deathbed

Contents

Illustrations

Acknowledgments

I am grateful to many people for their assistance, advice, and support during the long process that produced this book. From our first meeting as colleagues twenty-five years ago, Charles Rossman has been, professionally and personally, the most energetic and intelligent supporter of my work; his enthusiasm proved invaluable whenever I drew upon it. This project began with a seminar on death that I taught at the University of Texas. On the first occasion, it was team-taught with Betty Sue Flowers, from whose thinking on the subject I have learned much over the years. I am grateful to the students, both graduate and undergraduate, who took my courses on fictional death.

For over two decades I have discussed thanatological matters (among many others) with Michael Wheeler. I benefited greatly from our time as colleagues at the University of Lancaster and in Oxford, from his splendid book *Death and the Future Life in Victorian Literature and Theology*, and especially from our joint session at the London Institute of Contemporary Arts' conference, "Death and the Aesthetic," that celebrated the publication of Elisabeth Bronfen's book, *Over Her Dead Body: Death, Femininity and the Aesthetic*. I am grateful to the organizers, Helena Reckitt of the ICA and Anita Roy of Manchester University Press, since the rewriting I did for that occasion helped me to reconceive the entire book.

My work has benefited from the conversation, criticism, and support of Bernard Benstock, Marie Farge, Wayne Lesser, José Limon, Claude Levy, Hans Mark, Jeffrey Meyers, Neil Nehring, Thomas Palaima, Walt Rostow, Norman Sherry, John Slatin, Robert Twombly, Warwick Wadlington, and Thomas Whitbread. I am very grateful to Michael Levenson who, as the initial reader for Cambridge, offered enormously valuable criticism of the unfinished manuscript. Sue and Kurt Heinzelman and Janis and Evan Bergman-Carton have been wonderful colleagues and even better friends. The University of Texas Research Institute provided financial support including two semesters' leave; two Fulbright travel awards enabled me to work in England and France. I have had the benefit of excellent research assistants – Melissa Hirsch, Mary Mathis, and Ivana Slavnic – and of the most judicious and supportive of editors, Kevin Taylor, who has been unfailingly responsive and helpful to all my inquiries and concerns.

My greatest debt, in this and in all things, is to my wife, Elizabeth Butler Cullingford. Through constant questioning of my intentions and arguments, a kind of running domestic seminar, she made me think harder and more precisely about what I wanted this book to achieve. Through two close and painstaking readings of different versions of the manuscript, her rigorous, even ruthless, criticism helped to make it a book that at least seeks the level of her own high standards. By the end, her intimate collaboration was responsible for much of what the book achieves: she deserves its dedication on professional grounds alone. The mistakes and inadequacies remain my own.

Portions of this book have appeared in different form in *Mosaic* 15, 1 (Winter 1982); *Essays on the Contemporary British Novel.* Eds. Hedwig Bock and Albert Wertheim (Munich: Verlag, 1986); *On Miracle Ground II: Second International Lawrence Durrell Conference Proceedings.* Eds. Lawrence W. Markert and Carol Pierce (University of Baltimore Monographs, 1986); *The Modernists: Studies in a Literary Phenomenon.* Eds. Lawrence B. Gamache and Ian S. MacNiven (Fairleigh Dickinson University Press, 1987); *Graham Greene: A Revaluation.* Ed. Jeffrey Meyers (London: Macmillan, 1990).

Grateful acknowledgment is also due for the following extracts:

From *The Hour of Our Death* by Philippe Ariès. Copyright © 1977 by Editions du Seuil. Trans. H. Weaver. Copyright © 1980 by Alfred A. Knopf, Inc. Reprinted by permission of Random House, Inc. and Georges Borchardt, Inc.

From Graham Greene, letter to Vivien Dayrell-Browning, 10 March 1926. The Harry Ransom Humanities Research Center, University of Texas and David Higham Associates.

From John Lehmann, "Virginia Woolf's *Mrs. Dalloway*: A Reconsideration." Unpublished, undated. The Harry Ransom Humanities Research Center, University of Texas and John Lehmann.

From *Beloved* by Toni Morrison. Copyright © 1987 by Toni Morrison. Reprinted by permission of International Creative Management, Inc.

From Virginia Woolf, *Mrs. Dalloway*, Add MSS 51044–46. The British Library and Quentin Bell.

Introduction

Death and taxes, as American folk wisdom has it, are the immutable certainties of human existence. This adage implies nostalgia for transcendental signifiers, even unpleasant ones, in a world otherwise bereft of enduring truths and deities. Michel Foucault has shown that sex and madness, both read at times as natural, as anterior to their expressive forms, represent culturally contingent modes of discourse, concatenations of local factors, a semiotics of hierarchy and authority. Taxes, too, are multiply signified. More an imposition of social and political philosophy and power than of economic policy, they are direct or indirect, overt or covert, discriminatory rather than equitable, manipulated and evaded: never the stable, universal signifier of popular lore.

And what of death? Surely its substance, meaning, and inevitability are undeniable and fixed? Death comes to all; death waits for no one; death defines life from the moment it begins. Yet the same may be said of death as of sex and madness, and taxes. We seek to tame, control, order, evade, attain, summon, and dismiss death in as many ways, and with as varied success, as there are cultures and people, and thereby define death as it defines us. Death's innumerable vehicles – disease, famine, accident, old age, murder, suicide, execution, sacrifice, warfare – render a single model of dying, even so valuable a one as Elisabeth Kübler-Ross', reductive and false when applied as a rule rather than a tool.

The anthropocentrism and artifice of death are vividest in terminal visions and last words. Shakespeare's dying John of Gaunt evokes their power and appeal: "O, but they say the tongues of dying men / Enforce attention like deep harmony" (*Richard II* 2.1.5–6). The literature of last words represents appropriately idiosyncratic final self-projections. Though his letters speak of death as extinction, Henry James supposedly greeted its arrival with: "So here it is at last, the distinguished thing."[1] James' "at last" can be read variously: as the ultimate surrender, with relief, anxiety, or pride, to what can no longer be forestalled or evaded, or as the successful evocation of something long sought, a ritual completed. However read, James' salutation culminates a tradition in which nineteenth-century agnostics like John Stuart Mill saw death, of which the dying person should be fully cognizant, as life's climax.[2] If reports can be believed, appropriate dramatic final words include Goethe's "More light! More light!"; Hegel's "Only one man ever understood me ... And he didn't understand me"; Heine's "God will forgive me; it is His trade"; Thoreau's "One world at a time" (in response to "How does the opposite shore appear?"); Oscar Wilde's "I am dying, as I have lived, beyond my means"; Gertrude Stein's "What *is* the answer? ... In that case, what is the question?"

Such utterances seem *too* good, too apposite, mythic closure for the life such dying retrospectively reconfigures. The notion of final words, in fact, seems more fictive and ritualistic than mimetic. Goethe's supposed final cry for light, for example, has a dubious pedigree. An alternative tradition, of equally uncertain authenticity, makes Wilde's final words an aesthetic judgment on his French hotel's execrable wallpaper: "One of us has got to go."[3] And James, according to Edith Wharton, was behaving like one of his fictional interpreting consciousnesses: quoting "a voice distinctly not his own" that he heard in his room.[4] Whatever the imaginative projection at work here, it is unsurprising that death, for James, would "speak" with Jamesian rhetoric and sentiment. For James' "distinguished thing" is also the distinctive thing, not only transcending all else but different at each occurrence and requiring an appropriate acknowledgment and response.

Edwin Shneidman, a pioneer in thanatology, which derived from the work of Kübler-Ross and Geoffrey Gorer, writes that "Death is oxymoronic, a paradox made up of contrasting values, opposite trends, and even contradictory facts."[5] Ian Wilson tells of an Englishman and a Chinese visiting their deceased loved ones. The Englishman has brought flowers, the Chinese food. "Appalled at the apparent waste, the Englishman asks of the Chinese: 'When do your dead come to eat all this food.' 'When your dead come to smell your flowers,' replies the Chinese."[6] Frederick Hoffman writes, "Mortality attracts to itself all of the major images and metaphors of any culture ... Death has a special influence upon literary manners."[7]

For death, as Philippe Ariès and others have shown, is not only a biological occurrence but a complex of historically specific and materially determined events: a set of attitudes and a matter of perspective; a drama performed by and for the participants and their community; an experience created by and during its enactment; a determinant of narrative and ritual expression. It is in this sense that, as Yeats proclaims, "Man has created death."[8]

Why *fictional* death? Because death is central to representation and because it is represented as central in fictional texts. "Storytelling," as Hillis Miller writes, "is always after the fact, and it is always constructed over a loss."[9] A text, Walter Ong maintains, "is so much a thing of the past that it carries with it necessarily an aura of accomplished death."[10] Unless and until it touches someone near and dear or great and good, death is fictive for most of us during most of our lives: distant, other, abstract, a mythical construct. And unlike other experiences, death is fictional even when closest because it is always vicarious, never truly our own. As Kübler-Ross says, "death is never possible in regard to ourselves," never something lived through.[11] Our experience of death, then, lies between these two extremes, and in the mediated constructs through which we know it.

And why modernist death? Like Ariès, I acknowledge the difficulty (even arbitrariness) of dating cultural trends, of defining when dominant attitudes or practices end or begin. With Thomas Kuhn, I acknowledge that conflicting paradigms may coexist peacefully.[12] Literary periods, like Einstein's "fundamentals of scientific theory," are convenient fictions, retrospective narratives of shaping authority that serve the definer's purposes. They overlap: new ones begin before earlier ones end; trends continue even as they are superseded. Modernism's beginnings are located in the Renaissance (or "early modern period"); in the eighteenth century (with the rise of the middle class and mass literacy and communication); between 1815 and 1830;[13] in the Victorian period with the industrial revolution, Marx, Darwin, and the death of God; in 1900 with "the sudden irruption of forces totally new"[14] or with Victoria's death in 1901; with the outbreak of World War One, or with England's first conscript army in 1916.[15]

Literary modernism, conventionally dated 1890–1930, is commonly seen as beginning by rejecting the dead end of naturalism, with its pseudo-scientific emphasis on reportage. For Arthur

Symons, modernism was a "revolt against exteriority, against rhetoric, against a materialistic tradition," a spiritual liberation that assumed "the duties and responsibilities of ... sacred ritual,"[16] and it climaxed in the triumphant "blend of realism and symbolism pioneered by James and Conrad."[17] I have no quarrel with literary modernism's common dates and definitions, though I consider them convenient rather than "true" and often range beyond them. I will, for example, argue at times that modernism is bracketed by the two world wars – what Ford Madox Ford, describing the first, calls "this crack across the table of History" (*Parade's End* 510), a phrase equally applicable to the second: apocalypse then, and then again.

In this "century of death," as Gil Elliot and others have called it, death presses in "from all sides" and "the best way to distinguish the two or three literary generations of our century is in their manner of responding to the fact of death – that is, in their manner of somehow getting beyond it."[18] During the modernist period, death in Western culture and literature differs radically from what it was before and after. *Fictional Death and the Modernist Enterprise* investigates how modernist texts (and, concomitantly, pre- and postmodernist ones as well) reflect and challenge extra-literary explorations and expectations of death, how culture and literature create and read each other.

CHAPTER I

Fictional death and the modernist enterprise

Every story continued far enough ends in death;[1] yet every recounting suspends finality. In the paradigmatic *Thousand and One Nights*, Scheherazade's narrative simultaneously foregrounds and forestalls the death that inspires and requires it, and thereby exercises shaping authority that exceeds ordinary mortal limits.[2] Fictive titles often proclaim death's centrality in storytelling: Tolstoy's "The Death of Ivan Ilych," Mann's "Death in Venice," Joyce's "The Dead" and *Finnegans Wake*, Lawrence's *The Man Who Died*, Faulkner's *As I Lay Dying* and *Requiem for a Nun*, Hemingway's *For Whom the Bell Tolls*, Beckett's *Malone Dies*, for example. Other titles – Forster's *The Longest Journey* and *A Passage to India*, Lawrence's "The Woman Who Rode Away," Woolf's *The Voyage Out*, Ford's *The Rash Act*, Beckett's *The Unnamable* – reveal their thanatological significance only after we have read the texts they subtend. Like history, death is narrative as well as event: a process created, ordered, and performed by survivors, or sometimes non-survivors.

In "Four Quartets" T.S. Eliot writes, "human kind / Cannot bear very much reality."[3] But we can and we do: only reality must be sanctioned, "naturalized," by history and culture. For Gil Elliot, "The manner in which people die reflects more than any other fact the value of a society."[4] Concurring, the anthropologists Huntington and Metcalf maintain that in all societies "Life becomes transparent against the background of death, and fundamental social and cultural issues are revealed."[5] More than any other manifestation, narratives of death and dying reflect a culture's symbolic and mythic truths. Artifacts of death – rituals of dying and funeral, graveyards and tombs, wills and death certificates, the corpse itself – are as much communal constructs, dramatic and narrative performance, as are the texts that contain them.

For all its haphazardness, death long seemed an ordering principle, a force and form of moral and aesthetic meaning; in turn, it lent itself to appropriation by ritual and narrative, in which it served a climactic, shaping function. Ariès views medieval death as integral to everyday experience: in literature and in society death and dying were foreknown, expected, and accepted;[6] or so the record suggests, since those who "foresaw" deaths but did not die were unlikely to document the mistake. Much evidence supports Ariès' historiographical reconstruction, yet it is unlikely to be a full account of the past. Because I find his work stimulating and important, I want to consider its strengths and weaknesses.

Ariès' eclectic historiography has been challenged on grounds that period and cultural distinctions are matters of degree rather than absolute, and that histories of ideas make the past seem tidier than it was. Though admiring Ariès' capacious sweep, Robert Darnton warns that "Shifts in world view normally occur at a glacial pace, unmarked by events and without visible turning points." Noting the "heterogeneity and sparseness" of Ariès' documentation, Darnton argues that other evidence might tell a different, perhaps less astounding story. He ambiguously concludes: "The audacity of the undertaking must be admired, even if it bears no more relation to reality than the cartography of Amerigo Vespucci."[7]

Ariès himself, who calls his method "intuitive and subjective" (*Hour* xvii), first noted its limitations: he wrote mostly within and about a particular Catholic country with a unique history, and from his own cultural circumstances. Nonetheless, what Ian Morris calls Ariès' "great achievement" has been fruitful for historians, many of whom accept and deepen his insights.[8] Ariès' brilliance lies in his narrative power and aperçus, his opening of inquiry, rather than his historiography's tidy conclusiveness. Such inductive thinking now characterizes the work of anthropologists and ethnographers, who prefer the messy specifics of particular times and places to the tidy universals of paradigmatic templates. Ariès has aided the reenvisioning of cultures as unique rather than exemplary, an approach that empowers materialist investigations into the Western family and sexuality like those of Lawrence Stone, Michel Foucault, and Stephen Heath. It also grounds pioneering studies of death by Geoffrey Gorer, Elisabeth Kübler-Ross, Robert Kastenbaum, Avery Weisman, Edwin Shneidman, and many others. Such investigations convincingly argue that there is nothing "natural" about how a people tell their stories of sex or death. Both are products of culture: mediated, made, symbolic.

The major figures associated with the onset of European modernism – Marx, Darwin, Nietzsche, and Kierkegaard in the latter part of the nineteenth century; Einstein, van Gennep, and Freud after the turn of the century – produced radical reformulations of earlier paradigms of humankind and the universe, and thus of the meaning of death. Reorientations in physics, anthropology, and psychoanalysis provided cultural and historical contexts for modernist death. As Heisenberg comments, "Changes in the foundations of modern science may perhaps be viewed as symptoms of shifts in the fundamentals of our existence which then express themselves simultaneously in many places, be it in changes in our way of life or in our usual thought forms."[9] Each of these figures subverted the inherited cultural paradigms; yet in retrospect each seems more equivocal and less radical. Kuhn argues that scientific paradigms overlap, and what once seemed revolutionary may seem evolutionary a generation hence: it may even become reactionary by establishing a site of resistance to the *next* radical shift. In this, scientific revolutions parallel other cultural changes: literary modernism, for example, now often seems more conservative than innovative.

A second paradigm shift, toward the end of the modern period, had a similar impact. The 1920s saw reactions against the innovations of Einstein, van Gennep, and Freud. They led to quantum mechanics and then to chaos theory, to the kind of cultural studies associated with anthropologists like Clifford Geertz, and to post-Freudian psychoanalysis and literary postmodernism. Just as modernism both continued and reacted against Victorian paradigms, postmodernism rejects and extends modernism. Modernism's roots lie in the late nineteenth century, though its beginning may be said to climax with the Great War; postmodernism's roots lie in World War Two. Attitudes toward death also changed radically at the beginning and again at the end of the modern period. I will discuss these cultural transformations in order to distinguish modernist death from what preceded and what followed.

Enlightenment faith in progress and in our increasing comprehension of life and death retained potency throughout the nineteenth century. According to Habermas, Enlightenment thinkers expected "that the arts and sciences would promote not only the control of natural forces but also understanding of the world and of the self, moral progress, the justice of institutions and even the happiness of human beings."[10] The Newtonian Pierre Laplace (1749–1827) conflated theology, philosophy, and mathematics when he posited a powerful intelligence capable of embracing "in the same formula the movements of the greatest bodies of the universe and those of the lightest atom; for it, nothing would be uncertain and the future, as the past, would be present to its eyes."[11] Laplace, who supposedly told Napoleon "Give me the initial details and I will tell you the whole story of the world," maintained that all events follow nature's laws as necessarily as the sun's revolutions.[12]

Nearly a hundred years after Laplace, and as Einstein was beginning his work in relativity, Lord Kelvin (1824–1907) declared that scientists like himself would soon have nothing to do because physics, a coherent system, a closed set, was about to be totally understood. Only two major areas of exploration remained: the Michelson–Morley experiment concerning the existence of the ether, and blackbody radiation.[13] The results of these explorations, however, were astonishing and problematic rather than conclusive: the Michelson–Morley experiment led to special relativity; blackbody radiation to quantum mechanics. (Chaos theory or complexity seems likely to have as great an impact; see chapter 13 below.)

According to Abraham Pais, Einstein's biographer, "In all the history of physics, there has never been a period of transition as abrupt, as unanticipated, and over as wide a front as the decade 1895–1905."[14] The Harvard physicist Gerald Holton describes the predominant scientific (and cultural) worldview until the mid-nineteenth century as

> a static, homocentric, hierarchically ordered, harmoniously arranged cosmos . . . a finite universe in time and space; a divine temple, God-given, God-expressing, God-penetrated, knowable . . . This representation was gradually supplanted by another, particularly in the last half of the nineteenth century. The universe became unbounded, "restless," . . . a weakly coupled ensemble of infinitely many separate, individually sovereign parts and events. Though evolving, it is continually interrupted by random discontinuities on the cosmological scale as well as on the submicroscopic scale.[15]

What had seemed solidly anchored was suddenly cast adrift: nothing, it seemed, was possible without God and God was impossible.

Kuhn argues that a scientific revolution occurs when a once-honored theory is rejected in favor of another incompatible with it,[16] yet the extraordinary breakthroughs of this period, like literary modernism, affirmed received modes of apprehension even while innovating new ones. Inheriting a physics dominated by belief that both knowledge and the universe were finite and increasingly within our grasp, Einstein endorsed that belief. Relativity challenged Newtonian physics in certain fundamental ways; for example, by undermining the principle of simultaneity: "under relativity, as soon as either the particle or the scientist begins to move, the whole scheme of simultaneity becomes warped."[17] Yet Newtonian mechanics explained macrocosmic actions so well that the universe seemed manageable, comprehensible, divinely ordered.[18] According to Einstein, the enormous practical success of Newton's theory "may well have prevented him and the physicists of the eighteenth and nineteenth centuries from recognizing the fictitious character of the principles of his system." But by "fictitious" Einstein did not mean false; Newtonian principles were, rather, "free inventions of the human mind,"[19] and therefore as true in their way as relativity. Holton argues, in fact, that Einstein's special theory of relativity, like most scientific "revolutions," was fundamentally reactionary, a return to classical purity like that of the *Principia*.[20] Einstein considered relativity a natural development rather than a revolutionary act.[21] As Hans Mark has said, "Einstein was a Newtonian to the core."[22]

Einstein posited an equivalence and harmony between science and religion: "Science without religion is lame, religion without science is blind"; but religion had priority for him as it had for Newton.[23] Though he maintained that the mysterious is the "most beautiful experience we can have,"[24] Einstein echoes Laplace and Kelvin when he says, "The most incomprehensible thing about the universe is that it is comprehensible." Einstein saw modern physics, for all its revolutionary impact, as compatible with both Newtonian mechanics and faith in progress: relativity altered not the world but our perception of it. Like Laplace, Einstein spent much of his life on a theological quest for "that grail of science, the Grand Unified Theory or 'theory of everything.'"[25] The narrator of Salman Rushdie's postmodernist *Satanic Verses* mocks scientists like Einstein for seeking to resuscitate the God that Marx, Darwin, and Nietzsche had killed: "once they had proved the existence of a single unified force of which electromagnetism, gravity and the strong and weak forces of the new physics were all merely aspects, avatars, one might say, or angels, then what would we have but the oldest thing of all, a supreme entity controlling all creation" (81–2). Rushdie is right: Einstein's quarrel was not with those who preceded him, or with God, but with successors like Bohr and Heisenberg. He maintained a profound skepticism toward quantum mechanics because it relied on probabilistic uncertainty,[26] which he could not reconcile with a divine Creator or the traditional view of death as life's meaningful culmination.

Curiously, Einstein's antipathy toward quantum mechanics, which he first saw as logically inconsistent and then as an incomplete description of nature, was only strengthened by his inability to substantiate his opposition. In 1912 Einstein wrote, "The more success the quantum theory has, the sillier it looks"; and he never wavered from or succeeded in his quest for "a model of reality which shall represent events themselves and not merely the probability of their occurrence."[27] He maintained faith in what he called objective reality "although, up to now, *success* is against it."[28] He was especially upset because quantum mechanics rested on his own work, and it was as revolutionary *and* as conservative as relativity. Ironically, Steven Weinberg argues in *Dreams of a Final Theory*, it was Einstein's rejection of quantum mechanics that doomed his quest.

Modern science was most revolutionary in its subversion of faith in a finite, knowable universe. It is increasingly a matter of scientific, as well as literary, knowledge that what we "know" largely depends on where we stand; that some things are unknowable; and that much of the rest, like light, accords with self-contradictory principles. As early as 1924 Einstein wrote unhappily that there are "now two theories of light, both indispensable, and – as one must admit today despite twenty years of tremendous effort on the part of theoretical physicists – without any logical connection."[29] Depending on the measuring equipment, light proves to be a wave phenomenon or a stream of particles or, somehow, both. As if discussing a Jamesian interpreting consciousness or Yeats' dancer and dance, Holton writes that at the atomic level the system being observed and the measuring instruments form a single whole with the results depending heavily on the apparatus: "The study of nature is a study of artifacts that appear during an engagement between the scientist and the world in which he finds himself. And these artifacts themselves are seen through the lens of theory."[30]

In quantum mechanics, not experimental failure but paradoxes inhering in nature compel "a formulation of statistical laws." We can predict how, on average, a particle or a storm cloud or a person or a community will behave, though in neither nature nor human systems nor fictional representation does an "average" exist. Computation allows us to speak statistically about phenomena, but the process is irreversible: we can deduce nothing about particular particles, lives, or cultures once they are subsumed within the general. Beginning in the 1920s, Heisenberg's uncertainty principle, Bohr's theory of complementarity (which accepts dualities as irreconcilable), non-Euclidian geometry, Gödel's proof of mathematical indeterminacy, and Bell's theorem that "common sense" ideas about the macrocosmic as well as subatomic worlds are profoundly deficient[31] would seem definitively to have shattered Laplace and Condorcet's vision.

Since Einstein, the ontological status of scientific knowledge has been under assault. Experimental data seems increasingly to represent not the "real" world, but the relationship of scientist, equipment, and cultural context. Science and aesthetics have become complementary, with anthropologists, historians, biographers, and theoretical scientists often sounding like poets, philosophers, or literary theorists: "At least since Copernicus defended his theory as 'pleasing to the mind,' it has been an everyday fact in the life of scientists that some of the terms and attributes they use have for them great motivating power but cannot be subjected to contingency analysis." Heisenberg, rejecting a contemporary's view of wave mechanics, said, "The more I ponder the physical part of Schrödinger's theory, the more disgusting it appears to me," while of Heisenberg's approach Schrödinger in turn said, "I was frightened away [by it], if not repelled." The theoretical physicist Paul Dirac philosophized that a "theory that has some mathematical beauty is more likely to be correct than an ugly one that gives a detailed fit to some experiments."[32] Yet nature goes its messy, often unpredictable way, as when circular orbits, long a tenet of astronomical and religious faith, were displaced by Kepler's ellipses.[33]

In 1959, shortly before the emergence of chaos theory, Karl Popper romantically, but justifiably, summarized the state of the art:

Science is not a system of certain, or well-established, statements; nor is it a system which steadily advances towards a state of finality ... *We do not know: we can only guess.* And our guesses are guided by ... faith in laws, in regularities which we can uncover – discover. Like Bacon, we might describe our own contemporary science – "the method of reasoning which men now ordinarily apply to nature" – as consisting of "anticipations, rash and premature" and as "prejudices."[34]

Yet for Bohr and Heisenberg, quantum mechanics, like relativity before it, seemed so revolutionary and comprehensive that, echoing Kelvin, they pronounced the end of scientific revolution.[35]

The cosmologist Stephen Hawking reprised this theme in a 1980 lecture entitled, "Is the End in Sight for Theoretical Physics?" Hawking proclaimed that "We already know the physical laws that govern everything we experience in everyday life ... It is a tribute to how far we have come in theoretical physics that it now takes enormous machines and a great deal of money to perform an experiment whose results we cannot predict."[36] Yet, James Gleick writes, Hawking

recognized that understanding nature's laws on the terms of particle physics left unanswered the question of how to apply those laws to any but the simplest of systems. Predictability is one thing in a cloud chamber where two particles collide at the end of a race around an accelerator. It is something else altogether in the simplest tub of roiling fluid, or in the earth's weather, or in the human brain.[37]

Particle physicists, even agnostics like Steven Weinberg, continue to pursue Einstein's dream;[38] many chaologists, however, reject Einstein's dictum that God does not play dice with the universe. Niels Bohr said, "Nor is it our business to prescribe to God how He should run the world,"[39] while Joseph Ford maintains that God *does* play dice, "But they're loaded dice. And the main objective of physics now is to find out by what rules were they loaded and how can we use them for our own ends."[40] Suggesting that the question is not whether, "but *how* God plays dice," Ian Stewart makes a proposal that might have pleased even Einstein: "Either God is playing dice, or He's playing a deeper game that we have yet to fathom."[41]

Like anthropologists and historians who repudiate the notion that civilizations evolve, Gleick argues, Kuhn destroyed "the traditional view that science progresses by the accretion of knowledge, each discovery adding to the last, and that new theories emerge when new experimental facts require them. He deflated the view of science as an orderly process of asking questions and finding their answers."[42] Once the envy of the social sciences, scientific research now depends on preconceptions and accidents.[43] Not only is scientific "progress" discontinuous and disorderly, but it is as likely, or likelier, to produce Chernobyl or ozone depletion or AIDS as to cure tuberculosis. Where both life and death had seemed increasingly under scientific control, its promises and threats have become inextricable from each other.

In 1909, four years after Einstein published his work on special relativity, Arnold van Gennep, a founder of modern anthropology, produced his classic study of rites of passage. His Victorian predecessors, like Herbert Spencer, Lewis Henry Morgan, and Edward Taylor, who viewed Western civilization as the apex of social evolution and all Western ceremonial behavior as relics of superstitious eras, had traced civilization's evolution through progressively more complex, moral, and rational stages. Van Gennep, like his US contemporary Franz Boas, broke with this paradigm by discerning in rites of passage a universal structure and meaning; like Einstein, van Gennep saw a transcendent pattern in seemingly discrete events.[44] Dying, the ultimate rite of passage, has a structure and meaning paralleling other rituals, for death relates to life as marriage relates to being single: preliminal rites of separation, liminal transition rites, and postliminal rites of incorporation.[45] Positing a tripartite paradigm for all rituals of passage, van Gennep overrode both local differences and his predecessors' presuppositions about cultural hierarchies. Yet like Heisenberg and Bohr, modern anthropologists argued that not only what is observed and reported but also what exists depends largely on perspective, the cultural and personal lenses through which the world is viewed.

Reacting to van Gennep's kind of anthropology, Geertz postulated what has become basic to cultural studies and postmodernism:

> the image of a constant human nature independent of time, place, and circumstance ... may be an illusion ... what man is may be so entangled with where he is, who he is, and what he believes that it is inseparable from them ... modern anthropology ... is firm in the conviction that men unmodified by the customs of particular places do not in fact exist, have never existed, and most important, could not ... exist.[46]

Anthropologists like Geertz, who emphasize culture*s* (uncapitalized and plural), sound in some ways more like van Gennep's predecessors than like van Gennep. Tending, however, to view communities as inherently valuable rather than as occupying particular positions on some cultural scale, they pursue variation and uniqueness rather than essentialist common denominators and eternal truths about the human situation.

Not all of Geertz's contemporaries emphasize cultural distinctions. Lionel Tiger and Robin Fox, for example, adhere to what Geertz calls "the uniformitarian view of man," which seeks to transcend accidents of cultural difference.[47] Recent genetic studies of gender and of separated identical twins suggest a complex relationship between biology and environment. In their multicultural survey of funeral practices, Huntington and Metcalf reject the essentialist explanation of attitudes toward death, yet they do so in essentialist terms: "The baffling combination of the familiar and the strange, the universal in the cultural particular, confronts the anthropologist even when examining human sentiments, even human reactions to death."[48] The goal seems to be a balance between van Gennep and Geertz: the phrase "the universal in the cultural particular" is the essence of essentialism; but the ability to find "the familiar and the strange" in near and remote practices has become central to cultural studies. Focusing on cultural and social details, Geertz nonetheless reconciles these positions with a positivist formula van Gennep might have propounded: "the road to the general, to the revelatory simplicities of science, lies through a concern with the particular, the circumstantial, the concrete."[49]

Freud shared both van Gennep's essentialist approach to death and his view of life as a series of stages: "There is scarcely any other matter ... upon which our thoughts and feelings have changed so little since the very earliest times, and in which discarded forms have been so completely preserved ... as our relation to death. Two things account for our conservatism: the strength of our original emotional reaction to death and the insufficiency of our scientific knowledge about it" ("*Uncanny*" 241–2). What, Freud had earlier asked, "is the attitude of our unconscious towards the problem of death? The answer must be: almost exactly the same as that of primaeval man. In this respect, as in many others, the man of prehistoric times survives unchanged in our unconscious," and is manifested, for example, as "the doctrine of primal guilt, of original sin" (*War and Death* 296, 292). Focusing on acultural determinism, Freud speaks of destructiveness and the pleasure principle as equally fundamental to the "vacillating rhythm" of life (*Pleasure Principle*

41), yet he also asserts that the pleasure principle "seems actually to serve the death instincts" (63). He conceptualizes the desire to move beyond the pleasure principle as "*an urge inherent in organic life to restore an earlier* [inorganic] *state of things*" because "of the *conservative* nature of living substance" (36). Seeking his own key "to a universal logic of human social life," Freud formulated his theory of "death instincts," pronouncing that "*the aim of all life is death*" (38).

According to both Ernest Jones, Freud's biographer, and the psychoanalyst Erich Fromm, Freud derived the theory of the death instinct from obsessive self-absorption: "He thought of dying every day, after he was forty ... To assume that man needs to die because death is the hidden goal of his life might be considered a kind of comfort destined to alleviate his fear of death."[50] But the proximate, larger cause of Freud's postulating the death instinct was that extraordinary manifestation of man's destructiveness, the "terrible war which has just ended" (*Pleasure Principle* 12). The optimistic vision characteristic of Europe's middle class of Freud's time, which he had shared, seemed irreconcilable with the hate and destruction unleashed by the Great War.[51] As the underlying mechanism of Western society's tragedy, the repression theory underlies the death instinct, for Freud saw repression as creating civilization *and* its discontents. Hence, though he valorized both civilization and repression, Freud saw self-destructive contradictions within them.

Freud evinces his own contradictions in his correspondence with Einstein, *Why War?*, written shortly before Hitler's accession to power in 1933: he reaffirms his belief in death instincts even as he attempts to resuscitate the meliorist view of history. Maintaining that organic reasons oblige us to be pacifists who "have a *constitutional* intolerance of war," he prophesies "an end to the waging of war. By what paths or by what side-tracks this will come about we cannot guess. But one thing we *can* say: whatever fosters the growth of civilization works ... against war" (214–15). Freud's writings about war and death, more suggestive and problematic than definitive and conclusive, are amenable to multiple interpretations. Fromm says, "Freud's reliance on a 'constitutional' intolerance to war was ... an attempt to transcend the tragic perspective of his death instinct,"[52] while Girard, who links Freud to early ethnologists in seeking "to fathom the hidden meaning of primitive religions and to establish their essential unity," argues that the death wish is "a last surrender to mythological thinking, a final manifestation of that ancient belief that human violence can be attributed to some outside influence – to gods, to Fate, to some force men can hardly be expected to control . . . It is an act of evasion, an attempt to 'pass the buck.'"[53] Freud's "mythological thinking" also contains a gendered quality: unlike the generative process that culminates in childbirth, the death wish expresses patriarchal thinking that climaxed in World War One.

Fromm maintains that "aggression and destructiveness are not biologically given and spontaneously flowing impulses," and that Freud's elegantly simple vision contravenes historical reality.[54] Freud himself sometimes writes against both essentialism and the meliorist view of ethical progress:

> When the furious struggle of the present war has been decided, each one of the victorious fighters will return home joyfully to his wife and children, unchecked and undisturbed by thoughts of the enemies he has killed . . . primitive races . . . act differently in this respect, or did until they came under the influence of our civilization . . . when [savages] return victorious from the war-path they may not set foot in their villages or touch their wives till they have atoned for the murders they committed in war by penances which are often long and tedious . . . behind this superstition there lies concealed a vein of ethical sensitiveness which has been lost by us civilized men. (*War and Death* 295)

Yet the "primitive" rituals Freud describes may have been for purification rather than atonement: cleansing rather than penance is required for warriors to resume social life without threatening communal health and stability. Susceptible to multiple interpretations, the evidence may serve various historical reconstructions.

For all its contradictions and ambiguities, the death instinct, like van Gennep's rites of passage and Einsteinian relativity, assailed categorical thinking. Asserting an essentialist and archetypal vision that posits, in Einstein's phrase, an "objective reality" that is solid and stable, even if our comprehension falls short, Einstein, van Gennep, and Freud subverted hierarchical oppositions between civilized and uncivilized; science and religion; developed present and "primitive" past; history and myth; dying and other rites of passage. Yet their failure to reconcile essentialist ideas with material history, as much as their achievements, provoked a continuing controversy that helped to foster modernism.

British and American modernists like Conrad, Ford, Forster, Lawrence, Woolf, Hemingway, Faulkner, and Joyce have long been linked with popular conceptions and misconceptions of turn-of-the-century scientists, anthropologists, psychoanalysts, and historians. Lawrence Durrell, for one, saw Einstein's relativity theory as "vital to our understanding of the age we live in, and the literature which characterizes that age." He suggests that Joyce, Woolf, and Eliot, in turning from Newtonian mechanics to "the space–time continuum" and cyclical history, from objectivity to subjectivity, from external to psychological time, were replicating Einstein's worldview.[55] Yet, as Einstein exemplifies, technical innovation is not always accompanied by revolutionary political thought or religious iconoclasm. Eliot, Pound, and other literary modernists whom Einstein influenced were radical in formal expression but not substantively.

Durrell, as he later realized, expressed many common misconceptions: he erroneously saw Einstein as repudiating Newton, conflated relativity and quantum theory, and associated Einstein with the Principle of Indeterminacy, the breakdown of causality, and the provisional nature of truth (*Key* 29, 34), all of which Einstein rejected. Yet he correctly saw that the modernists were deeply implicated, often presciently, in the intellectual revisionism of their predecessors and contemporaries: as Friedman and Donley write, "Not since the Renaissance had so many creative people paid attention to what was going on in other fields."[56] Just as Henry Adams' *Education* employed Newton's second law of thermodynamics in theorizing how civilizations disintegrate,[57] modernists transmuted Marx, Darwin, Einstein, and Freud into literary currency. From William James' *Principles of Psychology* writers like Faulkner, Joyce, and Woolf (and scientists like Niels Bohr) took the "stream of consciousness" and the principle of complementarity, that is, the inseparability of thought and thinker, or of what Lily contemplates in *To the Lighthouse*: the relationship of "subject and object and the nature of reality" (38).[58] With Bergsonian duration[59] and new physical concepts of causality and simultaneity, time became subjective in Proust, Woolf, Joyce, and Faulkner. Open-ended fictional structures paralleled new notions of an expanding, infinite universe. The anthropological and Freudian quest for civilization's roots in "primitive" cultures found expression in writers like Lawrence, whose dismissal of "the old stable notion of the ego" also followed from the insights of Bergson and Freud. "Impressionistic" science, which, like impressionism in painting, emphasized the experimenter's stance and reaction, paralleled literary impressionism: the attempt to render precisely a unique angle of vision at a given instant. Woolf urged her contemporaries to "record the atoms as they fall upon the mind," to "trace the pattern, however disconnected and incoherent in appearance, which each sight or incident scores upon the consciousness" ("Modern Fiction" 155); and Ford Madox Ford, who called his *Joseph Conrad* "a work of art" dedicated "to the truth of the impression," considered his subjective rendering superior to mere "documentation."[60]

Refusing to resolve antinomies into a Hegelian synthesis, Kierkegaard's "either-or" helped induce the epistemological instability that characterizes modernism. "All our certitudes were going," Conrad's narrator says in "The Nigger of the 'Narcissus'" (*Great Short Works* 88); and the inability of Ford's narrator to tell his story sounds in his reiterated "I don't know ... It is all a darkness" (*Good Soldier* 12). Equally frustrated by narrative's failure, Faulkner's Mr. Compson despairs of understanding why Thomas Sutpen turned self-destructive just as the dream that had long inspired him seemed about to be fulfilled: "It's just incredible. It just does not explain. Or perhaps that's it: they don't explain and we are not supposed to know" (*Absalom* 100). Like Einstein, van Gennep, and Freud, such narrators seek, but fail to find, epistemological certitude in a world whose pieces no longer cohere. They do not challenge external reality's ontological status but, finding no way to comprehend it, they become disoriented by the events they filter, alter, and create by narrating. What *happens* in such texts is crucial, but it is revealed gradually, often grudgingly, and from conflicting angles and perspectives: understanding and reconstruction are always partial (both limited and subjective) and always in process.

Epistemological and religious incertitude help explain modernism's turn from stable rituals associated with Victorian dying. Modern novels are replete with characters of uncertain mortal (and moral) status, "grave" voices, revenants. No longer natural and culturally acceptable, fictional death became attenuated, denied, or horrific: initiatory or evaded rather than climactic. Subverting suspense, modern novels became circular and self-reflexive, returning repeatedly and ultimately to terminal events they rarely confront or transcend. Modernists elide the dying process (Woolf, Forster); refract it through untrustworthy memory (Marlow in *Heart of Darkness*, Stephen in *Ulysses*); base it in materiality (*Women in Love*, *As I Lay Dying*, "Snows of Kilimanjaro"); or foreground the complementarity of eros and thanatos (Lawrence's "The Woman Who Rode Away" and *The Man Who Died*; the "Hades" chapter of *Ulysses*).

Blanche du Bois in *A Streetcar Named Desire* says that "funerals are pretty compared to deaths ... Unless you were there at the bed when they cried out, 'Hold me!' you'd never suspect there was the struggle for breath and bleeding" (21–2). Yet like other death rituals, modern funerals are often elided (like Forster's Mrs. Wilcox's and Woolf's Mrs. Ramsay's), or emptied of traditional meaning, or transformed into horrific parody of communal ritual during which corpses fail to fill the coffin-shaped holes, like the one Faulkner draws in *As I Lay Dying* (82), at the center of survivors' lives. A gap, what Ariès calls "The empty space that death has created in the heart of life, the love of life, and the things and creatures of life" (*Hour* 327), remains in such texts. Repressed or inadequately represented, death leaks into language everywhere but the rhetoric is radically different from that of Victorian sentiment.[61]

Historically, modernism is bracketed by the world wars. The historian John Lukacs dates the twentieth century from 1914 (its end, he argues, occurred in 1989 with the demise of the Berlin Wall and Soviet hegemony in Eastern Europe). Dating modernism from England's 1916 Military Service Act, Paul Fussell argues that the world was different before the war: "The certainties were intact ... the Great War was perhaps the last to be conceived as taking place within a seamless, purposeful 'history' involving a coherent stream of time running from past through present to future ... where the values appeared stable and where the meanings of abstractions seemed permanent and reliable." The rupture, at first misread as continuity or historically sanctioned change, was widely welcomed as ending a complacent, stultifying culture and providing opportunity to sacrifice for an ideal. But far more was at stake, and lost. Fussell argues for the uniqueness of World War One: "Every war is ironic because ... worse than expected ... But the Great War was more ironic than any before or since. It was a hideous embarrassment to the prevailing Meliorist myth which had dominated the public consciousness for a century. It reversed the idea of Progress."[62]

Inaugurating what Langer calls "the age of atrocity," World War One produced fundamental changes in Western attitudes toward death. The war that was to be over by Christmas, and was to end all wars, metastasized like cancer and made continuing mass death a central feature of Western civilization. Olivia Bland suggests that the war ended lingering Victorian sentiment about death and dying, for people were finally unable to cope "with the very thought of death. Death and its trappings, mourning and elaborate funerals were pushed under the carpet and ignored."[63] Even when it was enacted, ritual was drained of meaning and authority; often it was elided as impossible or irrelevant.

World War One's casualties, Fussell maintains, included the "system of 'high' diction."[64] In 1908 Conrad could write unironically: "you cannot fail to see the power of mere words; such words as Glory, for instance, or Pity ... Shouted with perseverance, with ardour, with conviction, these two by their sound alone have set whole nations in motion and upheaved the dry, hard ground on which rests our whole social fabric ... Give me the right word and the right accent and I will move the world" (*Personal Record* 6). Hemingway maintained that the war debased such rhetoric: "There were many words that you could not stand to hear and finally only the names of places had dignity ... Abstract words such as glory, honor, courage, or hallow were obscene beside the concrete names of villages, the numbers of roads, the names of rivers, the numbers of regiments and the dates" (*Farewell to Arms* 185). The linguistic transformation is enacted in *The Good Soldier* (1915), which is set before (but written during) the war. Ford's narrator caricatures Edward Ashburnham whom he absurdly projects as his alter ego and eponymous hero: "For all good soldiers are sentimentalists – all good soldiers of that type. Their profession, for one thing, is full of the big words – 'courage,' 'loyalty,' 'honor,' 'constancy'" (26–7).

Yet at the same time, in a country still uninvolved in the Great War and that was never bombed or invaded, "the big words" were being enacted unironically. Determined to eradicate mourning, Hubert Eaton created Forest Lawn as if he inhabited a planet devoid of suffering and linguistic decay, with America the ideal Europe should have been and death the ideal life should have been. Espousing faith in divine benevolence that was cleanly, like muscular Christianity, Eaton built his California cemetery as a monument to "love, patriotism, and beauty," and all the other virtues that the US means to embody: "Tolerance, faith, humility, reverence, trust, truth, courage, vision, and determination – these are the virtues ... evoked ... throughout Forest Lawn."[65] Even after World War Two,

Faulkner, in his Nobel Prize speech, could extol "the old verities and truths of the heart ... the courage and honor and hope and pride and compassion and pity and sacrifice which have been the glory of [man's] past."[66] But Eaton and Faulkner, unlike Hemingway, were untouched by the horrors of European wars; they could, therefore, sustain a faith in progress and a rhetoric that sounds anachronistically hollow east of the Atlantic Ocean.

Even as World War One denied worth to individual life and death, civilian dying, increasingly the domain of medical personnel and hospitals, was becoming clinical, remote, and clandestine. Ostensibly opposed, killing and curing combined to distance death from the quotidian, to make it unknowable and unnameable. Accompanying the decline in traditional faith, the loss or hollowing of ritual created social and cultural gaps. R.W.B. Lewis asserts that twentieth-century literature "began on the note of death,"[67] but modernist fiction reflects society's refusal to countenance death's quotidian presence: deathbeds and dying were elided; death was past or future but rarely present, confronted, and mourned. When formally enacted, death's processes shifted from Victorian aestheticization (the death of Little Nell) to decaying material (Kafka's "Hunger Artist"; Hemingway's "Snows of Kilimanjaro"): the beautiful death became the elided or the dirty death (see chapter 4 below).

Gil Elliot sees the vast scale of man-made death as "the central moral as well as material fact of our time": our "century of death" is distinguished by a public commitment "to the preservation and care of life" but also to the replacement of disease and plague, which (prior to AIDS and the return of tuberculosis) seemed increasingly amenable to control, by extraordinary slaughter. The apparent paradox results from the fact "that one area of public death has been tackled and secured by the forces of reason; the other has not."[68] Foucault writes, "For millennia, man remained what he was for Aristotle: a living animal with the additional capacity for a political existence; modern man is an animal whose politics places his existence ... in question."[69] Shneidman speaks of our "oxymoronic century": great efforts are expended in saving individual lives and increasing mortality, at least for those well off, Caucasian, and Western. Yet "brutish wars, deliberate famines, planned starvations, police and government executions" have wiped out vast populations;[70] the estimates range from 150 to 200 million.

No moral reformation accompanied nineteenth-century technological advances. Producing both massive wealth and the living death of grinding poverty, the Industrial Revolution had a class-based impact on urban mortality rates.[71] By 1900 unchecked inventiveness, industrialization, and greed had produced healing and killing machines that gave those rich, white, and privileged greater control of life and death than ever before. Marx, who had seen such contradictions as inherent in capitalism, would not have been surprised. Fromm writes, "Capital for him was the manifestation of the past, of labor transformed and amassed into things; labor was the manifestation of *life*, of human energy applied to nature in the process of transforming it ... Who (what) was to rule over what (whom)? What is dead over what is alive, or what is alive over what is dead?" Paralleling Marx's thinking with Freud's death instinct, Fromm defines the "necrophilous" person as someone for whom "only the past is experienced as quite real, not the present or the future. What has been, i.e., what is dead, rules his life: institutions, laws, property, traditions, and possessions. Briefly, *things* rule *man*; *having* rules *being*; *the dead* rule *the living*."[72] What follows is war, between individuals and nations.

Instead of clashing, healing and killing are complementary: each requires and sustains the other. Modern warmakers harnessed healing to serve killing so as to guarantee sufficient participants. The *Herald* of 25 January 1890 editorialized on the irony:

> The epidemic of influenza has the one advantage that it is a preserver of the public peace. War is out of the question when armies are suffering from the prostrating effects of the grippe. We can fancy an army, say, of 200,000 men receiving orders to march to attack. The attacking army would have to leave at least 150,000 men in the hospital, and the sneezing of the remaining 50,000 would warn the enemy of their approach. We may be quite sure that no European war will break out until the influenza has vanished, especially as the disease has shown a marked fondness for soldiers.[73]

History's worst plague for the most people dead in the shortest time was probably the pandemic that began, apparently at a US military base, as the war was ending and medical science was coming into its own. In one-third the time, the 1918–19 influenza killed double or triple the estimated 9 to 10 million claimed by the war.[74] Although influenza still lacks a cure, war-related research produced many of the century's great medical advances; "wonder" drugs, for example, were fortuitous by-products of political and military necessity. Writing in the 1950s, Bertrand Russell dryly commented that atomic energy, which "has already proved itself very useful in medicine ... may in time cure nearly as many people as it will kill."[75]

Whether hiding and forestalling death in hospitals or enacting it massively in wars, modern technology removed death from the home and rendered it artificial, arranged, civilization's chief product; its dehumanized subjects were distanced from what had long been the "natural" site and processes of living and dying. Usurping nature's role, man's efficient machinery became so pervasive as to seem a fixture of the human condition, immune from interrogation. Foucault sees control personified by the doctor who supervises executions (as is now required by about half the US states, a practice condemned by the American Medical Association as unethical), "thus juxtaposing himself as the agent of welfare, as the alleviator of pain, with the official whose task it is to end life."[76] In a logical extension, many US states now perform executions by injection. Soldiers assail the "enemies" of the body politic; doctors "cure" it by extirpating virulent criminals.

Ariès suggests that, though it began in the Reformation, one great change in the history of death culminated at the start of the twentieth century when the centuries-old clerical control of dying ended (*Hour* 161). Emphasis on dying as a spiritual transition to final judgment deemphasized the life that preceded the final moment. When deemed tame, climactic, and appropriate, death occupied a privileged place in the life cycle. Ariès regrets modernist secularization because it downgraded death's impact and uniqueness, diluting and distributing it over the whole of life: "This life in which death was removed to a prudent distance seems less loving of things and people than the life in which death was the center" (314–15). Nostalgic for death's climactic function, Ariès mourns its reduction to "an intrinsic part of the fragile and empty existence of things" (332).

Decaying religious faith, waning belief in progress, changed perceptions of human existence after Darwin, Freud, and Einstein, and the trauma of the Great War destabilized traditional views of death's place in the cycle of mortality and immortality. Modernist fictional death, no longer tragic and consummatory, the ultimate and timely form of closure, became unpredictable, incoherent, often initiatory and pervasive. "The Death of Ivan Ilych," *The Man Who Died*, *As I Lay Dying*, and *Finnegans Wake* begin after the protagonist's death, an event to which they keep returning in search of lost meaning. As in Ambrose Bierce's "An Occurrence at Owl Creek Bridge," Joyce's "The Dead," and many of Forster's, Woolf's, and Lawrence's novels, death displaces life, or they seem to become interchangeable. Set in *Graves*end, *Heart of Darkness* begins and ends with England, now, as in Roman times, "one of the dark places of the earth." After opening with a discussion of marriage as impossible, *Women in Love* offers a trek through a Dantesque "country in an underworld ... a ghoulish replica of the real world" (11); and it ends with Rupert mourning the death of Gerald Crich, the god of that Hadean darkness. *Brighton Rock*'s first line anticipates the death that soon occurs. Sheldon Brivic's notion of "The Dead" as "a Gothic story of walking corpses"[77] fits all these texts.

Fussell's books on the world wars, *The Great War and Modern Memory* and *Wartime*, help to contextualize and frame the modern period. Fussell sees the wars enacting Marx's vision of history as repetition with a difference: first tragedy, then farce; or perhaps modernism and then postmodernism. Those like Fussell who fought in World War Two experienced "an unromantic and demoralizing sense that it had all been gone through before" (*Wartime* 132): World War One was tragic in destroying innocence, certainty, the sense of history as seamless and purposeful (*Great War* 18–21). In contrast, World War Two was not manichean conflict but costume drama ("American soldiers were issued white underwear and white towels, as if they were expected to be like other people – civilized and decent" [*Wartime* 5]), with a costume drama cast: "In advertising, the Allied war is fought by white Anglo-Saxons, officers or aviators, with neat, short hair, clear eyes, gleaming teeth, and well-defined jawlines" (*Wartime* 128). It played, he argues, as deadly farce: numerous strategic blunders, with many on both sides killed by what is now called "friendly fire"; rumors, mostly false (though the most horrific, that concerning the slaughter of Europe's Jews, proved true); and "chickenshit" (behavior that makes military life worse than it need be and has nothing to do with winning the war [*Wartime* 80]). Fussell argues that the total madness of World War Two made the "social and ethical norms" of the first seem retrospectively Victorian (*Wartime* 132). European monuments to the two wars materially enact Fussell's paradigm: those for what is still

1 G. Navaron, World War One monument, Saint Léger en Yvelines, France, 16 April 1993.

called the Great War are usually stone edifices occupying places of honor in the town square; those for the second, like self-reflexive postscripts or afterthoughts, are plaques attached to World War One structures (see illustration 1).

Trench warfare's lunacy seemed almost reasonable after the Holocaust: Germany's systematic destruction of much of its own population while it was fighting to conquer the world. Not only were German Jews unusually assimilated (and therefore likely to have supported the war effort), but vast resources were deployed in their annihilation. So outrageous was this action and so little sense did it seem to make from even a Nazi perspective that many then and since have refused to believed it, have denied its historical status. Fussell himself is susceptible to such amnesia. *Great War* builds on the power of shaping retrospection, both Fussell's and that of its participants. *Wartime*, however, marginalizes what, especially in hindsight, was central to World War Two: concentration camps and genocide. It occludes what it should remember.

The rhetorical shift Fussell associates with World War One seems especially germane to Holocaust writings. Discussing Raymond Federman's postmodern novel, *Take It or Leave It*, Brian McHale answers Adorno's question of how Holocaust survivors can write about the mass death they narrowly escaped: "One of Federman's solutions is *not* to write about it at all, but to let the blank spaces in the text ... speak for him ... It is the gaps that convey the meaning here, in a way that the shattered words *juif*, *cremation*, *lampshade*, *Auschwitz*, *responsabilité* ... could never have done had they been completed and integrated into some syntactical continuity."[78] In a sense, the second revolution in twentieth-century Western attitudes toward death, which began a decade after World War Two, sought to make the unsayable sayable again. Gorer's pioneering essay, "The Pornography of Death" (1955), shows how death became taboo, a matter of shame, guilt, abhorrence, and secrecy.[79] At the same time a young psychiatrist at Chicago's Billings Hospital, a recent immigrant who had worked with death camp survivors, was discovering how little she understood the cultural mores of a country that, having been spared the ravages of the world wars, was pervaded by Forest Lawn's ethic of thanatological oblivion.

Wanting to specialize in helping the dying, Elisabeth Kübler-Ross determined that greater scientific knowledge about death had produced the opposite of what was expected: *decreased* understanding and acceptance. Encountering a refusal to countenance death in the 1950s, Kübler-Ross writes: "The more we are making advancements in science, the more we seem to fear and deny the reality of death." In order to recuperate for dying patients the central role medical personnel had usurped, she tried to create seminars in which the terminally ill would teach medical interns about their experiences. What she met, however, was stonewalling: Chicago's largest hospital held no dying patients.[80] Ariès comments that "doctors lose their composure as they approach the floodgates through which the chaos of nature threatens to invade the rational city of man" (*Hour* 405). Dedicated to healing and trained to view death as failure, modern medical personnel were unable or unwilling to acknowledge their terminally ill patients.[81] Unsurprisingly, they often failed to help them during the most traumatic transition of their lives. For Ariès, "The ancient attitude in which death is close and familiar yet diminished and desensitized is too different from our own view, in which it is so terrifying that we no longer dare say its name" (*Hour* 28).

Beginning in the 1950s, however, thanatologists like Gorer, Kübler-Ross, Herman Feifel, Weisman, and Shneidman persisted in naming death despite the antipathy they aroused. Kübler-Ross' *On Death and Dying* recorded a cultural phenomenon in which death, once considered familial, personal, and natural, had become the prisoner of medical personnel who preached and practiced denial. But her pioneering work and writing both defined the condition and helped to change it. Her five-stage paradigm for the affective process of death and dying – denial ("No, not me"), anger ("Why me?"), bargaining ("Yes me, but ... "), despair ("Yes *ME*"), acceptance ("Yes ... me") – provided a new language for speaking about dying as natural rather than alien and mysterious.[82] Her model has been liberating for many: family and friends, medical personnel, and especially the dying, for as she surmised and then verified patients longed to break the conspiracy of silence surrounding them, and to speak and breathe freely and openly in the time they had left.

Kübler-Ross' model quickly gained such favor that, like van Gennep's schema, it is commonly extrapolated to analogous processes like mourning. Doctors and therapists who had denied that patients were dying invoked the Kübler-Ross model though, whether perversely or having missed the point, often as a template for measuring the "success" or "failure" of dying patients: like most revolutions the one Kübler-Ross inspired quickly produced its reaction. Seeking to reassert authority, medical personnel would seize the means she and others had provided for shifting the central role to the dying. Overriding those most intimately concerned, an extraordinary apparatus often prolonged the existence of terminal patients. The reasons are not always benign: a means of reasserting authority, doing it to show that it can be done, the hope of seeing patients through the "appropriate" stages. Further, since 50–60 percent of a lifetime's medical expenditure is incurred during the last sixty days of life, doctors and hospitals commonly give priority not to preventive medicine but to sustaining lives that can, at best, be briefly extended. Such practice has recently begun to wane: both rising costs and concern for patients' rights are leading to negotiated decisions that include those most affected by them.

Those disturbed by the misappropriations of Kübler-Ross' work often blame her for them. Kastenbaum faults the stage theory of dying "because the uncritical perpetuation of the one-path conception (a) impedes the appreciation and discovery of alternate approaches and (b) has the effect of stereotyping uncommon or idiosyncratic patterns as deviant."[83] Though admiring Kübler-Ross' work, Shneidman writes: "I do not believe that these are necessarily 'stages' of the dying process, and I am not convinced that they are lived through in that order, or, for that matter, in any universal order."[84] Kübler-Ross' stages, then, are no more "natural" than denial and medicalization or Victorian aestheticized death. But Kübler-Ross was more cautious about her work than many who adopted it for other ends. Her stages theory is a descriptive taxonomy rather than prescriptive or essentialist, a humane if problematic strategy rather than a claim to unmediated truth or a measure of medical success. Like Ariès, she provided not only practical guidance but also a cultural and literary model that is fruitful if wielded as a tool rather than a rule. It helped Angela Bourke, for example, discern stages of grieving in traditional Irish laments.[85] It helps us understand the depiction of dying in "The Death of Ivan Ilych," and in deceptive texts – "Occurrence at Owl Creek Bridge," *Pincher Martin*, Cheever's "The Swimmer" – whose transitional processes seem to be about survival, even triumphant self-assertion, but in which death is always the site of action, the possibility of its being evaded a delusion.

French historical materialists like Ariès abetted the cultural transformation that coincided with the emergence of chaos theory and postmodernism. Intending to trace earlier Western attitudes toward death and contrast them with contemporary views, Ariès began by locating the boundary and transition around the turn of the century, when the present seemed to begin. Surprised, however, at the extraordinary changes occurring as he started to write (around 1965), he revised his hypothesis: "the phenomenon that I believed to be contemporary had already been at least partly outmoded before my eyes" (*Hour* xvi). Philosophy had contemplated death since at least Plato's *Phaedo* and *The Republic*, though it was largely existentialists like Camus who continued the tradition in the twentieth century.[86] Traditional historians, however, had assumed that death "has no history." Unlike battles and reigns, cultural changes (what Darnton calls "the history of mentalities") are nebulous and difficult to document, so historians preferred "dramatic events to the great constants of the human condition."[87] But since Ariès, death's history has become prominent in thanatological study and thinking.

No longer dismissed as medical failure or just theological or philosophical speculation, death was suddenly available, widely discussed and debated. As throughout the nineteenth century, it was again part of medical study, the subject of sociological and legal investigation: "Shown the door by society, death is coming back in through the window, and it is returning just as quickly as it disappeared" (*Hour* 560). Shneidman says that the most impressive thing about death "is how much (and in how many different ways) various aspects of death and dying are currently undergoing dramatic changes . . . there is a new permissiveness regarding death, almost an urgency to speak and think about it."[88] Suppressed and occluded early in the modernist period, death at its end again became cultural currency; now it is central to disciplines like ethics, law, and biology, and to social sciences like anthropology, psychology, and sociology that assumed their modern forms, in part by tentatively acknowledging death, around the turn of the century.

Thus, Ariès encountered not death's continuing repression but its openness and availability. Instead of writing only about the great divide between Western attitudes before and after 1900, Ariès felt constrained to consider the later transition as well: in consequence, he wrote a very different book, less ideological and more eclectic, than he had intended. Concerning Western attitudes toward death, then, modernism begins with a shift to denial from the familial, climactic death central to Victorian life and letters; and ends with death's emergence from the closet and clinic into the light of academic study, media event, cultural phenomenon, casual conversation. For death as cultural topos has become susceptible to endless interpretation; has its history being written for the first time even as attitudes toward it undergo rapid alteration; and, as thanatological studies, cuts across and undermines traditional disciplinary and ontological distinctions. This study engages the changes in death in the literature, history, and culture preceding, between, and following these two remarkable transformations.

CHAPTER 2

Climactic death

In the West's dominant paradigm prior to the twentieth century, death is climactic, definitive, familiar, and imminent. Ariès maintains that a sense of life's fragility and death's certainty pervaded the medieval period, and that "writers focused their attention on the moment of death because it was surrounded by uncertainty and aroused the passionate interest of their contemporaries" (*Hour* 314). Death was supposedly preceded by fair warning, so that suitable preparation could be made. Garland describes the mythic origin of this belief: "the Greeks believed that some time in the past men had been able to foresee the moment when they would die. It was Prometheus, the friend of man, who deprived them of this disconcerting gift by instilling 'blind hopes' in their minds."[1] The change from hope to modern fear and denial accelerated during the nineteenth century, but as with other cultural shifts it was long in coming. Recounting the death of King George IV in 1830, the London *Times* commented: "His Majesty, far from being dismayed by the awful intelligence [of his imminent death], received it with the placid resignation of a Christian, and the fortitude of a man."[2] In the 1970s, after the second twentieth-century turn in Western attitudes toward death, John Phillips encountered elderly patients who predicted death with "placid resignation": "There was usually no obvious lethal disease process evident at the time, the electrocardiogram might be normal, the chest X-ray normal, the screening blood tests all normal, and yet death would occur, usually within 24–48 hours once the positive statement was made."[3] In pre-nineteenth-century representation, death climaxes both the life depicted and the text that contains and ritualizes it. By completing and terminating a rising action, this representation both culminates a cycle and sanctions its repetition.

Epic literature is defined by death: heroes kill their antagonists, visit underworlds, and then die themselves (like Arthur, Beowulf, and Roland) or else survive to anticipate death's imminence. Thus, a deadly double rhythm structures the epic: the climactic death of the antagonist, Hector, Penelope's suitors, Dido and Turnus, Grendel and his mother, Dante's compatriots, anticipates and necessitates the subsequent death of Achilles, Odysseus, Aeneas, Beowulf, Dante.

Proclaimed in *Beowulf, The Battle of Maldon*, and *The Song of Roland*, heroic codes are epic assertions of selfhood by protagonists who can die well because they have lived as if they were already dead, as if death were already experienced, assimilated, retrospective. Having traversed the gamut of human peril, they emerge like Stephen Crane's Henry Fleming in *The Red Badge of Courage*, who "had been to touch the great death, and found that, after all, it was but the great death" (109). Viewed in this way, living and dying become continuous rather than dichotomous, parts of a single extended process like that which Northrop Frye ascribes to the gods: "In the divine world the central process or movement is that of the death and rebirth, or the disappearance and return, or the incarnation and withdrawal, of a god ... the dying god is reborn as the same person. Hence the mythical or abstract structural principle of the cycle is that the continuum of identity in the individual life from birth to death is extended from death to rebirth."[4] Epic heroes are not gods nor are they resurrected; for them "the continuum of identity" results from their confronting death as ultimate validation for lives lived with extraordinary but untranscendent valor, an option unavailable to gods.

It is not that epic heroes fail to acknowledge their mortality; but they do so with the bravado of Tennyson's Ulysses:

> Death closes all; but something ere the end,
> Some work of noble note, may yet be done,
> Not unbecoming men that strove with Gods. (51–3)

No special mettle seems needed to confront death that life so lived – heroically, liminally – does not already require and inspire. Thus, the old retainer about to die at the end of *The Battle of Maldon* enunciates "with wonderful courage" the code that echoes in and defines Western heroic literature: "Mind must be the firmer, heart the more fierce, / Courage the greater, as our strength diminishes" (38). Similarly,

> When Roland sees the pagans closing in,
> His heart grows stronger, and prouder and more fierce.
> He'll yield to none, as long as he's alive. (158: 2124–6)

The more imminent the death, the fiercer the commitment to both material success and enacting a paradigm for those who follow.

Epic literature retains a strong focus on mortality. Having opted for eternal glory over long life in *The Iliad*, Achilles reappears in *The Odyssey* to say that he chose badly:

> Better, I say, to break sod as a farm hand
> for some poor country man, on iron rations,
> than lord it over all the exhausted dead. (11: 544–6)

Though they may "strive with Gods" and have lofty ambitions, to be mightiest or noblest among men, Achilles, Odysseus, Beowulf, and Roland remain earthbound. Even pious Aeneas, the most predetermined of epic heroes, is distracted by sensuality. Virgil defines an overarching purpose as the measure of Aeneas' actions; yet he seems less moved by the founding of Rome than by the doomed love between Aeneas and Dido, the terrible poignancy of her death, and the encounter in Hades when, reunited with her husband Sychaeus, she turns silently from Aeneas, her enemy, who "wept for her" – and also for himself. Foregrounding valor and codes of heroism, *Beowulf* yet remains based in the material. The dying Beowulf asks Wiglaf, his heir, to fetch the dragon's "priceless shimmering stones" so he can assure himself they are worth what they cost:

> once I
> have set eyes on such a store, it will be
> more easy for me to die, to abandon
> the life and land that have so long been mine. (2739–42)

Though he dies thanking God, Beowulf emphasizes his material success in bartering "my old life / for this treasure hoard" (2792–3).

No epic hero before Dante attains an afterlife correlating to earthly experience. The carefully calibrated *Commedia*, however, Christianizes the epic, making the afterworld consequent to this one. Dante creates and enters a religious and political world of the dead that implies Judgment, a secure cosmology. Unlike Achilles, Aeneas, and Beowulf, who end up with everyone else, Dante's shades inhabit an afterworld that corresponds to his view of what they deserve. So viewed, death becomes transitional rather than terminal, part of a continuum rather than disruptive.

Dantean echoes sound in many modernist texts, although post-Nietzschean modernists often elide not only death's traditional climactic function but also a life beyond. Lawrence struggled to imagine a world not controlled by the deathwish and Dantean teleology. Conrad's *Heart of Darkness* reenacts Dante's structure in Marlow's "weary pilgrimage amongst hints for nightmares" (29): "the gloomy circles of some Inferno" (31) become increasingly horrific on the journey to the Inner Station; the heart of darkness, the city of death, is the European "whited sepulchre" made from ivory extracted from Africa. Joyce, a Catholic apostate, invokes and assails the Dantean Inferno in *Portrait of the Artist*'s sermon on hell; he also names *Portrait*'s most spiteful character Dante and has Stephen at his nastiest open "the spiritual-heroic refrigerating apparatus, invented and patented in all countries by Dante Alighieri" (252). Baudelaire, Eliot, and Greene view limbo as worse than hell, neutrality worse than egregious sin, life itself as hell (see chapter 11 below).

From Chaucer to Bunyan, non-epical English protagonists usually respond to imminent extinction as if enacting Kübler-Ross' stages: with denial in order to avoid what still seems avoidable, then with anger, bargaining, despair, and ultimate acceptance. Death conceived as life's terminus, as inevitable and conclusive, implies that earthly existence is continually, and then finally, created in its image. Life is valued retrospectively rather than as lived; as Montaigne (echoing Seneca) writes, "the earlier acts of our lives must be proved on the touchstone of our last breath ... I have known many by their deaths confer a reputation for good or ill on their whole lives ... In judging another man's life, I always inquire how he behaved at the last."[5] This attitude toward death pervades medieval and Renaissance literature, as if taking its cue from Prospero who, at the end of *The Tempest*, proclaims that he will return from his atemporal island to Milan, the world of mortality and morality, "where / Every third thought shall be my grave" (5.1.310–11). In *The Commedia*, "The Pardoner's Tale," *Le Morte d'Arthur*, *Everyman*, *Dr. Faustus*, *Samson Agonistes*, and *Pilgrim's Progress*, "the time of death is every moment,"[6] and mortal continuity shares the focus of attention with posthumous survival.

Chaucer's Pardoner tells a tale in which living and dying change places. His greedy murderers, despite their boisterous vitality, are marked for death from the first. Resolved to seek and slay this "privee theef ... this false traytour Deeth" (lines 675, 699), Chaucer's allegorical drunken "riotoures" make a pledge whose meaning, which they never perceive, ironically expresses the shape and value of their lives: "To lyve and dyen ech of hem for oother" (703). They meet and threaten an old man, mock his Tithonus-like inability to die, and demand directions to "thilke traytour Deeth, / That in this contree alle oure freendes sleeth" (753–4). When they find golden treasure, the Pardoner scornfully comments, "No lenger thanne after Deeth they soughte" (772). But they abandon their quest not because it is no longer of interest, as they claim, but because it is fulfilled, as their subsequent murdering of each other instantiates.

King Arthur's story both enacts and violates the paradigm of climactic death. Malory's *Morte d'Arthur* begins with a death (King Uther's) and a birth (Arthur's), and ends with the king's death implicit in the catch phrase, "Long live the King," which celebrates political stability by mourning one king's death through proclaiming his successor. Early in the nineteenth century, the London *Morning Post* commented on the divine and legal sanction for this practice:

> When death strikes an exalted head ... it is not without its festivities. The cry of woe has scarcely ceased to sound for the departed, when the shout of gratulation is set up for his successor. It has been wisely provided by the Legislature that the Proclamation of a new Monarch shall immediately follow the demise of his predecessor, and that the Royal Authority, like the mantle of the Prophet, shall descend upon him at the very moment when the departing spirit is mounting to its God.[7]

Tennyson's *Idylls of the King* underscores such continuity, renewal through death and succession: "The old order changeth yielding place to new, / ... Lest one good custom should corrupt the world" (408–10). Malory's epitaph for Arthur, "*hic jacet Arthurus Rex, quondam Rex que futurus*" (391), like the title of T.H. White's Arthurian *Once and Future King*, proclaims, however, that Arthur is not only part of a cyclical process but that he contains the cycle, for its promise of an appropriate successor will be fulfilled only when Arthur returns as England's savior. But in all three versions the focus remains a great king's death, the demise of a romantic vision, and inconsolable grief for that loss.

Everyman also begins, in effect, with its protagonist's death; the play then dramatizes that fact, that process. Summoned and claimed by Death, Everyman responds with denial, with Kübler-Ross' "No, not me": "O Death! thou comest when I had thee least in mind!" He tries bargaining, offering Death a bribe in exchange for delay, and then rewriting his life, frantically searching for validation among worldly personifications, Fellowship, Kindred, Goods, all of whom reject his appeal. John Bunyan's *Pilgrim's Progress* (1678) similarly depicts a protagonist initially despairing over this world and the next: "I am condemned to die, and after that to come to judgement; and I find that I am not willing to do the first, nor able to do the second" (40). His plight is easier than Everyman's because, despite his family and home, he finds no value, nothing to which he wishes to cling, in "the wilderness of this world" (39), yet he too recoils from his doom. But once in motion along the anagogical equivalents of hazardous late seventeenth-century English roads, Pilgrim, like Everyman after accepting his fate, maintains a clear sense of purpose, one to which, though he stumbles on occasion, he always returns. The eschatology and structure of these works are identical: death, though metaphorically and literally present from the first, nonetheless occurs climactically, and as goal and vindication.

Fussell traces *Pilgrim's Progress*' appeal and decline as cultural currency between the world wars: "In the Great War it seemed the common property of both highly educated, 'literary' people and ordinary ones, and both called on it as a way of imposing some sense onto otherwise meaningless traumatic scenes and events ... by the ... Second World War this cultural resource has grown obsolete: *Pilgrim's Progress* is almost never invoked, let alone read." For Fussell this difference suggests "not just the obvious attenuation of Christian belief and context between the wars but something perhaps more disturbing, the enfeeblement of traditional education involving the English classics" (*Wartime* 232). The declining appeal of *Pilgrim's Progress*, however, might be better explained by shifting religious and literary sensibilities than by lower educational standards.

During medieval and Renaissance times, Ariès maintains, death was "the awareness by each person of a Destiny."[8] Marlowe's *Dr. Faustus*, like *Everyman* and *Pilgrim's Progress*, contextualizes mortality within the life to come even as its protagonist maintains a material focus to deny the spiritual. Girding himself to "fear not" as he performs black magic and exhorts the foul Mephostophilis to return in more pleasing guise (ironically, as "an old Franciscan friar" [1.3.14, 25]), Faustus deludes himself about the existence of that hell and damnation he himself evokes. He chides Mephostophilis on "these vain trifles of men's souls" (1.3.58), and instructs him on the afterworld:

> What, is great Mephostophilis so passionate
> For being deprived of the joys of Heaven?
> Learn thou of Faustus manly fortitude
> And scorn those joys thou never shalt possess. (1.3.80–3)

As self-deceived as Hamlet, who can speak of "The undiscovered country from whose bourn / No traveler returns" (3.1.80–1) after encountering a ghost, Faustus sees as metaphor – "I think hell's a fable" (2.1.124) – the afterworld that Mephostophilis' presence dramatizes.

> Think'st thou that Faustus is so fond to imagine
> That after this life there is any pain?
> No, these are trifles and mere old wives' tales. (2.1.130–2)

Mephostophilis' response replicates what his presence manifests to everyone but Faustus:

> But I am an instance to prove the contrary,
> For I tell thee I am damn'd, and now in Hell! (2.1.133–4)

Mephostophilis knows he may speak truthfully to one deafened by the delusion of life's self-sufficiency, and who, feeling himself invulnerable, blinds himself to what eyesight reveals. Even the rational skeptic Horatio, who presumed the Ghost to be nothing but "fantasy," acknowledges "the sensible and true avouch / Of mine own eyes" (1.1.23, 57–8).

As time runs out, Faustus seeks escape through the antithesis of what works for Everyman and Christian. They attain life beyond life by embracing what mortal existence valorized: Good Deeds on the one hand, Hope on the other. Faustus would despairingly deny his humanity, then his very existence: be lost "like a foggy mist / Into the entrails of yon laboring cloud"; or be "a creature wanting soul"; or metamorphose so that "This soul should fly from me and I be chang'd / Unto some brutish beast"; or have his soul "be changed into small water-drops / And fall into the ocean, ne'er be found"

(5.2.161–2, 172, 175–6, 185–6). Replicating the play's opening, when he contemptuously dismisses all human learning, Faustus rapidly, beautifully, but perversely rehearses all possible courses of action (except repentance) and finds them, rather than himself, wanting. Thus, though he cries out "O Christ, my saviour, my saviour!" (2.2.80) in a potential step toward salvation, Faustus is easily distracted by Lucifer's appearance, begs *his* pardon rather than Christ's, and becomes excited by the Seven Deadly Sins, whose beguiling pageantry he accepts as substantive: "That sight will be as pleasant to me as Paradise was to Adam the first day of his creation" (2.2.101–2). His final words, "O Mephostophilis," suggest a lover's cry and yielding. Fearfully compelled from the start by eternal punishment, the obverse of the extended pleasure he seeks from Mephostophilis, Faustus rushes headlong toward it throughout the play, taking most pleasure (as his fine poetry at the beginning and end, but nowhere else, suggests) in what he claims most to scorn or fear: all else for him is trifle. Like Mozart's Don Giovanni, Faustus defines his life retrospectively by the perverse death toward which he rushes, rather than by whatever might lie beyond.

Closely related to climactic death are "acceptance" of death and "appropriate" death, concepts that link protagonists' self-perception and perceptions others have of them. What is meant by acceptance of death? For Kübler-Ross it is "the final stage of growth": "it's really a victory."[9] Henry Murray examines Melville's writings for the meaning of accepting one's annihilation. About Melville's peaceful death, he asks:

> Did this last station of Melville's pilgrimage constitute a victory of the spirit, as some think? an ultimate reconciliation with God at the end of a lifelong quarrel? or was it a graceful acquiescence to the established morality and conventions of his world with Christian forgiveness toward those who had crushed him in their name? or a forthright *willing* of the obligatory? or was it an acknowledgement of defeat? a last-ditch surrender of his long quest for a new gospel of joy in this life? or was it a welcoming of death?[10]

Regardless of which interpretation might obtain, acceptance of death (whether one's own or another's, fictive or actual) includes the notion of appropriate death, which Avery Weisman defines as relatively free of pain and suffering, continued functioning on as high and effective a level as possible, and a confident yielding of control to others. "An appropriate death . . . is a death that someone might choose for himself – had he a choice."[11] Peter Brooks similarly speaks of "completion of the codes" provided by the "correct end" or "right death."[12]

Climactic death may or may not involve "acceptance" and may or may not be "appropriate," though often it is both. Everyman, Pilgrim, Faustus, and Don Giovanni all set themselves in opposition to death, but Everyman and Pilgrim "accept" death as not only inevitable but also as means to a better world beyond. Though Hamlet has sworn to avenge his father's murder, his ensuing actions seem attempts to avoid death, his own and others. Ultimately ensnared, however, he climactically accepts that the "readiness is all" (5.2.220), and so goes to kill and be killed.[13] Macbeth, who halfway through his play finds himself "in blood / Stepped in so far that … / Returning were as tedious as go o'er" (3.4.137–9), in the end refuses Macduff's demand that he surrender (5.8.28). Instead, he seeks an appropriate death: "Lay on, Macduff, / And damned be him that first cries 'Hold, enough!'" (5.8.33–4); so that, finally, we may say of Macbeth what was said of his equally traitorous predecessor as Thane of Cawdor (whose story, recounted at the beginning of the play, adumbrates Macbeth's): "Nothing in his life / Became him like the leaving it" (1.4.7–8).

Protagonists who accept death assert, in effect, its climactic and appropriate place in its fictive context. Oedipus at Colonus, Malory's and Tennyson's Arthurs, Roland, Milton's Samson – all seem to acknowledge that, in mortality, they have, as the Duke in *Measure for Measure* puts it, neither "youth nor age, / But, as it were, an after-dinner's sleep / Dreaming on both" (3.1.32–4), and they go, as Claudio in that play *says* he will, to "encounter darkness as a bride" (3.1.84). Few such protagonists appear in the modern novel, protagonists who, like Conrad's Lord Jim, assert and stage death as what Marlow calls "a last flicker of superb egoism" (251; see chapter 7 below). Neither the genre of the novel nor the twentieth century (nor Claudio when actually put to the test) has much to do with Aristotelian tragedy.

The protagonist's death, even when unwilled or opposed, may still be climactic and appropriate for reader or audience. Villains like Richard III or Macbeth die in a way that satisfies rather than upsets our expectations and needs, if not theirs. A sense of completion (disturbance followed by equilibrium) occurs at the end of works energized by some gross violation of decorum, regardless of whether the violation is malevolently motivated. In *Tamburlaine*, *Dr. Faustus*, *Richard III*, *King Lear* we (and the survivors) accept death as inevitable and appropriate, although the protagonists may not.

Milton's blinded Samson Agonistes, like Oedipus at Colonus, is marked for death from his first appearance. The goal is apotheosis; not merely fulfillment of the pattern of causality but its transcendence. As a way out of mortal anguish, Samson's death enacts the possibility of restoring light, "the prime work of God," to a world cast into unrelieved gloom (100, 70). He is already living

> a life half dead . . .
> Myself my sepulcher, a moving grave,
> Buried, yet not exempt,
> By privilege of death and burial,
> From worst of other evils, pains, and wrongs. (100–5)

At the end, the Chorus, like Greek choruses bemoaning untimely death, quickly finds consolation and comfort by inferring sacrificial meaning in what has occurred:

> O dearly bought revenge, yet glorious!
> Living or dying thou hast fulfilled
> The work for which thou wast foretold
> To Israel, and now li'st victorious
> Among thy slain self-killed;
> Not willingly, but tangled in the fold
> Of dire Necessity, whose law in death conjoined
> Thee with thy slaughtered foes. (1660–7)

The key phrase is "tangled in the fold / Of dire Necessity," for the paradigm evoked, one largely depleted of meaning for the modernists, is Christ's death, and the belief that every Christian death should "imitate" it. The great danger, which the Chorus addresses, is that martyrdom may seem, or become, self-glorifying suicide. Such a notion is rare in twentieth-century literature, though it remains central to faith-inspired work. Examining his motives as he awaits the king's murderous knights, Eliot's Thomas Becket finds that he fears this threat more than death:

> The last temptation is the greatest treason:
> To do the right deed for the wrong reason.[14]

At the end of *The Heart of the Matter*, Graham Greene reverses the situation: not a protagonist who awaits death and martyrdom for a transcendent cause, but one who commits suicide out of earthly love and despair of God. Expressing traditional Catholicism, Scobie's widow says he damned himself to save others. The priest, however, speaks Greene's more radical theology when, in offering consolation, he responds, "He never had any trust in mercy – except for other people" (306). The priest implies that, having risked damnation by committing a mortal sin out of love, Scobie has earned salvation.

Manoa, Samson's literal-minded father, exceeds the Chorus in hailing the glory of his son's death:

> Nothing is here for tears, nothing to wail
> Or knock the breast; no weakness, no contempt,
> Dispraise, or blame; nothing but well and fair,
> And what may quiet us in a death so noble. (1721–4)

Samson, God's "scourge and minister" (as Hamlet calls himself [3.4.182]), rebel and irritant, is thus happily dead, happy because his mode of departure both relieves his people and redeems his suffering, and because, as the Chorus and Manoa's final speeches suggest, he can now be safely honored, mourned, assimilated into ritual: defined. He ceases to remind, by his living presence, that he is other than what his eulogizers would have him be. They are, consequently, free to mythologize his life and death, to impose a retrospective pattern and to hail it as validating divine order, the antithesis of untidy mortal existence, especially Samson's.

For all their complexity and differences, the structures of these works are simple, tidy, classic. They represent one paradigm for the hero who, whether he acknowledges it from the first or needs to learn it, is death-obsessed and death-defined because it serves the story-teller's polemical purpose. Life for Everyman, Faustus, Samson, and other medieval and Renaissance protagonists is merely a stage (and the least important one in a larger process). Sir Walter Raleigh's "On the Life of Man" (1612), though it alludes to no life beyond the final curtain, makes the process explicit:

> Our graves that hide us from the searching sun
> Are like drawn curtains when the play is done.
> Thus march we, playing, to our latest rest,
> Only we die in earnest – that's no jest.

Such characters appear in this world in order to die, and so come to inhabit the absent eternity that may lie beyond the text that depicts, but never fully contains, their lives and deaths. Whatever validation exists in and for such lives reveals itself in the pattern that emerges during the experience and in meaning imposed retrospectively by survivors and commentators – both those within the work (the Pardoner, the choruses at the end of *Faustus* and *Samson*) and its reader or audience.

Moments of leave-taking are wholly self-validating and appropriate when the protagonist's experience of positive motion is unterminated by death. Everyman's last speech is not about death but life beyond it; Pilgrim is last seen entering the Celestial City and being "transfigured." Even more violative of the distinctiveness of life and death are untransitioned passages: those of the prophet Elijah, of Oedipus at Colonus, of Faithful in *Pilgrim's Progress*: "Now, I saw that there stood behind the multitude a chariot and a couple of horses, waiting for Faithful, who ... was taken up into it, and straightway was carried up through the clouds, with sound of trumpet, the nearest way to the Celestial Gate" (134).

In his speculations on dying, death, and the beyond, Thomas Browne considers the ambiguous condition of those who pass from this world to the next without dying: "*Enoch* and *Elias* [Elijah] without either tomb or buriall, in an anomalous state of being, are the great Examples of perpetuity, in their long and living memory, in strict account being still on this side death, and having a late part yet to act upon this stage of earth."[15] Among classical models, Browne might have included Menelaus who, as the sea-god Proteus prophetically informs him, will ultimately be conveyed, deathless, by immortals to the Elysian plain of eternal happiness, a fate granted him because, as Zeus's son-in-law, he has powerful relatives.

Prior to postmodernism, with its juxtaposed worlds or levels of being, the bourgeois novel provides few transcendent depictions. The most vivid exception is Joyce's rendering of Leopold Bloom as Elijah. As Odysseus, Bloom also has important connections, but his transcendence, though metaphoric and parodic, results rather from his unexpected and singularly courageous stand for tolerance and justice in the Cyclops' cave of xenophobic barbarism. His escape is triumphant:

> When, lo, there came about them all a great brightness and they beheld the chariot wherein He stood ascend to heaven. And they beheld Him in the chariot, clothed upon in the glory of the brightness, having raiment as of the sun, fair as the moon and terrible that for awe they durst not look

upon Him. And there came a voice out of heaven, calling: *Elijah! Elijah!* And He answered with a main cry: *Abba! Adonai!* And they beheld Him even Him, ben Bloom Elijah, amid clouds of angels ascend to the glory of the brightness at an angle of fortyfive degrees over Donohoe's in Little Green street like a shot off a shovel! (*Ulysses* 282–3)

Having stood up to the bullying Citizen's assault, Bloom earns something rare in modern fiction (or in the novel generally): heroic reward for heroic action. Bloom's exaltation exemplifies the "epiphany" Northrop Frye sees as characteristic of "romance": the moment when the central character arrives at "the mountain-top, the island, the tower, the lighthouse, and the ladder or staircase."[16] Joyce is mocking Bloom, who neither dies nor attains apotheosis, but he is, simultaneously, according him great respect for his startling and surpassing valor.

Since the novel that emerged in eighteenth-century England results from and expresses middle-class satisfaction with the world, it generally avoids the death obsession found in much medieval and Renaissance writing. (The sub-genre of the gothic provided an outlet for this morbidity.) In fact, it appears exactly when, as Foucault puts it, death in the form of epidemics and famine "was ceasing to torment life so directly ... In the space for movement thus conquered, and broadening and organizing that space, methods of power and knowledge assumed responsibility for the life processes and undertook to control and modify them."[17] Hence, the early novel's focus and values are domestic and conservative, its structure linear and climaxing with marriage, its complacent tone according with Marlow's pronouncement in *Chance*, Conrad's least modern novel, that "Pairing off is the fate of mankind" (426).

The "rise of the novel," as Ian Watt argues, results from combining the genres of romance, picaresque or rogue stories, and didactic fiction, and the superimposition upon this hybrid of bourgeois values. The basic premise is that this world matters supremely, that "all the varieties of human experience" are its subject-matter,[18] and that opportunities for succeeding materially (the only success that counts) are available for all who are worthy and industrious. Fielding's notion of a "comic epic poem in prose" (Preface to *Joseph Andrews*) characterizes the novel's origins, purpose, and structure. In early novels like *Moll Flanders*, *Pamela*, *Joseph Andrews*, *Tom Jones*, *Roderick Random*, *Humphrey Clinker*, *Pride and Prejudice*, *Emma*, protagonists are portrayed as initially outside the domestic design, seemingly too full of vitality and independence for their own good. Yet they triumph over physical or psychological obstacles and secure both respected places within society and appropriately desirable spouses, the two being interdependent. Such novels enact dramatic comedy as defined by Northrop Frye in "The Mythos of Spring": "What normally happens is that a young man wants a young woman, that his desire is resisted by some opposition, usually paternal, and that near the end of the play some twist in the plot enables the hero to have his will."[19] Sufficient time and opportunity exist for lives badly or oddly begun or lived to advance to forgiveness, material reward, and marriage.

These texts suggest that the world and the shaping word respond to desire and imagination, and they avoid confronting death, the telos in epic and tragedy. Yet almost immediately, perhaps in reaction to bourgeois smugness, a darker or tragic strain appears in fiction, and death rather than marriage becomes climax. Following *Don Quixote*, many novels treat social deviation and its consequences for protagonists who, often despite good intentions and natures, cannot be assimilated into community; for them, the wages of violating middle-class mores (usually sexual) are suffering and death. Richardson's Clarissa, seemingly headed, like most eighteenth-century female protagonists (and most male ones too for that matter), for an appropriate marriage, substitutes thanatos for eros after the process and script become reversed and corrupted: first she is drugged and raped, then she is wooed but not won. "My refuge must be death," she writes, "the most painful kind of which I would suffer, rather than be the wife of one who could act by me as the man [Lovelace] has acted. I have much more pleasure in thinking of death than of such a husband" (*Clarissa* 3: 507, 519). Thus, her brief adult life, and the book that lengthily expresses it, becomes a ritual, an exemplum, an *ars moriendi*: a counter-paradigm to Fielding's "comic epic poem in prose."

Clarissa depicts the Renaissance trope of death as sexual fulfillment, and climax as death. Dying is the ultimate orgasm; orgasm parallels, contains, and enacts the dying process. Richard Crashaw's "Hymn to Sainte Teresa" equates death's kiss with love's:

> His is the DART must make the DEATH
> Whose stroke shall tast thy hallow'd breath;
> A Dart thrice dip't in that rich flame

> Which writes thy spouse's radiant Name
> Upon the roof of Heav'n. (19–23)

Ariès writes, "At the end of the fifteenth century, we see the themes concerning death begin to take on an erotic meaning ... In the new iconography of the sixteenth century, Death raped the living. From the sixteenth to the eighteenth centuries, countless scenes or motifs in art and in literature associate death with love, Thanatos with Eros" (*Western Attitudes* 56–7). Such Jacobean and metaphysical themes and imagery regain their potency in *Clarissa.*

Clarissa had numerous nineteenth-century offspring. In *Wuthering Heights*, *The Scarlet Letter*, *Madame Bovary*, *Anna Karenina*, *The Return of the Native*, *The Mill on the Floss*, *Daisy Miller*, *Tess of the d'Urbervilles*, and *Jude the Obscure*, deviation is so great or the world so disapproving, or both, that the climax is death for the protagonist or the beloved. Death so represented precludes the possibility that a relationship, begun in violation, might be recast into a socially sanctioned form, yet it may enable the survivor to attain the beloved. The death of Bertha, the mad wife in *Jane Eyre*, frees Rochester from a destructive *wrong* marriage, and thus allows for a possible right one; Casaubon's death in *Middlemarch* similarly liberates Dorothea. In Jane Austen's *Emma*, the death of Mrs. Churchill, long assumed a hypochondriac, has a positive effect on everyone, as well as on her own good name. Death is:

> recommended as a clearer of ill-fame. Mrs. Churchill, after being disliked at least twenty-five years, was now spoken of with compassionate allowances. In one point she was fully justified. She had never been admitted before to be seriously ill. The event acquitted her of all the fancifulness, and all the selfishness of imaginary complaints. (266)

Emma and Knightly spend much of the novel as if awaiting the liberating death of Mr. Woodhouse, for while he lived "it must be only an engagement ... While her dear father lived, any change of condition must be impossible for her. She could never quit him" (299, 309), though they finally marry despite Mr. Woodhouse's obstinate failure to die.

Replicating the structure of Shakespeare's Romances, some Victorian novels depict tragic experience yielding to reconciliation after the release, through death, of the tension that has built throughout. *Wuthering Heights* and *Tess of the d'Urbervilles*, for example, depict the tormented, tautly rendered passion of Heathcliff and Catherine, of Tess and Angel, before reaching codas in which survivors embark on more stable and mundane relationships, the kind the world allows. To the extent that we find such endings satisfying rather than tacked-on (and only to that extent) such novels, for all their extravagance of style and emotion, retain their link with the genre's middle-class origins, with its orientation toward mundane success. Death may disrupt, but it is ultimately subsumed within an intelligible and overarching pattern – terminal for those who experience it, cathartic for those who bear witness – as the community reforms itself to seal the gap opened by death. Grand passions retain their intense impact, yet normative values are reasserted in the destruction of their violators. It is as if bursting fireworks burnt out to reveal not darkness beyond but what Wordsworth in the "Immortality Ode" calls "the light of common day" (line 77). Even such pyrotechnic fictions, with all their clash of "mighty opposites" (Hamlet's phrase) emphasize that the traditional novel negotiates its concern for life's continuity in this world. Thus they conclude, like *Paradise Lost*, on the cautiously upbeat note of a union between a man and a woman in love with each other and prepared to assert, together, their mortal frailty against a world that has demonstrated its antagonism, but has failed to destroy them. For such survivors, death becomes a closed option, or at least one deferred beyond the text. They are thus constrained to inhabit not Montaigne's world of retrospective death, but Samuel Johnson's post-epical one in which "It matters not how a man dies, but how he lives."[20]

CHAPTER 3

The "ars moriendi"

The ideal text of ideal dying, the *ars moriendi* can be written and performed only in a world with sufficient time and attention for ritual endings. Troubled by the danger of crossing the line between passive and active termination of life, Plato in *The Laws* denounced suicide as an act contravening God's will; yet Athenian justice compelled him to exempt certain self-inflicted deaths from his censure and to write, in effect, the first *ars moriendi*. Condemned to death by the state, Socrates argues "that a man should wait, and not take his own life *unless* God sends some constraint such as that which has now come upon me" (*Phaedo* 58; my emphasis). Instead of fleeing or playing passive victim (either of which, as Nietzsche and Rank emphasize, he could have done[1]), Socrates seizes the initiative and artfully shapes an appropriate end. After bathing "in order that the women may not have the trouble of washing my body after I am dead" (109), "dismissing the women so that there should be no weeping or display of violent emotion,"[2] quieting and consoling his already bereaved friends, and questioning his guard about exactly how to proceed, Socrates performs all the prescribed actions with dignity and authority, including drinking hemlock as if it were medicine to cure him of mortality. And he departs after the traditional thanks-offering for recovery from ill-health, here the long disease of life: "Crito, I owe a cock to Aesculapius [the god of healing]; will you remember to pay the debt?" (111). His last moments "have been both consciously articulated and consummately executed,"[3] and his death is a work of high aesthetic achievement.

Socrates' dying parallels that of Sophocles' Oedipus. At the end of *Oedipus Rex*, Oedipus commits self-mutilation out of loathing and despair, but also to free Thebes from the pollution that, despite his good intentions, he has caused as violator of incest and patricide taboos. Oedipus becomes surrogate victim, a sacrificial scapegoat chosen first to embody and then, in *Oedipus at Colonus*, to alleviate communal guilt, suffering, and infertility.[4] Thebes' famine and plague impel the opening action of *Oedipus Rex*. The supplicants recount their city's afflictions:

> Thebes, as you see yourself, is overwhelmed
> By the waves of death that break upon her head.
> No fruit comes from her blighted buds; her cattle
> Die in the fields; her wives bring forth dead children. (22–5)

Their appeal is an act of homage and repetition: Oedipus, their once and future savior, has already risked himself to save the city:

> we know that when you came here,
> You freed us from our bondage, the bitter tribute
> The Sphinx wrung from us by her sorceries ...
> Restore the state
> And keep it forever steadfast. Bring again
> The happiness and good fortune you once brought us. (35–7, 52–4)

But Oedipus can repeat earlier action only at the cost of his "happiness and good fortune." During the play, a figure of both noble compassion and violent self-assertion enacts an apparent paradox: Oedipus' actions dramatize his meriting the punishment that isolates him from community *and* he becomes worthy of the scapegoat's role.

In his mortality, conniving in his own punishment, and deferring of death Oedipus differs from fertility deities like Osiris, Dionysus, Attis, and Adonis. Yet his blinding, dethroning, and exiling are the symbolic equivalent of the sexual dismemberment associated with resurrection gods: Oedipus' self-blinding, according to Freud, "was simply a mitigated form of the punishment of castration – the only punishment that was adequate for him by the *lex talionis*."[5] Leading the assault upon himself, Oedipus engages in what Girard calls "unanimous violence": "Having plunged the community into strife, the surrogate victim restores peace and order by his departure. Whereas all the previous acts of violence compounded the violence, the violence directed against the surrogate victim banished all trace of violence."[6]

Like a slain and dismembered deity, then, he enacts the resurrection and renewal of the land in *Oedipus at Colonus*, which reverses the structure of *Oedipus Rex*: the later play begins with Oedipus as an old, blind beggar and ends with his transcendence. The conflict concerns the benefits awaiting the polis that provides Oedipus' final resting-place. Oedipus' refusal to return to Thebes and his cursing its political pretenders insure continuing civil strife and the deaths, first, of his sons who are also his brothers, and subsequently of his daughter who is also his sister. His choosing Colonus blesses nearby Athens and its ruler Theseus, who befriended him. Foreseeing his imminent death, "driven / by an insistent voice that comes from God," Oedipus leads his daughters and Theseus to "The holy and funereal ground where I / Must take this fated earth to be my shroud" (1599–1605). He prophesies Athens' happy future, bathes and dresses, comforts his already grieving daughters, exacts Theseus' promise to aid them, and then is carried off in a death "without lamentation, / Illness or suffering; indeed his end / Was wonderful if mortal's ever was" (1719–21). However Oedipus lived, "He died as he had wished" (1769): orchestrating the process, cursing his enemies, blessing his patron, heeding God's voice.

The hero's sacrifice, Bataille and Girard argue, may be essential for communal renewal, as well as for fertility rites. Girard sees in Sophocles' Oedipus plays "a pattern of transgression and salvation ... found in innumerable tales from folklore and mythology: in fairy stories, legends, and even in works of literature. A source of violence and disorder during his sojourn among men, the hero appears as a redeemer as soon as he has been eliminated." The initial violent act underlying ritual sacrifice "is unique and spontaneous. Ritual sacrifices, however, are multiple, endlessly repeated ... premeditated and fixed by custom. The ritual process aims at removing all element of chance and seeks to extract from the original violence some technique of cathartic appeasement."[7] Girard, an archetypal thinker, suggests that the motif of "surrogate victim," as exemplified by Oedipus, may underlie all mythology, rituals, and religion.

Oedipus' carefully crafted dying, which anticipates that of Socrates, "provides the fullest account of the beliefs surrounding the last moments of a hero's life that has come down to us."[8] It equilibrates a competition of interests between the simultaneously self-affirming and self-denying individual and the community whose mortal and moral limits he has transgressed and then transcended. Rarely do victims play so active and central a ritual role as do Oedipus and Socrates, yet when such an opportunity is offered and seized it may produce a remarkable conjunction of individual and communal interests rather than an Iphigenian drama of antagonism. Aristotle's notion of tragic catharsis derives from such a conjunction.

An anticipated, "proper" death affords opportunity to say goodbye, to bequeath property, to apologize, to make closure. Christian dying practice, however, emphasized the relationship between this world and the next: a deathbed confession to redeem a life of sin or, less commonly, a final accounting that demonstrates that one deserves salvation. The eighth-century Bede depicts the standard model in the dying Bishop Chad. Forewarned of his imminent death by "the voice of persons singing most sweetly and rejoicing, and appearing to descend from heaven," he summoned his monks to prepare them for his departure: "When they were come, he first admonished them to preserve the virtue of peace among themselves, and towards all others; and indefatigably to practise the rules of regular discipline." He then ordered them to return "to the church, and speak to the brethren, that they in their prayers recommend my passage to our Lord, and they be careful to provide for their own." After due preparation and at the promised time, "his soul being delivered from the prison of the body, the angels, as may justly be believed, attending him, he departed to the joys of heaven."[9]

Ariès equates all those who seize control of the process. For example, "Like Socrates, Hermes Trismegistus died in public, surrounded by his friends. 'Heretofore an exile, I am now returning to my homeland. Do not weep for me as if I were dead. I shall wait for you with the Sovereign Creator of the world'" (*Hour* 310). Treatises on dying well date from the early fifteenth century, when the soul's fate was no longer decided "in the vast reaches of the beyond." Judgment "was now enacted right in the bedroom of the sick person, around his bed" (*Hour* 107). Tracing the dying process, the 1418 *Ars Moriendi* instructs readers to practice rigorous meditation, contemplate the *memento mori*, and project themselves as *moriens* in preparation for dying.[10] The *ars moriendi* thus urges seizing control of the process and achieving a "proper death" by fulfilling social obligations and shriving one's soul.[11]

As I have suggested, epic heroes like Beowulf, Roland, and Arthur foreknow, accept, and enact death as a series of stages that generally includes a review of the life ending, regret for losses incurred, request for forgiveness, commending of friends and one's soul to God, final leavetaking, and occasionally instructions about burial (see Ariès, *Hour* 8–9, 14–17). Foreknowledge afforded sufficient time and opportunity to comport oneself properly, to become, like Socrates and Oedipus, as well as Don Quixote, Milton's Samson, and Bunyan's Pilgrim, priest rather than victim of the process. Even Hamlet, who has a presentiment of death and has already composed himself, manages, after being stabbed with the poisoned sword, to wound Laertes fatally, exact revenge against Claudius, exchange forgiveness with Laertes, outwrestle Horatio and demand that he live to "Report me and my cause aright / To the unsatisfied," and prophesy and endorse the choice of Fortinbras as Denmark's next king (5.2.305–58). Notions of proper dying were inscribed in medieval and Renaissance wills, in which the testator "expresses a feeling that is close to that of the artes moriendi: awareness of self; responsibility for one's destiny; the right and the duty to make arrangements for one's soul, body, and property; the importance of those last wishes" (*Hour* 201).

Both belief that death is foreknown and the notion of accepted and appropriate death diminished early in the seventeenth century. "After the split that divided the *literati* from traditional culture, presentiments of death were ranked with popular superstitions, even by writers who regarded them as poetic and venerable" (Ariès, *Hour* 8). Although belief that death provides warning has a long pedigree and remained powerful for later spiritual writers like Tolstoy ("The Death of Ivan Ilych," for example), it lost its predominance in Western culture. Here is one important explanation for changes in Western attitudes toward death in the modern era. When death no longer gave "advance warning, it ceased to be regarded as a necessity that, although frightening, was expected and accepted ... It destroyed the order of the world in which everyone believed; it became the absurd instrument of chance" (*Hour* 10). Precluding preparation and control, sudden death opens the possibility of being, like Hamlet's father, "Cut off even in the blossoms of my sin ... sent to my account / With all my imperfections on my head" (1.5.77–80). Sharing this fear, Othello urges Desdemona to pray before he murders her because "I would not kill thy unpreparèd spirit. / No, heaven forfend! I would not kill thy soul" (5.2.33–4). Similar weighing of the death moment prevents Hamlet from killing Claudius at prayer, "in the purging of his soul, / When he is fit and seasoned for his passage," for then he "goes to heaven" (3.3.85–6, 74).

All instances of death foreseen may lend themselves to the *ars moriendi*: death, according to ritual formula, before implicated witnesses. The performer seeks to accept and to craft an appropriate death even when it is externally imposed, as in capital punishment (Socrates) or battle (Arthur, Roland) or a duel (Hamlet). The iconography of St. Sebastian displays a near-naked body punctured by numerous arrows and a face with a beatific, masochistic, or simply content expression (see illustration 2); the martyr's death, a form of what K.R. Eissler calls "narcissistic gratification,"[12] clearly satisfied Sebastian. Except when motivated by despair, suicide, which Camus saw as an act "prepared within the silence of the heart, as is a great work of art,"[13] may also be performed as an *ars moriendi*.

History offers multiple responses to self-destruction. Ancient Athenian corpses of suicides would have their right hands cut off (to render the spirit harmless), while in first-century Athens they were tossed into a pit with murderers. In other parts of Greece, however, those wanting to commit suicide sought permission to do so from the senate; if the reasons were judged adequate, they were given hemlock free of charge. Yet as some contemporary opponents of euthanasia (a word from Greek meaning "easy death") fear might happen, what was permissible sometimes became mandatory: one "law decreed that anyone over the age of sixty was compelled to drink hemlock so that there should be enough food to go around for all."[14] The right to withhold and grant death can become authority to terminate life.[15]

In order that men might be as tranquil as gods, pre-Christian Epicureans and Stoics maintained that human happiness was independent of chance. They agreed with Socrates that only the good life is worth living: what matters is not when one dies but how, and dying well means escaping the danger of living badly. Marcus Aurelius wrote, "In all that you do or say or think, recollect that at any time the power of withdrawal from life is in your hands." Asserting that the way to avoid fearing death was to think of it constantly, Epictetus and Seneca saw suicide as reasonable, even desirable, if life became intolerable. Pliny tells of a Roman woman who, when her husband was found guilty of sedition and ordered to commit suicide, set the example: she plunged a dagger into her breast, "then presented it to her husband with that ever-memorable, I had almost said that divine expression, 'It does not hurt, my

2 Botticelli, *Saint Sebastian* (1474).

Paetus.'"[16] A Roman suicide might be performed as a public ritual: Petronius, to escape being killed by Nero, supposedly performed his death as an aesthetic act.[17] One aged woman "who, having explained to the citizen body her reasons for committing suicide, issued an invitation to Sextus Pompeius to attend her self-poisoning in the belief that his presence would render her death 'more distinguished.'"[18] Suicide remained honorable, as Shakespeare's tragedies of ancient Rome attest, for Elizabethans. *Julius Caesar*'s defeated conspirators perform "a Roman's part" by killing themselves (5.3.89). Horatio, who attempts to accompany Hamlet in death, insists, "I am more an antique Roman than a Dane" (*Hamlet* 5.2.343). The dying Antony, having fallen on his sword, speaks of himself as "a Roman by a Roman / Valiantly vanquished," while Cleopatra, preparing to follow him, says: "what's brave, what's noble / Let's do 't after the high Roman fashion / And make death proud to take us" (*Antony and Cleopatra* 4.15.59–60, 91–3).

But Roman morality shifted even before the Christian church was established. Acceptance of suicide was predicated on the view that the wellborn had the right to determine the standards by which they lived and were judged. As the Empire expanded and fostered multicultural mixing, however, alternative values gained support even in the capital; emperors increasingly intruded on and sought to limit the aristocracy's private morality; and traditional class lines and privileges became blurred. Then the official acceptance of Christianity, with its commandment against killing, strengthened Rome's initially mild ban against suicide.

Christianity is traditionally held to condemn suicides unequivocally in this world and the next. Long deemed the one unforgivable sin, the deliberate ending of one's life was inappropriate for individual determination, and lay under the severest moral and legal interdiction. As Helen Silving notes, however, "The Bible, perhaps in contrast to the Koran, contains no prohibition of suicide."[19] All six Old Testament suicides are reported without judgment made upon them.[20] Both St. Jerome and the Venerable Bede included Christ among the suicides.[21] Yet at the Council of Arles in 452, when it proscribed suicide, and at the Council of Toledo in 693 that made excommunication its punishment, the church read the Commandment against murder to include suicide, and eventually held that Judas' betrayal of Christ was a lesser sin than his suicide.[22]

From the Middle Ages through the eighteenth century, punishment for suicide included seizure of property, mutilation of the corpse, prohibition against burial in consecrated ground, and denial of church ritual.

Yet what Durkheim calls "altruistic suicide" was widely praised in the late Middle Ages and Renaissance. Thomas Elyot's influential *The Book Named the Governour* (1531) extols the Greek monarch Codrus for killing himself in order to preserve his people. As Shakespeare and others represented it, self-murder for the sake of a friend, master, spouse, nation, or faith was admirable. Suicide committed for honor (like that of Brutus and Othello), for love (Romeo and Juliet), to preserve chastity (Lucrece), for religious faith (martyrs), or for patriotism (Elyot's Codrus) evoked mostly positive responses from Shakespeare's contemporaries.[23] In fact, Christianity itself has always been ambivalent on the subject, exalting its martyrs and ascetics: " 'There be two sorts of voluntarie deathes,' says the Reverend Mr. Tuke [a popular contemporary of Shakespeare's], 'the one lawful and honest, such as the death of Martyrs, the other dishonest and unlawful, when men have neyther lawfull calling, nor honest endes, as of Peregrinus, who burnt himselfe in a pile of wood, thinking thereby to live forever in mens remembrance.' "[24] Martyrs may not technically be suicides but the church did some quick thinking in order to sanctify those who had, in violation of church doctrine, embraced death.

Outright condemnation was usually reserved for suicide committed from despair or a sense of utter sinfulness, which is why it is Despair who tempts the Red Cross Knight to kill himself in Spenser's *The Faerie Queene*, an allegorical quest for salvation. Such suicides were considered unpardonable because, unlike the "seven deadly sins," despair is detached from all desire and things, is beyond both repentance and sin, and rejects God's mercy.[25] Totally inner-directed, despair rejects the authority of religious structure by asserting an independence beyond its reach. Thus, Hamlet, in turmoil but not despair, rejects suicide because God has "fixed / His canon 'gainst self-slaughter" (1.2.131–2).

Declining anticipation of death was accompanied in the Renaissance by a revaluation, by humanists like Erasmus, of mundane existence. Church reformers, influenced by humanism, insisted that eternal judgment is based on how one lives one's life, not on last moments. In his posthumous *Biathanatos*, John Donne, born a

Catholic but an Anglican convert who became dean of St. Paul's Cathedral, urged sympathy and understanding, denying that suicide was invariably sinful even in instances of despair and arguing that such condemnation limited God's power. Even in Catholic France, the post-revolutionary National Assembly repealed all laws concerning suicide in 1790, and sanctions against it were not reinstated in the revised Penal Code of 1810 despite Napoleon's condemning a soldier, frustrated in love, who had committed suicide: "A French soldier ought to show as much courage in facing the adversities and afflictions of life as he shows in facing the bullets of a battery. Whoever commits suicide is a coward; he is a soldier who deserts the battlefield before victory."[26] Napoleon himself attempted suicide in 1814.

In *Ulysses* Leopold Bloom muses on the traditional treatment of suicides: "Refuse christian burial. They used to drive a stake of wood through his heart in the grave. As if it wasn't broken already" (80). Bloom is right: that was English law until the early nineteenth century, when harsh judgments accorded suicides were eased. Echoing *Hamlet*'s gravediggers, who quibble over whether Ophelia "willfully seeks her own salvation" and the appropriateness of her "maimèd rites" (5.1.2, 219), Blackstone defended the law:

> the law of England wisely and religiously considers, that no man hath a power to destroy life, but by commission from God, the author of it: and, as the suicide is guilty of a double offence; one spiritual, in invading the prerogative of the Almighty, and rushing into his immediate presence uncalled for; the other temporal, against the king, who hath an interest in the preservation of all his subjects; the law has therefore ranked this among the highest crimes, making it . . . a felony committed on oneself. A *felo de se* therefore is he that deliberately puts an end to his own existence, or commits any unlawful malicious act, the consequence of which is his own death.[27]

Suicide is a legal nightmare since perpetrator and victim are one, and the criminal rather than the crime is defined. Despite Blackstone's defense of the practice of "an ignominious burial in the highway,"[28] English law requiring that suicides be buried there with a stake driven through the heart was repealed in 1823; it remained, however, literature's way of dealing with vampires, into whom suicides were thought to turn.[29]

Henceforth, suicides were buried in churchyards, though without religious ceremony.[30] The relatively liberal Offences against the Person Act of 1861 declared attempted suicide a felony punishable by up to two years in prison.[31] Suicide, which remained a crime in England until 1961, is still so designated in several US states; but since the weakening of Christian prohibition late in the nineteenth century, the West has increasingly treated suicide as a medical rather than a legal or moral problem.[32] Recent cases in both countries have focused, rather, on the "crime" of assisting suicide, whereas doctors in the modern period (as with the terminally ill Freud[33]) often followed patients' wishes in alleviating pain even, or sometimes especially, if death were hastened. Today Catholicism holds that suicides acted while insane, which allows a church funeral and burial.[34]

In the line that includes Plato, Seneca, and Montaigne, Camus in "An Absurd Reasoning" maintains that philosophy concerns the practice of dying, a notion he took to its logical conclusion: "There is but one truly serious philosophical problem, and that is suicide. Judging whether life is or is not worth living amounts to answering the fundamental question of philosophy."[35] Camus implies that death, conceived and written as an aesthetic and spiritual accomplishment, is worth dying, and worth dying well. Frederick Hoffman contemplates fictional protagonists who literalize Camus's logic: "Often the hero wills his death as an active and violent proof of man's triumph over the threat of death," like Kirillov in Dostoevsky's *The Possessed*.[36] In the modern period, suicide was a powerful motif, first as trope and then as reality, for Hemingway and Woolf.

Rilke's *Notebooks* (written 1903–10) foresaw a twentieth-century environment unconducive to the *ars moriendi*:

> Where production is so enormous an individual death is not so nicely carried out; but then that doesn't matter. It is quantity that counts. Who cares anything today for a finely-finished death? No one. Even the rich, who could after all afford this luxury of dying in full detail, are beginning to be careless and indifferent; the wish to have a death of one's own is growing ever rarer. A while yet, and it will be just as rare as a life of one's own. (17)

Bemoaning the loss of both appropriate death and appropriate life, Rilke anticipated the anonymity and emptiness of modern mass existence and dying.

The *ars moriendi* tradition inaugurated by Socrates and perpetuated by Christianity was largely played out by the modernist period, given its quietus by Nietzsche. In "The Problem of Socrates," Nietzsche views the death-orientation of Socrates (whom Shelley called "the Jesus Christ of Greece") as anticipating Christianity's denigration of life: "Socrates *wanted* to die: not Athens, but he himself chose the hemlock; he forced Athens to sentence him." Socrates and Plato, Nietzsche insists, are "symptoms of degeneration, tools of the Greek dissolution ... Socrates was a misunderstanding; *the whole improvement-morality, including the Christian, was a misunderstanding*."[37] After Christ's, Socrates' is Western culture's most problematic death. Jacques Choron maintains that Socrates "sees his manner of dying not as a suicide but as self-execution, which is only another form of capital punishment, to which he has been condemned, no matter how unjustly, by his judges."[38] But Socrates need not have cooperated; and his doing so fits Durkheim's classic definition: "the term *suicide is applied to all cases of death resulting directly or indirectly from a positive or negative act of the victim himself, which he knows will produce this result*."[39] Choron also argues that "there are reasons to believe that [hemlock] was given to Socrates as a special favor, and the possibility of a quick and painless death may have been a factor in the refusal of the seventy-year-old Socrates to escape."[40] Others maintain, however, that the "high aesthetic achievement" (see illustration 3) was Plato's rather than Socrates':

> Socrates's ending was most likely given a latter-day Hollywood-like treatment by his chronicler Plato. For death by coniine, a poisonous alkaloid of the hemlock plant, is marked not only by ascending motor paralysis, as Plato recorded, but also by intense nausea, vomiting, and limb-flailing convulsions – unpleasantries that are found nowhere in Plato's noble end to the life of his friend and teacher ... The description of a calm and painless death that must have been neither tranquil nor without discomfort was most certainly Plato's final tribute to his dear friend.[41]

D.H. Lawrence, following Nietzsche, blamed "the coming of Socrates and 'the spirit'" for two millennia of "living in a dead or dying cosmos," for all subsequent "religions have been religions of the dead body and the postponed reward: eschatological, to use a pet word of the philosophers."[42] Emma Bovary's agonized dying may be read as Flaubert's attempt to correct the record.

Several modernist texts reconceive and satirize Socrates' sacrificial bird. In *The Good Soldier* Ford's conventional John Dowell

3 Studio of Jacques-Louis David (1748–1825), *The Death of Socrates*.

speaks cryptically of convention as "the cock that the whole of this society owes to Æsculapius" (37). In *Ulysses*, Bloom sympathetically imagines Paddy Dignam's final moments with his now-orphaned son: "Poor boy! Was he there when the father? Both unconscious. Lighten up at the last moment and recognise for the last time. All he might have done. I owe three shillings to O'Grady. Would he understand?" (85). Lawrence reverses the meaning of Socrates' bird in *The Escaped Cock* (Lawrence's original and preferred title for *The Man Who Died*). As Hinz and Teunissen write, "Socrates signaled the decline of the Greek world when he perverted the offering designed as thanksgiving for the restoration of life into a token tribute for having been released from the 'illness' of life; the man who died owes a cock to Asclepius for being cured of the sickness of the Socratic mentality."[43] Socrates' cock signaled his release from material being; Lawrence's punningly announces erotic resurrection. Modernism could only mock a tradition it could no longer sustain.

The *ars moriendi* failed when sudden death, "regarded as ignominious and shameful" in medieval times because it could be neither anticipated nor ritualized, "a strange and monstrous thing that nobody dared talk about" (Ariès, *Hour* 10–11), became again, as Erasmus maintains it had been in antiquity, most desirable. Joyce's Bloom marks the cultural change:

– [Patrick Dignam] had a sudden death, poor fellow, [Power] said.
– The best death, Mr. Bloom said.
Their wideopen eyes looked at him.
– No suffering, he said. A moment and all is over. Like dying in sleep.
(*Ulysses* 79)

Sudden death provokes awe and mute fear in Power, a Catholic, because it takes one "Unhouseled, disappointed, unaneled" (*Hamlet* 1.5.78). For the Protestant Jeremy Taylor, "sudden death is but a sudden joy, if it takes a man in the state and exercises of virtue: and it is only then an evil, when it finds a man unready."[44] Bloom, a humanist and Jewish apostate who lacks belief in damnation, would not feel the force of this religious difference. Wishing to minimize suffering and maximize pleasure in a secular age, Bloom sees *only* sudden death (or death during sleep or unconsciousness) as acceptable.

Tracing what they consider the debasement of a once vigorous practice, Huntington and Metcalf regret the decline represented by texts like Robert Neale's *The Art of Dying* (1973), which

> stress an almost Buddhist resignation in the face of one's own death and the death of others. The earlier volumes urge that the sinner "look on death" in order to wake the fires of conscience; the latest writers advise a sidelong glance in order to avoid psychological maladjustment. In the Middle Ages men and women made themselves masters of their own deaths. In America, the archetypal land of enterprise, self-made men are reduced to puppets.[45]

This cultural transformation led to a conspiracy of silence and willed ignorance that continued into the post-World War Two period. *Death Be Not Proud* (1949), which might have taken Beckett's title, "The Unnamable," is a moving yet ultimately life-denying account of the death from a brain tumor of John Gunther's seventeen-year-old son. Every effort was made to avoid mentioning death for fear of invoking it; family and friends connived to keep the dying person from knowing of its imminence in order, it seems, to distance him from his own experience. In anguish, Gunther denied his son both knowledge of what was happening and voice in the process and resulting book. Desperate to evade the inevitable, Gunther filled his time and pages with medical details, and imposed and then wrote what he considered an appropriate death for his son: "He died absolutely without fear, and without pain, and without knowing that he was going to die."[46] Ariès' medieval man would read Gunther's well-intentioned conclusion with horror and outrage. Edward Albee's play *All Over* (1971) takes Gunther's attitude to its logical extreme: we see only survivors because a huge screen hides the hospital bed from the audience as well as from family and friends; for all we, and they, can tell the dying man is already gone.

Rather than deny death, many societies enacted ritual sacrifice to control it. What Bataille calls "the religious act above all others"[47] seeks to socialize and delimit death, removing it from the individual's domain and transforming it, on the communal level, into an aesthetic and spiritual work. Communities seek to propitiate the gods, regulate the most traumatic of transitions, and deflect a perceived or anticipated threat. Girard argues that "Sacrifice is the boon worthy above all others of being preserved, celebrated and memorialized, reiterated and reenacted in a thousand different forms, for it alone can prevent transcendental violence from turning back into reciprocal violence, the violence that really hurts, setting man against man and threatening the total destruction of the community."[48] The belief that death can be controlled through its enactment is powerful and enticing; but like capital punishment it requires communal willingness to find or create victims and to assume the murderer's role, and it comes with no guarantees. And it is disastrous in modern texts.

Lawrence's "The Woman Who Rode Away" (1925) is a deflationary version of the Socratic or Oedipal paradigm of victim as agent in which death is pervasive and yet never occurs. The eponymous woman has an uncertain identity (she is never named), inhabits and embodies an "unliving" environment, seeks riddling answers from mysterious deities, and makes a desperate journey for self-knowledge and death. Like the later *Lady Chatterley's Lover*, the story begins with an unfulfilled woman disconnected from her children and a husband who defines himself through his work, who fails her sexually and morally, and who personifies the landscape he has helped to despoil with his now exhausted mines. In "Why the Novel Matters," Lawrence writes that "in the novel ... when the man goes dead, the woman goes inert" (*Posthumous Papers* 538). So the passive, dehumanized woman of this fairy tale is characterized negatively from the first, by her antipathy to a loveless marriage and to the stultifying ugliness of her surroundings. Married life, constituted in terms of property and ownership, had become "an invincible slavery: and her conscious development had stopped mysteriously with her marriage" (*Short Stories* 2: 546–9). Her environment entraps and devitalizes her: "when you looked up from this shut-in flowered patio, you saw the huge pink cone of the silver-mud refuse, and the machinery of the extracting plant against heaven above. No more" (546). Her life devoid of spiritual dimension, she is moved only by what she imagines "*lives* in the hills and the mountains," her "vague enthusiasm for unknown Indians," and what she envisions as their wonderful "old, old religions and mysteries" (548–9). Her ride into the hills, then, is a forlorn quest for expansiveness, for the freedom and identity denied her by social constraints, for an "immensity" that, Bataille suggests, "spells death to the [wo]man it attracts."[49]

Kate Millett asserts that this story "is Lawrence's most impassioned statement of the doctrine of male supremacy and the penis as deity," and that the woman's "fatalism is never explained, save in

Lawrence's obsessive wish to murder her."[50] Yet Lawrence's male narrator provides motivation for her suicidal despair while deprecating her search for "primitivism" as "crazy plans." Her journey, he maintains, is doomed from its inception: "She was overcome by a foolish romanticism more unreal than a girl's. She felt it was her destiny to wander into the secret haunts of these timeless, mysterious, marvellous Indians of the mountains" (549). Though she flees a land and a life where all is dead for her – "Deadness within deadness" (547) – she seems beyond death even as she seeks it. In the cold dawn after her first night spent in the open, "She lay wrapped in her blanket looking at the stars, listening to her horse shivering and feeling like a woman who has died and passed beyond" (552), a sensation reiterated as a refrain. She contemplates returning home, but finds herself unable to do so:

> And now, as she neared, more or less, her destination, she began to go vague and disheartened ... if she had had any will of her own left, she would have turned back, to the village, to be protected and sent home to her husband.
>
> But she had no will of her own. (552–3)

From the dead land she has left, she arrives at the dead land that is her destination and destiny. Although she has been victimized by white males, her Indian captors seem far worse: "remote, inhuman" (557), the antithesis of the primitivistic ideal Lawrence sought elsewhere. The corn they grow is stunted, their village "bare and arid [with] no sign of moving life"; "the stream was dry, like summer, dried up by the frozenness of the head-waters" (579); and the old chief's fingers on her naked body are "as if Death itself were touching her" (564).

On her first night of captivity, Lawrence's woman anticipates (desires?) sexual assault that never comes: "she had a moment's thrill of fear and anxiety, seeing the dark forms cross and pass silently in the moonlight. Would they attack her now?" (557). But she misreads their interest in her: with passion on neither side, both eroticism and sacrifice are drained of climactic import. The woman's journey is, at least in part, a flight from sexuality – from a husband who, for all his deadness, "admired her body" intensely – to a desired transcendence that is really denial: "she did not feel shamed in her nakedness. She only felt sad and lost ... She was only utterly strange and beyond herself, as if her body were not her own" (564).

Her journey is circular: from empty passion to empty passion. At the sacrificial age of thirty-three, she came willingly, in fulfillment of an Indian legend, "to serve the gods of the Chilchui"; and she continues unresisting up to her ritual death, which is poised to occur as the story ends. The white woman's sacrifice is the Indians' attempt to regain potency and renew the land by reclaiming their gods from European conquerors:

> we shall have the sun on our right hand and the moon on our left. So we can bring the rain down out of the blue meadows, and up out of the black; and we can call the wind that tells the corn to grow, when we ask him, and we shall make the clouds to break, and the sheep to have twin lambs. And we shall be full of power, like a spring day. But the white people will be a hard winter, without snow. (575)

Though the Indians sound like Lawrence in *Apocalypse* (46–7), their hope is as forlorn as the woman's search for meaning. For all the sublimated eroticism of the ritual, these curiously asexual men show "no more sign of interest in her than if she had been a piece of venison they were bringing home from the hunt" (557), for she is alien and they devitalized. They respond to her "impersonally ... with a mystic hatred," treating her solely as the victim she had been in her own community, and chose to be in theirs. Yet they seem more eager to destroy her as a woman than as a racial enemy:

> her kind of womanhood, intensely personal and individual, was to be obliterated again, and the great primeval symbols were to tower once more over the fallen individual independence of woman. The sharpness and the quivering nervous consciousness of the highly-bred white woman was to be destroyed again, womanhood was to be cast once more into the great stream of impersonal sex and impersonal passion. (569)

For all their masculine prowess, the Indians "have no sex"; and the sacrifice itself is anti-climactic despite its sexual charge. Knowing she is "going to die," the woman is carried naked beneath a "fanged inverted pinnacle of ice" and pinned onto a sacrificial altar in a "cave that like a dark socket bored a cavity, an orifice" (579). Inside, "the old, old priest" is "naked and in a state of barbaric ecstasy." The woman is laid "on a large flat stone, the four powerful men holding her by the outstretched arms and legs"; poised over her, their long knives ready, two priests await the full penetration of the dying sun's rays into "the far end of the funnel-shaped cavity ... into the hollow of the cave, to the innermost."[51]

The scene replays the endings of numerous late- and post-Victorian texts in which men, insecure in their masculinity, reassert it by destroying women. The masculine authority represented in such fiction had long seemed natural, but it was increasingly challenged as the nineteenth century came to a close. Discussing Stoker's *The Lair of the White Worm* (1911), Gilbert and Gubar write, "As in so many turn-of-the-century fantasies, a group of men have bonded in order to achieve a ceremonial assertion of phallic authority that should free all men from the unmanning enslavement of Her land and return the relations between the sexes to the 'proper' balance of male dominance, female submission."[52] This "balance" was increasingly challenged during the modern period because of the destabilizing of gender relations by the suffragist movement and the World War.

Lawrence both accepts and interrogates the premises of this fictional genre by making the woman already beyond what she fearfully desires, the men asexual primitives, and the ending a non-action, poised in mid-sentence: "The mastery that man must hold, and that passes from race to race" (581). Like sacrificial ritual itself, this line pretends potency but lacks action, lacks verb and object; it both presumes and withholds the sacrificial act. The woman's death, since it occurs before the story begins, is already past; since it is elided at the climactic moment, it remains suspended, deferred. As in Baudelaire and Eliot, the final limbo status seems the worst of all: the absence of climactic death creates an ending that lacks dignity as well as definitiveness. The Indians, who are Other before they are Men, are similarly cheated. They are, the last clause implies, already disinherited; their ritual represents not possible renewal but the last impotent gasp of an already, perhaps always already, dead people, a gesture forever frozen and desiccated despite the *pretended* force of the story's final "race to race."[53] For Lawrence, modernity destroyed community, both primitive and civilized, so the quest to renew vitality in ritual sacrifice, whether or not it ever worked, is unviable. Despite Kate Millett, the story cannot be read straightforwardly, as Lawrence's displacing of Christianity with a new religion of death.

Communities seeking to form or sustain themselves by appropriating and ritualizing death are, as "The Woman Who Rode Away" suggests, primitivistic or anachronistic. They contrast with the substitution of civil justice for the cycle of personal revenge, the symbolic beginning of Western civilization, that concludes Aeschylus' *Oresteia.* Like Girard, Bataille sees sacrifice as retaining its symbolic power, as in the Catholic mass: "in essence the sacramental quality of primitive sacrifices is analogous to the comparable element in contemporary religions."[54] What Girard calls "the sacrificial crisis" (ritual enacted despite its being emptied of sacrality) threatens the social fabric,[55] a trope common in twentieth-century texts written by Americans or set in the US, where World War One's pointless sacrifices had not come. Fictional rituals of violent scapegoating like Faulkner's "Dry September," "Pantaloon in Black," *Light in August*, and *Intruder in the Dust*; Clark's *The Ox-Bow Incident*; and Jackson's "The Lottery" share the anachronistic quality of "The Woman Who Rode Away."

The requisite conditions for unanimous sacrificial violence include a small but not quite closed community that, fearing life to be more complex, less amenable to control, than it had long seemed, feels threatened and asserts its need to sustain, unquestioningly, attitudes and values whose façades are cracking. "Dry September" (1931) is a racially eroticized replay of ritual sacrifice gone awry. Set in a turn-of-the-century Southern town, it begins in a barbershop, a traditional male preserve appropriate to locker-room jokes rather than the enactment of violence or sex. But in this arid land and time – "the bloody September twilight, aftermath of sixty-two rainless days" – sterile men desperate to escape stagnant weather and lives feel impelled to "manly" action by a rumor of rape that spread "like a fire in dry grass" (169). For the martial McLendon, who "had commanded troops at the front in France and had been decorated for valor" (171), imaginative projection transcends event: "Happen? What the hell difference does it make? Are you going to let the black sons get away with it until one really does it?" (172). To wait on facts as Hawkshaw, the ineffectual voice of reason, urges is to be a "nigger lover" – and probably effeminate. And to be female is to be effaced, either as stereotype (the phrase "white woman" occurs six times in the first four pages) or as victim. Both story and town are full of voyeurs who, when they finally act, do so out of leering and frustrated sexuality that emerges as violence rather than eroticism. Hence, they perform a lynching in order to defend the "honor" of Minnie Cooper, the pathetic spinster who, in her own "dry September," has apparently been driven to delusion and hysteria by sexual frustration. All eyes finally turn to her as she bursts into uncontrollable laughter over the irony that the men who never knocked at her door eagerly kill in order to preserve her good name, which no one cares about or believes was violated.

The story elides crucial explanations and actions – how the rumor started, the lynching, Hawkshaw's return to the barbershop – so the final scene offers no advance on the opening. It dramatizes the sterile and destructive consequences of desacralized racial scapegoating while restoring the circumstances in which it occurs. Returning home in midnight's continuing aridity after having killed to "defend" white womanhood, McLendon brutalizes his long-suffering wife. He finds no more sexual release, however, in beating her than he did in the lynching of the innocent black man. Impotence and rage are as unbearable and stifling at the end as at the beginning: in unintentionally self-mocking post-coital action he futilely mops his sweat "and, with his body pressed against the dusty screen, he stood panting. The dark world seemed to lie stricken beneath the cold moon and the lidless stars" (183).

A similar paradigm operates in Clark's *Ox-Bow Incident* (1940). Determined to enact frontier justice rather than wait on facts or law, "a lawless mob" (41) forms in a Western town as "dead as a Piute graveyard" (5). As in "Dry September," action overrides doubts as soon as "a leader; somebody they can blame," here called a "scapegoat" (74, 264), appears. Claiming to embody community, the self-appointed, even self-deputized posse feels free to act as much against communal institutions as against those it labels criminal, as Davies, the Hawkshaw figure, makes explicit:

> "it's infinitely more deadly when the law is disregarded by men pretending to act for justice than when it's simply inefficient, or even than when its elected administrators are crooked." ... he said a lynch gang ... doesn't ever really judge, but just acts on what it's already decided to do, each man afraid to disagree with the rest. He tried to prove to us that lynchers knew they were wrong; that their secrecy proved it, and their sense of guilt afterward. (61–2)

The novel climaxes with a mock trial: the accused cattle rustlers speak in their own defense and a jury vote is taken in which five men stand out against the unanimity of "the pack." For the large majority, the logic of their presence makes immediate hanging inevitable: as Davies says, "We're doing it because we're in the pack, because we're afraid not to be in the pack ... we don't dare resist the pack" (139–40). The guilty loquacity of Faulkner's and

Clark's self-appointed vigilantes, their need constantly to outtalk doubt about what they are doing and to recommit themselves to mob action, emphasizes the perverseness of such sacrifice, and insures violence's failure and repetition.

Finally, Shirley Jackson's "The Lottery" (1949) enacts scapegoat ritual in a mid-Western agricultural town where annual sacrifice is the community's self-defining act. Other forms of communal gathering – "the square dances, the teenage club, the Halloween program" (138) – are ends in themselves, pleasurable actions, and only secondarily express social identity.[56] The annual lottery, to select someone for stoning, is meant to insure that the land will be fruitful and the community endure through sacrificing a randomly (and therefore supernaturally) chosen member. The ritual, having existed longer than anyone remembers, represents continuity, history, tradition, the known, an assertion, as in all ritual, of a future that replicates the past. The presumption seems to be, "if this death, then no other," a comforting thought that makes death seem subject to human control: regular, predictable, tame. Thus, despite the story's mounting horror (resulting from the narrator's flat, reportorial recounting; our growing awareness of what is happening; and a zeroing in on Tessie Hutchinson, this year's victim), the ritual is represented as superficially plausible: no deaths *have* occurred since last year's lottery.

The woman who rode away retains to the end such dignity and purposefulness as anonymity allows. Mrs. Hutchinson, however, quarrels with the lottery not in principle but in being selected. She is first marked by her absence, then by her haste not to be late (for what turns out to be her own death and funeral). She is defined by stereotypical ordinariness: her taciturn husband, her three children, her casual garrulousness, her having washed up before coming out ("Wouldn't have me leave m'dishes in the sink, now, would you, Joe?" [140]), her sudden sense of injustice as the lot falls first on her family and then on her: "It wasn't fair!" Like scapegoat figures before her, she is constrained to assume "a dual connotation. On the one hand ... a woebegone figure, an object of scorn who is also weighed down with guilt ... On the other hand ... surrounded by a quasi-religious aura of veneration ... a sort of cult object."[57] Stripped of distinguishing features, she stands, isolated and important, but also unwilling, as her community's victim and salvation, before being stoned to death in the story's final line: " 'It isn't fair, it isn't right,' Mrs. Hutchinson screamed, and then they were upon her" (145). Girard maintains that in sacrifice communal survival is at stake, the renewal of the land that always verges on becoming waste: "The act of collective murder is seen as the source of all abundance; the principle of procreation is attributed to it, and all those plants that are useful to man; everything beneficial and nutritive is said to take root in the body of the primordial victim." But, he adds, unanimity is required; even the victim must consent: "the abstention of a single participant renders the sacrifice even worse than useless – it makes it dangerous."[58] Hence, Tessie's dismay at being chosen evokes the response "Be a good sport" from other participants, those for whom the lottery is again validated by its having spared them.

Girard is, of course, discussing the past or "primitive" societies. What makes "The Lottery" powerful and surreal is its deploying archaic ritual in a contemporary setting. It speaks, however, to the same instinct that sought to elide death: the desire to keep it under wraps, define and regularize it, make it part of community rather than the ultimate threat. Girard considers how communal violence gets transformed into sacred action: "A collective murder that brings about the restoration of order imposes a kind of ritualistic framework on the savage fury of the group, all of whose members are out for one another's blood. Murder becomes sacrifice; the angry free-for-all that preceded it is transformed into a ritual dispute over the choice of the most suitable victim, one that satisfies the piety of the faithful or has been selected by the god. In effect, the real question behind these preliminaries is, Who will kill whom?"[59] The philosophical basis here is Hobbesian materialism, the notion that in the "war of all against all" egoistic self-expression is checked only by an absolute authority, or by Freudian repression. The lottery both provides an outlet for the desire to kill and controls its consequences. The communal hope is that such ritual can propitiate the deity (whether transcendent or internal), and that death itself can be wholly ritualized, made to happen only in the regular and prescribed time and way, within both the story's ritual of the lottery and the ritual story called "The Lottery." Tessie's failure to be "a good sport," however, subverts such expectation and exposes a debased community stubbornly reenacting anachronistic ritual. It anticipated the US lottery that determined who would be sent to die in Vietnam.

Western civilization, which has defined itself in history largely through acts of conquest, genocide, slavery, and exploiting "those who have a different complexion or slightly flatter noses than ourselves" (*Heart of Darkness* 215), produced a literature of power structures and slaughter, and of individuals desperately seeking identity before being sacrificed for someone else's ideal. Around 1900, Foucault suggests, the balance of power began to shift: "For a long time, one of the characteristic privileges of sovereign power was the right to decide life and death . . . By the time the right of life and death was framed by the classical theoreticians, it was in a considerably diminished form."[60]

Yet by means of technologies of killing and healing, and the patterns and demands of ritual sacrifice that continue within them, such authority became more powerful than ever in the modern period even as belief in its efficacy and meaning waned.

CHAPTER 4

Dying in bed

The bed situates the fundamental human actions, those Eliot's Apeneck Sweeney reduces to "Birth, and copulation, and death. / That's all the facts when you come to brass tacks" ("Fragment of an Agon" 38–9). John Bishop notes that the word "bed," where people asleep are "dead to the world," "derives from the proto-Indo-European root ... meaning 'to dig or bury.'" It stands, he adds, "in an oddly complementary relation to the word 'cemetery,' which derives from the Greek *koimötörion* ('sleeping room,' 'dormitory') – in turn from the verb *koima* ('to put to bed')." Hence, "we drift through sleep in places primordially conceived as burial sites and are laid to rest at our wakes in places originally designating bedrooms."[1] Such etymological transformation underlies the laying out of corpses in "the Slumber-Room" (as in Waugh's *Loved One*).

Ariès argues that the "clericalization of death" in the thirteenth century erased the interval between death and judgment: judgment came down to earth and was enacted around the deathbed as a result of actions occurring there. The soul's fate came to depend not on prior actions, but solely on the dying moment, the moment of truth, when everything was won or lost.[2] Hence, at the end of Marlowe's *Dr. Faustus* angels and demons struggle for Faustus' soul. The possibility of last-minute confession or conversion defined the dying process, so that in extreme cases a doctor's first duty was to summon a priest.

The dying moment's cultural prominence is crucial in *Othello*, which introduced the bed onto the stark English stage. Shakespeare dramatizes the eros/thanatos trope that "occurs in nearly every culture in the world": alleged infidelity transforms the site of consummation into a deathbed.[3] Shakespeare had earlier sketched the trope in *Hamlet*'s graveyard scene. Gertrude speaks of eros become thanatos:

I hoped thou shouldst have been my Hamlet's wife.
I thought thy bride-bed to have decked, sweet maid,
And not t'have strewed thy grave. (5.1.244–6)

As if on cue, Hamlet leaps into the grave to seize pride of place, over Laertes, in loving the dead Ophelia.

Rhetorically if not consciously, Desdemona anticipates the substitution of funeral for marital rites. On being ordered by Othello "to bed on th' instant," she asks Emilia to "shroud" her in "one of these same [wedding] sheets" if she should die, sings the willow song of disappointed love, and implies her willingness to surrender "all the world" (4.3.8–86). Desdemona's despondency anticipates and climaxes almost immediately not in marital consummation but in her murder, which Othello finds easier to perform than lovemaking. Yet believing in the dying moment's supreme significance, Othello tells Desdemona, "I would not kill thy unpreparèd spirit . . . I would not kill thy soul." Self-appointed priest of the deathbed ritual, Othello enumerates its stages: prayer, preparing one's spirit for death and reconciling one's self "to heaven and grace," the confession of sins and appeal for mercy (5.2.26–61).

The paradigm of "the good death" that Shakespeare evokes in *Richard II* and *Othello* is what Huizinga calls "a great cultural idea."[4] Reality was often quite different, "for in the age of the Black Death people died miserably and profligately. In times of famine, corpses were found with grass in their mouths. In times of plague, the dying were often abandoned and their bodies piled up or tossed without ceremony into mass graves."[5] Or at least this was true of the lower classes, for "great cultural ideas" are often class-inflected; people who matter socially and politically are likeliest to have plays written about them and to have "important" deaths and funerals. With or without plague, peasants rarely enjoy "good deaths."

Dying confession retained great force during the Renaissance, but the Reformation shifted the focus from the deathbed to making death part of daily religious practice, undermining the last moment's spiritual significance. *Othello*, in fact, enacts the transition: in order to exculpate Othello, Desdemona dies absurdly claiming that she has suffocated herself. For this lie Othello, invoking the letter of church doctrine, would damn her: "She's like a liar gone to burning hell!" Emilia, however, powerfully reinterprets the dying moment: "O, the more angel she, / And you the blacker devil!" (5.2.129–35). We are meant to understand that Desdemona attains salvation because of her blameless life, which her dying lie enhances rather than negates. She lived, as Calvin exhorted, "with death always before our eyes." Jeremy Taylor compared deathbed repentance to "washing the corpse, it is cleanly and civil, but makes no change deeper than the skin." The illumination of the last moment "is the greatest mockery of God in the world" because it renders one "useless and intolerable to the world [by] permitting all impiety with the greatest impunity and encouragement."[6] Presumably the reverse is also true, so that Othello is as wrong about Desdemona's dying as about her life. Like Calvin, Taylor urged the contemplation of death throughout life: "repentance being the renewing of a holy life . . . it is a contradiction to say, that a Man can live a holy life upon his deathbed."[7] Taylor's scenario displaces the art of dying with that of living, in effect spreading the deathbed scene over a lifetime and affecting every day of that life. The spiritual treatises of the sixteenth and seventeenth centuries sought not to prepare the dying for death, but to teach the living to meditate on death so that they might learn to live well (*Hour* 299–301).

Enlightenment thinkers generally affirmed a rigid separation between life and death, viewed doubts about the firmness of these categories as superstition, and expressed little interest in the transition between them. For the most part they shared Samuel Johnson's view that "It matters not how a man dies, but how he lives. The act of dying is not of importance, it lasts so short a time."[8] Nineteenth-century thanatology was altogether different. Victorian literature is replete with funerals: Dickens, for example, depicts numerous burials, as well as the digging-up of corpses. Reverence for what Hardy called "the sacredness of last words" (*Mayor of Casterbridge* 332) and the belief that death was susceptible to understanding and control restored the deathbed to prominence in many Victorian novels and most biographies.[9] These representations occurred within highly conventionalized social customs and funerary rituals meant to ease the transition from death to grave. Consolatory Christian literature emphasized the continuity between this life and the next, particularly the idea of heaven as community (*Hour* 19). Culturally central and openly acknowledged, death for the Victorians "was no mystery, except in the sense that death is always a mystery."[10]

Generally conceived as climactic, familiar, even domestic, death was a drama centered on the dying person, the protagonist, with family, friends, and often strangers participating and bearing witness. Ian Wilson comments, "up to a century ago death was a social event, the tolling of the bell that signified the giving of the Last Rites being a call for even complete strangers to hurry to a dying person's bedside."[11] Public and available, Victorian deathbed scenes were emotionally extravagant, crowded and full of activity: "Hence the profound significance of Pascal's remark that one dies alone, for at that time one was never physically alone at the moment of death" (*Hour* 19). Dickens' Scrooge is deemed not to have been "natural in his lifetime" because if "he had been, he'd have had somebody to look after him when he was struck with Death, instead of lying gasping out his last there, alone by himself" ("Christmas Carol" 472). Pascal's statement resonated less in the modern period when dying alone in a hospital room was likely.

Deathbed scenes feature prominently in Dickens' *The Old Curiosity Shop*, *Dombey and Son*, *Bleak House*, and *Hard Times*; Charlotte Brontë's *Jane Eyre*; and Browning's "The Bishop Orders His Tomb" and *The Ring and the Book*, and in nineteenth-century US literature like Cooper's *The Prairie*, Stowe's *Uncle Tom's Cabin*, Dickinson's "I Heard a Fly Buzz When I Died." Harking back to the *ars moriendi* tradition, the moment of dying reclaimed aesthetic and spiritual significance: climaxing the life conceived as a work of art and launching the soul into the next world. Such occasions enact a vision of a stable quotidian order and a direct link between this world and the next.

Protagonists of Victorian deathbeds, with their aesthetic and spiritual orientation, were often children (Little Nell in *The Old Curiosity Shop*, Little Johnny in *Our Mutual Friend*, Little Eva in *Uncle Tom's Cabin*), women (Helen Burns in *Jane Eyre*), or unconscious rather than active heroic figures, often voiceless at the end, susceptible to sentimentality because dematerialized and passive, effaced even before death. In *Jane Eyre*, the virtuous Helen Burns, who says her dying is a journey "to my long home – my last home . . . I am very happy, Jane . . . I am going to God" (70–1), dies peacefully asleep in Jane's arms. Unaltered by death, Little Nell's corpse images "her tranquil beauty and profound repose . . . her former self lay there . . . that same sweet face . . . the same mild lively look" (539) – a death mourned by an entire culture, but sentimentalized by no one, Morley suggests, more than her author: "Dickens was moved to forget his grammar: 'Nobody shall miss her like I shall. It is such a very painful thing to me, that I really cannot express my sorrow.'"[12] Catherine's death in *Wuthering Heights* is aestheticized as a peaceful drift: "She drew a sigh, and stretched herself, like a child reviving, and sinking again to sleep." Death, Nelly Dean claims, restores Catherine to the innocent state before passion claimed her: "She *lies* with a sweet smile on her face; and her latest ideas wandered back to pleasant early days. Her life closed in a pleasant dream." But Heathcliff, echoing Othello, insists on the punning falsity of Nelly's recreation: "Why, she's a *liar* to the end!" (183; my emphasis). He demands that Catherine's spirit remain true by staying with him: "Where is she? Not *there* – not in heaven – not perished – where? . . . You said I killed you – haunt me then! The murdered *do* haunt their murderers. I believe – I know that ghosts *have* wandered on earth" (183).

Victorian men, like Heathcliff himself, Stephen Blackpool in *Hard Times*, and Casaubon in *Middlemarch*, are usually denied peaceful, sentimentalizing passage from life to death: they go from authority status to corpse without transition. For both genders, the exceptions to these generalizations are marginal figures: the "worldly, selfish, graceless, thankless, religionless" Rose Dawson of *Vanity Fair* (142), the doomed criminal Magwitch in *Great Expectations*, the outcast Jo, prayerless but saintly, in *Bleak House*, who dies choosing his "berryin ground" and in hopes of light to come (571–2).

Toward the end of the nineteenth century, F.W. Farrar, the writer and preacher who witnessed many deathbed scenes, gave testimony that supports Jeremy Taylor's Protestantism rather than Victorian convention: "Those scenes have left on my mind the deep conviction that a death-bed very rarely makes any observable difference in the general habit of mind of the dying . . . I find the strongest possible disinclination to speak of religious subjects, or the habit of fencing off all approach to anything like a heart-searching intercourse . . . so far as I have seen, they die, in nine cases out of ten, exactly as they have lived."[13] Numerous doctors, scientists, and clergymen testify to the peacefulness and absence of fear and terror of those on the verge of death. The Canadian doctor William Osler found only 18 percent of the 500 whose deaths he witnessed suffered physical pain, and only three expressed terror or remorse; the physician and medical researcher Lewis Thomas saw "agony in death only once."[14]

Michael Wheeler cites Walton's *The Last Moments of HRH The*

4 W.I. Walton, *The Last Moments of HRH The Prince Consort*, lithograph (1862).

Prince Consort (see illustration 4) as the apogee of the public deathbed scene. Depicting numerous doctors and statesmen, as well as the grieving royal family, Walton's picture of the state bed-chamber "not only suppresses emotion, but also conceals a potential for sexual irony, with the children of the fruitful marriage gathered near the bed. The overt analysis of the relationship between *eros* and *thanatos* ... was largely the preserve of the Gothic in the nineteenth century, where the 'normal' (and safe) compartmentalizing of birth, marriage, and death was disrupted."[15] What Walton suppresses is unwittingly implied in the crude cut-out, "The Death of the Prince Consort at Buckingham Palace" (illustration 5), a close-up of the same moment showing only the loving family, the children owing their existence to erotic acts performed in the depicted bed by the dying Albert and his grieving wife.

For Victorians, death's personal meaning had been sustained by faith in progress, a utopian expectation that the world, becoming both morally better and increasingly comprehensible, would lead to a better one, both here and beyond. This faith began to unravel by the end of the century, at least in part because material advances subverted rather than strengthened it. Ian Wilson writes, "When

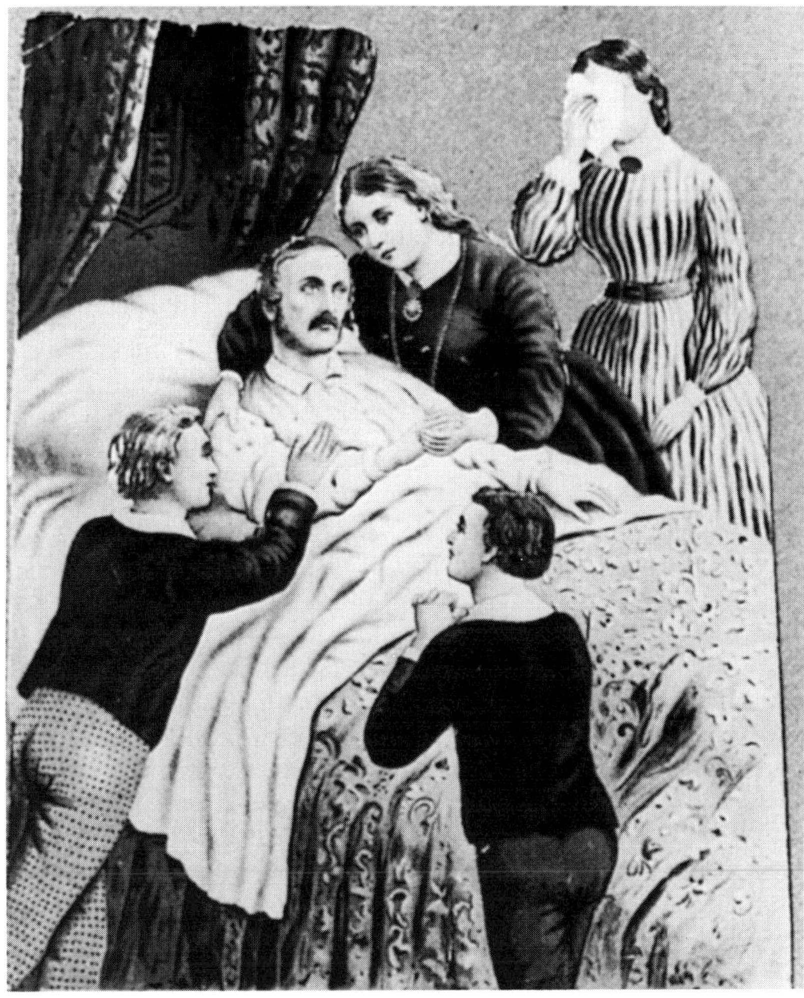

5 Anon., "The Death of the Prince Consort at Buckingham Palace" (late nineteenth century).

medical knowledge dramatically improved in the nineteenth century the incidence of misdiagnoses of death increased."[16] Definitions of death and the determination of the death moment – like the distinction between life and death – became *more* dubious as medical personnel learned how difficult the line is to draw. Holding up a mirror to check for breath (or a feather, as Lear does with

Cordelia) became insufficient to overcome the growing fear of live burial. Joyce's Bloom's wonders, "And if he was alive all the time? Whew! By jingo, that would be awful! ... They ought to have some law to pierce the heart and make sure or an electric clock or a telephone in the coffin and some kind of a canvas airhole. Flag of distress" (*Ulysses* 91). Technology increased both sophistication and incertitude concerning the death moment. Lack of breath as determinant yielded to cardiac arrest and then to a flat electroencephalogram or electrocardiogram: what had seemed instantaneous and obvious became marked by stages and doubt. In consequence, doctors sought "to 'redefine' death, with few confident that they have yet reached any totally unimpeachable formula,"[17] or that they ever will.

Like the collapse of sexual taboos around the turn of the century, modernist reconceptualized dying followed from the cultural rediscovery of the body that the eighteenth-century Swift, for one, had obsessively detailed in the Brobdingnag section of *Gulliver's Travels*, but that Victorians like Dickens and Trollope had elided. Despite the openness and emotional intensity of Victorian deathbeds, the dying material body was covered and denied as the site of both lust and mortality; dying could then be romanticized and aestheticized, a practice far removed from de Sade's claim that "there is no better way to know death than to link it with some licentious image."[18] Though birth, copulation, and death often occurred in the same Victorian bed, writers like Dickens, George Eliot, and Thackeray sought, if often unsuccessfully, to suppress the erotic rhetoric of their deathbed scenes.[19] Continental writers like Balzac, Flaubert, Zola, Tolstoy, and Dostoevsky depict not the Victorian "beautiful death," with its spiritual orientation, but material mortality in their characters' "dirty death."[20] With almost Jacobean morbidity, Flaubert traces the effects of poison, assailing what had been the site of lust, as it disfigures Emma Bovary while killing her; Tolstoy's teleology seeks spiritual transcendence, but he obsessively details Ivan Ilych's material disintegration.

The nauseating spectacle, disgusting odor, and terrible screaming of Emma and Ivan drive from the deathbed those who, in a Victorian depiction, would have gathered, borne witness, and sought enlightenment. In England, the change is adumbrated by Hardy, the most modern of Victorians, who sought, "without a mincing of words," to explore the strongest of passions. *Jude the Obscure* details both illicit love and the consequent decay of the once erotic substance that comprises the "dirty death." Jude is abandoned in his dying by both his spiritual wife, Sue Bridehead, and his physical one, Arabella. Tragedy follows from Sue's antagonism toward the body; Hardy writes, "though she has children, her intimacies with Jude have never been more than occasional." Everything follows inexorably from her scrupulousness and their failed passion: ostracism because they live together unmarried; poverty; the deaths of the children; their return to earlier, disastrous, spouses ("Weddings be funerals ... nowadays," Mrs. Edlin comments [316]); Jude's illness and dying. His whispering, through "parched lips," *Job*'s curse at having been born is counterpoised with the "Hurrah!" of revelers (321), as the indifferent Arabella hurries disgustedly from his deathbed to seek new pleasure.

The turn from Victorian deathbed conventions appears in the effect of maternal dying on the lives of three modernists: Woolf, Joyce, and Lawrence. All three mothers died at home, surrounded by their families who had gathered to bear witness. But the Victorian paradigm was radically ruptured in each case: the dying was agony for the mother and agonizing for the rest; surviving fathers, self-pitying bullies all, were self-obsessed; children did not properly grieve; the dead mothers, unappeased, became haunting presences. For all three writers, the failed ritual of the maternal deathbed continued to recur: attempting to free themselves, they repeatedly wrote of or around or through it.

Woolf was the youngest of the three, only thirteen, when her mother died in 1895. Her reaction at the deathbed was to laugh – to hide tears? because of others' Victorian posturing? because the worst was finally over? because "I felt nothing whatever"?[21] Then she envisioned a man sitting on the deathbed. Mark Spilka argues, plausibly, that the ghost was Herbert Duckworth, Julia Stephen's first husband, whom she had apparently loved deeply but who had died after only three years of marriage.[22] Woolf writes of Duckworth, "how completely he satisfied her is proved by the collapse, the complete collapse into which she fell when he died. All her gaiety, all her sociability left her. She was as unhappy as it is possible for anyone to be ... Stella once told me that she used to lie upon his grave ... As she was undemonstrative that seems a superlative expression of her grief." Stella Duckworth, with whom Woolf shared this vision, seemed to acknowledge that the apparition was indeed her father: "'It's nice that she shouldn't be alone', Stella said after a moment's pause" (*Moments of Being* 90, 92). Though Leslie Stephen demanded comforting from his women, Woolf failed to provide solace on this occasion: "My father staggered from the bedroom as we came. I stretched out my arms to stop him, but he brushed past me, crying out something I could not catch; distraught" (*Moments of Being* 91).

Joyce depended greatly on his mother, but the relationship had to be on his terms. When she was dying (in 1903), he refused her plea that he make confession and take communion, and he took pride in not praying for her at the end; but the night of her death he went to her room to see her ghost. Richard Ellmann writes: "His mother was part of the stable world he was engaged in renouncing; yet he did not want her to renounce him. If she died he could neither hurt nor please her; death was abandonment of response to him." The drunken John Joyce, more overtly self-centered, cried out to his dying wife, "I can't do any more. If you can't get well, die. Die and be damned to you!" After her death, he self-pityingly anticipated his own, and then imagined that his children longed for it.[23]

Lawrence rushed the first copy of *The White Peacock* into his dying mother's hands (in 1910), but though the inscription he had written for her was read out, she turned away and never mentioned it. Having loved his mother "almost with a husband and wife love" and having been "born hating my father" so much that he could wish him in hell (*Letters* 1: 3 December 1910, 190; 20 February 1911, 232), Lawrence could yet describe his mother's dying with increasing distance and aesthetic disdain: "It is a continuous 'We watched her breathing through the night' [from Thomas Hood's "The Death-Bed"] . . . and still she is here, and it is the old slow horror. I think Tom Hood's woman looked sad but beautiful: but my mother is a sight to see and be silent about for ever . . . Banal! . . . The desire of my life, at present, is to have mother buried." He then says he has just proposed marriage to Louise Burrows (*Letters* 1: 5 December 1910, 192–3). The most dominated by his mother in life, Lawrence performed an exorcism during her dying; subsequently, as *Sons and Lovers*' autobiographical Paul Morel, he both failed to mourn her and, driven by impatience at her lingering, performed euthanasia to get free of her. Afterward, Paul and his sister, like Virginia Woolf, "laughed together like two conspiring children. On top of all their horror flicked this little sanity" (394).

Yet Lawrence remained sufficiently haunted to emulate Flaubert and Tolstoy in emphasizing bodily disintegration, the moral corruption manifested as physical rot on the still-inhabited body, as with Thomas Crich's death in *Women in Love*. Similarly reacting against Victorian conventions, modernist texts like Mann's *Death in Venice*, Faulkner's *As I Lay Dying* and "A Rose for Emily," and Hemingway's "The Snows of Kilimanjaro" inscribe a pattern of material and psychological decay within the topos of the deathbed monologue. Hemingway's story begins with a conversation in which Harry, dying like Ivan Ilych of an insignificant wound, insists that his rotting body's gangrenous stink, like Nietzsche's decomposing God, signals his impending death, as the presence of gathering vultures testifies. Faulkner's Addie Bundren, "no more than a bundle of rotten sticks" before she dies, is driven by a "furious desire to hide that abject nakedness which we bring here with us, carry with us into operating rooms, carry stubbornly and furiously with us into the earth again" (43–5). Taken on a horrific ten-day journey to the cemetery in Jefferson, her unembalmed corpse is exposed to the world by the stench one witness compares to "a piece of rotten cheese coming into an ant-hill" (193), the circling vultures (116, 177, 185, 200), and the astonished gazes of those the family passes. Darl, the one son sane enough to try to cremate the corpse, is sent by the family to an asylum in order to escape having to pay for the barn he burns down.

The war writers of this period and after (Remarque, Barbusse, Sartre, and Genet) similarly depicted the "dirty death" in which "the idea of death and the fear that it inspires open the sphincters and thus re-create in a completely healthy body the sordid realities of disease" (*Hour* 569). The naturalistic emphasis of Zola and Dreiser mocks the Christian promise that, at the Resurrection, the dead will arise and regain their own, transfigured bodies.[24] Nineteenth-century English novels had an ethos controlled by women, the arbiters of the domestic sphere, as writers, characters, and readers. Just as doctors were preempting midwives, modernists attempted a male takeover of dying by removing civilian death from the family setting to the realms of medical personnel and the funeral industry. When dying and death left the home people became less familiar and less comfortable with what they looked like, and less willing to contemplate them. It was rare in nineteenth-century life or literature that someone had not witnessed a dying and paid respect to a "beautiful corpse"; in the first half of the twentieth century it was rare to have this experience.[25] The modern emphasis, unlike the Victorian, was on making death private, even secret; for the decline of traditional religious faith transferred to death the sense of shame and fear previously associated with sex. According to Gorer, whose perspective is more class-based than Ariès', the chances of dying alone increase higher up the social scale. Working classes, which preserved customs like drawing the blinds and covering mirrors after a death, tend to be more familiar with death and less frightened of it, and to pay respect to the body before burial, because their deaths are likelier to occur at home.[26]

The officer in Kafka's "In the Penal Colony" nostalgically compares the modern emphasis on the meaninglessness of dying with the way it used to be: "How we all absorbed the look of transfiguration on the face of the sufferer, how we bathed our cheeks in the radiance of that justice, achieved at last and fading so quickly" (209). With the tradition beyond resuscitation, the officer seeks to enact it one last time, on himself; but his dying becomes, instead, a horrific echo of deathbed meaning: "The Harrow was not writing, it was only jabbing, and the bed was not turning the body over but only bringing it up quivering against the needles. The explorer wanted to do something, if possible, to bring the whole machine to a standstill, for this was no exquisite torture such as the officer desired, this was plain murder." In the end, "no sign was visible of the promised redemption; what the others had found in the machine the officer had not found" (224–5). The sacrificial act, whether of self or other, seems devoid of meaning in a world lacking transcendent signification.

Religious novelists commonly sustain the deathbed's fictive and spiritual power. Martin du Gard's *Jean Barois* (1913) and Cather's *Death Comes for the Archbishop* (1927) replicate Othello's belief that the final drama can outweigh a lifetime's actions, and that engaged survivors can enter vicariously into the process. Cather's narrator says, "there was always hope that the dying man might reveal something of what he alone could see; that his countenance, if not his lips, would speak, and on his features would fall some light or shadow from beyond" (170). Some go further, seeking not only to discern meaning but, like Othello, to impose it. In *Jean Barois*, Barois' father, a religious skeptic throughout his life, apologizes to his son for his dying weakness and then confesses and receives communion. Barois himself later repeats his father's action. As soon as he dies, however, his pious wife finds an atheistical "testament" he had written in order to disavow, in advance, any conversion he might undergo. Watching as she burns it, the priest becomes complicit in her retrospective rewriting of Barois' life in order to make it conform to its final moments.[27]

Catholic converts like Greene and Waugh risked anachronism to reassert the potency of deathbed confessions. In *Brighton Rock* (1938) Greene posits possible repentance for the evil Pinkie "between the stirrup and the ground,"[28] and the whiskey priest in *The Power and the Glory* (1940) walks cheerfully into a deathtrap in order to hear a murderer's dying confession, for "a Christian could believe that the soul ... held absolution and peace at the final moment, after a lifetime of the most hideous crime ... He had heard men talk of the unfairness of a deathbed repentance – as if it was an easy thing to break the habit of a life whether to do good or evil" (254). The priest fails; the murderer, still "bent on vicarious violence," dies without confessing; and though the priest whispers "the words of conditional absolution, in case, for one second before it crossed the border, the spirit had repented," he prays "without conviction" (255). Greene believed in the power and meaning of the final moment, but not in our ability to take advantage of it.

Conversely, Waugh climaxes what he calls "the fierce little human tragedy" (318) of *Brideshead Revisited* (1944) with a dying moment that saves both protagonist and witnesses. The apostate Lord Marchmain, who "lay dying, wearing himself down in the struggle to live" (304), makes the sign of the cross at the end (307). Waugh's stock Irish priest, Father Mackay, comments: "Well, now, and that was a beautiful thing to see. I've known it happen that way again and again. The devil resists to the last moment and then the Grace of God is too much for him" (307–8). Marchmain's dying gesture, it is implied, exculpates him from a life of sinful indulgence; it also destroys the adulterous relationship between the deathbed witnesses, his daughter Julia and Charles Ryder, the novel's protagonist. Despite having argued vehemently against summoning the priest, Charles himself kneels and prays: "O God, if there is a God, forgive him his sins, if there is such a thing as sin." And after Marchmain makes his sign, Charles thinks, "Then I knew that the sign I had asked for was not a little thing, not a passing nod of recognition, and a phrase came back to me from my childhood of the veil of the temple being rent from top to bottom" (307). Similarly affected, Julia ends their "sinful" relationship; Charles converts to Catholicism.

Instead of being either "beautiful" or "dirty," dying was often elided from both experience and literature during the modern period. This cultural shift gained impetus in this century's second decade because war took death from the bed to the trenches, and because medical developments gave patients, for the first time in history, more likelihood of being helped than harmed by doctors:[29] a change that moved death from the domestic to the clinical bed. The extraordinary technologies of modern medicine and mass slaughter effectively silenced, denied, and emptied death of traditional meaning, thus precluding an appropriate end. The liminal figure, reduced to a thing or statistic, was effaced or else transformed into an object of political, commercial, and technological transactions. Writing of intensive hospital care, Richard Macksey seems to be describing the war machine: "The full panoply of 'life-support systems,' the technology of death, has even made the previously unequivocal threshold between life and death exceedingly ambiguous . . . The untender mercies of the modern comprehensive medical center hardly leave much of a stage for the departing protagonist."[30]

Childbirth underwent an identical change: in the nineteenth century it commonly occurred among family members at home, and on the bed of conception and dying. During the modern period, birth was taken from midwives and hospitalized at least partly as a male attempt to eliminate what Lawrence called "the Magna Mater" (*Letters* 3: 5 December 1918, 302): female control of "the mysteries" – as mother, lover, layer-out.[31] Seeing a midwife, Stephen Dedalus thinks, "One of her sisterhood lugged me squealing into life" (*Ulysses* 32); but in the novel's present, Mina Purefoy gives birth in a hospital, "Horne's house" (316). Both shifts are linked with suffrage and the war: as women claimed places in the male work world, politics, and higher education, men denied them their traditional roles as midwives (who had often been burned as witches) and guardians of the corpse: domestic, reproductive, and ritual roles. Modern doctors initiated into technology seemed more trustworthy intercessors in dying and death than the women who, as Joyce suggests in "The Sisters" and Lawrence shows in "Odour of Chrysanthemums," had usually washed and prepared the dead for burial.[32] In *Witches, Midwives and Nurses*, Ehrenreich and English depict medicine as an ages-old arena of gender struggle. They link medieval Europe's suppression of witches and the rise of the male-dominated medical profession in the US as aspects of the male takeover of health care, and see a return of female healers as central to the women's movement.

Through at least the 1970s, hospitals would shift into high gear for seriously ill patients. Doctors, who increasingly viewed themselves as wonderworkers to whom, from the onset of fatal illness, the dying "belonged," asserted authority and expertise. Patients mattered only as cases, and any possibility of death was suppressed as unthinkable: its occurrence was viewed as failure in our success-oriented culture. David Wheeler writes, "Death and dying arouse *mutual* fears in doctor and patient, particularly in an age in which faith in God has for many been displaced by faith in science."[33] Medical personnel who refuse to acknowledge a patient's terminal condition are of little assistance during life's most traumatic transition. In fact, just as priests in ancient Greece avoided the dying for fear of contamination and because their offices were thought to be inefficacious during the ritual disposing of the dead,[34] doctors often absented themselves at the end. Death was left for menials to tidy away,[35] as in "sickness unto death" tales like Tolstoy's *Ivan Ilych* and Kafka's *The Metamorphosis* and "A Hunger Artist." Then, pursuing the logic of the post-Victorian shift from climactic deathbeds, the male-dominated funeral industry refocused attention to rituals of burial and survival.

In the decades after Greene's and Waugh's novels of Catholic conversion (see chapter 1 above), depersonalized dying and death were increasingly challenged by pioneering studies like Gorer's "Pornography of Death," Kübler-Ross' hands-on treatment of terminal patients and her influential writings, the work of thanatologists like Edwin Shneidman, "historians of mentalities" like Philippe Ariès, the hospice and dying-at-home movement, and the notion of rational suicide and patient rights. Despite the antipathy her project aroused, Kübler-Ross persisted in recording how death, considered familial, personal, and natural prior to the twentieth century, had become captive of a predominantly male medical establishment that preached and practiced denial. Her work and writing not only defined the modern condition, but helped to change it, and restore something of the traditional female role. Death's return has been sudden, profound, and widespread: ejected by Western society, it is returning as quickly as it disappeared (*Hour* 560). Hospice and dying-at-home movements are restoring the *ars moriendi* and deathbeds to cultural practice (see chapter 13 below). Death is reclaiming centerstage in medical discussion and treatment, academic study, postmodern fiction, and AIDS narratives.

CHAPTER 5

Artifices of mortality

Yeats' speaker in "The Tower" (1926) simultaneously proclaims and bequeaths his credo:

> It is time that I wrote my will . . .
> And I declare my faith:
> I mock Plotinus' thought
> And cry in Plato's teeth,
> Death and life were not
> Till man made up the whole,
> Made lock, stock and barrel
> Out of his bitter soul,
> Aye, sun and moon and star, all,
> And further add to that
> That, being dead we rise,
> Dream and so create
> Translunar Paradise.[1]

Yeats places man at the center, in his faith and will, making "out of his bitter soul" the whole that is death and life and "Translunar Paradise." The process of dreaming and creating is enacted in "Sailing to Byzantium" (1927) when an old man, no longer at home in *that* "country" – Ireland, the West, mortality – journeys from fecundity and flux ("Those dying generations . . . the mackerel-crowded seas"), eastward, back in time, toward spirituality, in order to be gathered into the "artifice of eternity." For eternity here *is* artifice, a culture-specific construct that, like other aesthetic creations, reflects and perpetuates social meaning. The death for which the speaker prays depends on conscious choice and shaping, an opting "out of nature" and entry into a realm of unending singing. Both death and eternity, then, are wrought, formed, in this exceptional case "Of hammered gold and gold enamelling" by "Grecian goldsmiths."[2] Ironically, in Yeats' imagination nature and artifact intersect and create each other. In one of the poem's earliest comments, T. Sturge Moore shrewdly notes, "a goldsmith's bird is as much nature as a man's body, especially if it only sings like Homer and Shakespeare of what is past or passing or to come to Lords and Ladies."[3]

Nature and artifice meet in the accoutrements of death: wills and death certificates, burial containers and sites, tombs, effigies, and epitaphs, the corpse itself – the most transparent forms of self-representation. From them may be adduced both significant cultural transformations and the interests of those who control death's processes: medical professionals, coroners, morticians, religious and political leaders, lawyers, and florists, plus those who write about them. This chapter examines death's artifacts, the constructs that comprise a culture's, including modernism's, artifices of mortality.

WILLS AND TESTAMENTS

In reconstructing Western attitudes toward death, Ariès scoured funerary artifacts. Wills proved especially revealing sources of information (*Hour* xv). In antiquity and again after the eighteenth century, wills were private legal documents that primarily concerned transmittal of property. For medieval Christians, however, the focus was not the life ending and what was left behind, but what lay beyond.[4] Between the twelfth and eighteenth centuries, the will "was primarily a religious document, required by the Church even of the poorest persons . . . a sacramental, like holy water; the Church enforced its use, making it obligatory under pain of excommunication. Anyone who died intestate could not, in principle, be buried in a church or cemetery" (*Hour* 189). Yet, Ragon suggests, looking forward and looking back are inextricably connected: fourteenth-century nobility "ruined itself in pious donations intended to redeem a life that was hardly pious."[5] Wills specified the number of masses, up to 10,000;[6] their material concerns included expressions of affection; redressing of wrongs and forgiveness of injuries; warnings against premature burial; choice of burial site; instructions regarding the funeral procession and service, epitaphs, memorial plaques, material bequests.

In the Renaissance, wills and testaments became a literary genre in which poets commented on life's brevity and death's certainty (Ariès, *Hour* 198–201). Like Yeats' "The Tower," such documents enact the testator's faith through distributing alms, charitable endowments, and pious bequests, which Ben Jonson's *Volpone* satirizes as material negotiation. Thus a correlation, unknown in pre-Christian times and rare in the twentieth century, was established between wealth and death. Since deathbed bequests assured salvation, they retroactively validated avarice: "The will served both to justify the love of earth and to make an investment in heaven, thanks to the transition of a good death" (*Hour* 189–94, 606).

This situation contextualizes *The Merchant of Venice*'s casket plot, appropriately so called since it originates in a will. Considering her father's testament an "artifice of eternity" through which paternal authority posthumously controls the living, Portia complains that "I may neither choose who I would, nor refuse who I dislike, so is the will of a living daughter curb'd by the will of a dead father" (1.2.23–5). But Portia never contests her maid Nerissa's statement:

> Your father was ever virtuous, and holy men at their death have good inspirations; therefore the lott'ry that he hath devis'd in these three chests of gold, silver, and lead, whereof who chooses his meaning chooses you, will no doubt never be chosen by any rightly but one who you shall rightly love. (1.2.27–32)

Rather than repudiate her dead father's will, Portia engages the process it imposes for determining her husband. Whether jokingly or not, she tells Nerissa to "set a deep glass of Rhenish wine on the contrary casket" (1.2.94) to distract an undesirable suitor. She gives Bassanio, the suitor she desires, numerous verbal clues, urging him to "tarry ... Before you *hazard*" and to "Beshrew your *eyes*," for, unlikely as it seems, "I stand for *sacrifice*" (3.2.1–2, 14, 57; my emphases). She commands a song to be played, that, using strong "-ed" rhymes, warns against "fancy" based on eyesight and steers Bassanio to the visually unappealing lead casket ("Who chooseth me must give and hazard all he hath") that contains "Fair Portia's counterfeit!" (2.7.9; 3.2.115). Thus aligning her father's will and her own, Portia gains the husband she desires while following the letter, and perhaps even the spirit, of her father's testament.[7]

Shakespeare manipulates and correlates wealth, love, and death in order to validate Portia's father. Bassanio is initially depicted as a fortune-hunter who has been profligate with his own property ("I have disabled mine estate"), then with that of Antonio, whom he owes the most (1.1.124, 131), and presumably with others' as well. Worse, in order to recoup, with one roll of the dice, all he has lost, Bassanio seeks a second fortune from Antonio, even though his hazard jeopardizes not his own but Antonio's life. Bassanio reveals much by the order in which he initially enumerates Portia's qualities:

> In Belmont is a lady *richly left*;
> And she is *fair* and, fairer than that word,
> Of wondrous *virtues*. (1.1.161–3; my emphases)

The implicit question is whether Bassanio's character or his situation is speaking: he will prove himself worthy of Portia (and her riches and love) only by reversing these priorities. What a modern writer might represent as an intolerable imposition on an intelligent and willful woman, Shakespeare justifies by reflecting contemporary testamentary practice: as Nerissa implies, the right attitude toward Portia's wealth defines the husband who will love her properly.

Until the mid-eighteenth century, wills had two main sections: pious clauses (the more important part) and the distribution of wealth. With the church as broker, the will was an insurance policy between the individual and God: its premiums paid in temporal currency but its payoff eternal wealth in heaven. In the eighteenth century, however, the moral and material emphasis of Portia's father's will became the norm: obligations to heirs gained precedence over charitable contributions and pious endowments as the testament's focus "shifted from philanthropy to family management" (*Hour* 191, 196–7). In analyzing thousands of eighteenth-century Provençal wills, Michel Vovelle found a pattern of increasing simplicity, indifference to the place of burial, and secularization.[8]

Victorian wills and legacies were essentially legalistic and material: would heirs receive the bequest provided by the laws of inheritance? The answer was usually unambiguous, and the dual concern of earlier wills became a target of *Volpone*-like satire. Browning's "The Bishop Orders His Tomb at Saint Praxed's Church," for example, scathingly depicts a Renaissance bishop, "dying by degrees," and against his will. While denouncing vanity in a church devoted to a virgin martyr who gave her wealth to the poor, Browning's bishop surrounds himself with his possessions and sons, neither of which his calling allowed him. Ruskin praised the poem's superb representation "of the Renaissance spirit – its worldliness, inconsistency, pride, hypocrisy, ignorance of itself, love of art, of luxury, and of good Latin."[9] Mouthing deathbed pieties as he boasts of worldly success, the bishop orders a rich tomb, decorated with erotic figures out of Greek mythology, that commands the best view of the altar. He reluctantly dispenses the material goods – "all have I bequeathed you, villas, all" – that he would retain in this world or take with him to the next. He embodies what Ariès calls "precapitalist man who wants to 'go to his grave loaded with gold and riches' and to hold on to his fortune *in aeternum*, because he is hungry for it and cannot separate himself from it without a violent conversion. He accepted the idea of dying, but he could not bring himself to 'leave houses and orchards and gardens'" (*Hour* 194). Bequeathing great wealth rather than moral treasure, Browning's bishop anticipates the capitalist accumulation and bequeathing of vast fortunes – by men with names like Carnegie, Guggenheim, Morgan, Nobel, Rhodes, Rockefeller, and Vanderbilt – in the nineteenth century. Though ruthless and acquisitive, these men are now mostly known for the philanthropic foundations, libraries, museums, scholarships, and peace prizes they established through their willed rewriting of their lives.

Where Browning satirizes the spiritual pretensions of a materialist, Dickens, for whom wills and legacies were a central interest, targets a material process for an age whose materialism displaced spiritual worth. Saturated in London's toxic industrial fog, *Bleak House* elaborates a legacy case, concerning how the trusts under a Jarndyce will were to be administered, that lasts for decades: "one of the greatest Chancery suits known ... a monument of Chancery practice" (22). In terms that suggest *Bleak House* itself, Dickens proclaims:

> This is the Court of Chancery; which has its decaying houses and its blighted lands in every shire; which has its worn-out lunatic in every madhouse, and its dead in every churchyard ... which gives to monied might, the means abundantly of wearying out the right; which so exhausts finances, patience, courage, hope; so overthrows the brain and breaks the heart; that there is not an honourable man among its practitioners who would not give – who does not often give – the warning, "Suffer any wrong that can be done you, rather than come here!" (6–7)

Richard Carstone, the would-be beneficiary who mistakenly banks on law and capital, dies despairingly when the case absorbs in costs all of the disputed estate (760, 763).

Our Mutual Friend, which reconfigures *The Merchant of Venice*'s casket plot, also turns on a legacy. John Harmon has been left his father's fortune on condition that he marry Bella Wilfer, though she complains of having been "left to him in a will, like a dozen of spoons" (37). Since he has never met her and has been abroad for years, he can return disguised in order to determine his *own* will, whether, like Portia's suitors, to "take his chance between Yes and No" (460). John and Bella meet, fall in love, marry, and live for a time on his earnings. Finally, he reclaims his identity and his legacy: a union of wills and love that parallels Portia's.

Dickens' characters, however, take a tortuous and hazardous course to fulfill this will. Presumed to have been "Found Drowned" at the beginning by Gaffer Hexam, a "bird of prey" who fishes for bodies in the Thames, a disguised John Harmon inspects his own supposed corpse. Bella's self-pity and greed are more harshly portrayed than Bassanio's: " 'I am sure,' said she . . . I am one of the most unfortunate girls that ever lived . . . what a glimpse of wealth I had, and how it melted away, and how I am here in this ridiculous mourning – which I hate! – a kind of widow who never was married' " (36). But like Bassanio she attains a saving self-awareness – "what a mercenary little wretch I am" (459) – that leads ultimately to reformation.

Like *Bleak House*, saturated in fog symbolic of money, deceit, and death, *Our Mutual Friend* is encased in "mummy-dust," in which, as Peter Ackroyd writes, "Ancient myth and modern urban life co-exist and interpenetrate . . . the ash and dirt of London are thus placed within a perennial myth of death and rebirth." Dickens' London embodies national decay resulting from sterile commercialism in which monetary worth alone determines value.[10] Dickens nostalgically recalls a time when plot, setting, and character development could affirm the mythic vision of a dead father's will; but he places them in a deadly industrial environment where material death mocks such meaning.

As he often does, Hardy recasts the Victorian paradigm within what he calls "the ache of modernism." *The Mayor of Casterbridge* first enacts sin, repentance, and forgiveness, and then reenacts it as sin, despair, and death. Having failed his second test as badly as the first, the dying Henchard writes a will that addresses the usual concerns, but with no sense of spiritual survival or immortality. To negate himself he need only preclude human action and memory.

"MICHAEL HENCHARD'S WILL

"That Elizabeth-Jane Farfrae be not told of my death, or made to grieve on account of me.

"& that I be not bury'd in consecrated ground.
"& that no sexton be asked to toll the bell.
"& that nobody is wished to see my dead body.
"& that no murners walk behind me at my funeral.
"& that no flours be planted on my grave.
"& that no man remember me." (331)[11]

Hardy's poem, "His Immortality," locates the soul's survival, no longer conceivable as literal, in "each faithful heart / Of those bereft," and traces its fading, shrinking, and finally "Dying amid the dark."[12] Henchard's self-judgment, with its harsh, reiterated "& that no," would hasten rather than lengthen the process of the soul's fading, to unwish not his death but his life. His will, which his survivors respect, enters, at the end, into an uneasy balance, "due to the persistence of the unforeseen," between "unbroken tranquillity" and the "general drama of pain" (333). Elizabeth-Jane and Farfrae's happy marriage allows Henchard's life and will to be read as aberrant, yet it cannot negate the centrality of Henchard's fate to the novel's vision.

Legacies are usually ironic, bleak, and complexly enacted in modernist texts. Forster's *Howards End* is one of the least bleak, unless one is inclined to defend stereotypical upper-class bullies. Forster depicts Mrs. Wilcox's husband and son acting to thwart her dying wish to leave Howards End to Margaret Schlegel, for whom Mrs. Wilcox feels spiritual rather than familial kinship. Their unwarranted interference, which only delays the bequest, redounds solely against the men. Legacies are far harsher in both Fitzgerald's *The Beautiful and Damned* and Faulkner's "The Bear": inheritance both bequeaths riches and renders them valueless. After the protracted, *Bleak House*-like legal battle, Fitzgerald's Anthony Patch, in a final chapter ironically called "No Matter!", goes insane at the moment of success. Faulkner's Ike, reading the ledgers that serve as his grandfather's legacy, uncovers a family history replete with slavery's horrors, including incest, forced miscegenation, and suicide, that leads to his repudiation (see chapter 8 below).

The concept of a "living will"[13] is a byproduct of advanced technology that initially seemed an unquestionable good: to prolong life while minimizing pain and suffering. Recent cultural changes, however, argue that such "good" can sometimes do harm, that life holds dubious value for irreversibly comatose patients connected to machines that perform or control bodily functions. The emotional and financial costs can be extremely high for everyone concerned, the benefits negligible or non-existent. Testaments used to concern before and after: life, death, and the relationship between them. Living wills shift the focus to van Gennep's middle term: the problematic process of dying.

DEATH CERTIFICATES

Like other versions of fictional death, the death certificate, which Shneidman calls "that special form which gives operational meaning to death," is culturally specific rather than universal, different in different places and times, and replete with assumptions about human mortality. Its social functions include helping to determine property and pension rights, settling life insurance claims, charting genealogies, studying demographics and diseases, and assisting in crime detection. A legal text in which false statements are misdemeanors in much of the US, it is "badly flawed" because most states require a declaration of causality in terms of the "NASH classification" system: "Accident, suicide or homicide," with "natural" causes implicit if none of these three is specified.[14] Though possible causes may be too numerous to list, the death certificate lacks categories like "undetermined" and "pending," and ignores the degree of intentionality, short of suicide.

Peschel and Peschel suggest we have regressed in this area:

> Years ago, before the World Health Organization established strict rules for filling out death certificates, some physicians answered these questions quite colorfully. One old certificate read, "Cause of death: blow on the head with an ax. Contributory cause: another man's wife." Now, however, the "blow on the head with an ax" . . . would be certified as "skull fracture with laceration of brain" . . . and as "homicide." How much less revealing! . . . another old-time doctor wrote in response to the question about the cause of death of a person who had died suddenly: "Don't know. Died without the aid of a physician."[15]

Such narratives inscribe cultural realities beyond what boxes on a standard form allow.

Sounding like Virginia Woolf attacking Bennett, Wells, and Galsworthy for failing to create characters to live in their carefully constructed edifices, Shneidman considers the certificate "Cartesian and apsychological in spirit," reducing people to "biological machines to which things happen, rather than vital, introspective, unique individuals who often unconsciously play a decisive role in their own fate. In other words, it leaves the person out." His desire to "put the person in" echoes numerous modernist discussions (by Ford, Woolf, Lawrence) on the centrality of character. Shneidman's death certificate would include the type of death (for example, brain death or somatic, that is, cessation of bodily functioning); causes like execution, warfare, and police action; an acknowledgment that death is dual (one experience for the decedent, another for survivors); and, most importantly, the extent to which the decedent's psychological state ("intentioned, subintentioned, or unintentioned") contributed to the death.[16] Shneidman's proposal has much to recommend it, though it is often impossible to determine the deceased's desire to die, and death certificates are no better than the physicians who complete them.[17]

The English death certificate, which has undergone significant changes over the years, is different. It assumed roughly its modern form in 1837 (the year Victoria became queen) probably because of social reform movements, especially the growing concern for public health. Since 1927 it has had two parts: causes leading to death, and indirect or subordinate causes. Since 1949 greater detail has been required about those causes.[18] Instead of listing categories to check, the item labeled "Cause of death" requires a prose response (a narrative) and the respondent's signature. In addition, a far older document remains in use for aristocrats and important public officials: not a form but a formulaic narrative of social success that interweaves genealogy, chronology, a curriculum vitae, and a curriculum funerae. Beginning with a boldly painted coat of arms, it recounts, in elegant (if understated) prose, the deceased's titles and achievements, funeral details, family relations and descendants. Although legal forms have been required for a century and a half the practice continues. Being formulaic, the story is both easily told and one that only a class-based society wants to keep telling.

THE CORPSE

The corpse is death's central artifact, a powerful object and symbol that connects individual fate to social order. Despite its representation of ghosts and underworlds, Western rhetoric distinguishes dying from the dead. Discussing Keats' "Ode to a Nightingale," Lionel Trilling marks their boundary:

It is not uncommon for poetry to represent death as a positive and pleasurable experience. Death and dying seem naturally to associate themselves with love – the words are used to express the ultimate degree of erotic pleasure, and all great love stories end in death, as if this were the sign and validation of the lovers' passion ... But if the words "die" and "death" can suggest a pleasurable and even a voluptuous experience, the word "dead" cannot; it is a harsh, grim word, meaning all that we can conceive of insentience.[19]

After exhausting the alternatives, Hamlet jarringly proclaims, "Horatio, I am dead" (5.2.340); Lear's anguish over Cordelia, announced in harsh monosyllables, is equally definitive:

> She's gone forever.
> *I know* when one is *dead* and when one lives;
> *She's dead as earth.* (5.3.264–6)

Lear's echo sounds in the startling opening of Dickens' "Christmas Carol": "Marley was *dead*, to begin with. There is *no doubt* whatever about that ... Old Marley was *as dead as a door-nail*" (422; my emphases). Frost's "The Death of the Hired Man" also ends abruptly:

> Warren returned – too soon, it seemed to her,
> Slipped to her side, caught up her hand and waited.
> "Warren?" she questioned.
> "Dead," was all he answered.

Set at a deathbed hidden behind a screen, Albee's *All Over* opens with the Mistress, in response to the Wife's "Is he dead?", quoting the dying man:

> once he said to me, "I wish people wouldn't say that other people 'are dead.'" I asked him why ... and he pointed out that the verb to be was not, to his mind, appropriate to a state of ... non-being. That one cannot ... *be* dead ... one could be dying, or have died ... but could not ... be ... dead. (3–4)

Postmodernist texts like Stoppard's *Rosencrantz and Guildenstern Are Dead* and Swift's *Waterland* enact Trilling's distinction. Stoppard's Guildenstern insists that "Dying is not romantic, and death is not a game which will soon be over ... Death is not anything ... death is not ... It's the absence of presence, nothing more ... the endless time of never coming back ... a gap you can't see, and when the wind blows through it, it makes no sound" (124). Unlike Lear,

Swift's narrator distinguishes not between "dead" and "dying" but between "dead" and "gone": " 'dead' is a blunt word for a blunt and natural phenomenon. 'Gone' – awesome and open-ended – required Explanation" (244).

Huntington and Metcalf argue that the vitality of a culture or ideology "depends upon its ability to channel the power of such mordant symbols as the corpse,"[20] to assimilate the products of "dying," the embodiment of "dead." Asserting the corpse's essentialist significance, E.O. James discusses the attraction/repulsion tension it induces. The corpse inspires

> horror and dread ... as a "daemonic-sacred object ritually unclean" and taboo, and, therefore, to be avoided and disposed of as summarily as possible so that a dangerous source of contagion may be removed. Conversely, it is also alluring, "fascinating" and compelling, arousing ... love, mercy, pity and comfort, drawing the mourners into a sacramental relationship with the deceased ... Thus arises the dual desire to shun and eliminate a dreaded object and to enter into closer relations with the mysterious "other world" ... Out of this "numinous" situation a complex ritual has developed in the cult of the dead which has found expression in a doctrine of immortality.[21]

Bodily corruption is universal; its metaphorical significance varies greatly: in treating the corpse, a society enacts its profoundest understanding of death and life.[22] Van Gennep sees rituals of mutilation and scarification inscribing a culture's moral and social values: "the human body has been treated like a simple piece of wood which each has cut and trimmed to suit him."[23] Huntington and Metcalf suggest that what is true of the living body is true of the dead one: "If the human body in life provides such a reservoir of moral representations, this same body after death carries its own possibilities for symbolic expression."[24]

What, in fact, is the social worth of a corpse? In ancient Greece, the corpse was sacred, or at least it became so, as *The Iliad* and Sophocles' *Antigone* demonstrate, through the performance of rituals that determine the soul's fate. Creon learns to his sorrow that, while it is patriotic to defend one's city against assailants, it is blasphemy to refuse even a traitor proper burial. The corpse, Garland writes, "is sacred because the dead person, in the initial period after his decease, lacks a proper social identity in either world." The focus of concern was spiritual, not material: the Greeks were not obsessed with the corpse as a site of pollution, and it "inspired little horror.

There are few references in Greek literature to the maggots and worms with which certain Christian theologians are so engrossed," and which pervaded medieval art and literature. The Homeric corpse could even be a thing of beauty, its potential pollution curtailed by ritual cremation.[25]

Early Christians, who believed in bodily resurrection, opposed the ancient practice of cremation. It was outlawed around the thirteenth century when, according to Ariès, the clergy began to control the vigil, mourning, and funeral procession, investing it, and themselves, with mystery through concealment.

> The dead body, formerly a familiar object and an image of repose, came to possess such power that the sight of it became unbearable. Now, and for centuries to come, it was removed from view, hidden in a box, under a monument, where it was no longer visible. The concealment of the body is a major cultural event, for like all things related to death, it is also charged with a symbolism that was primarily ecclesiastical . . . The refusal to see the corpse was not a denial of physical individuality but a denial of physical death.

Or at least it was at a certain social level, for this "strange repugnance" occurred within what Ariès calls "the age of the macabre," when images of decomposition were common and concealment and denial were unavailable to lower classes (*Hour* 168, 171–2). The laity also retained control at the social pinnacle. Of the Earl of Derby's funeral in 1572, Lawrence Stone writes, "Though the service took place in church, the master of ceremonies was not the parson but the heralds, and the affair was characterized more by the rituals of antiquarian feudalism than by those of Christianity."[26] College of Arms heralds retain this function today.

Control and custom shifted early in the nineteenth century. Ragon hyperbolically writes, "The first cremation since the fall of the Roman Empire took place in Italy in 1822, when, in an act of romantic homage, Byron set fire to Shelley's drowned body [see illustration 6]. But the cremation of the poet Shelley, performed in a spirit of identification with the ancient Greek poets, was a gesture that found no imitators," until the 1872 establishment of the New York cremation society.[27] The Victorian obsession with "decent burial," which opposed cremation, created health problems because of delays (in order to raise money or gather the family) and overcrowding. Scarcity of space, Morley writes, "meant that recently interred corpses were constantly disturbed; it was this that made the

6 Louis-Edouard Fournier, *The Funeral of Shelley* (1889).

system of interment a 'gross indecency towards the dead'. In order to make room, corpses not a week buried were chopped up and burnt."[28] England's Cremation Society was established in 1874 in response to such problems, though cremation was not legalized until 1902, years after crematoria were built.

Bloom's thoughts at Glasnevin recapitulate the church's position, "Cremation better. Priests dead against it," while mocking the belief: "Get up! Last day! Then every fellow mousing around for his liver and his lights and the rest of his traps. Find damn all of himself that morning. Pennyweight of powder in a skull. Twelve grammes one pennyweight. Troy measure" (*Ulysses* 94, 87). In *The Loved One* Waugh is similarly ironic about modern funeral practice: "Normal disposal is by inhumement, entombment, inurnment or immurement, but many people just lately prefer insarcophagusment" (43). Catholicism officially abandoned in 1964 what it had long ceased to insist on, material resurrection; but not until 1968 were more than half the deceased cremated, a development connected with sanitation concerns, cost, and the decline in formalized mourning and institutionalized religion.[29] Though still less common than burial in Catholic countries like France, cremation, because cleaner and cheaper and requiring less space, is increasingly popular.

With cremation unavailable, Victorian funerary customs, like other laws and practices, were particularly harsh toward the poor. Enacting Marx's notion of capitalism as the economics of the dead past, a new discourse of corpses meant, Thomas Laqueur writes, that the poor "who in life could not sell their labor for sufficient money to provide for a decent interment were of value only when they no longer owned their labor or their bodies, i.e., when they were dead. While an individual living had no rights in his body, dead he could become the property of someone else." The 1832 Anatomy Act, based in part on New York's 1789 Anatomy Act, allowed doctors to claim paupers' bodies for dissection.[30]

Chaucer's "Pardoner's Tale" depicts material wealth transmuted into death; the antithesis, death changed into wealth, corpses from ends to means, became commonplace in the eighteenth and nineteenth centuries. Scrooge views the gleeful looters of his body "with a detestation and disgust, which could hardly have been greater, though they had been obscene demons, marketing the corpse itself" (474). *Our Mutual Friend* opens with two "birds of prey" discussing money and the dead. Gaffer Hexam, who forages in the Thames for corpses, parodies Shylock when he rhetorically asks: "Has a dead man any use for money? Is it possible for a dead man to have money? What world does a dead man belong to? T'other world. What world does money belong to? This world. How can money be a corpse's? Can a corpse own it, want it, spend it, claim it, miss it?" (4). Gaffer's logic was enacted by "resurrection men," ironically so termed because, Michael Wheeler writes, their trade was "a demonic version of the gospel's promise of life coming out of death."[31] Often they went from robbing to exhuming corpses; and then to murdering social outcasts and selling their bodies to anatomists, positivists for whom dissection led to enlightenment.

The earliest recorded case of grave-robbing in London occurred in 1777; the body business was booming by 1800.[32] The most famous suppliers of corpses, Burke and Hare, were technically not resurrectionists because, as Burke testified, "neither Hare nor myself ever got a body from a churchyard. All we sold were murdered, save the first one, which was that of the woman who died a natural death."[33] The irony of the term "resurrectionist" was compounded by the belief that mutilating the corpse, the soul's cover, prevented salvation, a belief that underlay modern embalming. Men like Burke and Hare, and Bishop and Williams, appear frequently in nineteenth-century fiction. Jerry Cruncher embodies *A Tale of Two Cities*' theme of "buried alive" and "recalled to life"; Durdles in *The Mystery of Edwin Drood* confesses to "a touch of the Tombatism" from "always prowling among old graves and ruins, like a Ghoule" (30, 103);[34] and Injun Joe in *Tom Sawyer*, after helping to unearth a corpse, avenges a grudge he bears his doctor-employer by murdering him at the gravesite (91). Dylan Thomas' screenplay, *The Doctor and the Devils*, set in early nineteenth-century Edinburgh, dramatizes the dealings of anatomist Robert Knox with Burke and Hare. Justifying his trade with resurrection men, the self-righteous Doctor Rock absurdly argues: "the practice of Anatomy is absolutely vital to the *progress* of medicine. Remember that the progress of medicine is vital to the progress of mankind. And mankind is worth fighting for: killing and lying and dying for" (167). Despising "the dirty devices of the world" of "active evil" he inhabits, Rock believes himself immune until his name becomes "a ghost to frighten children." He finally acknowledges having connived at murder, having set himself up "as a little god over death" (19, 62, 169–70).

Modernist texts are often skeptical toward dying and its product, the material object needing disposal. No bodies remain after the elided deaths of Forster's Mrs. Wilcox and Woolf's Mrs. Ramsay. In *Heart of Darkness* Marlow links the emptiness of Kurtz's life with his absence at his own death: "The voice was gone. What else had been there? But I am of course aware that next day the pilgrims buried *something* in a muddy hole" (86; my emphasis). Marlow's "of course" asserts more than he knows. In *Absalom, Absalom!* Faulkner literalizes such retrospective emptying out when Rosa Coldfield tries to explicate her relationship with Charles Bon: "*I never saw him. I never even saw him dead. I heard an echo, but not the shot; I saw a closed door but did not enter it . . . One day he was not. Then he was. Then he was not . . . For all I was allowed to know, we had no corpse . . . he was absent, and he was; he returned, and he was not; three women put something into the earth and covered it, and he had never been*" (150–3). Never fully accepted when alive, Bon in death compels no satisfactory ritual of closure; his unlived life leaves no corpse.

Echoing Thomas' Dr. Rock, some contemporary medical practitioners find neither metaphysical absence nor meaning, but only social or material worth, some *thing*, in fatally afflicted patients. Having studied emergency room practice, David Sudnow reached two disturbing conclusions concerning a corpse's social worth. First, the treatment given to someone labeled "DOA" (dead on arrival) by the ambulance driver varies enormously depending upon the patient's perceived age, social background, and moral character. Least likely to be treated and quickest to be pronounced dead are suicides, dope addicts, prostitutes, violent criminals, vagrants, and wifebeaters.[35] Second, echoing nineteenth-century practice, DOAs are sometimes treated as fodder for internists. Sudnow cites the case of a woman who, having attempted suicide by gunshot, arrived

> quite alive and talkative . . . in great pain and very fearful. She was told that she would need immediate surgery, and was taken off to the OR . . . One doctor said aloud, quite near her stretcher, "I can't get my heart into saving her, so we might as well have some fun out of it." During the operation, the doctors regarded her body much as they would during an autopsy.[36]

The socially unworthy are considered discardable, depersonalized grist for an internist's sense of fun.

In an age of interchangeable body parts, Waugh satirically calls the heart "a small inexpensive organ of local manufacture" (*Loved One* 135); Bloom calculates a corpse's worth more generously: "what price the fellow in the six feet by two with his toes to the daisies? ... It's the blood sinking in the earth gives new life ... Every man his price. Well preserved fat corpse, gentleman, epicure, invaluable for fruit garden. A bargain. By carcass of William Wilkinson, auditor and accountant, lately deceased, three pounds thirteen and six. With thanks" (*Ulysses* 87, 89). Bloom values the corpse because it partakes of earthly renewal, the life cycle.

Embalming, however, turns the corpse into artifice, the opposite of natural renewal, while precluding its use by anatomists. Originating in Egypt before 3000 BC, embalming (now called prepping in the trade) became a morticians' competition to make lifelike corpses. A lost art for 2000 years, embalming was unavailable in the Middle Ages when, for example, England's Henry II died in France in July 1189; pageantry was curtailed and the rotting corpse hastily buried in a nearby abbey. Evisceration, which became fashionable in the thirteenth century, allowed for extended funeral ritual and the transporting of dead war heroes home from the battlefield. Despite the church, which urged that the body remain intact for resurrection, dispensations were commonly granted the wealthy.

Modern embalming, in which the arteries are injected with a preservative, became possible in the seventeenth century with William Harvey's discovery of blood circulation. Yet embalming became controversial even as the practice spread; Stone writes that a revolt, especially of women, occurred against its invasiveness: they expressed "their new-found sense of individuality by refusing to submit their bodies to gruesome mangling by the embalmer's knife, a refusal which automatically made necessary a swifter and therefore more economical interment."[37] Similarly repelled, England's George III refused to have his body "undergo any surgical operation ... his Majesty having in his life-time always expressed an aversion to ... embalming."[38] Despite similar opposition, George IV was embalmed because his funeral was delayed.[39] The US Civil War, with its vast numbers of dead to be shipped home, the slow pageantry of Lincoln's return to Illinois after his assassination, and growing health concerns made embalming increasingly common, and led to widespread misconceptions (until the Federal Trade Commission's 1984 reformed Funeral Rule) that it is legally mandated, regardless of survivors' wishes, even for those to be cremated. The rule in *The Loved One* is: "Embalmment of course, and after that incineration or not, according to taste" (42).

Waugh comments: the embalmed "body does not decay; it lives on more chic in death than ever before, in its undestructable Class A steel and concrete shelf; the soul goes straight from the Slumber Room to Paradise, where it enjoys endless infancy."[40] Morticians replace the signs of death with the illusion of life, a pretense aimed at reassuring the living (*Hour* 599–600). As Jessica Mitford's *American Way of Death* (1963) demonstrates, expensive caskets, elaborately impersonal ceremonies, and solitary gravestones with name and dates, like embalming, express capitalist values; her Marxist critique evoked virulent assaults and communist charges. Like Kübler-Ross, Mitford both depicted an unhealthy cultural condition and helped to transform it. A backlash against lavish and dishonest funeral practice led to consumer-oriented regulation of the funeral industry, memorial societies, reduced funeral expenditure, and inexpensive choices in bodily disposal.

Embalming is a coverup, or would be if its product were not manifestly hollow, like Lenin's shell in Red Square that symbolized the regime he installed and embodied, both alive and dead.[41] In *Women in Love*, Mrs. Crich sees her husband's corpse lying "in repose, as if gently asleep, so gently, so peacefully, like a young man sleeping in purity." She speaks bitterly of his looking "beautiful as if life had never touched you – never touched you. – God send I look different – I hope I shall look my years, when I am dead" (335). That which arouses her fury is the embalmer's ideal. Corpses in *The Loved One*, no matter how disfigured by age or dying, are placed in "the Slumber Room" after being restored to "buoyant life, transfigured with peace and happiness" (51). Though "he came of a generation which enjoys a vicarious intimacy with death" and works at the Happier Hunting Ground, the pet imitation of Whispering Glades, Dennis had never "seen a human corpse" (37). He was startled by the hanging body he had discovered, "with eyes red and horribly starting from their sockets, the cheeks mottled in indigo like the marbled end-papers of a ledger and the tongue swollen and protruding like an end of black sausage" (45). The wax effigy produced by embalming, however, is far more grotesque: "the face was entirely horrible; as ageless as a tortoise and as inhuman; a painted and smirking obscene travesty by comparison with which the devil-mask Dennis had found in the noose was a festive adornment, a thing an uncle might don at a Christmas party" (75).

But embalmed corpses prove functional as erotic messengers and messages: a debased courtship ritual. Fixed with "the Radiant Childhood smile" (68) by the Senior Mortician and embalmer Mr. Joyboy, they are sent to the cosmetician Aimée Thanatogenos, whose name, like the book's title, transgresses what Geertz calls the "razor-thin dimensions of the line dividing reason from unreason, eros from thanatos."[42] Joyboy tells her: "When I send a Loved One in to you, Miss Thanatogenos, I feel as though I were speaking to you through him ... Of recent weeks the expressions that greeted Aimée from the trolley had *waxed* from serenity to jubilance" (70, 99; my emphasis). And when Aimée and Joyboy become engaged, "The corpses who came to Aimée for her ministrations now grinned with triumph" (136). The grin, however, proves to be that of death, which shortly claims the despairing Aimée. Even before she dies, her wooers, Joyboy and Dennis, had devitalized and embalmed her, in the image of their own needs, as a cultural artifact. Unlike the corpse of modernist fiction, Aimée's is all too present where it should not be, on Joyboy's trolley, so Joyboy and Dennis remove her to the Happier Hunting Ground's crematorium for clandestine disposal. Dennis recites, to no one since Joyboy has fled, a plagiarized poem from Poe that he has "written for the occasion" (162); he then settles down "to await his loved one's final combustion" (164).

Memorial services, secular funerals without corpses, can be read as either the ultimate denial of death that Waugh is satirizing or as part of the postmodern reconfiguring of the relationship between life and death. My experience is that they have proliferated in recent years as a reaction against rather than a continuation of a debased cultural practice. An embalmed shell pretending to be someone asleep in evening clothes denies what has transpired; it partakes of the distancing and pretense that pre-packaged funerals offer. The interplay of personal memories and stark absence, however, provides intimate and vivid representation of the person being mourned and of mortality's and memory's meaning and limits.

BURIAL SITES

Cemeteries, among the most widely read of cultural anthropological texts, are the oldest of human cities: "Mid the uneasy wanderings of paleolithic man, the dead were the first to have a permanent dwelling."[43] Archaeologists study grave assemblages not because they are morbid but because material patterns at burial sites may provide what Karen Campbell calls "the most heavily laden symbol that any civilization creates for itself."[44] Though the data may provoke disagreement or uncertainty, the accoutrements of cemeteries provide unique information about the ideologies and values of ancient societies since the artifacts of burial – bone and stone – may survive, even for millennia. Maeterlinck endorsed the Egyptians' desire to prolong the life of their dead because the longer the dead live in the environment and the memory of the living, the wiser and happier the living will be.[45] We cannot know whether Egyptians were indeed wise and happy in denying mortality; or whether Etruscans, as Lawrence claims, lived peaceful, natural lives because, their tombs suggest, they envisaged death not as passage and judgment, but as continuous with life.

Pre-Christian signs in Europe indicate that the ancients, for all their familiarity with death and honoring of burial places as sites of transition, feared the proximity of the dead. As if anticipating modern health concerns, they considered the dead to be impure; if they were near, they might return and contaminate the living. To avoid contact, the living separated themselves from the abode of the dead, which is why ancient cemeteries (like those lining the roads into Rome and the Etruscan tombs Lawrence visited) were located outside towns and clearly demarcated. But early Christians, believing in bodily resurrection and worshipping martyrs and their tombs, lacked this aversion to the dead; and unconcerned familiarity with the places and artifacts of burial predominated between about 400 and 1800: hence the word "cemetery," which derived from the Greek for sleeping chamber. During this period of rapprochement between living and dead, towns and villages were invaded by cemeteries, the first bedroom communities, which were then surrounded by habitation.[46]

After the reversal, houses and public squares were built above charnels. People who lived in cemeteries, like John O'Connell, the caretaker of Glasnevin in *Ulysses*, presumably became oblivious to the sight of burials and the proximity of large common graves, which were left uncovered until they were full. Despite church objections, townspeople came for mundane as well as spiritual purposes: "The disapproval of the synods, reiterated fruitlessly as it was for centuries, tells us that the cemeteries continued to be used for recreation, and for the games that accompanied the markets and fairs ... Market-place; place for announcements, auctions, proclamations, sentences; scene of community gatherings; promenade; athletic field; haven for illicit encounters and dubious professions ... the cemetery was the public square ... the center of collective life" (*Hour* 64, 69–70).

Ariès dates the end of this period and practice around 1800, when shifting cultural mores supposedly no longer tolerated this closeness between living and dead, yet it continued into the nineteenth century. Devastating cholera epidemics beginning in 1831 were largely responsible for the establishment of commercial cemeteries like Highgate. The 1831 opening of new burial sites at St. Martin-in-the-Fields, as described by *The Sunday Times*, recalls what had earlier been commonplace: "Crowds of ladies perambulated the vaults for some time, and the whole had more the appearance of a fashionable parade than a grim repository of decaying mortality." Highgate was founded in 1839 as an antidote to London's appalling graveyards (with their unsanitary overcrowding and grave-robbing), and as a sylvan retreat where death could be sentimentalized as sleep. Considered by some to be a principal source of poisonous exhalations,[47] graveyards came increasingly under the scrutiny of health officials, reformers, and moralists. In 1843, the Victorian landscape gardener J.C. Loudon inveighed against the danger "of the effluvia of decomposition" from unsealed coffins, multiple gravesite occupancy, reuse of sites, shallow graves, and above-ground catacombs.[48]

Loudon, who designed a model cemetery that became influential (for example, on Forest Lawn), "defined the main object of a burial ground as the disposal of the dead in such a way that their decomposition would not injure the living, either by affecting their health or by shocking their feelings, opinions, or prejudices ... The secondary object of the burial ground was the improvement of the 'moral sentiments and general taste of all classes, and more especially of the great masses of society.'" His design included an arboretum, with trees and plants labeled and properly kept, classical architecture and sculpture, straight roads for solemnity and grandeur, green paths between the graves, sun, air, and open space. Morley discusses the "Victorian preoccupation" with the cemetery's moral, educational, and aesthetic significance. It was also an important locus of self-discovery in Victorian and modern fiction.

Wuthering Heights ends with Lockwood standing amid the gravestones of those who he is convinced sleep peacefully "in that quiet earth" (363). In *Great Expectations*, however, the cemetery is the site of nativity and identity as well as of moral awakening. Pip reads his patronymic in the churchyard: "I give Pirrip as my father's family name, on the authority of his tombstone." Of his parents and five dead siblings, he says, "my first fancies regarding what they were like, were unreasonably derived from their tombstones," and in this un-Loudon-like setting he enters into consciousness: "My first most vivid and broad impressions of the identity of things, seems to me to have been gained on a memorable raw afternoon towards evening. At such a time I found out for certain, that this bleak place overgrown with nettles was the churchyard ... and that the small bundle of shivers growing afraid of it all and beginning to cry, was Pip" (1–2). Precisely at this moment, as if enacting David Copperfield's early fear of his father rising from the grave, Pip is seized by Magwitch, threatened with extinction, and startled onto the path of initiation into his own life.

Echoing *Wuthering Heights*, modernist texts like James's "The Beast in the Jungle" and Joyce's "The Dead" also end at gravesites. Here too the living protagonists seem less vital than those dead and buried, and they participate in their own lives as if by rote, posthumously. Both James and Joyce adumbrate the Victorian notion of the cemetery as the site of moral education, the place where, at story's end, life's trappings are displaced by death's. John Marcher, who "had been the man of his time, *the* man, to whom nothing on earth was to have happened," encounters passion (both eros and thanatos) at the cemetery when he sees "the raw glare" of grief on "the face of a fellow mortal," a man "deeply stricken" by loss. Turning to May Bartram's tombstone, Marcher reads there "the open page of his story. The name on the table smote him as the passage of his neighbour had done, and what it said to him, full in the face, was that *she* was what he had missed." With the shock of that sight he finally realizes that she had offered him escape from the living death of his life: "The escape would have been to love her; then, *then* he would have lived." With typical Jamesean irony, Marcher misses life in awaiting it and discovers it only in confronting its absence.

Equally aloof from his own "mechanical" life (185), Gabriel Conroy is similarly responsible for the deadened existence of the woman who shares his life. Where May dies after Marcher misses what she offers him, Gretta is "perished alive" in her loveless marriage (177). Like the "lugubrious" dinner subject (monks who "slept in their coffins"), Gabriel's life "was buried in a silence" (201) of self-consciousness and thwarted emotion. His epiphany echoes Marcher's obsession with the beast that seems always about to spring: "A vague terror seized Gabriel as if . . . some impalpable and vindictive being was coming against him, gathering forces against him in its vague world" (220). Gabriel too sees in another what he "had never felt . . . himself": "the full glory of some passion," which he now experiences vicariously by envisioning himself approaching "the lonely churchyard on the hill where Michael Furey lay buried" (223).[49]

The peaceful, nurtured settings of modern cemeteries (a revival of ancient Greco-Roman practice) exclude both passion and the surrounding world. They are usually located in urban settings (largely because towns have overtaken and surrounded them), but prettified and distinct: in a curious historic reversal, the city of the dead is now protected from everyday pollution. The cemetery's death- (and therefore life-) denying message dates from the Great War, which, Ragon writes, "brought about the creation of specifically military cemeteries, with their endless rows of identical crosses . . . in their impeccable symmetry of identical graves they . . . suggest the discipline of the serried ranks of the army." Before the nineteenth century, "all great battles that left a region littered with dead sowed terror all around, for, very often, plague or cholera followed. The soldiers, stripped of their uniforms, were buried on the spot in common graves, and the officers were buried in the nearest church."[50] Great War cemeteries simultaneously assert and subvert the individual identity and meaning of lives both raised to heroic stature and reduced to pieces of an endless pattern. Though first employed during medieval plagues, mass graves, Fussell writes, "pertain especially to the twentieth century. There are 2500 British war cemeteries in France and Belgium." The bodies below the rows of headstones, he suggests, are often "buried in mass graves, with the headstones disposed in rows to convey the illusion that each soldier has his individual place." What changed was perhaps less substance (below ground) than appearance (rows of crosses), though it is debatable whether Fussell's point is strengthened or weakened by the occasional Star of David (see illustration 7). These cemeteries, Fussell adds, are also peculiar sign systems that, "both pretty and bizarre, fertile with roses," project "an almost unendurably ironic

7 Herman Manasse, Meuse-Argonne World War I cemetery, Romagne, Meuse, France.

peacefulness. They memorialize not just the men buried in them, but the talents for weighty public rhetoric of Rudyard Kipling. He was called on to devise almost all the verbal formulas employed by the Imperial War Graves Commission."[51]

Similar rhetoric and architecture dominate Waugh's Whispering Glades, the "great necropolis" (*Loved One* 38) based on California's Forest Lawn, that monument to American nostalgia for Victorian taste and belief in progress.[52] During the war but far removed from it, Hubert Eaton's 1917 "Builder's Creed" proclaimed his intent to create a cemetery

> as unlike other cemeteries as sunshine is unlike darkness, as eternal life is unlike death. I shall try to build at Forest Lawn a great park, devoid of misshapen monuments and other customary signs of earthly death, but filled with towering trees, sweeping lawns, splashing fountains, singing birds, beautiful statuary, cheerful flowers, noble memorial architecture with interiors full of light and color, and redolent of the world's best history and romances. [See illustration 8.][53]

8 Forest Lawn, Glendale, California.

Forest Lawn replaced vertical tombstones with tablets flush with vast lawns, thanatological statuary and edifices with copies of Old World art and architecture grander, better made, more permanent than the originals. Waugh's Whispering Glades self-reflexively boasts: "This is more than a replica, it is a reconstruction. A building-again of what those old craftsmen sought to do with their rude implements of by-gone ages. Time has worked its mischief on the beautiful original. Here you see it as the first builders dreamed of it long ago." Yet, Dennis Barlow notes, movie sets seem solider than Whispering Glades' buildings, which are as deceptive as World War One cemeteries. At Whispering Glades' trysting-place, modeled on Yeats' "Lake Isle of Innisfree," nature, like death, is transmogrified into artifact: the boatman who carries Dennis across says, "They got bee-hives," but no bees: "Once they had bees, too, but folks was always getting stung so now it's done mechanical and scientific; no sore fannies and plenty of poetry" (*Loved One* 78, 40, 82).

9 Ernesto Gazzeri, "The Mystery of Life," Forest Lawn, Glendale, California.

Forest Lawn, Oring writes, "is dedicated to the stirring of national as well as domestic sentiments ... Besides love, patriotism, and beauty ... Forest Lawn is clearly committed ... to the formation of what might be called 'good character.'" Forest Lawn promulgates virtues central to the national mythos: tolerance, faith, humility, reverence, trust, truth, courage, vision, and determination. The religious message is represented by "a smiling Christ, a Christ that 'loved you and me,' what Eaton called an 'American Christ.'" The afterlife is also American: material yet asexual, even puritanical.[54] Glorifying a stylized body, scores of statues depict the beauty of imitation flesh: "Forest Lawn acknowledges the physical beauty of its statuary, it does not entertain the notion of its sensuality. Beautiful, yes; erotic, no."[55] The most famous statue, "The Mystery of Life," enacts the stages of human existence (see illustration 9). Forest Lawn's popularity (500,000 visitors annually, Southern California's most popular tourist site prior to Disneyland's opening) and appeal as a marriage site (25,000 weddings performed there by the mid-1980s) attest to Eaton's commercial perspicacity.

The semiotics of cemeteries, what they reveal and what they conceal, compel contemporary anthropological attention. Examining recent massacre gravesites in order to reconstruct atrocities, forensic experts in Argentina, Chile, Guatemala, Bolivia, and Iraq use the term "cultural artifacts" to refer not to grave ornaments or pottery shards but to bullets lodged in shattered bone. The absence of evidence can also be culturally significant. When in 1991 archaeologists in Manhattan uncovered the site known in the eighteenth century as the Negroes Burial Ground, now preserved as the African Burial Grounds and the Commons Historic District, the only possession they found in one grave, a brass finger ring, spoke eloquently of its occupant's social status.[56]

TOMBS AND MONUMENTS

Tombs and monuments are as culturally revealing as wills and burial sites. They inscribe and narrate values and attitudes toward life in this world and the next: grief, guilt, pride, fear, sometimes even pleasure. The ancient and venerable practice of erecting memorials materially complements the rituals devoted to the interment, housing, and equipping of the dead for the journey beyond the grave. The Egyptians elaborately housed their royal dead in anticipation of passage to judgment; funerary monuments expressed the Greek conception of the dead as beings raised to a higher state of dignity.[57] Yet Maeterlinck argues that Western treatment of the dead is tinged with absurdity: "Having passed through the portal, they must silently reproach us for having imprisoned them in their nauseating boxes and their ridiculous or hideous monuments."[58] Though marking gravesites with inscriptions was uncommon until the late eighteenth century, it had become so widespread by the mid-nineteenth that Victorian reformers, targeting its abuses, argued that monuments should remain inside the church and burials outside: "Rather than erect proud and ugly monuments, a person of rank and wealth was advised to build or restore a parish church, a chapel, school, alms house, or hospital."[59] This aesthetic and practical argument had limited appeal.

Victorian tombs were often gendered. *Great Expectations* begins with the orphaned Pip envisaging his parents through their tombstones: "The shape of the letters on my father's gave me an odd idea that he was a square, stout, dark man, with curly black hair. From the character and turn of the inscription, '*Also Georgiana Wife of the Above*,' I drew a childish conclusion that my mother was freckled and sickly" (1). She is also something of an afterthought in death, as she presumably was in life. Dickens underscores this point when he has Pip, scared witless by Magwitch and his demand for his mother, point to the tomb: "Also Georgiana. That's my mother" (3). As Hillis Miller says, "A gravestone is the sign of an absence,"[60] one that Dickens has Scrooge contemplate with horror when, from the other end of the mortal spectrum from Pip's (a life *already* badly lived), he reads "upon the stone of the neglected grave his own name" ("Christmas Carol" 479).

Lawrence, in contrast, read the Etruscan tombs he visited in Spring 1927 as depicting what he had long sought, Christianity's antithesis, "the vital past which he felt had been lost in the process of civilization."[61] Lawrence reconstructs a simple, natural, and pleasant culture: "death, to the Etruscan, was a pleasant continuance of life, with jewels and wine and flutes playing for the dance. It was neither an ecstasy of bliss, a heaven, nor a purgatory of torment. It was just a natural continuance of the fullness of life. Everything was in terms of life, of living." Etruscans buried their dead, in appropriate finery, within elaborate tomb-cities, in tombs decorated with scenes of banqueting, ritual, and lovemaking. Lawrence was most impressed with the Etruscan emphasis on fertility, on life triumphing over death: "in stone, unmistakable, and everywhere, around these tombs" are "the phallic symbol" and a "Noah's Ark box, the *arx*, the womb . . . in which lies the mystery of eternal life, the manna and the mysteries" (*Etruscan Places* 1, 12–14).

Were the Etruscans really as Lawrence represents them? We cannot know since, as he says, they were culturally destroyed and assimilated by the efficient Romans, leaving behind nothing but the tombs and their conquerers' accounts. Yet, Richard Aldington comments, Lawrence "found in the Etruscans (or lent them, it doesn't matter) a conception of life such as he believed in himself."[62] Unlike that reincarnation of Rome, the modern industrial society, they represented his ideal of bodily awareness, his ethic of vitality; and his Etruscan vision found immediate expression in the first part of *The Escaped Cock*, which was published "under the emasculated title, *The Man Who Died*,"[63] and in everything else he wrote during his remaining three years.

Before the twentieth century, Michel Ragon writes, European war monuments, like those commemorating the 1870 war, followed ancient Athenian necrological custom in being placed away from villages, on battlefields, so "they did not become active symbols." Those for what is still commonly called the Great War, however, are located in towns, and replicate the gendered tombstones of Pip's parents. Usually phallic stone columns (often identical because mass-produced), they occupy an honored place in the town square. They were erected, for example, in every French village except Thierville (the only one to suffer no loss of life in the wars since 1870), 36,000 in all, between 1920 and 1925. World War One memorials, a collective cenotaph, became the national emblem; ceremonies of ancestor worship, which had disappeared from the Christian West, occur annually at these sites as a secular cult of the dead that, for many, replace an enfeebled church authority.[64] These memorials are modern because of the technology that produced them, but also in incorporating products of that technology like unexploded shells.[65] Memorials for World War Two, in which France's quick surrender produced far fewer deaths, are simple plaques attached to sides of existing columns ("Also Georgiana") rather than free-standing equivalents (see illustration 1).

Monuments, like official history and mass gravesites, serve political ends, like the Warsaw ghetto memorial (erected 1948) that became a symbol and site of resistance to communist rule. They may also deceive by enshrining lies that repeat the horrors they ostensibly commemorate. Largely in response to Yevtushenko's anguished "Babi Yar" (1961) – "No gravestone stands on Babi Yar / Only coarse earth heaped roughly on the gash" – a monument to the 1941 massacre was finally built in 1974. But it glibly referenced all "victims of Fascism" while effacing the Jews; its central figure was a communist resistance fighter; and it stood not at the ravine but some distance from it: at the site of erasure, where corpses were burned. A new monument, a large bronze menorah at the end of a brick road that follows the Jewish victims' final mile, was erected at Babi Yar by the post-Soviet Ukrainian government in 1991. Though not intended to rewrite history, the symbolic graveyard designed by Adam Haupt and Franciszek Duszenko and erected at Treblinka in 1964 yet invokes a double sense. Its 17,000 granite stones, roughly carved yet tidily aligned, memorialize 850,000 Jews murdered at this deathcamp (but not buried under these stones) and also Poland's lost Jewish villages.[66]

Public monuments like pyramids and mausoleums assert a culture's imperious, if hollow, triumph over death, like Shelley's "Ozymandias, King of Kings," whose self-proclaimed glory is mocked by the reclaiming desert: "Round the decay / Of that colossal Wreck, boundless and bare / The lone and level sands stretch far away." Memorial scrolls to honor war dead or presidential statuary in Washington, DC, empty tombs devoid of corpses, often seem erected so that souvenir-hawkers may thrive rather than so that people may remember and learn from history. Yet as if countering Kipling's rhetoric and traditional funereal deceptions, Washington's eloquently understated Vietnam Memorial seems the ultimate postmodern memorial, one that materially replicates the American-Jewish custom of reading out, on Yom Hashoah (April 18), the names of Nazi victims.

Some, however, oppose all war memorials. W.D. Ehrhart, a marine decorated for valor in Vietnam, writes:

> I didn't want a monument,
> not even one as sober as that
> vast black wall of broken lives . . .
> I didn't want a road beside the Delaware
> River with a sign proclaiming:
> "Vietnam Veterans Memorial Highway." . . .
> What I wanted
> was an end to monuments.[67]

Perhaps, despite the flamboyant and irrational public discourse during and after the 1991 Gulf War, Ehrhart's type of monument-weariness, as well as the dichotomy between the victory claimed and the disaster wrought, may spare us tasteless and distorting monuments to Operation Desert Storm.

CHAPTER 6

Funerals and stories

History is the story, or stories, of death. And just as "history" means both past events and their retrospective retelling, so death is narrative as well as occurrence, both the dying process and rituals of grieving and reconstitution performed by survivors. An imminent death reshapes the life it culminates, so that it seems always to have been headed toward its particular end. Narrative performs an analogous function by ordering the experience it seeks to comprehend, making it seem predetermined rather than chaotic. Tolstoy's "Death of Ivan Ilych" depicts the processes as synchronic: the dying Ivan reconceives his life, completing the process in time to live well as he dies. Beginning with Ivan's funeral, a cynical, bitter account, Tolstoy then uses Ivan's final experience to reconceive it. Reread subsequently, the opening becomes an ironic warning about narratives of death and mourning, and about living and dying.

Like the *ars moriendi*, every story both implies and denies death, sustains its fictionality and fictionalizes its inevitability. Forster writes, "Scheherazade avoided her fate because she knew how to wield the weapon of suspense – the only literary tool that has any effect upon tyrants and savages."[1] Communities domesticate or socialize death, as opposed to challenging or denying it, by containing it within rites of separation and reincorporation. In Kafka's parable, "Leopards in the Temple": "Leopards break into the temple and drink to the dregs what is in the sacrificial pitchers; this is repeated over and over again; finally it can be calculated in advance, and it becomes a part of the ceremony."[2] Nature's random destructiveness receives human meaning and dimension, the order of artifice, within communal practice. Beginning where experience ends, both narrative and funeral concern absence, separation, displacement; both seek to shape and regularize transitional processes, to "tame" death, which always threatens to become anarchic, by making it comprehensible, socially acceptable, and necessary.[3] Every marriage ceremony, initiation rite, sacrifice, and funeral has one purpose: to preserve or restore communal well-being, which is endangered by unlicensed sexuality, unfettered masculinity, unpropitiated deities, and death. Like surgical operations, rituals require great care in performance; even then things may go wrong. This chapter examines communal and literary reactions to death, common features of funeral practices widely separated historically and geographically, and differences that result from local circumstances.

Anthropologists consider death rituals among the most interesting, challenging, and accessible material for understanding people and culture.[4] According to Lawrence Stone, Peking man was ritually burying his dead by 500,000 BC, and burial rituals were highly developed by 50,000 BC; by 7000 BC ancestor worship was flourishing at Ur.[5] Spengler viewed disposal of the dead as expressing how a people link their historic past with their conception of death and what lies beyond. Ancient Egyptians, for example, asserted their faith in mortality against time's depredations by embalming "even their history in chronological dates and figures . . . Today, pathetic symbols of the will to endure, the bodies of the great Pharaohs lie in our museums, their faces still recognizable."[6] They remain preserved, if not for the next world at least in this one.

Funerals are the most elaborate and important ceremonies for the Lodagaa of West Africa,[7] in traditional Malagasy societies,[8] for the Maoris[9] – in fact, for most cultures. Some observers view ritual burial as the defining act of civilization.[10] Elements of ritual exorcism, Frazer suggests, include persuasion, fraud, force, paying money for passage to the afterworld, and instructing spirits on the correct route.[11] Huntington and Metcalf explore the bases of death's intense emotional impact on survivors: shock, fear (for one's own life and death's power in general), sadness for the other's loss of life, loneliness, anger, and antipathy toward the corpse.[12]

Fear, grief, or joy usually determines the communal response to death.[13] Some argue that fear is universal, essential, fundamental to *all* human activity.[14] Death inspires fear, Frazer maintains, not because it is terminal but, on the contrary, because of belief that spirits survive, remain near, and cause "many of the ills which beset this our mortal life on earth." The dead seek company among the living in order to bear their souls with them to the unknown world beyond the grave.[15] Such belief, Frazer maintains, originated in pre-historical times, remains widespread, and is viewed skeptically only in advanced civilizations.[16] Commenting on Faulkner's story, "The Old People," Cleanth Brooks says that the dead "haunt the earth because they hate to leave it . . . they could not be expected to prefer 'the scoured and icy stars' when there is the earth itself for them to haunt – the beautiful and inexhaustible earth."[17] The phenomenon recurs in texts ranging from *Wuthering Heights* to "The Dead."

Considering themselves perpetual, societies experience death as intrusive, unnatural, a threat to survival,[18] less Henry James' "distinguished thing" than an anti-social surprise. Though constantly threatened by brute reality killing its members, society recuperates faith in its immortality, and the body politic that death has assailed is reconstituted, by the performance of restorative ceremonies. Viewing funerals as rites of passage, van Gennep considered them double-edged: they acknowledge the desire to maintain the bond between the living and dead, and the need to sever it so that the will to live can be asserted over the tendency to despair. In his pioneering study of early Indonesian burial customs, van Gennep's contemporary Robert Hertz saw the deceased during the "intermediary period" as neither alive nor finally dead. While the corpse rots, the soul wanders aimlessly (as in Catholic limbo), and both threaten individual and communal health.

Weakened by the loss of a member and endangered by potential additional losses, the community assumes ritual responsibility through ceremonies that isolate the deceased and the bereaved, constituting them as a special group: the dead are separated from the living, and the living are incorporated into the world of the dead from the moment of death until the body is disposed (Ariès, *Hour* 603). Such rituals, which are synchronic for the deceased and the bereaved,[19] maintain social continuity by preventing survivors from yielding to the impulse to flee in panic or follow the deceased into the grave.[20] When the transition ends, the deceased enters the realm of the dead and mourners rejoin the community; a feast is held to honor the now dry bones, celebrate the soul's arrival in the land of ancestors, and mark the survivors' reentry into society.

"The Kaddish," the Jewish prayer for the dead, contains no reference to death or the deceased; its unqualified praise of God underscores ritual's focus on the living, on continuity despite traumatic loss.[21] That it is recited by mourners at the regular weekly service emphasizes ritual's attempt to reintegrate the bereaved, separated out by their contact with death, into the social structure that would otherwise remain doubly bereft, unhealed, and hence in continuing danger. The last word, Hertz writes, remains with life: "at whatever stage of religious evolution we place ourselves, the notion of death is linked with that of resurrection; exclusion is always followed by a new integration." Only when the process ends can society, its peace and wholeness recovered, reconstitute the body politic and thus "triumph over death."[22]

Death rituals enact the tripartite structure van Gennep posited for dying. Garland views the ancient Greek funeral, for example, as "a three-act drama with precise regulations governing the most minute details of procedure [for] the laying out of the body ... its conveyance to the place of interment ... and finally the deposition of its cremated or inhumed remains."[23] Ceremonies of mourning, which conclude both Homeric epics, serve to rehabilitate the commonweal, to close the breach opened by loss, even if, as with Troy's performing Hector's funeral at the end of *The Iliad*, it survives only for the ritual's duration.

Analyzing contemporary death rituals in rural Greece, Loring Danforth similarly depicts a tripartite aesthetic structure. She compares the corpse, the soul, and the mourners to "three actors in a ritual drama, linked symbolically to one another as they move together through the three phases of the rite of passage: separation, transition, and incorporation." The ritual seeks to effect an untroubled transit for the three participants: "The remains of the dead must be properly disposed of, the soul must arrive at the proper destination, and the mourners must be reincorporated into the flow of everyday social life."[24] The importance of such ritual performance has been noted by numerous social commentators. Nina Witoszek, for example, calls contemporary Ireland – with its spectacular funerals, political manifestations in cemeteries, and pilgrimages to graves of patriotic heroes – a *Theatrum Mortis* in which funeral ceremonies are the culture's central symbolic vehicle.[25]

Commitment to mortality and human continuity underlies the celebratory as well as fearful response to death, one that may erase the line between erotic and thanatological ceremonies. Joseph Henderson writes that the "initiation rite celebrated in the Eleusinian mysteries (the rites of worship of the fertility goddesses Demeter and

Persephone) was not considered appropriate merely for those who sought to live life more abundantly; it was also used as a preparation for death, as if death also required an initiatory rite of passage of the same kind."[26] Conversely, the view of funeral as initiation rite, like birth or marriage, makes it a ceremony in which anxiety is mixed with joy, or in which the celebratory may even predominate. The Bara of Madagascar, for example, view dying as a movement "from a state of mediated equilibrium between order and vitality to a state of pure, fatal order ... The sex and sex-related activities of the funeral nights are symbolic ammunition in the open warfare between the extreme ends of the polar continuum of the human condition." Erotic energy is asserted against thanatological stasis: "The continuity of the living is a more palpable reality than the continuity of the dead. Consequently, it is common for life values of sexuality and fertility to dominate the symbolism of funerals."[27]

Reenacting a Nigerian funeral, Norman Iles sees sexuality as its central theme: it might "seem a contradiction to us, a happy funeral ... Its purpose is not to express grief, but to overcome it by relating the happy things, and the lasting ones. The tribe wants to sing that life is worth living, and keeps its purpose."[28] The songs and dances Iles reproduces, with their overt sexual symbolism and evoking of ancestors and children, make the funeral a fertility rite, an affirmation of human and natural continuity, the cycle within which loss and grief may be subsumed, even transcended. Graham Greene's John Hargreaves, in *The Human Factor*, echoes Iles: "I used to enjoy funerals in Africa. Lots of music – even if the only instruments were pots and pans and empty sardine tins. They made one think that death after all might be a lot of fun" (205). Whether feast, dance, or sex, the funeral's last, reintegrative, stage suggests a joyous holiday, what Joyce calls "funferal" (*Finnegans Wake* 304).

Funeral and story meet in eulogy, ritual retelling of goodness confronting adversity that celebrates and completes a life, though formulaic praise may submerge the unique individual beneath the prototype as earth contains the corpse. In Western practice, funerals without eulogy can seem parsimonious, devoid of substance, *Hamlet* without Hamlet; for in the public address of praise that Aristotle calls the *epideictic*, we reconstitute ourselves as moral beings. Despite Antony's claim that he comes "to bury Caesar, not to praise him" (*Julius Caesar* 3.2.76), his funeral oration recreates a paragon of virtue that the conspirators, having killed a different Caesar, had not anticipated. Antony's rhetorical power enables him to rewrite history and manipulate the plebeians' actions. Yet eulogy carried to excess may empty ritual of meaning and vitality. Garland writes, "In Thessalian and Boeotian funerary inscriptions the dead are commonly accorded the title *hêrôs* (hero), even in the case of persons of no consequence. In Athens this usage was regarded as sufficiently exotic to provoke from Plato Comicus the remark: 'Why don't you hang yourself and become a Theban hero?' "[29]

John McManamon surveys the tradition, beginning around 1400, of the tripartite pattern of ritual eulogy: exordium, praise, and peroration. The deceased was the excuse and occasion for expatiating on the humanist agenda and extolling its political and social benefits.[30] Twain satirizes such funereal invention when Tom, Joe, and Huck, having feigned death, fulfill the ultimate childhood fantasy: watching the town perform their funeral and hearing the minister relate "many a touching incident in the lives of the departed ... which illustrated their sweet, generous natures ... how noble and beautiful those episodes were ... that at the time they occurred ... seemed rank rascalities, well deserving the cowhide" (*Tom Sawyer* 151). Freud comments, "Towards the actual person who has died we adopt a special attitude – something almost like admiration for someone who has accomplished a very difficult task. We suspend criticism of him, overlook his possible misdeeds, declare that '*de mortuis nil nisi bonum*', and think it justifiable to set out all that is most favourable to his memory in the funeral oration and upon the tombstone."[31] In a remarkable exception to common practice, the *Morning Chronicle* of London refused to rewrite the past upon King George III's death: "We should belie all the history of our times, and of our uniform opinions for the last forty years, if we were to say that his late Majesty's reign had been fortunate."[32]

Pastoral elegy, a kind of eulogy once removed, is the most conventionalized form of the survivor's art, yet it retains great potency. A mode of mediation and mourning that Thomas Browne called a "ceremony of bravery," elegy enacts the irony that the world, debilitated by loss, reaffirms itself in the returning spring. Elegy's speaker, both set apart and representing a community of mourners, envisions the deceased journeying deeper into death, warns that such fate is universal, and seeks to confound death either by imagining resurrection or by redefining mortality.[33] Milton's "Lycidas," Shelley's "Adonais," Arnold's "Thyrsis," Tennyson's *In Memoriam*, and Auden's "In Memory of W.B. Yeats" honor the dead subject who, literally or figuratively a poet himself, is silenced by both death and narrative. Pastoral elegy aestheticizes and romanticizes loss, then depicts it as natural and ultimately desirable because of the art it inspires. What elegy ultimately celebrates is less the dead poet and his spiritual triumph over death than the coming to full creative power of the living one who, first outraged by death, is inspired to art that reenacts it. Claiming his predecessor's empty place, the elegist seizes the authority of authorship from the inert hand of the "great man" whose greatness he reconstructs only to usurp.[34] But such triumph is only temporary since not only the predecessor's achievement but also his fall is paradigmatic. At its best, elegy, like eulogy, blends inherited form and felt experience, revivifies and again terminates the predecessor's life, presages and forestalls the elegist's similar fate. Coming into his own by evoking and then displacing the voice death has silenced, the elegist must in turn yield to *his* successor. Perhaps only when both death and the shaping aesthetic response are given their proper due can rituals of funeral and story properly work their healing magic.

During the late medieval and early modern periods, the funeral's purpose and enactment were primarily spiritual, "essentially an occasion for Masses," rather than secular: "After the thirteenth century, it is as if the mentality that until then had been developed in the hothouse environment of the cloisters spread to the world at large ... This was a great change, the greatest until the secularization of death in the twentieth century" (*Hour* 173, 161). Yet because of deference paid to title and status, ostentatious rituals persisted in England until around 1600, when economic moves led to nocturnal, torchlight funerals for noblemen and courtiers to minimize show.[35] The belief became widespread, Laqueur argues, that "God's judgement of the soul was beyond human influence and one's earthly reputation was too deeply grounded in the world order to be susceptible to human judgement."[36]

The rising middle class, however, inaugurated a counter-trend. As other transactions became commodified, the bourgeoisie, eager to secure its new social status, purchased funerals previously available only to aristocrats. In response, undertaking as a profession was established by 1800. Early undertakers were craftsmen, often carpenters; increasingly, they assumed the functions of laying out, hiring carriages, and organizing the ritual. In the eighteenth and nineteenth centuries, undertakers, called "Dismal Traders," were generally treated with contempt "as purveyors of falseness ... men who traded in lies and deception" because they furnished commoners' funerals as grandly as those of nobility or gentry, and paraded death's corruption in finery for money. Yet, Laqueur maintains, seventeenth-century falseness became nineteenth-century truth: "death became the occasion for a final accounting, a stocktaking of worldly success. The funeral became a consumption good whose cost was clearly evident and could be matched with exquisite precision to the class and degree of 'respectability,' to use that new nineteenth-century term, of the deceased."[37]

Lending itself to abuse and hypocrisy, such display climaxed in what Morley calls "that quintessence of sentiment and gentility, the Victorian funeral," whose prodigality enacted the belief that it was as "necessary to maintain the standards of one's class in death as in life, and, if possible, even to use death as a means of further social advancement." Funeral and mourning practices perform a culture's social agenda, as in the Victorian obsession with public grieving: "Grief was a pre-eminent feeling; even where there was a cause for grief, it seems that it often became necessary to force it, and it is quite clear that a show of exaggerated grief became a mark of would-be gentility." Even if grief seems natural and universal, it may be ordered and qualified by communal and gendered forms and norms. Mourning customs were far heavier for women than men: "wives often stayed at home while husbands – although it was *their* blood relation who had died – could go to a party ... it was, explicitly, 'a survival of the outward expression of the inferiority of women' since 'the inferior always expresses grief for the superior.'"[38]

Opulent funerals, an early nineteenth-century norm, gradually inspired hostile reactions based on what Morley enumerates as "utilitarian puritanism, a new Catholicism conscious of its medieval heritage and impatient of Caesarean imagery, an Evangelicalism with its emphasis on 'works', and a sense that proper class distinctions were being obscured to an extent where it seemed almost necessary to impose funerary sumptuary laws."[39] Climaxing with the parliamentary *Report from the Select Committee on the Health of Towns* (1840) and Edwin Chadwick's *A Report on the Results of the Special Inquiry into the Practice of Interment in Towns* (1843), complaints against excess culminated in the 1850 Metropolitan Interments Act, which began to contain lavish funerals.

Customs change slowly. *The Times* of 2 February 1875 complained: within the last half century "prodigious funerals, awful hearses drawn by preternatural quadrupeds, clouds of black plumes, solid and magnificent oak coffins instead of the sepulchral elm, coffin within coffin, lead, brick graves, and capacious catacombs have spread downwards far beyond the select circle once privileged to illustrate the vanity of human greatness."[40] Continuing their funereal traditions, royalty and aristocracy produced the most prodigious of all Victorian funerals, the Duke of Wellington's, in 1852. Rejecting all concern for expense (the funeral car alone cost £11,000) and equating expenditure with "moral grandeur," England performed "a funeral pomp as striking as any that ever awaited the lifeless forms of humanity"[41]; it was "theatrical, eccentric, powerful and imperially pagan; it compelled admiration."[42] Changing mores can, however, be inferred from the insistent tone and defensive rhetorical questioning of this contemporary account:

> public feeling will not be satisfied unless *every* service, *every* officer of State, *every* great institution of the realm, *every* relic of ancient chivalry, takes its due place and share in this national act ... We are often told ... that the days of pageantry are gone by. How can that be said when there is *not a* single office, *not a* herald, *not a* form, *not a* name, in the description of the 'Proceeding' at the funeral of the Duke of Albemarle [1670] which does not still survive?[43]

Morley suggests that the last great universal demonstration of mourning occurred for Queen Victoria in 1901,[44] though altered fashion and the Queen's detailed instructions made Victorian England's terminal ritual less elaborate than Wellington's.[45]

Victorian lower classes were kept in place, in part, by their internalized desire for a good funeral. Like Sally in *Oliver Twist*, the poor hoarded money to avoid the "disgrace" of a parish funeral. This displacement of earthly concerns onto the funeral, and the beyond, enacts a conservative ideology that justifies harsh political and economic conditions by promising their reversal in the afterlife.[46] Whereas pagan kings and nobles tried to take their material wealth with them in order to live well in both worlds, contemporary governments, Freud suggests, "believe that they cannot maintain moral order among the living if they do not uphold the prospect of a better life hereafter as a recompense for mundane existence."[47] The poor and suffering are unlikely to seek earthly redress if they are promised ultimate reward not *despite* but because of their low status, so long as they are properly buried.

Nineteenth-century fictional narrators like Lockwood in *Wuthering Heights*, *Moby-Dick*'s Ishmael, and Pip in *Great Expectations* elegize powerful dead predecessors. Like funeral ritual, narrative reconstruction requires, as Horatio implies at the end of *Hamlet*, articulate witnesses both to recount the deaths that occurred and to contain the energy that threatens its survivors. Such narrators enter the moral universe, in which both choice and story are both possible and necessary, by transforming and aestheticizing what was experienced as "carnal, bloody, and unnatural acts, / ... accidental judgments, casual slaughters, / ... deaths put on by cunning and forced cause" (*Hamlet* 5.2.383–5). Climactic deaths of vigorous, doomed characters like Catherine and Heathcliff, Ahab, and Magwitch can be rendered meaningful and cathartic through retrospective celebrating and ordering. Thus, *Moby-Dick*'s Epilogue is more beginning than end: "The drama's done. Why then here does any one step forth? – Because one did survive the wreck" (565). Invoking the refrain that signals each narrative of death and destruction brought by *Job*'s messengers, "And I only am escaped alone to tell thee," Ishmael's "stepping forth" proclaims him both survivor and eulogist, a priest in the ritual recounting of dead to whom drowning has denied proper burial. Having gone to the abyss of annihilation, "the closing vortex" into which the *Pequod* is sucked, Ishmael, saved by Queequeg's coffin, floats alone on the "dirge-like main." Ishmael embodies and articulates with confidence (justified or not) the experience of becoming an "orphan," Melville's word for him and the last word of *Moby-Dick*. He becomes, like the Ancient Mariner and the survivors of Stephen Crane's "The Open Boat," an "interpreter." As orphan and interpreter, he can begin his narrative with an act of self-naming: "Call me Ishmael."

Twain's depiction of empty eulogy and disrupted funeral in *Tom Sawyer* parodies nineteenth-century ritual norms and narratives, modes that scarcely survived into the modern period's radically different conditions. In her "biography" of World War One, Barbara Tuchman records what she considers the last moment of a stable order. Edward VII's funeral in May 1910 was a ritual of finality, of a world ending: "the greatest assemblage of royalty and rank ever gathered in one place and, of its kind, the last."[48] Occurring shortly afterward, World War One, with its vast numbers of sudden dead who could not be properly memorialized, overwhelmed and disabled the last remnant of the Victorian apparatus of mourning: "The stage had become too wide for propriety."[49] Ritual was cheapened, hollowed, and its demise contributed to modernist malaise and dis-ease.

Chapter 4 above discusses the "dirty death" as a modern alternative to the Victorian "beautiful death." Like mass war and hospitals, which distanced or hid death, however, modern fiction often elides death altogether: characters suddenly disappear rather than enact the dying process. In Conrad, Joyce, Forster, and Woolf, death may be past or future, anticipated or survived; rarely is it confronted and ritualized. Death's focus shifts from the drama's central actor to survivors' regrouping and recounting techniques, from the immediate and literal to the mediated, metaphoric, and retrospective. And like dying, funeral rituals were often elided or depleted of meaning: increasingly professionalized, funerals offered little consolation when death became, as the influential anthropologist James Frazer noted, final rather than an opening to salvation.

Modernism's fictive tone is often elegiac, but the genre of loss, mourning, and reconstruction is as maimed as burial rituals on which it is predicated. Discussing that key text on the cusp of the Victorian/modernist turn, Hardy's *Jude the Obscure*, Irving Howe speaks of the breakdown of plot with its purposeful action, causal sequence, climax, and an impression of completeness that "comes from the sense that the action of a novel, as given shape by the plot, has exhausted its possibilities of significant extension; the problems and premises with which it began have reached an appropriate terminus." Traditional plots assume a rational structure in human conduct, one that can be ascertained, and that provides meaning and order. But modernist texts, unfolding not through plot but a series of discontinuous situations, question these assumptions.[50] In consequence, such fiction rarely tells a consoling story that compensates for the loss of social observance and leads to healing.

Conrad's *Heart of Darkness* exemplifies and enacts the breakdown of ritual and narrative recreation. It is a fiction replete with empty holes made by purposeless actions: a French man-of-war incomprehensibly shells the bush (222); Marlow nearly stumbles into "a vast artificial hole [that] somebody had been digging on the slope" (225); the Eldorado Exploring Expedition seeks to "tear treasure out of the bowels of the land" (241). One basic reason for digging holes in the earth is to perform a burial. Claiming that "*humanitas*" derives "first and properly from *humando*, burying,"[51] Vico in *The New Science* derives our humanity largely from our being the only species that buries its dead. Others have similarly argued that the first cities were built for the dead, an architecture linguistically inscribed in the etymological linkage of the common form for town ("burg" or "borough") with its cognate, "bury." Marlow asserts the need for funereal ritual when, referring to rotting hippo, he says that survival *on* the earth requires "the faith in your ability for the digging of unostentatious holes to bury the stuff in – your power of devotion, not to yourself, but to an obscure, back-breaking business" (261). But *Heart of Darkness* has as many unburied corpses as empty holes: when Marlow meets Fresleven, "my predecessor, the grass growing through his ribs was tall enough to hide his bones" (217); a "dead" railway truck looks like "the carcass of some animal" (224); workers are "moribund shapes . . . free as air – and nearly as thin" (226); carriers die in harness, and stay there; on the road Marlow encounters "the body of a middle-aged negro, with a bullet-hole in the forehead" (229); and he unceremoniously dumps his dead helmsman overboard in an act he ironically calls a "simple funeral" (263). As for Kurtz, Marlow awkwardly says, "I went no more near" him after his death; he wonders whether anything remains now that the voice is gone; and he scarcely acknowledges that the "next day the pilgrims buried *something* in a muddy hole" (284; my emphasis).

Maintaining that wrestling with death "is the most unexciting contest you can imagine" (284), Marlow deploys imagery of failed vision to represent his near-death experience in *Heart of Darkness*: Kurtz's "soul was mad. Being alone in the wilderness, it had *looked within* itself, and, by heavens! I tell you, it had gone mad. I had – for my sin, I suppose – to go through the ordeal of *looking into* it myself . . . His was an *impenetrable darkness*. I *looked at* him as you *peer down* at a man who is lying at *the bottom* of a precipice where *the sun never shines*" (280, 283; my emphases). Marlow's imagery and verbs of seeing and not seeing foreground his voyeurism, his participating and withholding of himself, his entering deeply but vicariously into Kurtz's doom:

> It is *his* extremity that *I* seem to have lived through. True, *he* had made that last stride, *he* had stepped over the edge, while *I* had been permitted to draw back my hesitating foot. And perhaps in this is the whole difference;

perhaps all the wisdom, and all truth, and all sincerity, are just compressed into that inappreciable moment of time in which *we* step over the threshold of the invisible. (285; my emphases)

Marlow's shift to "we" echoes his earlier suggestion that he and Kurtz had been jointly inhumed: Kurtz "was as good as buried. And for a moment it seemed to me as if I also were buried in a vast grave full of unspeakable secrets" (275). But though he sees himself as being "so to speak, numbered with the dead" (282) by the pilgrims who nearly buried him (284, 285), Marlow stops short of the edge. He is, as Robert Detweiler says of authors who portray the death moment, doubly a failure:[52] constrained to imagine what he fails to share, simultaneously creating and destroying another's consciousness.

Marlow, who is himself nothing but a voice, elegizes and displaces his predecessor, Kurtz, a voracious mouth, "a gorgeous eloquence" (288) that still spoke "from beyond the threshold of an eternal darkness" (290), in order to pronounce "judgment upon the adventures of his soul on this earth" (284). Trailing Kurtz through the jungle, Marlow "confounded the beat of the drum [that signals Kurtz's coming and his imminent death] with the beating of my heart" (278), fusing ritual rhythm and identity. Discussing the percussive noise often heard at African funerals, Huntington and Metcalf comment, "it is a natural symbol for marking a temporal change in status, especially one as irreversible as death. Furthermore, the drumbeat has an obvious affinity with the heartbeat and rhythm of life. Or equally, it can resound with the hollow finality of death."[53] This ritual equivocation sounds throughout *Heart of Darkness*, helping to enact the title's compelling rhythm, with its interplay of sound and sight, abundance and depletion, life and death.

Marlow exemplifies narrators whose stories ultimately fail to encompass and comprehend the deaths they recount. Kurtz triumphs by stepping into the dark and judging with almost his last breath, "He cried in a whisper at some image, at some vision ... 'The horror! The horror!'" Marlow calls Kurtz's cry "the expression of some sort of belief; it had candour, it had conviction ... it had the appalling face of a glimpsed truth ... It was an affirmation, a moral victory paid for by innumerable defeats, by abominable terrors, by abominable satisfactions. But it was a victory!" (283–5). Yet just as Marlow deprived Kurtz of funeral ceremony by neither participating in nor narrating it, so he denies him appropriate eulogy: instead of "a glimpsed truth," Marlow tells the Intended that Kurtz's last word was "your name" (292). Having said earlier that he detested mendacity because "There is a taint of death, a flavour of mortality in lies" (237), Marlow acknowledges the harm he has done when he says, "I laid the ghost of his gifts at last with a lie." Failing to bury Kurtz or to honor his "moral victory," Marlow remains haunted by "the disinterred body of Mr. Kurtz saying, 'My intended'" (260). Perverting the mourning process, Marlow allows Kurtz only "unspeakable rites" (262) that turn the Intended's keening into inappropriate triumph and vindication, "an exulting and terrible cry."

Enacting the story's title, Marlow's heart, having resonated with the drums announcing Kurtz, now "stopped dead" before the woman to whom he has lied because the truth "would have been too dark – too dark altogether" (292). Conrad's dark truth is that the torch Kurtz brought to the Congo failed to illuminate his experience of darkness. Rather, it enabled Europeans, all of whom "contributed" to Kurtz's making (261), to remain self-deceived about their motivation, to see greed and savagery as what Marlow calls "an idea; and an unselfish belief in the idea – something you can set up, and bow down before, and offer a sacrifice to" (215). Marlow performs this pagan ritual before the Intended when, instead of rendering "that justice which was [Kurtz's] due," he worships at the shrine of Victorian hypocrisy that sends Europe's exemplars off to conquer and die in the name of Christianity or the white man's burden: "a heavenly mission to civilize" (215).

In thus deforming his story, or telling two contradictory ones, Marlow denies justice to his dead. Like a modernist Ancient Mariner without a moral, Marlow, a failed priest who betrays Kurtz's last vision by turning him into a Theban hero, dooms himself to retelling his tale, repeating ritual motions as hollow as Kurtz and *his* story. Like Eliot's Prufrock, narrators like Marlow proffer revision rather than vision. They can never tell their stories for the first time since they subvert the narrative as it unfolds; nor can they tell them finally since, as with unburied and improperly mourned dead, the failure to enact ritual leaves it undone. Marlow began by reading the past back from the present, "And this also ... has been one of the dark places of the earth" (213), so the story's final image, of a "somber" waterway leading out of Gravesend "into the heart of an immense darkness" (292), projects that past forward into future narrative reenactments in which no one is properly ritualized or laid to rest, and no ghosts exorcised.

Ford Madox Ford, Conrad's collaborator on three novels, retells *Heart of Darkness*' tragedy as farce in *The Good Soldier*. His parodic Marlow, John Dowell, begins with, "This is the saddest story I have ever heard," a passive construction implying that he recounts a life that is past, over and done with; and also someone else's, something read rather than experienced. Ford's original title, "The Saddest Story," was changed at his publisher's insistence because the book appeared when "the darkest days of the war were upon us" (Preface xx–xxi), but the war is embedded in the text. Dowell tautologically says, "I call this the Saddest Story rather than 'The Ashburnham Tragedy,' just because it is so sad, just because there was no current to draw things along to a swift and inevitable end. There is about this story none of the elevation that accompanies tragedy; there is about it no nemesis, no destiny" (164). Dowell's modern concept of plot – "no current . . . inevitable end . . . no nemesis, no destiny" – helps to explain what happened to tragedy (a religious genre) once Christianity's teleology had lost its potency. Story rather than tragedy, sad rather than cathartic, *The Good Soldier* exemplifies how culture and literature are mutually informing: when death became anticlimactic, tragedy became impossible.

Numerous traces of Conrad's Lord Jim, a romantic failure aspiring to tragic status, recur in *The Good Soldier*. Inhabitants of "an intolerable universe," both Jim and Edward are "luckless" victims of what Dowell calls "blind and inscrutable destiny" (54, 49), while Edward and Leonora, like Jim, "were only poor wretches creeping over this earth in the shadow of an eternal wrath. It is very terrible" (70). Seeking to escape an intolerable situation, Nancy romantically announces that, like Jim, she will flee "To the ends of the earth" because she and Edward, echoing *Lord Jim*'s reiterated judgment of its protagonist as "not good enough" (94, 99, 101, 102, 194), "are not worth it" (*Good Soldier* 216). Dowell concurs: Marlow had told Jewel that "the world did not want [Jim]" (193), so Dowell's final comment on Edward, who is about to commit suicide, is "I didn't think he was wanted in the world" (256). For good or ill, tragic heroes always matter.

Exploring the pathos of his life, Dowell seeks to become survivor, priest, and storyteller. But his performance is hapless: because his dead were never fully alive for him he has no way to mourn them.

His recounting is incoherent, lacking communal sanction or solace, a series of repetitions and contradictions rather than substance or meaningful danger. His life's smooth veneer was shattered by sudden revelations and Florence and Edward's anticlimactic deaths, both suicidal victims of passions they failed to control and that Dowell never comprehends.[54] By circumlocution and narrative deflection, Dowell both asserts and denies significance to their deaths. He ends the book's first half by setting the scene of Florence's apparent suicide (102); he then relates Leonora's telling him that Florence was Edward's mistress and that she killed herself, and he responds with total lack of feeling, an "extraordinary sense of leisure" (104–5). Seeking to order a past he can neither recount nor escape but only replicate, Dowell says: "it is all over. Not one of us has got what he really wanted . . . what I wanted mostly was to cease being a nurse-attendant. Well, I am a nurse-attendant. Edward wanted Nancy Rufford and I have got her. Only she is mad" (237). Despite his asserting "it is all over," the past is never buried or expiated, ritualized or mourned, but only repeated as self-mockery. He ends with an account of Edward's suicide that contradicts his earlier version (195), and his ludicrous failure to elegize the dead: "I wanted to say: 'God bless you,' for I also am a sentimentalist. But I thought that perhaps that would not be quite English good form" (256).

Dowell experiences not only others' lives but his own through his narratival attempt to construct his story rather than through a Proustian search for a lost past. His approach subverts coherence, so events fail to connect causally or even sequentially. They become discrete, isolatable, like pieces of broken or disassembled statues arranged for separate viewing rather than made part of larger wholes. Unable to write tragedy, Dowell ultimately offers self-canceling multiple endings. He announces, "There is not even any villain in the story" (165), and then both that Leonora "took on the complexion of a mad woman; of a woman very wicked; of the villain of the piece" (240) and that "The villains – for obviously Edward and the girl were villains – have been punished by suicide and madness" (252). Finally, asserting that everything turned out wrong (237), and yet that the story has "a happy ending with wedding bells and all . . . A happy ending, that is what it works out at" (252), he concludes by both valorizing and subverting the genre that has proved impossible: "there was a great deal of imbecility about the closing scenes of the Ashburnham tragedy" (238).

The Good Soldier brilliantly demonstrates what happens to a form when the culture that created it loses confidence in the securities of plot, which is predicated on coherence, causality, an end in view. If death is an accident of an absurd universe rather than a meaningful culmination of human action, then plot becomes creaky fiction. Ford offers not only the commonest fare of traditional structure and climax (death and marriage), but also affairs, madness, dramatic revelations, and the like. None of it works as it used to, none of it matters enough to displace the spectacle of a woefully inadequate narrator failing to live his life or tell his tale. Virginia Woolf says that a free writer would "base his work upon his own feeling and not upon convention, there would be no plot, no comedy, no tragedy, no love interest or catastrophe in the accepted style . . . Is it not the task of the novelist to convey this varying, this unknown and uncircumscribed spirit, whatever aberration or complexity it may display?"[55] Woolf's formula perfectly fits *The Good Soldier*'s struggle with genre, structure, and substance.

Dowell inhabits a culture that drained ritual of meaning, and put nothing in its place. His never-consummated marriage creates a void at the center of his life and story; and, as a wealthy gentleman of leisure, he lacks Marlow's opportunity to ground his being in work: "the chance to find yourself. Your own reality – for yourself, not for others" (44). Having missed his own marriage, Dowell also elides his wife's death (merely describing her as "lying, quite respectably arranged ... on her bed" [102]) and funeral, calling himself "the titular possessor of the corpse" (108). Rituals of marriage and death remain unperformed in a story whose end replicates and mocks its beginning: "So here I am very much where I started thirteen years ago. I am the attendant, not the husband, of a beautiful girl, who pays no attention to me" (236). Dowell's lack of affect made Florence dead for him (as he was for her) throughout their loveless marriage, so that he cannot mourn her; Nancy's madness parallels the earlier relationship, but is worse because more hopeless. No one in tragedy is the same at the end because meaningful death and suffering have occurred; ending as he began, Dowell neither exorcises his ghosts nor reintegrates himself into society. Tragedy and elegy are replete with loss, with what has been and is no more; *The Good Soldier* laments emptiness, not a life fulfilled and ended, but one never lived. Anticipating the failure of Faulkner's Uncle Ike to make and experience significant choices, unable to tell the story he intends, Dowell incarnates no one so much as Tithonus, for whom only life's negatives accrue: forever undead, unburied, and unmourned.

Funerals and mourning are based, in part, on the belief that the unpropitiated dead seek company among the living, and that proper ritual prevents the dead from taking the living with them.[56] Modernist culture, with its positivist orientation, lost much of the energy that sustained rites of transition like funerals along with belief in their ability to insure that the deceased enter the realm of the dead and that survivors reenter community. Yet a rationalist, secular, anti-superstitious age produced James, Conrad, Ford, Woolf, Joyce, and others whose writings are replete with revenants, ghostly presences, and those Eliot called the "partly living."

Joyce's "The Dead," Ellmann writes, "begins with a party and ends with a corpse, so entwining 'funferal' and 'funeral' as in the wake of Finnegan."[57] The story depicts the hold that the dead, when ritual fails, can retain on the living. Gretta Conroy tells her husband that she was in the convent when she learned that Michael Furey, the young man who had loved her (and whose name suggests both heavenly retribution and violent passion), had died and been buried. Having missed his proffered love, as well as his dying and funeral, Gretta finds that Michael remains undead and unburied for her. When Bartell D'Arcy sings "The Lass of Aughrim," a song of seduction, abandonment, and perhaps death that Michael used to sing, Gretta, standing in an attitude that strikes Gabriel as symbolic of "grace and mystery," hears a call from the world of shades. For Michael Furey, love had led to death; the process is now reversed, as Gretta's excitement at recalling her dead lover unintentionally arouses in Gabriel a "keen pang of lust." But when Gretta, responding to her husband's jealous probing, says of Michael, "I think he died for me," Gabriel feels his hold on everyday reality shaken: a "vague terror seized Gabriel at this answer as if . . . some impalpable and vindictive being was coming against him, gathering forces against him in its vague world" (210–20).

The dead have been invoked by and against the living throughout the story. The atmosphere of both the party and the story is one of funereal gloom: with its representation of Romeo and Juliet and "the two murdered princes in the Tower" (186); its conversations about dead writers and singers, and monks who sleep in their coffins; and with earlier generations romanticized in Gabriel's after-dinner speech, whose elegiac tone suggests a funeral oration for what he calls "the memory of those dead and gone great ones whose fame the world will not willingly let die" (203). Finally, Gretta's memory of Michael Furey evokes "this figure from the dead" as if she had borne him. Three times Gabriel asks if she loved Michael Furey; twice she ignores the question to continue her own narrative; the third time she says, "I was great with him at that time," as if alluding not to love but to imminent birth. Gabriel, after the epiphanic vision of his blindness and self-absorption, imaginatively answers the call made by the "few light taps upon the pane" that echo the sound of gravel that Michael Furey had thrown against Gretta's window the night he had caught "his death in the rain." Leaving the site of lust, Gabriel's soul "approached that region where dwell the vast hosts of the dead. He was conscious of, but could not apprehend, their wayward and flickering existence. His own identity was fading out into a grey impalpable world: the solid world itself which these dead had one time reared and lived in was dissolving and dwindling" (219–23). Gabriel's sudden expansive empathy leads him not to the ecstasy for which he had lusted, but to escape, whether temporarily or in death is uncertain, his material being.

The meaning of this controversial ending depends partly on whether the story is read within *Dubliners*. As the book's culminating section, "The Dead" is usually seen as fulfilling the motifs of frustration, sterility, and moral paralysis of the first fourteen stories. Gabriel's epiphany, then, acknowledges that he is a dead member of a dead society, and it transports him (literally or metaphorically) to the land of the dead. On its own, however, the story seems one of spiritual development, and the final vision potential redemption. Gabriel's snow vision associates him with the dead *or* the story is one of maturation, and the "West," to which Gabriel now realizes he will journey, represents a possible rebirth, through coming to terms with a death culture, for him and Ireland.[58]

Joyce saw Ireland as paralyzed by its dead but unburied past. In a 1907 lecture, delivered shortly after he completed "The Dead," he depicts contemporary Ireland on its "death bed where the poor, anaemic, almost lifeless, body lies in agony, the rulers give orders and the priests administer last rites." It would not be resuscitated, he adds, by the Nationalist Revival then gathering force: "Ancient Ireland is dead just as ancient Egypt is dead. Its death chant has been sung, and on its gravestone has been placed the seal." Ireland's only hope, Joyce maintains, is "to have done once and for all with failure. If she is truly capable of reviving, let her awake, or let her cover up her head and lie down decently in her grave forever."[59] A culture that fails to lay its dead to proper rest devitalizes its present by obsessively rewriting and repeating its past; it becomes a nation of Ancient Mariners: "the greatest talkers since the time of the Greeks."[60]

Joyce assailed his fellow countrymen for failing to propitiate those who died in a still incomplete, and often betrayed, political and cultural revolution. When Irish Home Rule was approved in 1912, he predicted that "there will be a ghost at the banquet – the shade of Charles Parnell ... The ghost of the 'uncrowned king' will weigh on the hearts of ... the new Ireland."[61] Joyce's first known literary effort, written when he was nine, was a poem, "Et Tu, Healy," linking Parnell's fall, a "moral assassination,"[62] to Julius Caesar's murder and the great Irish theme of betrayal. Joyce variously blamed Parnell's political allies, Irish bishops, the press, the Irish parliamentary party, the Irish "rabblement": "In his final desperate appeal to his countrymen, he begged them not to throw him as a sop to the English wolves howling around them. It redounds to their honour that they did not fail this appeal. They did not throw him to the English wolves; they tore him to pieces themselves."[63] The self-appointed "Parnell of art,"[64] Joyce asserted betrayal as central in his life and writing, and proudly claimed Parnell's enemies as his own.

In "Parnell's Funeral," Yeats maintains that had Parnell's heirs eaten his heart, thus performing the ritual of incorporating the dead into the living, demagoguery and civil rancor would not have "won the day." Joyce himself never shook off his obsession with Parnell, the Arthur-like king who would return to lead his people to nationhood, or with Ireland, whose wake he spent seventeen years celebrating. Radical ambivalence lies at the heart of "The Dead": the West (where Gretta comes from and where the nationalist Miss Ivors wants Gabriel to visit) represents both the "real" Ireland and the mythical land of the dead. For an ex-Catholic, the meaning of death was as problematic as the narrative of "The Dead," another instance, as with tragedy, of form following function. Hence, the final equation of "all the living and the dead" (224) renders mortality, like Irish history, opaque and elusive.

Joyce's life and writings enact the paradigm he critiqued in his fellow countrymen: obsessed with a past he could neither experience nor let go, Joyce could neither live in Ireland nor escape its grip. Dead it may have been; but its haunting presence remained. Ellmann writes, "That the dead do not stay buried is . . . a theme of Joyce from the beginning to the end of his work. Finnegan is not the only corpse to be resurrected."[65] In *Ulysses* the man drowned nine days before bobs up in both Bloom's and Stephen's thoughts (18, 38, 62); and both are haunted, in different ways, by their dead. Joyce had rejected his dying mother's plea that he make his confession and take communion.[66] Typically, he portrays the incident as worse than it was: Stephen refuses when his mother begs him "with her last breath to kneel down and pray for her." Buck Mulligan says, "The aunt thinks you killed your mother" (5; the phrase recurs in Stephen's thoughts 35). Stephen's response, "Someone killed her" (5), can be read as bitterness or indifference, like Joyce's mocking misprint in the telegram that summoned Stephen back from Paris: "Nother dying. Come home" (35). Stephen's conscience makes him wonder whether he bears responsibility for this death that is and is not just a*nother*. Recalling that Mulligan had saved men from drowning (4, 38), Stephen thinks that *he* could have saved the drowned man (and his mother) only if he had been assured of his own safety: "If I had land under my feet. I want his life still to be his, mine to be mine. A drowning man. His human eyes scream to me out of horror of his death. I . . . With him together down . . . I could not save *her*. Waters: bitter death: lost" (38; my emphasis). Who is lost? one wonders.

Ellmann suggests that Joyce, having seen his mother's ghost, transformed her into Stephen's.[67] Joyce implies that the refusal of one ritual, bedside prayer for the dying, ruined another: the funeral and mourning of Stephen's mother that are also elided. Like Hamlet, who found no appropriate way to mourn the father whose death and funeral he had missed, Stephen is visited by a guilt-inducing parental ghost: "Silently, in a dream she had come to him after her death, her wasted body within its loose brown graveclothes giving off an odour of wax and rosewood, her breath, that had been upon him, mute, reproachful, a faint odour of wetted ashes" (5; also 9, 23, 473–5). Stephen fears that this "reproachful" ghost – "Ghoul! Chewer of corpses!" (9; also 474) – will replicate Hamlet's fate: "No, mother! Let me be and let me live" (9).

Also haunted by his dead, his father and son, Bloom, unlike

Stephen, seems pre-modernist in mourning both and fearing neither, and his Jewishness links him to an ancient humanist tradition. Recalling his father's dying wish that he care for his dog, Bloom responds very differently from Stephen: "Thy will be done. We obey them in the grave" (75). Though Rudolph committed suicide to escape a painful terminal illness, the inquest provided Bloom with a healing story: "Verdict: overdose. Death by misadventure" (80). Bloom imagines Rudy alive, and then happily recalls his conception (73–4); a tiny coffin evokes not only Bloom's sympathy for its inhabitant but also a memory of Rudy during his brief life (79). Bloom's trip to Glasnevin cemetery enables him to bid Paddy Dignam a ritual farewell, while acknowledging propinquity's role in mourning: "More dead for her [Dignam's wife] than for me" (84). His participation in the service serves also, and more importantly, to reinvoke Bloom's own dead – "poor papa ... Mamma, poor mamma, and little Rudy" (91) – whom he then remourns and reburies. The conjunction of Paddy Dignam and Bloom's father is dramatized by Dignam's later appearing to Bloom as the Ghost in *Hamlet*: "Bloom, I am Paddy Dignam's spirit. List, list, O list!" (385). Though a half-rotted corpse, he returns not for revenge but to vouch for Bloom to the Watch, ask tenderly after his wife, and make a final ritual request: "Pray for the repose of his soul" (387). He then departs and haunts Bloom no more.

In contrast, Stephen's "Dance of death" (472) summons a horrific apparition of his mother caught between two worlds. She rises, "emaciated ... stark through the floor, in leper grey ... her face worn and noseless, green with gravemould ... She fixes her bluecircled hollow eyesockets on Stephen and opens her toothless mouth uttering a silent word" (473). Responding to Stephen's denial of responsibility ("Cancer did it, not I. Destiny"), she demands that he repent, and offers him the ritual that he, a modernist ex-Catholic, had refused her: "I pray for you in my other world" (474). As she draws "near and nearer," warning Stephen of divine retribution to come, he hears "the agony of her deathrattle" and lashes out, smashing the chandelier: "Time's livid final flame leaps and, in the following darkness, ruin of all space, shattered glass and toppling masonry" (475). The passage enacts apocalypse in terms of Einsteinian space/time.

Bloom first conflates Stephen and Rudy in "Hades" and "Oxen of the Sun," the chapters of death and birth. Hearing Simon "Full of his son," Bloom thinks: "He is right. Something to hand on. If little Rudy had lived. See him grow up. Hear his voice in the house. Walking beside Molly in an Eton suit. My son" (73). In "Oxen of the Sun," the birth cry of Mina Purefoy's son awakens paternal feelings in Bloom, "the meekest man and the kindest," but who "had of his body no manchild for an heir." So he "looked upon him his friend's son and was shut up in sorrow for his forepassed happiness and as sad as he was that him failed a son of such gentle courage ... so grieved he also in no less measure for young Stephen for that he lived riotously with those wastrels and murdered his goods with whores" (318–20). The final vision in "Circe," the chapter of apocalypse and resurrection, evokes Yeats, merges Stephen and Rudy, and lays *Ulysses*' ghosts.

Bloom stands paternally over the fallen Stephen, whom he has rescued, while Stephen murmurs lines from Yeats' "Who Goes with Fergus?", a song he sang to his mother, at her request, on her deathbed and that has run through his head all day (8, 9, 41, 474, 496). Bending to listen, Bloom sympathetically misunderstands Stephen's words, conflating the maternal figure, the death song, and an erotic blessing: "Face reminds me of his poor mother. In the shady wood. The deep white breast. Ferguson, I think I caught. A girl. Some girl. Best thing could happen him." Suddenly the final vision appears, a Yeatsean figure transformed into the son who might have been, "a fairy boy of eleven, a changeling," to whom Bloom lovingly, "wonderstruck, calls inaudibly": "Rudy!" (497).

Anticipating his return to the conjugal bed in "Ithaca," Bloom evaded death in "Hades": "Plenty to see and hear and feel yet. Feel live warm beings near you. Let them sleep in their maggoty beds. They are not going to get me this innings. Warm beds: warm fullblooded life" (94; Bloom commonly uses such imagery for Molly: 50, 84, 138, 604). If, as many critics maintain, Bloom returns at the end to full conjugal relations with his wife after years of white marriage ("Could never like it again after Rudy" [137]), one explanation is that, unlike Stephen, Bloom has successfully confronted his ghosts.

Against the modernist grain, Yeats' "Lapis Lazuli" celebrates ritual's transformative power:

> All perform their tragic play,
> There struts Hamlet, there is Lear,
> That's Ophelia, that Cordelia;

Yet they, should the last scene be there,
The great stage curtain about to drop,
If worthy their prominent part in the play,
Do not break up their lines to weep.
They know that Hamlet and Lear are gay;
Gaiety transfiguring all that dread.[68]

Modernist elegies abandoned tragedy, though they had little difficulty performing "all that dread." *Heart of Darkness* and *The Good Soldier* memorialize a world, devoid of healing ceremony, that devalued all the stages of traditional ritual: living becomes horrific or vacuous when dying is denied and death evaded. Joyce's "The Dead" teases by evoking and interrogating the passions of the past, but it leaves ambiguous whether they are now possible for Gretta and Gabriel. Like *To the Lighthouse* (see chapter 10 below), *Ulysses* is that rare modernist text that unflinchingly conjures its dead with love as well as dread, and then enacts a drama and vision of transfiguring gaiety.

CHAPTER 7

Life after life

In 1857, two years before Darwin's *Origin of Species*, an eminent marine biologist and Royal Society Fellow, shaken to the depths of what he considered his immortal soul by the evolution revolution, propounded an ingenious scheme for reconciling new geological findings with fundamentalism. Fossil evidence indisputably existed, Philip Henry Gosse acknowledged, but it was God who, following "the law of organic creation," created plants and animals with the "retrospective marks" of their "specific identity." Just as "the absolute necessity of retrospective phenomena in newly-created organisms" required that the first tree have rings and the first man a navel as a relic of a birth that never occurred, so the world was "created with fossil skeletons in its crust" – skeletons of animals that never existed.[1] They were put there, according to the seventeenth-century Archbishop Ussher, at nine in the morning of 26 October 4004 BC.

Gosse was ridiculed both then and subsequently for treating the earth as God's great deception, what John Fowles calls "the most incomprehensible cover-up operation ever attributed to divinity by man" (*French Lieutenant's Woman* 131–2). Yet Gosse, who anticipated and tried to disarm this attack, was seeking a solution to a genuine problem: how to reconcile faith with scientific knowledge. Not everyone has Gosse's problem: science (or history) has made many atheists; others deny a relationship between faith and mundane reality; still others read Genesis allegorically, mythically. Though little interested in organized religion, Einstein held to his credo that "Science without religion is lame, religion without science is blind."[2] His relativity thesis, in contradistinction to Heisenberg's indeterminacy principle, propounded differences that were perspectival, not absolute: where one stood determined how things *seemed* rather than what they were. For Einstein, "God did not play dice with the universe," and "the most incomprehensible thing about the universe is that it is comprehensible." In this spirit he spent much of his life seeking a unified field theory, what Pais calls his "quest for harmony,"[3] that like God comprehended and connected the universe's fundamental forces.

As nineteenth-century scientists expanded the known material universe, what they could accomplish seemed boundless. Centuries of belief that knowledge and the universe were finite and increasingly comprehensible climaxed with Condorcet's pronouncement envisaging infinite perfectibility: "Thanks to the progress of the sciences, men will reach a stage in the future when he [*sic*] can eliminate death ... Science will have conquered death. And then one will no longer die."[4] Spiritualism, "the child of scientific naturalism and rational explanation," promulgated a harmonizing Einsteinian vision of nature and the supernatural. Traditional afterlifes were not products of logical positivists, but spiritualists emulated positivistic science in seeking to identify how the world beyond was constructed and regulated.[5] Despite Darwin's intention in *The Origin of Species* to challenge anthropocentric assumptions about evolution and progress, spiritualists appropriated scientific materialism to depict the afterworld and express assurance in our ability to know and contact it. At a time when traditional faith and classical physics were under assault, spiritualists, steeped in both orthodox science and established religion, were viewed as heretical by both.[6] Like Hardy, who tried "to reconcile a scientific view of life with the emotional and spiritual, so that they may not be inter-destructive,"[7] they challenged the tenets of a materialistic age that seemed increasingly antithetical to the spiritual. Yet many viewed empirical science and belief in ghosts as compatible, and expected that, as Alex Owen writes, "scientific epistemology would verify the materiality of the unseen world."[8] The quest was for a faith or power that could be sustained or wielded despite, or by means of, scientific methodology.

Such a quest had many motives and assumed many forms. In "Passage to India" (1871), Whitman's journey on "the seas of God" is grounded in the material girdling of the globe represented, from East to West, by the opening of the Suez Canal, the laying of the first trans-Atlantic cable, and the completion of the continental railroad – all in the late 1860s. Madame Blavatsky explicitly rejected spiritualism: "We assert that the spirits of the dead cannot return to earth" – though she added, "save in rare and exceptional cases."[9] Repudiating both evolutionary science and Christianity, she saw Cosmic Ideation instantiated in Cosmic Substance, a dynamic process or bridging that reveals Divine Thought as the Laws of Nature.[10] She asserted an esoteric authority in *Isis Unveiled* and *The Secret Doctrine*; her project, "The Synthesis of Science, Religion, and Philosophy," though she "opposed the contemporary developments of all three,"[11] demonstrates theosophy's inclusive breadth.

Modernist art was enriched by presumptions of posthumous survival or unknown realities. Avant-garde artists like Duchamp, Kupka, and Kandinsky were both drawn to theosophy and convinced that science could teach them about reality's fluid and transparent nature, forms existing beneath material surfaces, and the ethereal nature of art as a medium of radiation between creator and congenial receiver.[12] Gilbert and Gubar argue that theosophy shook "the hegemony of patriarchal rationalism" by offering "alternative historical and theological possibilities" and raising "the possibilities of disorderly female rule,"[13] which partly explains why Blavatsky's ideas, so important in creating the intellectual climate between the 1880s and 1930s, largely disappeared in discussions of the period. The art historian Maurice Tuchman suggests that the theosophical content of modern art receives little attention because Hitler's interest in the occult made mystical beliefs shameful.[14] Desiring the power promised by the occult, Hitler appropriated theosophy's "Svastika,"[15] even while proscribing organizations like Yeats' Order of the Golden Dawn.[16] Like modernism, theosophy "cut both ways": it established secret societies that engendered elitism, conspiracy, and paranoia, but in seeking "to form the nucleus of a Universal Brotherhood of Humanity without distinction of race, colour, or creed,"[17] it inspired nationalist, socialist, and suffragist movements.

What seems most impossible today is what Gosse attempted: to reconcile fundamentalism and Darwinism in the light of twentieth-century debunking: Biblical Higher Criticism, the Gnostic Gospels, scientific analysis of the Shroud of Turin that dates it from the Middle Ages, disproof of miracles generally. Yet technological breakthroughs around the turn of the century – Roentgen's X-rays, Marconi's radio waves, electromagnetism – also seemed miraculous and inexplicable. They did not so much illuminate the known as reveal the vastness of the unknown: visible light represented only a small fraction of reality's spectrum, and beyond and beneath both sense and imagination lay previously unsuspected realities and dimensions, whether extraterrestrial or spiritual. Perhaps God and an afterlife lay in one of them awaiting discovery by faith-driven scientists like Edison, who built a receiving set designed to capture and magnify messages from spirits. Similarly inspired, Robert Millikan, head of the California Institute of Technology and a Nobel laureate in physics, campaigned throughout the US during the 1920s for a reconciliation between science and religion.

In their quest, spiritualists had to rewrite the myths of underworld visitation, like Persephone's, that inscribe the notion of reluctant, or impossible, return. Extra months or years granted clinical death survivors are today considered especially precious, a sign of God's or at least technology's grace. Such revivals, like sudden death (once most feared, now deemed most desirable), were not always so acclaimed. Fishermen, for example, traditionally do not swim, fearing prolonged dying should they fall into cold fishing waters but also because of superstition about returning. Recoverers from apparent death were considered tainted, outcast, as dangerous to social order as improperly buried dead.

Such revenants, Garland writes, were called "second-fated ones" or "persons with two fates." Having been "dead" and yet rejected by the powers below, they were considered impure, taboo, and had to undergo rituals associated with childbirth.[18] Such doubling of life, its instability and unpredictability at odds with expectations of contained and reliable categories, creates a sense of unease that Freud calls "the uncanny," and that many experience "in the highest degree in relation to death and dead bodies, to the return of the dead, and to spirits and ghosts."[19] The debate about posthumous survival was lively and varied throughout the modern period. In *The Double* (1914) Rank contextualizes the discussion within concepts of the soul:

> an image as closely similar as possible to the physical self, hence a true double ... the idea of the soul originally coincided completely with that of a second body ... Later, it became an immaterial concept with the increasing reality-experience of man, who does not want to admit that death is everlasting annihilation ... the primitive belief in souls is originally nothing else than a kind of belief in immortality which energetically denies the power of death; and even today the essential content of the belief in the soul ... has not become other, nor much more, than that.[20]

Freud similarly posited an explanation based on the primitive belief that the dead survive and appear at scenes of former activities. "As soon as something *actually happens* in our lives which seems to confirm the old, discarded beliefs we get a feeling of the uncanny ... Conversely, anyone who ... rid[s] himself of animistic beliefs will be insensible to this type of the uncanny" (247–8). Freud, however, cites instances of its recurrence.

In contemplating the recoiling from death and the belief in posthumous survival, which he roots in nineteenth-century romanticism, Rank quotes Edmund Spiess on the power of self-love and the instinct for self-preservation. These emotions produce "the deep and powerful longing to escape death or the submergence into nothingness, and the hope of again awakening to a new life and to a new era of continuing development. The thought of losing oneself is so unbearable for man, and it is this thought which makes death so terrible for him."[21] Perhaps it can follow into the beyond and pull back even reluctant "second-fated ones."

Many of Gosse's contemporaries (and ours), and by no means only the crackpots, deployed science to enact such longing and hope in order to *prove* God's existence, or at least a world beyond this one. H. Rider Haggard, Henry James, Sr., Arthur Conan Doyle, Upton Sinclair, Yeats, Jung, Houdini, Rilke, and Mann participated in seances, experimented with clairvoyance, telepathy, and automatic writing, even became theosophists, attempting to marry science and faith, to "prove" the existence of spirits. Even Houdini, Rilke, and Mann, in whom dubiety accompanied desire, sought to replicate something like medieval deathbed ritual, the *ars moriendi*, in which the dead could be properly evoked and mourned.

Freud, just after the war, cast his reaction to this phenomenon in cautious litotes. Lectures

> undertake to tell us how to get into touch with the souls of the departed; and it *cannot* be *denied* that *not* a few of the most able and penetrating minds among our men of science have come to the conclusion ... that a contact of this kind is *not impossible*. Since almost all of us still think as savages do on this topic, it is *no matter for surprise* that the primitive fear of the dead is still so strong within us and always ready to come to the surface on any provocation.[22]

Bertrand Russell, who thought as a rational skeptic rather than "as savages do," asserted a strictly material basis of identity and thought: "Our memories and habits are bound up with the structure of the brain ... [and] it seems scarcely probable that the mind survives the total destruction of brain structure which occurs at death." He concluded, "It is not rational arguments but emotions that cause belief in a future life."[23] His was not, however, the predominant view.

The emotions Russell scorned have a long pedigree. The hypothesis that a spirit's "ethereal body" was composed of "spirit matter"[24] derives from the ether theory that dates from the fifth-century BC philosopher Anaxagoras. It became crucial to classical physics, which, based in objects and forces acting upon them, maintained for centuries that events are explicable in terms of things. Gary Zukav summarizes what was both "commonsense" and mystic belief: "the entire universe lies in and is permeated by an invisible, tasteless, odorless substance that has no properties at all, and exists simply because it has to exist so that light waves can have something to propagate in. For light to travel as waves, according to the theory, something has to be waving ... The ether theory was the last attempt to explain the universe by explaining some*thing*."[25] The Michelson–Morley experiment (1887), designed to determine definitively how the ether worked, proved instead its non-existence.

Erecting the special theory of relativity (1905) on ether's non-existence, Einstein asserted, Zukav writes, "that electromagnetic fields involve no object whatever, that they are not states of the ether medium, but 'ultimate, irreducible realities' in themselves ... Both relativity and quantum theory heralded the unprecedented remoteness from experience which has characterized physical theory ever since."[26] What science now shows us, Heinz Pagels writes, sounds almost theosophical: "the visible world is neither matter nor spirit; the visible world is the invisible organization of energy."[27] Encountering natural paradox and epistemological limits, twentieth-century physics destroyed the millennia-old faith that the universe and knowledge were, no matter how vast, finite and knowable. Yet such radical reformulation transforms science and impacts society only over time; much remains unchanged (Newton's laws of thermodynamics and classical causality still explain many phenomena); and culture reacts haphazardly and slowly.

Ether retained metaphoric currency upon which early twentieth-century writers drew to express the mysterious and ineffable, and to sustain a human correspondence with the macrocosm. Willfully anachronistic in the service of his theology, Milton depicted a geocentric universe in *Paradise Lost*. Modern novels like Chopin's *The Awakening* (1899), Wharton's *Ethan Frome* (1911), and Lawrence's *Women in Love* (1920), all of which shocked contemporary readers for their treatment of forbidden passion and the lack of saving spirituality, employed the concept of the ether to represent what had become attenuated. In *The Awakening* the ether signifies absent presence, the immaterial plenitude that seemingly sustains two lovers: "There was *not a particle* of earth beneath their feet. Their heads might have been turned upside-down, so absolutely did they tread upon blue *ether*" (22). The imagined ether instantiates a series of harsher negatives in *Ethan Frome*, all that Ethan desires and seems momentarily promised, but that lies beyond his reach: "The night was perfectly still, and the air so dry and pure that it gave *little* sensation of cold. The effect produced on Frome was rather of a complete *absence* of atmosphere, as though *nothing less tenuous than ether* intervened between the white earth under his feet and the metallic dome overhead" (27). And in *Women in Love*, Gerald reacts to Gudrun's being wounded by Winifred's rabbit in erotic and cosmic terms: "They were implicated with each other in abhorrent mysteries ... The long, shallow red rip seemed torn across his own brain, tearing the surface of his ultimate consciousness, letting through the forever *un*conscious, *un*thinkable red *ether* of the beyond, the obscene beyond" (242; my emphases). Here too the negatives associated with the ether bode ill.

Whatever spiritualists and mediums found, posthumous existence, and mock versions of it, became a leitmotif of modernist writing: numerous protagonists die early, and then get on, more or less badly, with their lives. Arthur Symons spoke metaphorically of symbolism spiritualizing literature, which thereby becomes "a kind of religion, with all the duties and responsibilities of the sacred ritual."[28] After assailing the "Edwardians" as materialists, Woolf praised the "Georgians" (Forster, Lawrence, Lytton Strachey, Eliot, Joyce) for their spirituality. She thought *Ulysses* an "illiterate, underbred book" that seems written by "a self taught working man ... egotistic, insistent, raw, striking, & ultimately nauseating" (*Diaries* 2: 16 August 1922, 189), but she continued to admire Hades, the funereal scene where spiritual and material meet, as offering "life itself": "with its brilliancy, its sordidity, its incoherence, its sudden lightning flashes of significance."[29]

Modernist writers often metaphorized what earlier literature literalized. In Dante's *Inferno*, one of the fraudulent counsellers, thinking himself secure from earthly judgment, from having his story revealed, tells the still-alive Dante:

> If I believed that my reply were made
> To one who could revisit earth, this flame
> Would be at rest, and its commotion laid.
> But seeing that alive none ever came
> Back from this deep, if it be truth I hear,
> I answer without dread of injured fame. (27: 61–6)

In making this passage the epigraph to "Prufrock," Eliot updates and domesticates the interplay of shameful death and shameful life. Prufrock absurdly tries out various great parts – John the Baptist, Hamlet – and then opts for "Lazarus, come from the dead, / Come back to tell you all, I shall tell you all." But his return is greeted with ennui; his new understanding, which impresses no one, converts into no worldly currency. Dubious spirits also appear in James, Rilke, Joyce, Forster, and Woolf; corpses take on a life of their own (like *Ulysses*' drowned man); and protagonists survive their dying in Machado de Assis' *Epitaph of a Small Winner*, Bierce's "An Occurrence at Owl Creek Bridge," *Lord Jim*, *Ethan Frome*, *The Man Who Died*, *As I Lay Dying*, *Finnegans Wake*, Golding's *Pincher Martin*, among others.

The paradigm of death as initiation in modernist fiction appears in *Epitaph of a Small Winner* (1880), whose posthumous narrator proclaims it the "work of a man already dead," one "written here in the world beyond" (17), in "Hamlet's 'undiscovered country'" (20). The book's first chapter, "The Death of the Author," inaugurates a posthumous narrative:

> I hesitated some time, not knowing whether to open these memoirs at the beginning or at the end, *i.e.*, whether to start with my birth or with my death. Granted, the usual practice is to begin with one's birth, but two considerations led me to adopt a different method: the first is that, properly speaking, I am a deceased writer not in the sense of one who has written and is now deceased, but in the sense of one who has died and is now writing, a writer for whom the grave was really a new cradle; the second is that the book would thus gain in merriment and novelty. (19)

Death-haunted and self-reflexive, *Epitaph* concerns both the life of its protagonist/narrator, Braz Cubas, and his self-assertive narrating. Never has looseness of form and chronology, for example, been more appropriate: "this book is written leisurely, with the leisureliness of a man no longer troubled by the flight of time" (24). Unlike the dead who speak in seances much as they did when alive,[30] Cubas knows that his readers inhabit a realm different from his:

> the book is tedious, it smells of the tomb, it has a *rigor mortis* about it; a serious fault, and yet a relatively small one, for the great defect of this book is you, reader. You want to live fast, to get to the end, and the book ambles along slowly; you like straight, solid narrative and a smooth style, but this book and my style are like a pair of drunks. (143)

No longer the feared or anticipated end of human action, death, like childhood for adults, is known and past, assimilated; Cubas embodies the perspective and attributes of gods, for whom traditional plot structure is inappropriate. In contrast to Dante's evil counseller, Cubas proclaims his indifference to earthly judgment: "Perhaps the reader is astonished by the frankness with which I expose and emphasize my mediocrity; let him remember that frankness is the virtue most appropriate to a defunct." Alive, one feels shame, hypocrisy. "But in death, what a difference! what relief! what freedom! . . . public opinion loses its power as soon as we enter the territory of death . . . we dead folk are not concerned about its judgment" (74–5).

Like most of Cubas' assertions, this one rings both true and false: dead modernist narrators are neither freer nor more reliable than live ones. Cubas self-consciously addresses his audience in order to justify himself and his methodology. "Observe now with what skill, with what art, I make the biggest transition in this book. Observe . . . Did you note carefully? No apparent seams or joints, nothing to upset the reader's habitual attentive calm, absolutely nothing. Thus the book has all the advantages of system and method without the rigidity that they generally entail" (37). Cubas pretends to worry about his effect on readers. Having described his mother's death, he concludes: "A sad chapter. Let us move on to a happier one" (73). About a later chapter, he writes, "Perhaps I shall eliminate the preceding chapter" (144) – but obviously he does not. Nor does he erase "Deleted," the chapter about which he says, "I have half a mind to delete this chapter. Some may find it offensive. Yet, after all, these are my memoirs, prudish reader, not yours . . . Yes, I shall definitely delete this chapter" (180). Like Sterne's still-unborn narrator in *Tristram Shandy* and Ford's devitalized Dowell in *The Good Soldier*, the dead Cubas insists "How much better it would be to tell things smoothly, without all these jolts! . . . I retie the thread of the narrative from time to time, only to break it again" (145). Nonetheless, he continues as before: "The last chapter left me so sad that I had half a mind not to write this one, but to rest a while, to purge my spirit of the melancholy that had saturated it, and to continue a little later. But no, perhaps you are pressed for time" (201).

Existing beyond time, Cubas offers a postmortem narrative that lacks teleology since it has nowhere to go, no meaning to provide since meaning is past. Toward the end he responds with mock exasperation to his reader's putative misunderstanding of his shifting attitudes and styles: "My dear critic . . . I do not mean . . . to suggest that I am older than when I began to write the book. Death does not age one . . . in writing each phase of the story of my life I feel the corresponding emotion or attitude, which is of course reflected in my style. Good God, do I have to explain everything!" (227). Cubas' trope for both art and mortality is a palimpsest whose multiple layers may be read simultaneously: "man is a thinking erratum. Each period in life is a new edition that corrects the preceding one and that in turn will be corrected by the next, until publication of the definitive edition, which the publisher donates to the worms" (81). Cubas constantly writes and rewrites himself, juxtaposing original and emendation, telling and untelling his story. His concluding chapter, "Negatives," offers a sardonic bow toward oblivion:

> Adding up and balancing all these items, a person will conclude that my accounts showed neither a surplus nor a deficit and consequently that I died quits with life. And he will conclude falsely; for, upon arriving on this other side of the mystery, I found that I had a small surplus, which provides the final negative of this chapter of negatives: I had no progeny, I transmitted to no one the legacy of our misery. (251)

Like Greek tragic choruses, *Epitaph of a Small Winner*, like all epitaphs, speaks to the terrors, desires, and beliefs of the living, to the love of story and hope for survival. Like other modernist voices from beyond the grave, Cubas' insists he is alive and well and living – somewhere; even if he has yet to encounter God. Cynical and self-mocking, the storyteller yet affirms narrative's power to comprehend death.

Like de Assis, Conrad and Joyce depict death in terms of boundary collapse, but more speculatively and metaphorically. In "The Sisters," Old Cotter, an unsympathetic character, hints at the dead priest's sexual perversity: "there was something queer ... there was something uncanny about him" (*Dubliners* 9–10). Marlow, in "the sepulchral city" before setting out for the Congo, says that the old woman knitting black wool caused an "eerie feeling" to come over him: "She seemed uncanny and fateful" (*Heart of Darkness* 219). An uncanny effect, arising out of repression and fear, results when the distinction between imagined and lived experience is effaced, as happens when one crosses, and then recrosses, between life and death. E.T.A. Hoffmann, whom Rank discusses in this context, wrote, "Seized by thoughts of death: doubles."[31]

The archetypal story of doubles and death, the one informing all subsequent ones, is Poe's "William Wilson" (1839). The narrator and his double, who initially seem discrete, were born on the same day, have the same name, look alike, wear the same clothes. At school, where they arrive and leave the same day, they are for a time inseparable, bound, at least on the narrator's part, by animosity that is really self-loathing. Bent on a life of evil, the narrator is repeatedly exposed and thwarted by his double, "my arch-enemy and evil genius" (445), whom he finally assaults and kills. The action, however, turns out to be suicide, not murder, as his double's and the story's last words emphasize: "*You have conquered, and I yield. Yet, henceforward art thou also dead – dead to the World, to Heaven and to Hope! In me didst thou exist – and, in my death, see by this image, which is thine own, how utterly thou hast murdered thyself*" (448). Defined variously – alter ego, conscience, soul, good and bad angel, unconscious, second fate, revenant, "secret sharer" – Gothic doubles became a staple of modernist plots and structures.

Posthumous, doubled existence is dramatized by Conrad, Forster, Lawrence, Woolf, Ford, among others. Conrad's *Lord Jim* depicts its protagonist's quest for death as expressing what Freud calls the "compulsion to repeat" both action and recounting,[32] for the *Patna*'s story "seemed to live, with a sort of uncanny vitality, in the minds of men, on the tips of their tongues" (84).[33] Wilde's Dorian Gray says, "I have no terror of Death. It is only the coming of Death that terrifies me," about which Rank comments: "Thus we have the strange paradox of the suicide who voluntarily seeks death in order to free himself of the intolerable thanatophobia."[34] Jim recoils fearfully, Marlow suggests, not from death but from its unexpectedness, its failure to conform to his imagining: "he was afraid of the emergency ... He might have been resigned to die, but I suspect he wanted to die without added terrors, quietly, in a sort of peaceful trance" (54). But then, Marlow adds, "It is always the unexpected that happens" (58).

The unexpected "rash act" early in *Lord Jim* is Captain Brierly's suicide; he kills himself as surrogate for Jim. But it also adumbrates Jim's own metaphorical and spiritual suicide: like Brierly's, Jim's death is both an act of supreme arrogance and an admission "of unmitigated guilt" (36). In deserting the *Patna* Jim takes a leap "into an everlasting deep hole" (68) that recalls Kurtz and the "impenetrable darkness … lying at the bottom of a precipice where the sun never shines" from which Marlow drew back in *Heart of Darkness* (283). Marlow says of Jim what he said of Kurtz on the verge of death: "He had tumbled from a height he could never scale again" (*Lord Jim* 68–9). Unlike epic visitors to Hades, Jim plunges into his abyss not in quest of understanding (though perforce he gains self-knowledge, more than he would like), but in abandonment of selfhood and the moral universe. Afterward, Jim grandiosely pronounces, " 'Everything was gone and – all was over … ' he fetched a deep sigh … 'with me.' " Marlow mockingly concurs: "His saved life was over … Annihilation – hey! And all the time it was only a clouded sky, a sea that did not break, the air that did not stir. Only a night; only a silence" (70). Jim's consequent journeying ever Eastward, a journey from one form of death to another, and from retelling to retelling, makes the two halves of this doubled fiction each other's uncanny mirror image.

Through Marlow and Stein, Jim seeks a second life, what he naively calls "a clean slate … clean slate" (159), on which to write a new self, to reclaim innocence repeatedly lost, and whose loss he has ignored, in previous incarnations. Rank says, "a person's past inescapably clings to him and … it becomes his fate as soon as he tries to get rid of it."[35] Conrad offers no possibility of new life, of a return being anything but repetition. Sympathetic in most things, Marlow, with a weariness born of experience, mocks Jim's exuberance for this undertaking: "A clean slate, did he say? As if the initial word of each our destiny were not *graven* in imperishable characters upon the face of a rock!" (113; my emphasis). Marlow's deadly pun is appropriate: both "grave" and "engrave" derive from Old English for "dig," and one meaning of "grave" is "graven": carved, sculpted, written. This image of imperturbable stolidity and inexorable destiny is replicated in Doramin's "imposing, monumental" bulk – "immense and heavy, like a figure of a man roughly fashioned of stone" (158–9) – and then in Jim after Dain Waris' death and just before he goes to be killed by Doramin: "He sat like a stone figure" (248).

For Marlow, Patusan represents an alien dimension, "a star of the fifth magnitude," a place "of no earthly importance to anybody" (133), a story scarcely worth telling. Marlow both does and does not subscribe to Jim's assertion of pristine possibility: in going to Patusan, he says, Jim "left his earthly failings behind him and what sort of reputation he had, and there was a totally new set of conditions for his imaginative faculty to work upon. Entirely new, entirely remarkable" (133). But Patusan, which Stein seems once before to have "used as a grave," serves to fulfill Brierly's injunction to bury Jim "twenty feet underground" (41, 122, 134). For Jim, as the captain who carries him there malappropriately pronounces, "was already 'in the similitude of a corpse ... Already like the body of one deported'" (147). Marlow later seems to agree with his "privileged reader" (214) that actions there – a realm forever "motionless, unfaded, with its life arrested, in an unchanging light" – signify nothing morally or aesthetically. Upon leaving Patusan and Jim for the final time, Marlow says, "I had turned away from the picture and was going back to the world where events move, men change, light flickers, life flows ... But as to what I was leaving behind, I cannot imagine any alteration" (200).

Conrad's imagery is more reliable than his narrators. Jim resembles Hamlet in having bad dreams, seeking oblivion, and entering a grave he will soon inhabit. Of his experience in an open boat after deserting the *Patna*, Jim says, "We were like men walled up quick in a roomy grave. No concern with anything on earth. Nobody to pass an opinion. Nothing mattered ... No fear, no law, no sounds, no eyes – not even our own" (74). Marlow depicts Jim's origins and termination in similar terms. The "quiet corner" of England that houses his father's parsonage is "as free of danger or strife as a tomb" (208), while Patusan "was a great peace, as if the earth had been one grave ... This was, indeed, one of the lost, forgotten, unknown places of the earth" (196). Jim embraces there, in the already grieving "melancholy figure" of Jewel, "the shadow of a cruel wisdom buried in a lonely grave, looking on wistfully, helplessly, with sealed lips" (168). No return from this afterlife is possible: "Once he got in, it would be for the outside world as though he had never existed ... 'Never existed – that's it, by Jove!' [Jim] murmured to himself" (142). Triumphant in Patusan, Jim exults: "I feel as if nothing could touch me" (147). And Marlow, who saw Jim on the *Patna* as victim "of a fiendish and appalling joke ... planned by the tremendous disdain of the Dark Powers" (74), comments that "Perhaps, indeed, nothing could touch him since he had survived the assault of the dark powers" (151).

Analyzing the uncanny, Freud found himself led back

> to the old, animistic conception of the universe. This was characterized by the idea that the world was peopled with the spirits of human beings; by the subject's narcissistic overvaluation of his own mental processes; by the belief in the omnipotence of thoughts and the technique of magic based on that belief ... as well as by all the other creations with the help of which man ... strove to fend off the manifest prohibitions of reality. (240)

Marlow's representation of Jim's encounter with mysterious forces enacts Freud's "uncanny." Jim's "narcissistic overvaluation" manifests itself in his love of Patusan and its people "with a sort of fierce egoism, with a contemptuous tenderness" (152) and in his Brierly-like rushing to die with "a last flicker of superb egoism" (251). Conrad's imagery, however, suggests that Jim's life, like his actions in Patusan, is not susceptible to "the manifest prohibitions of reality" because he essentially did *not* survive his journey to the abyss any more than Coleridge's Ancient Mariner, who is claimed by Life-in-Death. Marlow describes Jim just after the *Patna*'s accident as "a doomed man aware of his fate, surveying the silent company of the dead. They *were* dead! Nothing could save them!" (53). Jim undergoes a moral and spiritual suicide early on; the subsequent working out of his fate, the second closing of his life, is "graven in imperishable characters."

Jim exists between *Patna* and Patusan posthumously. As chandler for Egström, he takes great risks to be first to greet ships, appearing suddenly beside them, even in squalls, as "a yelling fiend ... more like a demon than a man" (118). Twice within a dozen lines, before and after learning why Jim flees, Egström says that the earth is not big enough to hold him (118–19), his meaning seeming to shift from Jim's rushing over its terrestrial surface to his failure to stay buried beneath it. Four times within the next chapter's first few lines, Marlow uses "ghost" or "shade" to represent Jim's wrestling with his uncanny double: "what I could never make up my mind about was whether his line of conduct amounted to shirking his ghost or to facing him out" (119).

Jim's material death is sealed by his meeting Gentleman Brown who, Marlow says, "sails into Jim's history, a blind accomplice of the Dark Powers" (215). Jim acknowledges his pattern of repeated failure when, just before going to die, he uses the same metaphor: "the dark powers should not rob him twice of his peace" (248). Marlow introduces Brown with a double focus on death. He wonders how Jim would have narrated his own dying: "He has confided so much in me that at times it seems as though he must come in presently and tell the story in his own words" (208). Then Marlow tells of hearing Brown, "a few hours before he gave up his arrogant ghost" (209), speaking his "broken, violent speech . . . with the very hand of Death upon his throat" (225), consoled on his deathbed by his treachery "like a memory of an indomitable defiance" (245). Brown plays a complex of doubling roles: destiny, nemesis, alter ego.

Marlow speaks of the dying Brown as he has of Jim: his "intense egoism, inflamed by resistance, tearing the soul to pieces, and giving factitious vigour to the body" (209). Alone of the book's characters in sharing an honorific title with Jim (in fact, "gentleman" is the only one Jim claims for himself [80]), Brown enters Patusan "tired of his life, and not afraid of death" (216). Surrounded but apparently ignored, he and his men "seemed to be forgotten, . . . as if they had been dead already" (220). Brown, who "hated Jim at first sight," stands with him "on the opposite poles of that conception of life which includes all mankind" (231–2), insisting on an equivalence between them: " 'Let us agree,' said I, 'that we are both dead men, and let us talk on that basis, as equals. We are all equal before death' " (232). Brown proves himself Jim's insidious double: parallel lives have led to Patusan, where Brown makes his "subtle reference to their common blood, an assumption of common experience; a sickening suggestion of common guilt, of secret knowledge that was like a bond of their minds and of their hearts" (235). Such racial sharing explains why Jim's great friend Dain Waris "was still one of *them*," while Brown, like Jim, "was one of *us*" (220).

According to Rank, "the uncanny double is clearly an independent and visible cleavage of the ego (shadow, reflection)," which is why "the life of the double is linked quite closely to that of the individual himself."[36] Following Rank, Freud wrote that the double, the most prominent theme connected with uncanniness, was originally a denial of death's power; but when the soul can no longer be preserved in "the soil of unbounded self-love ... the 'double' reverses its aspect. From having been an assurance of immortality, it becomes the uncanny harbinger of death,"[37] which is why twins are killed in certain cultures. Embodying the "dark powers" that lie without and within Jim, Brown both incarnates Hardy's "crass casualty" and precludes a possible saving beyond. For all Jim's staging of it, his death becomes meaningless in the modernist context: tragedy has become anachronistic, and the consequences of trying to live out a defunct genre prove not just disastrous, but bathetic, uncathartic.

Jewel denounces Jim for having left her "as if I had been worse than death" (212). Having "beheld the face of that opportunity which, like an Eastern bride, had come veiled to his side," Jim marries death instead: "He goes away from a living woman to celebrate his pitiless wedding with a shadowy ideal of conduct" (253). The survivors end in Stein's "cold abode of despair": "uninhabited and uninhabitable," a place entered, like the Intended's funereal house in *Heart of Darkness*, "as you would a scrubbed cave underground" (211). Jim becomes a shade among shades, "a disembodied spirit astray amongst the passions of his earth, ready to surrender himself faithfully to the claim of his own world of shades" (253). As at the end of "The Beast in the Jungle," "The Dead," and *The Good Soldier*, living and dead become interchangeable, indistinguishable: Marlow calls himself "an evoked ghost"; Jewel "is leading a sort of soundless, inert life in Stein's house"; and Stein himself, "aged greatly of late" and about to depart, waves farewell "sadly at his butterflies," totems of dead souls he has avidly collected (253).

Like Jim, Wharton's Ethan Frome also begins as "the ruin of a man" (3), one already "dead and in hell now!" (6). A posthumous survivor of a suicidal crash that was "More'n enough to kill most men" (6), he exists "in a depth of moral isolation too remote for casual access" (14), beyond passions he could neither enact nor deny. Like Jim, Frome inhabits a dead community (8), a static, "exanimate" world (19) in which "A dead cucumber-vine dangled from the porch like the crape streamer tied to the door for a death" (51), and the kitchen he enters after the dry cold of the night has "the deadly chill of a vault" (53). His world is not only his, it is him: he incarnates "its frozen woe," his "diminished dwelling the image of his own shrunken body" (21). The reverse unfolding of his story, like the darkness enclosing Kurtz's, occurs within "the blackness of the hemlock-shaded lane," its occasional "ghostly landmark" being a farmhouse as "mute and cold as a grave-stone" (48, 23).

Like Dickens' Pip, he had as a boy found his identity speaking from a headstone: "SACRED TO THE MEMORY OF ETHAN FROME AND ENDURANCE HIS WIFE, WHO DWELLED TOGETHER IN PEACE FOR FIFTY YEARS" (80). In her Introduction, Wharton calls her figures "granite outcroppings; but half-emerged from the soil, and scarcely more articulate" (vi). Her barren New England landscape suggests a graveyard and, by extension, the corpses buried there. In "A Christmas Carol" Scrooge had managed to "sponge away the writing on this stone!"; but Ethan's fate, like Jim's, is graven in imperishable characters on "the Frome grave-stones slanted at crazy angles through the snow ... For years that quiet company had mocked his restlessness, his desire for change and freedom. 'We never got away – how should you?' seemed to be written on every headstone; and whenever he went in or out of his gate he thought with a shiver: 'I shall just go on living here till I join them'" (49–50), for "There was no way out – none" (134). Graveyard imagery resurfaces when Mattie, "the embodied instrument of fate," urges Ethan, as both despair at their imminent parting, to crash the sled into a tree: "The spruces swathed them in blackness and silence. They might have been in their coffins underground" (167). The image recurs at the end when Mrs. Hale, one of the narrator's sources, says, "There was one day ... when they all thought Mattie couldn't live. Well, I say it's a pity she *did* ... if she'd ha' died, Ethan might ha' lived; and the way they are now, I don't see's there's much difference between the Fromes up at the farm and the Fromes down in the graveyard; 'cept that down there they're all quiet, and the women have got to hold their tongues" (180–1).

Writing of what he calls Hardy's "uncanny foresight" in *Satires of Circumstance* (1914), "a medium for perceiving the events of the war just beginning," Fussell notes the funerary materials of these poems: "graves, headstones, 'clay cadavers,' coffins, skeletons, and rot. The favorite rhetorical situation is the speaking of the dead."[38] Gilbert and Gubar comment on how young men, "entering the polluted realm of the trenches ... understood themselves to have been exiled from the very culture they had been deputized to defend." An uncanny sense results because the "inhabitants of this sepulchral dream kingdom felt themselves to become ... ghosts even when they were still alive ... Forced over the borders of civilization into a country of paradox and pollution, the men of war were transformed into dead-alive beings whose fates could no longer be determined according to the rules that had governed western history from time immemorial."[39] Hence, the war intensified interest in what Fussell calls "very un-modern superstitions, talismans, wonders, miracles, relics, legends, and rumors"[40] – and the already widespread efforts to contact the dead. Two antithetical impulses were at work. First, the war's carnage and the flu epidemic that seemed its byproduct confirmed for many the Darwinian implication that there was no God, thus climaxing the turn from Victorian sentimentalizing of death that began decades before. Second, as death became both endemic and distanced, either geographically or in hospitals, elaborate funerals and mourning declined rapidly.[41] Yet as millions died and many lost someone close, the absence of corpses and rituals of separation and farewell stood faith on its head: death rather than posthumous survival became problematic and dubious, so many sought comfort by contacting the spirit world.

Katherine Anne Porter's "Pale Horse, Pale Rider" (1939) depicts a return from clinical death based on Porter's own experiences during the war and the 1918–19 flu epidemic.[42] It begins with Miranda awakening, in a bed in which "too many have died ... already," imagining herself on a horse trying to "outrun Death and the Devil" (114), returning reluctantly to consciousness and a headache that "had started with the war" (119). The world of Miranda and Adam, who met when he came to town to write his will before going to war, is antithetical to "the simple and lovely miracle" (125) of the innocence their names suggest. Miranda tries not to love Adam: "he was not for her nor for any woman, being beyond experience already, committed without any knowledge or act of his own to death" (129). But they already inhabit a deathworld, "funerals all day and ambulances all night" (146), because this "funny new disease ... seems to be a plague ... something out of the Middle Ages" (126). In intensifying pain, of mind and heart as well as body, as Adam's leave ends, Miranda collapses with flu into a nightmare in which Adam, repeatedly shot with arrows, arises "unwounded and alive ... in a perpetual death and resurrection." When she interposes herself, crying "It's my turn now, why must you always be the one to die?", the arrow strikes through her heart and into his, "and he lay dead, and still she lived" (152). The nightmare is prophetic: she alone is doomed to survive.

After travelling the "road to death" (156), Miranda enters a soundless, beautiful world where it was always morning; she encounters everyone she has ever known, their faces "transfigured each in its own beauty ... their eyes were clear and untroubled as good weather, and they cast no shadows" (159). Recalled to life by thoughts of death, she returns to "a terrible compelling pain running through her veins like heavy fire, the stench of corruption filled her nostrils, the sweetish sickening smell of rotting flesh and pus ... the smell of death was in her own body" (159). Her reentry, on Armistice Day, echoes Marlow's return to Brussels after Kurtz's death in the Congo: "Miranda looked about her with the covertly hostile eyes of an alien who does not like the country in which he finds himself, does not understand the language nor wish to learn it, does not mean to live there and yet is helpless, unable to leave it at his will" (161). A "salvaged creature," a "second-fated" one ungratefully "snatched back from death" by modern technology, she grieves "shamelessly, in pity for herself and her lost rapture," and for being set "once more safely in the road that would lead her again to death" (161–2) – only without Adam, who died of the flu when she did. His ghost, "more alive than she was," appears briefly at her summons; but when she makes a further appeal in order to be able to say, "I believe ... I believe," the room was "silent, empty, the shade was gone from it." After war, after plague, after death, there would now, whether she cares or not, "be time for everything" (165).

Ford's 1930s novels, *The Rash Act* and *Henry for Hugh*, also deploy the trope of posthumous existence. Parodying Poe's uncanny tale, "William Wilson," Ford posits two similar figures, male cousins of the same age, with nearly identical names, plights, and appearances: a series of doublings that also extends to plot. The epigraph to the first of these novels provides a source for its title: " 'The rash act,' the coroner said, 'seems to have been inspired by a number of motives, not the least amongst which was the prevailing dissoluteness and consequent depression that are now world wide.' *Times Law Reports*, July 14, 1931." Ford also knew Conrad's use of "the rash act" in reference to Captain Brierly, a judge at Jim's Court of Inquiry. Brierly's mate, who speaks the phrase, tells Marlow, "he was probably holding silent inquiry into his own case. The verdict must have been of unmitigated guilt, and he took the secret of the evidence with him in that leap into the sea" (*Lord Jim* 40, 36).

In *The Rash Act* Henry Martin Aluin Smith and Hugh Monckton Allard Smith contemplate suicide in the same place at the same time. Only one of them is successful: "Hugh Monckton was lying on his face in the place where Henry Martin had meant to lie . . . That fellow had succeeded in killing himself when he, Henry Martin, had ignominiously failed" (221–2). But Henry Martin, who had envied his double's life, is taken for him when he awakens; and, in the sequel, *Henry for Hugh*, gets to live the other's life, "his posthumous capacity" (167), and finds that the two converge: he has become a shade in his own revised existence.

William Golding's late-modernist *Pincher Martin* (1956), a reprise of Tolstoy's "Ivan Ilych" and Bierce's "Occurrence at Owl Creek Bridge," texts whose endings rewrite both the fiction and the life it recapitulates, depicts the notion that drowning persons reprise their lives. The book interweaves two other stories as well. The first, which alternates with flashbacks during the first nine-tenths of the book, depicts Martin's agonizing attempt to cling to life, health, and sanity on a rock in the Atlantic Ocean. Occupying the novel's last five pages, the second reveals that Martin did *not* suffer because he was dead all along. Hence the bulk of the novel's action, the attempt at survival plus the flashbacks, must fit into the instant of dying, which, in retrospect, *seems* to occur on the second page, in mid-cry, "Moth-" (8), though this is uncertain. The book's last line – "He didn't even have time to kick off his seaboots" (190) – contradicts or places under erasure, but does not cancel, his earlier divesting himself of them: "He felt a weight pulling him down . . . He got his right leg across his left thigh and heaved with sodden hands. The seaboot slipped down his calf and he kicked it free . . . He forced his left leg up, wrestled with the second boot and got it free. Both boots had left him" (7–8). In fact, a reiterated regret (12, 34, 83, 186) is that he had kicked off his boots and lost them in the water.

What are we to make of this rewriting of the novel by its last few pages? We are asked, in effect, to choose between Martin's agony and despair over perhaps a week and most of the book, and his apparently instantaneous death. Both versions stake their claim: the first by its intensity and length, the second by its apparent factual basis and concluding position. Wanting it both ways, Golding, off somewhere paring his fingernails like Stephen Dedalus' God, refuses to intervene, to adjudicate. The two versions contradict and subvert each other, yet remain in dynamic equilibrium, each held in the other's orbit. The alive-dead Martin inhabits a realm that both incorporates and denies traditional time and space: on the rock, "Time stretched on, indifferently" (166), and his body appears, at the end, on a beach rather than in mid-ocean. We encounter, therefore, someone who dies on the book's first or second page (though we learn this only at the end), yet who fights for life as fiercely as any literary character. One analogy, made late in the book, is with King Lear's defiant confrontation with nature's storms and violence. In both *King Lear* and *Pincher Martin*, external frenzy seems almost a byproduct (and healthier version) of humankind's outrages against nature, community, and self. In the agony and intensity of their defiance, Lear and Martin attain a dignity and vitality that create meaning and validation for lives badly lived. Like both Macbeth and Macbeth's predecessor as Thane of Cawdor, it may be said of Martin – whether he died instantaneously or after long anguish or, somehow, both – that "Nothing in his life / Became him like the leaving it" (1.4.7–8).

Science continues to serve those who would link matter and spirit, posthumous survival. Heinz Pagels examines how quantum mechanics was used to "prove" identity between physics and metaphysics, the reality of telepathy.[43] Bodies are weighed at the moment of death, a practice dating back to ancient Egypt, in order to demonstrate that they become lighter because something ("the soul") has departed. Cryogenicists freeze bodies upon death in anticipation of their being restored to life in this world rather than judged in the next. Mathematicians, like Dale Kohler in Updike's novel *Roger's Version*, use computers to seek God as well as the patterns underlying chaos. Space exploration is partly motivated by the desire to see Who as well as what is out there, while astronomers often seem on a spiritual as well as physical quest.[44] Even Roman Catholicism, long at odds with scientific advancement, has acknowledged that Galileo was right, and Pope Pius XII, addressing the Pontifical Academy of Science in 1951, spoke of contemporary cosmology as meaning that "true science to an ever-increasing degree discovers God as though God were waiting behind each closed door opened by science."[45]

But success in such ventures seems increasingly unlikely, for science and mathematics are moving in the opposite direction from that in which theosophists and spiritualists tried to go. Epistemology, like "commonsense," has been subverted, since the turn of the century, by Einsteinian relativity and Heisenberg's uncertainty principle; non-Euclidian geometry, Gödel's proof, Bell's theorem, and fractal mathematics; the new sciences of chaos and complexity; Penrose's demonstration that artificial intelligence can never equal the workings of the human mind.[46] In nothing more than the shattering of faith in ultimate human omniscience has twentieth-century science been revolutionary. Not only is the spiritual realm unwilling to yield its secrets to rational inquiry, neither, it turns out, is this one – at least not to the extent expected.

In consequence, the "advancement of knowledge" has slowed, and even reversed itself. What had long seemed amenable to ultimate understanding (like weather) has declined rather than expanded because of the impossibility of knowing initial conditions sufficiently: much that we "know" depends on where we stand or is intrinsically unknowable or accords with self-contradictory principles. Some of this, like the wave/particle paradox,[47] resulted from the scientific revolution of the modern period. Quantum mechanics requires us to speak of how, *on average*, a particle behaves and where it is located, though an "average" particle, like an "average" person, exists only as an imaginative construct. More rethinking of traditional categories – science and religion, self and other, ultimately life and death – is resulting from chaos and complexity theory.

In the 1970s and 1980s, the quest to transcend scientific and mortal limits inspired books like Raymond Moody's bestseller, *Life After Life*, and the establishment of NDE (Near-Death Experience) support groups.[48] Unlike spiritualism, the life-after-life phenomenon seeks not to prove that God and an afterworld exist beyond this one, but rather to represent the experiences of people who, having been clinically dead, claim already to have been there, met Him, and, Lazarus-like, returned to tell us all. Yet no one, according to Moody, "has described the cartoonist's heaven of pearly gates, golden streets, and winged, harp-playing angels, nor a hell of flames and demons with pitchforks."[49] *Life After Life* depicts two types of "posthumous" experience. In the first, or *local* version, the clinically dead witness actions around or near their bodies, and return able to describe what occurred around them or even in the next room.

The second version, the *peripatetic*, usually involves a journey through a dark tunnel to a white light, a white-robed figure, and a paradisal milieu. Accounts of such occurrences feature non-traumatic death (like Ivan Ilych's after he breaks through his "black hole" into the light), what Moody calls "intense feelings of joy, love and peace" during the "posthumous" experience, and the trauma of returning. Twenty percent of near-death accounts incorporate "*both* out-of-the-body and out-of-this-world elements."[50] Most accounts suggest that those who return are at peace with their lives, no longer afraid of death, though Christine Brooke-Rose's novel, *Such* (1966), depicts a Lazarus figure adrift between two worlds, neither of which accommodates him.

Various mundane explanations for posthumous experiences have been offered. Accounts of those merely *threatened* by death, it turns out, parallel those who have been clinically dead: a sense of joy and calm, a review of one's life, a vision of intense light. Common to both experiences is stress or anxiety, which produces chemical alterations that may cause those affected to recall accounts they heard or read; the condition known as hypoxia (lack of oxygen) can cause tunnel vision, intoxication, and euphoria.[51] Freud writes, "There is something about anxiety that protects its subject against fright and so against fright-neuroses,"[52] and that may shut down pain and induce pleasurable visions.

Perhaps the most elegant materialist explanation for peripatetic adventuring is Carl Sagan's paradigm of a vestigial birth memory,[53] which accords with Rank's linking "the death problem" to "the trauma of birth." Rank writes, "with the thought of death is connected from the beginning a strong unconscious sense of pleasure associated with the return to the mother's womb."[54] Such linkage occurs commonly among non-Western people: the Bara of Madagascar, for example, "invariably use the metaphor of birth ... when asked to comment on the meaning of burial ... Just as one must be born into the world of the living, so must one also be born out of it and into the world of the dead."[55] In *Aspects of the Novel*, Forster writes: "let us think of people as starting life with an experience they forget and ending it with one which they anticipate but cannot understand" (56); in "What I Believe" he says, "The memory of birth and the expectation of death always lurk within the human being ... Naked I came into the world, naked I shall go out of it!"[56] Salman Rushdie literalizes rebirth in his postmodern novel, *The Satanic Verses*, which begins with a plane exploding and two of its passengers falling without parachutes as through "the birth canal," and then resuming, or re-initiating, their lives after landing: "'To be born again,' sang Gibreel Farishta tumbling from the heavens, 'first you have to die. Ho ji! Ho ji! To land upon the bosomy earth, first one needs to fly'" (3–4).

Sagan's thesis recalls Freud's "uncanny" as a reappearance of material repressed from childhood. According to Freud, "It often happens that neurotic men declare that they feel there is something uncanny about the female genital organs. This *unheimlich* place, however, is the entrance to the former *Heim* [home] of all human beings, to the place where each one of us lived once upon a time and in the beginning."[57] But since "posthumous" experience is not limited to "neurotic men," perhaps the unconscious conceives the trauma of departing this world as a repetition of entering it. It might, consequently, be revealing to compare accounts by men and women, as well as ones by people born vaginally and those delivered by Caesarean methods, for whom female genital organs are likely to signify very differently.

It would also be instructive to juxtapose recollections of religious and non-religious revenants, for the wish or belief may inspire the experience, or "memory" of it. After reviewing non-spiritual explanations, Ian Wilson concludes, "case after case attests that in principle *real* recall of information beyond the reach of the physical senses is achieved."[58] Yet, like Kurtz and Marlow in the Congo, those entering alien realms tend to find what they bring: the paradise gained is culturally specific. After a heart attack, the Swedish writer and secularist, Artur Lundkvist, spent two months in a coma before recovering fully: he experienced an extraordinary voyage into his own past and psyche, the world's problems and future, his own poetic metaphors come to life – but he never encountered God.[59]

CHAPTER 8

Survivors of apocalypse

In 1917, Einstein denounced the West's use of its great material knowledge: "Our much vaunted progress in technology, generally of civilization, is like the axe in the hand of a pathological criminal." In 1932 he maintained that "if the workers of this world, men and women, decide not to manufacture and transport ammunition, it would stop war for all time."[1] Einstein's pacifist stance, which he sustained until Hitler's rise to power in 1933, was rooted in manichean pessimism and the Western world's "apocalyptic legacy."[2] As if taking his cue from Einstein, Gil Elliot writes that the "scale of man-made death is the central moral as well as material fact of our time." Examination of earlier historical times "shows the twentieth century to be incomparably the more violent period."[3] Creating a reign of terror that dwarfed natural disasters (especially as they retreated before medical and technological advances), the modern military–industrial complex seemed to have gone berserk. Fussell writes that endless war became

> seriously available to the imagination around 1916. Events, never far behindhand in fleshing out the nightmares of imagination, obliged with the Spanish War, the Second World War, the Greek War, the Korean War, the Arab-Israeli War, and the Vietnam War ... Thus the drift of modern history domesticates the fantastic and normalizes the unspeakable. And the catastrophe that begins it is the Great War.[4]

Massive, continuing devastation became civilization's norm, with civilian deaths from war rising steadily from 5 percent in World World One to 91 percent in Vietnam.[5]

Conrad's prescient *Heart of Darkness* locates the roots of modernity's malaise within modes of exploitation, of self as well as others. Hillis Miller reads the nightmare tale as parable, a genre "oriented toward the future, toward last things ... Apocalypse *means* unveiling; an apocalypse is a narrative unveiling or revelation ... *Heart of*

Darkness is perhaps most explicitly apocalyptic in announcing the end, the end of Western civilization, or of Western imperialism, the reversal of idealism into savagery."[6] Malcolm Bradbury also views World World One as the apocalypse that led to modernism: "It expressed itself, again and again, as violation, intrusion, wound, the source of psychic anxiety, generational instability, and of the mechanistic inhumanity that prevails in, say, Lawrence's *Lady Chatterley's Lover* – a novel dominated by the 'false, inhuman bruise of the war.'"[7]

Apocalypse defined the world inhabited by trench soldiers; retaining it within their psyches the war's survivors – Graves, Sassoon, Frederic Manning, T.E. Lawrence – often expressed it as desire for degradation, usually sexual. According to Victorian convention, soldiers are more manly, more sexually charged, than civilians – imagery that feeds the culture's need for willing recruits. "What makes them so is their youth, their athleticism, their relative cleanliness, their uniforms, and their heroic readiness, like Adonis or St. Sebastian, for 'sacrifice.'" Fussell notes "a curious intercourse between [war and love]. The language of military attack – *assault, impact, thrust, penetration* – has always overlapped with that of sexual importunity." Discussing war literature in terms of masturbation, exhibitionism, and homoeroticism, Fussell adds, "War and sexuality are linked in more literal ways as well. That a successful campaign promises rape as well as looting has been understood from the beginning. Prolonged sexual deprivation will necessitate official brothels" for soldiers, and promote sexual liberty at home: "On the one hand, sanctioned public mass murder. On the other, unlawful secret individual love."[8]

Military gear for World War One often did the opposite of the expected: it unmanned and emasculated. Gilbert and Gubar write,

> the gloomily bruised modernist antiheroes churned out by the war [Eliot's sterile Fisher King, Hemingway's emasculated Jake Barnes, Ford's symbolically sacrificed O Nine Morgan, Lawrence's paralyzed Clifford Chatterley] suffer specifically from *sexual* wounds, as if, having traveled literally or figuratively through no man's land, all have become not just no-men, nobodies, but *not* men, *un*men. That twentieth-century Everyman, the faceless cipher, their authors seem to suggest, is not just publicly powerless, he is privately impotent.[9]

In Lawrence's *Kangaroo* (1923), Somers echoes Freud when he imagines brutalized men returning from war to their wives having lost their heads, "their inward, individual integrity," and more: "Awful years [1916–19] – the years when the damage was done. The years when the world lost its real manhood. Not for lack of courage to face death. Plenty of superb courage to face death. But no courage in any man to face his own isolated soul, and abide by its decision" (217). Gilbert and Gubar comment,

> the war to which so many men had gone in the hope of becoming heroes ended up emasculating them, confining them as closely as any Victorian women had been confined ... the symptoms of shell-shock were precisely the same as those of the most common hysterical disorders of peacetime ... what had been predominantly a disease of women before the war became a disease of men in combat.[10]

A hallmark of modern fiction, failed masculinity, is enacted repeatedly in novels written during or after the war: by the cuckolded Dowell in Ford's *Good Soldier* and Bloom in *Ulysses*, the paralyzed Mark in Ford's *Parade's End*, Aldington's sexually inadequate George Winterbourne in *Death of a Hero*, Faulkner's gelded Benjy in *The Sound and the Fury* and castrated Joe Christmas in *Light in August*.[11]

Modernist protagonists are devitalized and emasculated; after the Nietzschean death of God, as Foucault suggests, apocalypse seemed likely to lead to the end of the human species, "erased, like a face drawn in sand at the edge of the sea."[12] Modernist novels were written out of the detritus of Western civilization that survived World War One. Death and destruction – immense, indiscriminate, and manufactured – provided the context for Ford's *The Good Soldier*; Lawrence's *The Rainbow*, *Women in Love*, and *Lady Chatterley's Lover*; Joyce's *Ulysses*; Woolf's *Jacob's Room*, *Mrs. Dalloway*, and *To the Lighthouse*; Fitzgerald's *The Great Gatsby*; Hemingway's *The Sun Also Rises*, and much of Faulkner's fiction. The war is foregrounded in Dos Passos' *Three Soldiers*, Cummings' *The Enormous Room*, Ford's *Parade's End*, Faulkner's *Soldiers' Pay*, Hemingway's *A Farewell to Arms*. These texts share an atmosphere of universal doom, an apocalyptic world view.[13]

Adapting Northrop Frye's terms, Fussell speaks of the literature of World War One within the "ironic" mode – which follows the modes of "myth, romance, and the 'high mimetic' of epic and tragedy," in all of which "the hero's power of action is greater than ours," and "the mode in which the hero's power of action is like ours ... the 'low mimetic,' say, of the eighteenth- and nineteenth-century novel." In its late phase, as after the war, "the ironic mode seizes upon 'demonic' imagery," nightmare and apocalypse, before the return to the cycle's first phase, that of myth and ritual.[14] Powerlessness and mass death pervade this literature, defining the modernist context within which it and its fictionalized worlds exist.

World War One and its aftermath made it impossible to sustain earlier dominant tropes of progress, faith in a divine presence in human history, heroic presumptions about battle and masculinist values. Much of the trauma and disorientation of the war had to do with its assault on patriarchy: modernism coincided not only with the suffragists and growing demands for women's rights, but with the loss of a male generation, the entry of women into workplaces they had never entered before, the use of technology (a masculine product and image) for mass destruction, and the subversion of what had seemed essential about gender and gender relationships.

Rather than find solace in the new dispensation, many modernists enacted strategies for evading or assailing it. They espoused political or religious ideologies that were conservative or even reactionary, simultaneously romanticized and patronized "primitive" cultures in distant parts of the world or in the past, or sought to resuscitate moribund rituals. In these ways, historical continuity might be set right again, or the causes of disaster pinpointed, or at least, as in Pound's gendering of civilization as "an old bitch gone in the teeth," blame properly placed. As Gilbert and Gubar argue, Ezra Pound was "representative rather than idiosyncratic when, in 'Hugh Selwyn Mauberley' (1920) he metaphorized the society for which the war had been fought as female." Emancipation of women through and following the war provoked a strong misogynistic backlash.[15] Instead of assailing the death culture that masculinist history had constructed many sought to revivify it.

One means of recuperating death as ritual (discussed in chapter 3 above) is human sacrifice; another is to turn it into sport: either a hunt (animal sacrifice) or an arena game staged before an audience (or community), often with one of the combatants representing the community and expected to kill "the enemy." Roman gladiatorial combat, for example, was a way of saying, to paraphrase Villiers de l'Isle Adam's *Axel*, "as for dying, our slaves can do it for us."[16] Both Faulkner and Hemingway, who came of age during World War One, were rejected by the US Army, and began writing in the aftermath of the war's devastation. Seeking order and meaning that would reaffirm individual identity (especially a traditional masculinist one) in a world suddenly uncongenial to it, they explored social confrontations with mortal limits and worth by enacting the trope of dangerous games.[17]

Faulkner joined the Canadian Air Force, but failed to cross the ocean before the Armistice. He regretted missing out and for years fostered the myth that he *had* participated. Though this war did not haunt Faulkner, it served as backdrop for two of his first three novels, *Soldiers' Pay* (1926) and *Flags in the Dust* (1973; first published as *Sartoris* in 1929), and was foregrounded in his late anti-war novel, *A Fable* (1954). Often archly self-conscious, *Soldiers' Pay* is *negative* autobiography: not a fictionalized war experience but an imaginative construct Faulkner imposed on paper after failing to impose it on his life. Just after the war, Lieutenant Donald Mahon, a shell-shocked mindless vegetable, returns home amid raucous soldiers. He is less the novel's protagonist than its absent center: "His body is already dead." Spoiled by war, he is doubly its spoil: both its devastation and its appropriate reward. Often called "Loot," he is the prize other characters contest, both product and horrific booty of organized killing and dying.

Even less than World War One did other large historical events of his time – the rise of fascism, the Spanish Civil War, Stalinism, World War Two – compel Faulkner's imagination. His "great war" was the one that stained the soil and people he knew and whose impact, therefore, seemed more immediate, far greater, and more enduring. Reading back through the war he had missed to the Civil War and its consequences, Faulkner found a pre-capitalist society that, for all its failings, seemed congenial to individual identity. Even while condemning slavery as dehumanizing, Faulkner mixed memory and desire into a pre-modernist version of manhood that romanticized the antebellum South, asserted frontier values and initiation rites, and downplayed the role of women, even as social and procreative beings. Like Cooper, writing *The Leatherstocking Tales* removed from the events he depicted, Faulkner imagined a green world in which how *men* lived and died mattered supremely. For him, authorial self-assertion led to the creation, or recreation, of Yoknapatawpha, "a cosmos of my own. I can move these people around like God."[18]

Though set in 1919, *Flags in the Dust*, with its tone "of savage nostalgia," is obsessed with dead Civil War figures rather than the attenuated survivors of the just-ended war. Yet all are equally mocked when, in the novel's penultimate scene, Aunt Jenny visits her ghosts in the Sartoris graveyard, "those fool pompous men lying there with their marble mottoes and things." Faulkner's ironic intertext, *The Song of Roland*, lends a romantic patina to the elegiac ending, evoking "ghosts of glamorous and old disastrous things. And if they were just glamorous enough, there would be a Sartoris in them, and then they were sure to be disastrous . . . For there is death in the sound of it, and a glamorous fatality, like silver pennons down-rushing at sunset, or a dying fall of horns along the road to Roncevaux" (432–3). Yet as the novel reaches for lost glory, it demonstrates that no golden age ever existed: only time and longing, memory that remembers memory remembering, allow anyone to think otherwise.

Faulkner's hunting stories, concerning the loss of wilderness, frontier, the natural environment, depict history as the story of men confronting nature simply and directly as they assert or seek stereotypical masculine values: courage, physical daring, *virtu*, male bonding, what Hemingway calls "grace under pressure." The hunt motif represents nostalgia for a lost manichean world in which winners and losers are differentiated absolutely and the successful confronting of physical challenge evokes moral approbation. Quintessential American heroes (Huck Finn, Henderson the Rain King, Yossarian in Heller's *Catch-22*) seek such a world, and such values, in order to escape civilization's ambiguous threats and frustrations.

This mythical world of pre-lapsarian innocence, freedom, independence, a property- and class-less condition in which *men* partake of nature's bounty, is lost in our becoming creatures of society's constricting and unresolvable complexities. Yet Faulkner is also modernist in critiquing what he evokes: his hunting stories are set late in the nineteenth century, *after* the Civil War, the central event in Faulkner's history. That is, from beyond World War One, he wrote post-Civil War stories at whose center lies an imagined pre-war golden age. Yet he also demonstrates this vision's failure: the fall into modernity was always implicit in the "innocence" he represents. For *The Big Woods*, a collection of hunting stories that recall when the hunt was a ritual of renewal and masculinity rather than an exercise in nostalgia and ending, Faulkner wrote linking passages about the death of the wood and its ritual hunt. Thus, even as these stories evoke that dead past, they reenact its death. He represents the hunt, then, not as a recapturable ritual, but as one whose loss he elegizes.

Go Down, Moses (1942), and especially its central story "The Bear," emblematizes Faulkner's radical ambivalence toward what he seeks. The first story, "Was," begins with a static, verbless assertion: "Isaac McCaslin, 'Uncle Ike', past seventy and nearer eighty than he ever corroborated any more, a widower now and uncle to half a county and father to no one" (3). In "Delta Autumn," the book's penultimate story and the last in which Ike appears, he is confronted by an "almost white" woman, a distant cousin who is a child of enforced miscegenation. Appealing for his sympathy and support, she concludes with these damning words: "Old man . . . have you lived so long and forgotten so much that you don't remember anything you ever knew or felt or even heard about love?" (363). In "The Old People," the fairly straightforward hunting story that immediately precedes "The Bear," Ike is initiated into manhood through learning to shoot, successfully killing his first deer at twelve, and being marked with its blood by his mentor, Sam Fathers. Ike would seem, by training and instinct, to instantiate all that Faulkner longed to recapture, yet his fate, which is initially and ultimately the crucial issue of *Go Down, Moses*, suggests modernist impotence instead. The key questions are why does Ike, who seems likely to fulfill Faulkner's nostalgic quest, go so wrong? Why does he choose to live the life he does and why are the results of that decision so dire? And how does his decision help to create the context of modernism out of which Faulkner writes *Go Down, Moses*?

"The Bear" traces Ike's education in the woods during six years, from age ten to sixteen, from his first experience of the annual hunt to the climactic moment when Lion and Boon Hogganbeck kill the old bear. The emphasis is on "*men*, hunters, with the will and hardihood to endure and the humility and skill to survive, and the dogs and the bear and deer juxtaposed and reliefed against it" (191): not who possesses a deed to the land but who proves worthy of it. Prior to the bear's climactic killing, the hunt takes the form of a dangerous game, "the best game of all, the best of all breathing and forever the best of all listening . . . the yearly pageant-rite of the old bear's furious immortality" (192–4), of a ritual of masculine renewal that seems eternal. Its terms, firmly prescribed by setting and tradition, are "ordered and compelled by and within the wilderness in the ancient and unremitting contest according to the ancient and immitigable rules" (191–2), like those of controlled death in sacrifice.

Under Sam Fathers' tutelage and priesthood, Ike passes all the tests of the wilderness, and so attains such knowledge and wisdom as it has to offer about the world it represents and about himself. "He entered his *novitiate* to the *true* wilderness with Sam beside him as he had begun his *apprenticeship in miniature to manhood* after the rabbits and such with Sam beside him . . . It seemed to him that at the age of ten he was witnessing *his own birth*" (195; my emphases). Sam teaches Ike the lore of the woods and the requisite virtues (humility, patience, courage, pride) so that at thirteen Ike was already "a better woodsman than most grown men" (210), and at sixteen, on the day of the final hunt, he is honored by being given the best mount, the only one the old bear cannot spook.

Ike's education and spiritual initiation had proceeded without female intervention: "If Sam Fathers had been his mentor and the backyard rabbits and squirrels his kindergarten, then the wilderness the old bear ran was his college and the old *male* bear itself, so long *unwifed* and childless as to have become its own *ungendered progenitor*, was his alma mater" (210; my emphases). Ultimately surpassing even Sam, Ike becomes father to himself, his "own ungendered progenitor": "he was teaching himself to be better than a fair woodsman without even knowing he was doing it" (205). When Sam, guardian of the ritual hunt, tells Ike he will never see Ben while he carries his gun – "'You will have to choose,' Sam said" (206) – Ike can surrender masculinist identity: "He had left the gun; by his own will and relinquishment he had accepted not a gambit, not a choice, but a condition in which not only the bear's heretofore inviolable anonymity but all the ancient rules and balances of hunter and hunted had been abrogated" (207). Then, realizing "He was still tainted" (208), Ike ungenders himself by laying aside technology's remaining trappings, his watch and compass, and thereby gains an extraordinary accolade: the soundless, motionless, "dimensionless" meeting with Old Ben. Through initiation, the hunt ritual, and Ike's self-generation, Faulkner would seem to have found all he sought to validate in the South's past, yet what Ike embodies is undermined and betrayed throughout, and largely by Ike himself.

The land's owner, Major de Spain, is responsible for the demise of the world entrusted to his care: suggesting that capitalism destroys masculinity, Faulkner depicts both wilderness and ritual hunt as doomed when de Spain sells the wood for lumber. Through right of ownership, he had earlier arrogated to himself the Jehovah-like authority of apocalyptic judgment. Ben, he asserts, has killed a colt, and all is changed: "He has broken the rules. I didn't think he would have done that. He has killed mine and McCaslin's dogs, but that was all right. We gambled the dogs against him; we gave each other warning. But now he has come into my house and destroyed my property, out of season too. He broke the rules" (214). No one objects to this absurd invocation of inappropriate capitalist values, and so the last hunt – its participants a curious rabble of townspeople, farmers, loggers, poor white trash – mockingly reenacts the Southern defense of a debased social construct, the final charge of an already defeated army: "so that when they went into the woods this morning Major de Spain led a party almost as strong, excepting that some of them were not armed, as some he had led in the last darkening days of '64 and '65" (236).

But just as the South, myth and nation, is doomed, with or without de Spain to lead it, so are the wilderness and the bear, already anachronistic, "out of an old dead time, a phantom, epitome and apotheosis of the old wild life" (193), by the time Ike is ten. Ike and Sam Fathers, men of the wilderness, play passive parts in the deaths of Old Ben and the woods he symbolizes. The refrain in the first part of the story is "So he [Ike] should have hated and feared Lion" (209, 212, 226), yet Ben's conqueror is welcomed and trained for the job. Ike, however, already knows at the age of ten that he will never fire his gun at Old Ben (203); his subsequently relinquishing it in order to encounter him, then, sacrifices no usable weapon. Yet Ike and Sam agree that Ben's killer "must be one of us" (212), and when de Spain pronounces Old Ben's doom, Ike realizes that Sam, "*was glad ... He was old ... It was almost over now and he was glad*" (215). With the wilderness' death, the role of womenless fathers ceases to be viable.

Ike also welcomes his own part in ending what cannot endure, of what, given Faulkner's post-war perspective, is already dead:

> It seemed to him that there was a fatality in it. It seemed to him that something, he didn't know what, was beginning; had already begun. It was like the last act on a set stage. It was the beginning of the end of something, he didn't know what except that he would not grieve. He would be humble

and proud that he had been found worthy to be a part of it too or even just to see it too. (226)

That last phrase is revealing, for Faulkner's emphasis throughout "The Bear" is on passivity, on learning *not* to shoot; and when the crisis comes Ike and Sam are inactive, voyeurs at the kill.

What are we to make of this *anti*-hunt climax to Ike's role as Adamic figure in the American Eden? Is Ike a trailblazer or a moral cipher? Should we admire him as a young initiate, or as one who later rejects his early folly, or both, or neither? "The Bear" depicts Ike's education beyond his initiation, an experience that, like all desacralized death rituals, becomes irrelevant when the world whose values it replicates and sustains is over. With the final hunt that culminates in Old Ben's killing and industrialization laying the woods waste, "The Bear" enacts the history and mythos of a pristine South that culminates in a present that is both post-Civil War and post-world war. Ike has learned the master's lessons: humility, patience, abnegation, all the negative virtues. So at the climax both he and Sam are effectively absent, or worse: Sam, though "markless" as the dying wilderness, collapses fatally when Ben falls. Characteristically, Ike's one resolute action in all of *Go Down, Moses* is relinquishment, and what he relinquishes is his patrimony, his inherited masculine identity: that which gives him a name and a link to the past, and therefore a future as well. That relinquishment of responsibility provokes the young woman's disdain in "Delta Autumn," and the dismay of Compson, who has loved and trusted Ike: "I don't believe you just quit. It looks like you just quit but I have watched you in the woods too much and I don't believe you just quit even if it does look damn like it" (309). But quit is exactly what Ike has done, as Faulkner himself complained in an interview: "I think a man ought to do more than just repudiate. He should have been more affirmative instead of just shunning people."[19] Ike also knows this, knowing "that no man is ever free and probably could not bear it if he were" (281). No wonder he becomes merely Uncle Ike: lacking surname, having surrendered the active roles of husband, which he briefly plays, and of father that, for all his desiring a son, he never manages. He becomes, like "the old male bear itself, so long unwifed and childless[, his] own ungendered progenitor" (210). All the negatives accrue to Ike: property-less, powerless, nameless, heirless. Having rejected his life, Ike finds death a grace that *Go Down, Moses* denies him: only the long, Tithonus-like dying remains.

Hemingway, who sought death all his life, joined the Red Cross as an ambulance driver, made it to the Italian front where, within a week, he received the wound he wore like a medal all his life and that infused all his writing. The son of a suicide, Hemingway, like Greene, contemplated killing himself on numerous occasions; when he finally succeeded his suicide seemed to trigger others: his sister, his brother, and Adriana Ivancich, whom he had loved. Hemingway actively pursued death in order to test and demonstrate his prowess to himself as well as others, and to transform the confrontation into both sport and art, and his life into achievement wrested from the brink of annihilation. He used death to define his characters and himself: as accidental and temporary survivors whose lives are predicated on how they respond to both violence and more insidious threats.

Death is not always a derivative of war for Hemingway. *To Have and Have Not* (1937), which climaxes with its dying hero gasping, "No matter how a man alone ain't got no bloody fucking chance" (225), is commonly read as marking a significant change from rugged individualism and toward a concern for political action. Old Santiago in *The Old Man and the Sea* (1952) knows death as a familiar, integral not to history's larger destructive events but to quotidian reality. Yet it was World War One and the wound it gave him that largely determined, or over-determined, Hemingway's response to death and his strategies of survival.

Believing in the war as a "crusade for democracy" and anticipating that it would serve his writing, Hemingway eagerly sought martial action and felt only contempt for "military politicians of the rear." As he subsequently wrote, "any experience of war is invaluable to a writer."[20] He also liked the way he looked in uniform and the status it conferred: "Our uniforms are regular United States Army officers' and look like a million dollars. Privates and non-coms must salute us" (*Letters*, 14 May 1918, 6). His wound, which remained psychically significant, fulfilled a juvenile fantasy. He reveled in his medals and promotion and his sense of being newly appreciated: "It's the next best thing to getting killed and reading your own obituary" (*Letters*, 18 August 1918, 13). His good fortune at being alive "conclusively proved that I can't be killed" (*Letters*, 11 September 1918, 18). Retrospectively, he characterized himself as "not . . . at all hard boiled since July 8 1918 – on the night of which I discovered that that also was Vanity" (*Letters*, 21 December 1926, 240). Yet undeterred, he went subsequently to the Greco-Turk war, the Spanish Civil War, and World War Two.

The wars and wounds that inspired Hemingway maimed, unmanned, and destroyed many of his protagonists. The autobiographical Nick Adams returns home shell-shocked in "Big Two-Hearted River"; Jake Barnes' wound renders him impotent, an embodiment of the spiritual wasteland who finds no way to shore his fragments against his ruin. Lt. Henry, seeking to escape a similar fate in *A Farewell to Arms* (1929), finds death pursuing him like an avenging fury and assailing the "separate peace" he and Catherine had sought away from the world's self-destruction. Robert Jordan, like Conrad's Marlow in *Heart of Darkness* in that "he did not give any importance to what happened to himself" (*For Whom the Bell Tolls* 4), finds meaning only in fighting and dying bravely for another's hopeless cause. In *Across the River and Into the Trees* (1950), Richard Cantwell, like Hemingway before him, revisits the scene of his wounding at the Italian front thirty years earlier in World War One. He "relieved himself in the exact place," and then completes "the monument" by digging a hole in which to bury his excrement and a 10,000 lira note, the amount that came with his medals: "It's fine now, he thought. It has merde, money, blood . . . It's a wonderful monument. It has everything. Fertility, money, blood and iron. Sounds like a nation. Where fertility, money, blood and iron is, there is the fatherland" (18–19). In this extraordinary passage, which echoes Bismark's "blood and iron" and Marx's conflating of death and money, Hemingway erects the perfect memorial to war's masculinist values.

Hemingway's most extensive attempt to bury, or sublimate, the war was expressed in masculinist quests: a cult of athletic prowess, sexual promiscuity (four marriages and many mistresses), and the surrogate and dramaturgical experience of controlled violence. His greatest need was to challenge himself in "dangerous games" while adhering to their "fundamental rules": big-game hunting, deep-sea fishing, boxing, or bullfighting. Throughout his writing and a life of physical risk-taking, Hemingway projected himself literally and imaginatively from fear of lost manhood: the result was both numerous triumphs and recurring confirmations of loss and failure.

Like "The Bear," "The Short Happy Life of Francis Macomber"

(whose working titles included "Marriage is a Dangerous Game" and "The More Dangerous Game"[21]) both enacts and betrays the rules of the hunt that supposedly convert it from gratuitous violence into ritual. The notion of proving one's moral worth through exercising physical prowess is prominent in many cultures. Eliade suggests that such a principle has force and authority in a spiritual context: "For religious man, reactualization of ... mythical events constitutes his greatest hope ... it is by virtue of this eternal return to the sources of the sacred and the real that human existence appears to be saved from nothingness and death." Yet the "perspective changes completely when the sense of *the religiousness of the cosmos becomes lost ... repetition emptied of its religious content necessarily leads to a pessimistic vision of existence ... when it is desacralized*, cyclic time becomes terrifying."[22]

Hemingway's story, like Faulkner's, depicts a protagonist who fights not merely for survival, but for mythic values that, though vestigial memory insists they once had meaning, civilization and mass destruction render fatuous. Robert Wilson, the white hunter who leads the safari, enunciates and embodies the hunt's rules: you don't shoot from cars; despite the danger, you don't abandon wounded animals; you don't send in beaters to flush them out ("Somebody bound to get mauled" [17]); and you don't talk about your clients. Wilson speaks often about what people are and are not supposed to do, even while maintaining that talk is opposed to rules, which are inherited, tradition-sanctioned, tacit. After assuring Macomber that hunters "never talk about our clients," he adds: "You can be quite easy on that. It's supposed to be bad form to ask us not to talk though" (7). When Macomber rattles on about his embarrassment at Margot's having witnessed his cowardice, Wilson thinks: "I should think it would be even more unpleasant to do it ... wife or no wife, or to talk about it having done it" (11). Responding to Macomber's angry, jealous suggestion that he hunt alone while Margot and Wilson stay in camp the day after they sleep together, Wilson says: "Can't do that ... Wouldn't talk rot if I were you" (24).

Only once does Wilson, touched by Macomber's sudden fearlessness, reveal something about himself. He quotes the Shakespearean line that expresses his credo: "By my troth, I care not; a man can die but once; we owe God a death and let it go which way it will he that dies this year is quit for the next." But immediately he regrets "having brought out this thing he had lived by": "You're not supposed to mention it ... Much more fashionable to say you're scared ... Doesn't do to talk too much about all this. Talk the whole thing away. No pleasure in anything if you mouth it up too much" (32–3). Wilson might be even more embarrassed if he knew the source of his credo: a character named Feeble, one of Falstaff's conscripts for the royal wars in *2 Henry IV* (3.2.229–33). Himself dismissive of honor and advocating cowardice when it comes to saving himself (*1 Henry IV* 5.1.129–40), Falstaff says: "And for a retreat, how swiftly will this Feeble the woman's tailor run off!" (*2 Henry IV* 3.2.262–4).

Macomber is Wilson's antithesis. For Wilson, the safari is vocation, a means of personal fulfillment, a primitive sacred ritual in which animals are adversarial, not merely passive (human) victims. Macomber acts out a cinematic idyll, one inspired by the banal desire to demonstrate his dubious masculinity to his beautiful, spiteful wife, whom his cowardice has driven to adultery. Understanding none of the rules, Macomber wants always to talk: about lying awake at night listening to the lion's roar, about his cowardice, about Margot's unfaithfulness, about his sudden sense of living, "for the first time in his life," beyond fear. Yet Macomber's moral role (like the story's title, which seems ironic but is also meant literally) may be greater than that of Wilson, who grudgingly comes to respect him and who himself violates the rules he claims to espouse. Wilson's values are made most explicit in his attitude toward rich female clients: "he made his living by them; and their standards were his standards ... in all except the shooting. He had his own standards about the killing and they could live up to them or get some one else to hunt them" (26). Yet Wilson's standards are elastic, *ad hoc*: whipping the natives (though it is illegal) rather than fining them, carrying "a double cot on safari to accommodate any windfalls he might receive," mouthing his vapid credo at the first blush of empathy.

Most violative, however, are his using the car to chase buffalo and then, implicitly, asking that it be kept secret: "Wouldn't mention it to any one though. It's illegal ... I'd lose my license for one thing. Other unpleasantnesses ... I'd be out of business" (30). His position near the end, then, replicates Macomber's at the beginning, as if implying that Macomber has morally triumphed through ceremonial initiation. Though Wilson serves as priest in the ritual hunt its values prove meaningless for him, rote learning rather than sacred belief. He seems, in fact, a burlesque figure: often speaking the choppy sentences of a mock noble savage, unwittingly undercutting everything he claims to embody, and finally posed vacuously over the bodies of Macomber and the wild buffalo, dead in an instant. "'Hell of a good bull,' his brain registered automatically. 'A good fifty inches, or better. Better'" (36). "Automatically" – the adverb reveals the rote quality of Wilson's "code." He is what Marlow calls Kurtz, hollow at the core, and his syntax, which is meant to be spare, clean, objective, and manly, is also self-parodic. Since Hemingway himself often affected what came to be known as "Hemingway Choctaw,"[23] he must at some level have known how difficult it is to take seriously.

Macomber has risked, gained, and lost all. At one point, Wilson thinks, "If they got buff today there would only be rhino to come and the poor man would have gone through his dangerous game and things might pick up" (26). The hunt, seemingly parodic of ritual initiation into manhood for Macomber, becomes what it parodies. During the buffalo hunt, Wilson realizes the genuineness of Macomber's alteration: "Look at the beggar now, Wilson thought. It's that some of them stay little boys so long, Wilson thought. Sometimes all their lives. Their figures stay boyish when they're fifty. The great American boy-men. Damned strange people. But he liked this Macomber now. Damned strange fellow. Probably meant the end of cuckoldry too" (33). This last is literalized within moments when Macomber is "accidentally" killed by Margot who, presumably, also perceives and fears the change in him. Hemingway's point seems clear: the cuckold who becomes hero of the hunt will refuse to countenance continuing betrayal by the wife Hemingway portrays as stereotypical bitch. In consequence, Macomber becomes not only hunter but hunted, simultaneously victor and victim of the most dangerous game. Conquering his fear of death, he lives, briefly, as "a man," and dies as Hemingway himself presumably sought to die.

Bullfighting, which Hemingway called "an art, a tragedy, and a business,"[24] is the form of controlled violence, of ritual death as sport and artifice, he explored most extensively. He wrote, "It's just like having a ringside seat at the war with nothing going to happen to you" (*Letters*, 17–18 July 1923, 88). Bullfighting is pivotal in *The Sun Also Rises* (1926), which climaxes when the impotent aficionado,

Jake Barnes, betrays its spiritual meaning by pimping for Brett Ashley with the young bullfighter Romero. Hemingway explored the subject in a long article, "Bullfighting, Sport and Industry" (1930), and in two subsequent books: *Death in the Afternoon* (1932) and *The Dangerous Summer* (1960), the latter "a book about death written by a lusty sixty-year-old man who had reason to fear that his own death was imminent."[25]

His fullest disquisition on bullfighting is *Death in the Afternoon*, which he calls "A Natural History of the Dead" (133). Hemingway maintains that Spaniards, "as they have common sense ... are interested in death and do not spend their lives avoiding the thought of it and hoping it does not exist only to discover it when they come to die" (264). Castillians, he says,

> know death is the unescapable reality, the one thing any man may be sure of; the only security ... They think a great deal about death and when they have a religion they have one which believes that life is much shorter than death. Having this feeling they take an intelligent interest in death and when they can see it being given, avoided, refused and accepted in the afternoon for a nominal price of admission they pay their money and go to the bull ring. (266)

Whether or not Hemingway represents the Spanish view of bullfighting,[26] he is, like Lawrence and other modernists, indulging in what Freud called "the primitive" to satisfy his own needs.

Hemingway's "quarrel with androgyny"[27] and his need to experience heroism in a world he saw as having ended battlefield killing caused him to romanticize rituals of dangerous games, especially the bullfight, the "only place where you could see life and death, i.e., violent death now that the wars were over" (2). The impulse behind the bullfight, Hemingway maintains, is pagan: "I suppose, from a modern moral point of view, that is, Christian point of view, the whole bullfight is indefensible; there is certainly much cruelty, there is always danger, either sought or unlooked for, and there is always death" (1). Hemingway's equation of modern morality with Christianity is curious, and certainly one that Lawrence, who considered bullfighting and Christianity equally repugnant and death-obsessed, rejected.

Hemingway saw the bullfight, from the matador's perspective, as eros triumphing over thanatos. The great bullfighter "must love to kill ... he must have a spiritual enjoyment of the moment of killing. Killing cleanly and in a way which gives you aesthetic pleasure and pride has always been one of the greatest enjoyments of a part of the human race ... One of its greatest pleasures ... is the feeling of rebellion against death which comes from its administering" (232–3). The question of whose death occurs must never be in doubt: always the bull's, never the bullfighter's. Bullfights, Hemingway insists, would be *less* interesting if the bulls (which are always killed either during or after the fight) were allowed to survive, having learned from their experience, to fight again.

Hemingway maintains that "the bull learns so rapidly in the ring that if the bullfight drags, is badly done, or is prolonged an extra ten minutes he becomes almost unkillable by the means prescribed in the rules of the spectacle" (107). Bullfighting, therefore, "is based on the fact that it is the first meeting between the wild animal and a dismounted man" (21). Experienced bulls would be dangerously unpredictable, threatening not only the matador but ritual itself, and thereby communal order. The animal is killed; the man avoids death.

Hemingway's obsession with aestheticized ritual and dramaturgy leads to his dismissing the horses' fate: "I believe that the tragedy of the bullfight is so well ordered and so strongly disciplined by ritual that a person feeling the whole tragedy cannot separate the minor comic-tragedy of the horse [when it is gored] so as to feel it emotionally" (8). Lawrence, a writer of very different sensibility, mocks the notion of "manly hunt"[28] and anti-romantically depicts a horse's death in the bullring as *faux* eroticism: "the horse was up-ended absurdly, one of the bull's horns between his hind legs and deep in his inside. Down went the horse, collapsing in front, but his rear was still heaved up, with the bull's horn working vigorously up and down inside him, while he lay on his neck all twisted. And a huge heap of bowels coming out. And a nauseous stench" (*Plumed Serpent* 13). In the entire bullfight, Lawrence insists, "There was no glamour, no charm" (8). The difference parallels that between the Victorian aestheticized death and the modernist "dirty death," as Hemingway acknowledges at times. In *The Sun Also Rises*, Montoya, the priest of the bullfight, forgives Jake his friends at first; yet they were "something shameful between us, like the spilling open of the horses in bull-fighting" (132). The comparison of Jake's friends to the horses' spilled guts anticipates Jake's shameful introduction of Romero and Brett, a betrayal that results in Jake's being excommunicated from the brotherhood of initiates.

Knowing better, Hemingway insists that controlled violence, with its designated victim, like Agamemnon's daughter Iphigenia, kept ignorant of her role, is cathartic, a formal social process that reenacts a familiar script as sport, play, storytelling, or sacrificial ritual. *Death in the Afternoon* suggests the "challenge" and "jousting" Foucault finds in eighteenth-century public executions: "If the executioner triumphed, if he managed to cut off the head with a single blow, he 'showed it to the people, put it down on the ground and then waved to the public who greatly applauded his skill by clapping' ... Conversely, if he failed, if he did not succeed in killing the 'patient' as required, he was liable to punishment,"[29] though not, presumably, to death.

For Hemingway bullfighting is "the most dangerous game" because it "is the only art in which the artist is in danger of death and in which the degree of brilliance in the performance is left to the fighter's honor" (91). His bullfighter is an executioner who risks death:

> the matador, if he knows his profession, can increase the amount of the danger of death that he runs exactly as much as he wishes. He should, however, increase this danger, *within the rules provided for his protection* ... it is to his credit if he does something that he knows how to do in a highly dangerous but still geometrically possible manner. It is to his discredit if he runs danger through ignorance, through disregard of the fundamental rules, through physical or mental slowness, or through blind folly. (21)

The antithesis of such controlling artifice, of ritual death, is not extended life, but anarchic death, like the rule-less mêlées that occur in small towns:

> Sometimes the bull is killed if the town has the money to afford it, or if the populace gets out of control; every one swarming on him at once with knives, daggers, butcher knives and rocks; a man perhaps between his horns, being swung up and down, another flying through the air, surely several holding his tail, a swarm of choppers, thrusters and stabbers pushing into him, laying on him or cutting up at him until he sways and goes down. All amateur or group killing is a very barbarous, messy, though exciting business and is a long way from the ritual of the formal bullfight. (24)

The bullfighter, though usually "frightened at some moment *before* the fight begins," must manifest during it that bravery which is "the ability temporarily to ignore possible consequences" or, even better, "the ability not to give a damn for possible consequences" (58):

the greatest emotional appeal of bullfighting is the feeling of immortality that the bullfighter feels in the middle of a great faena and that he gives to the spectators. He is performing a work of art and he is playing with death, bringing it closer, closer, closer, to himself, a death that you know is in the horns because you have the canvas-covered bodies of the horses on the sand to prove it. He gives the feeling of his immortality, and, as you watch it, it becomes yours. Then when it belongs to both of you, he proves it with the sword. (213)

Though he may feel himself a god at moments, the bullfighter is rather a priest, not a rule-maker but guardian and orchestrator of ritual he inherits; and the bull, his sacrificial victim, is like a man playing cards, "having learned the rules, through having them forced on him and through losing; and now, having his fortune and life at stake, gives much importance to the game and the rules, finding them forced upon him, and does his best with utmost seriousness. It is up to the bullfighter to make the bull play and to enforce the rules. The bull has no desire to play, only to kill" (147). Hemingway speaks of the bullfight, on those occasions (rarer than he suggests) when they are properly enacted, as "tragedy; the death of the bull, which is played, more or less well, by the bull and the man involved and in which there is danger for the man but certain death for the animal" (16).

The successful matador participates fully in ritual ecstasy, which Hemingway deems sexually climactic: "the beauty of the moment of killing is that flash when man and bull form one figure as the sword goes all the way in, the man leaning after it, death uniting the two figures in the emotional, aesthetic, and artistic climax of the fight" (247). But ultimately bullfighters, like Roman gladiators, perform not for themselves but for spectators, who frame and sanction the ritual, aficionados within whom exists "this sense of the tragedy and ritual of the fight" (9). Sharing Hemingway's voyeurism, Bataille writes that spectators experience sacrificial meaning:

This sacramental element is the revelation of continuity through the death of a discontinuous being to those who watch it as a solemn rite. A violent death disrupts the creature's discontinuity: what remains, what the tense onlookers experience in the succeeding silence, is the continuity of all existence with which the victim is now one. Only a spectacular killing carried out as the solemn and collective nature of religion dictates has the power to reveal what normally escapes notice.[30]

Ritual performance requires validation through repetition. Bullfighting, Hemingway notes, "is an impermanent art as singing and the dance are, one of those that Leonardo advised men to avoid, and when the performer is gone the art exists only in the memory of those who have seen it and dies with them ... It is an art that deals with death and death wipes it out" (99). Yet Hemingway evokes at the beginning, and implicitly throughout *Death in the Afternoon*, the theme of "eternizing" self-validation, the trope of the maker of texts that endure. "I was trying to learn to write, commencing with the simplest things, and one of the simplest things of all and the most fundamental is violent death" (2). Unlike the matador, the writer, as Faulkner maintained, *is* or can be a god, one who makes worlds by observing, encompassing, and rewriting inherited rules and rituals. The bullfight, then, exists both in its observers' minds and in the interplay of memory and recreation perpetuated in Hemingway's texts.

Hemingway responded to apocalypse, then, by reconceiving death as ritual and tragedy in his life and in his writing, which was for him, as for Harry in "The Snows of Kilimanjaro," the most dangerous game, a matter of living or dying. As if prophesying his own suicide, Hemingway inscribes Harry's capitulation to comfort and women, his betrayal of talent and work, as the gangrene that decays his still-living body: "What was his talent anyway? It was a talent all right but instead of using it, he had traded on it ... he had chosen to make his living with something else instead of a pen or a pencil" (60), with, that is, his penis. And now the moral rot of his social disease is killing him.

In their only significant exchange of letters and comments on each other, Faulkner faulted Hemingway in terms reminiscent of Hemingway's critique of Harry. Hemingway, Faulkner suggests, failed to take the risks that matter for a writer, the kind that, gallantly overreaching, are bound to fail: "Hemingway taught himself a pattern, a method which he could use and he stuck to that without splashing around to try to experiment. It had nothing to do with the value of the work at all. It was simply on the degree of the attempt to reach the unattainable dream, to accomplish more than any flesh and blood man could accomplish, could touch."[31] Literal-minded and obsessed with defining wounds and masculine prowess, Hemingway responded to what he took to be Faulkner's charge that his was a *physical* cowardice: he had General Charles Lanham write to tell Faulkner about his bravery in battle. And after reading *Big Woods* Hemingway turned what he mistakenly thought Faulkner had said into his own accusation of cowardice: "I would be a little more moved if he [Faulkner] hunted animals that ran both ways" (*Letters*, 14 November 1955, 850). Hemingway was the most materialist of modernists in his life-long obsession with the meaning and death he knew most intimately in his body. For all his efforts, it was bound to betray him in the end.

CHAPTER 9

E.M. Forster

Forster was both younger and older than his contemporaries: he outlived them all but had virtually finished with fiction before most of them began, and five of his six novels were written before World War One. (Even the exception, *A Passage to India* [1924], was begun before the war, in 1912.) Yet, as Forster wrote of his own novels and those of his compeers, "even when they are not directly about a war – like the works of Lytton Strachey or Joyce or Virginia Woolf – they still display unrest or disillusionment or anxiety, they are still the products of a civilisation which feels itself insecure . . . [Such prose] is the product of people who have war on their mind" (*Two Cheers* 272). Though Forster's novels are more social comedy than elegy (Woolf's term), death casts as long a shadow in them as in those of any of his contemporaries.[1]

For all his humanism, Forster struck early reviewers as cavalier, even profligate, in disposing of his characters. One insisted that Forster "deals out death to any one of his characters on the slightest provocation."[2] In one of the first extended essays on Forster after *A Passage to India* was published, Edward Shanks, longing for tidy Victorian structures and climaxes, assailed Forster as if he were responsible for the modern world's messiness: "Sudden death is worse than a commonplace with Mr. Forster, it is a vicious habit . . . His sudden deaths, sudden as they are, are announced with all possible calm."[3] The truth is more complex: death both inspires and enacts what is central to Forster's plots; but its representation is often ambiguous, playful as well as serious, positive as well as negative, appropriate even if unforeseen. Forsterian death is shocking because still meaningful and yet undramatized, disorienting because unique and individual, surprising in its ability still to surprise, and it occurs in a world increasingly defined by anonymous death.

Unlike Hemingway's quarrel with androgyny, Forster's was with heterosexuality: it raised fundamental questions concerning his relationship with death, which Forster usually represented as a consequence of failed erotic love. In "What I Believe," he writes, "Two cheers are quite enough [for democracy]: there is no occasion to give three. Only Love the Beloved Republic deserves that" (*Two Cheers* 70). After Oscar Wilde's trial, however, Forster had good reason to keep secret the particular form of his own "Beloved Republic," although, as Carolyn Heilbrun shows, his novels quietly interrogate and disorient accepted gender relationships that no longer seemed essential or stable: few of his central relationships enact heterosexual love. Even when one is fully and sympathetically portrayed, like that of George Emerson and Lucy Honeychurch in *A Room with a View*, Forster destabilizes inherited norms. George breaks new ground when he admits to Lucy his complicity in the masculine habit of telling women what to do: "it lies very deep, and men and women must fight it together before they shall enter the garden." And he thinks, "I want you to have your own thoughts even when I hold you in my arms" (195).

In *Howards End*, Margaret Schlegel finds in Mrs. Wilcox a female progenitor from whom she receives, and can then bequeath, what remains of value in her culture.[4] Unable to love men, scarcely remembering her child's father, Helen wonders: "Is it some awful, appalling, criminal defect?" Margaret responds by confessing that she does "not love children. I am thankful to have none" (338–9). Lionel Trilling suggests an imaginative failure in Forster's displacement of "too thoroughly gelded" males by "the Eternal Feminine";[5] but Trilling's thinking, not Forster's, was bound by traditional gender categories. In *A Passage to India*, Heilbrun argues, the unfeminine Adela Quested – "Hysterical, unsatisfied, uncharming, unpretty" – becomes heroic by making "a fool of herself in the cause of justice ... The woman who is hero does not fulfill herself by being wife or mother or lover; she makes decisions, she affects events which shake the world."[6] The novel's remarkable relationships are atypical ones between Fielding and Aziz, and Aziz and Mrs. Moore.

Charles Herriton's death, which occurs before the beginning of Forster's first novel, *Where Angels Fear to Tread* (1905), impels his widow, Lilia, on an Italian journey. She seeks both adventure and escape from her dead husband's continuing domination in the form of his family's stultifying conventionality and manipulation; and finds both in a precipitous Italian marriage, a "brief and inevitable tragedy" (41). The marriage is disastrous not only in suburban English terms, but also because freedom in Italian society, "the brotherhood of man," is denied women (47), who are men's possessions (55): Gino "had a good strong will when he chose to use it, and would not have had the least scruple in using bolts and locks to put it into effect" (58). After Lilia is "tamed" (59), she romanticizes the England she had fled: "It seemed impossible that such a free, happy life could exist" (62). When she learns of Gino's infidelity, she determines to have a child, a son, in order to win him back (61). "His one desire was to become the father of a man like himself . . . it was the first great desire, the first great passion of his life" (67). Her death in childbirth is dismissively announced: "As for Lilia, some one said to her, 'It is a beautiful boy!' But she had died in giving birth to him" (68). Yet the birth instigates the novel's subsequent events that climax in the Herritons' abducting and accidentally killing the baby whose birth caused Lilia's death.

Forster is parodying Victorian death in childbirth as a strong narrative strategy, as in the birth and death of the two Catherines in *Wuthering Heights* (180). As a homosexual who questioned gender norms, he was dubious about marriage and childbirth, the Victorian "angel in the house," and the babies and husband who defined her role. This doubt produced Helen's unsentimental view of husbands, Margaret's of children, and the killing of Lilia's baby. Forster also challenged Victorian conventions of dying, in which death was both trope and fact. Death's "big" fictional effect results from its being used as novelistic climax or closure. What seems off-key about Forster's deaths is their occurring at odd places in the narrative and producing little impact. He seems to expend his emotional capital, as well as his characters, recklessly, and without reaping the traditional affective benefit. In the process, and despite the conventional quality of his prose, he helps to define the modern novel.

Some critics defend Forster's sudden and seemingly capricious deaths. Trilling, who links them with Hardy's "crass casualty" ("Hap," *Complete Poems* 9), notes that both oppose industrialism and organized religion. The destruction of the rural world and society in the nineteenth century created widespread disorientation and unsettlement; the loss of faith resulted in an analogous spiritual restlessness. Those affected lost assurance of their place in this world as well as the next: chance and synchronicity displaced certitude and causality. As Jacques Barzun writes, "we blame Hardy for failing to show adequate cause when the lack of adequate cause is what Hardy is trying to show."[7] The comment applies equally to Forster.

In *The Longest Journey* (1907), Gerald's surprising death, occurring just before he is to marry Agnes, is announced even more brutally than those of Lilia and her baby: "Gerald died that afternoon. He was broken up in the football match" (55). This is especially startling since, for Forster, football of course meant soccer, supposedly a non-violent sport, for the players if not the fans. Rendered tone deaf by heterosexist bias, Trilling argues that a humanizing duality of vision complicates Forster's treatment of the death: "Forster can despise Gerald of *The Longest Journey* because Gerald is a prig and a bully, but he can invest Gerald's death with a kind of primitive dignity, telling us of the maid-servants who weep, 'They had not liked Gerald, but he was a man, they were women, he had died.'"[8] Forster's tone, however, smacks less of "primitive dignity" than sardonic irony. Like Twain, he mocks social structures that compel women to perform ritual eulogy for men, even men they dislike. After World War One, Twain's and Forster's parodying, rather than the rhetoric of Eaton's Forest Lawn and Faulkner's Nobel Prize speech, became eulogy's modern norm.

The death of the brainless Gerald who had "the figure of a Greek athlete" frees him from all mortal failings, at least for the romanticizing Rickie. Gerald becomes mythologized: forever young and fair, an embodiment of ideal passion against which Rickie measures himself, and inevitably falls short. Like the spouse's death in *Where Angels Fear to Tread*, that of the fiancé in *The Longest Journey* leads to an inappropriate marriage and deaths of child and parent, for Rickie, denying his own deepest desires, marries the rebounding Agnes, a fatal mistake based on lies and self-deception rather than sexual honesty. Eventually, after a child is born and dies, and a low-class half-brother appears whom Agnes urges him to deny, Rickie flees and dies himself almost immediately thereafter. Run over by a train while doing "a man's duty," rescuing his drunken brother, Rickie receives a decidedly unclassical eulogy as "one who has failed in all he undertook; one of the thousands whose dust returns to the dust, accomplishing nothing in the interval. Agnes and I buried him to the sound of our cracked bell, and pretended that he had once been alive" (303).[9] Rickie's death is sudden, but neither capricious nor inappropriate, for in this book whose dedication reads "Fratribus" it allows for the birth of his brother's daughter, who is named for his mother. In this ending of renewal, Claude Summers suggests, "Forster implies the symbolic achievement of the physically impossible: fraternity has begotten progeny."[10] Wholly unsentimentalized, marriage seems scarcely relevant.

That rare Forsterian event, a happy marriage, occurs in *A Room with a View* (1908), but it was a near thing. George and Lucy first make serendipitous physical contact because of a stranger's death they both witness. The novel's first draft depicts not the stabbing but only its aftermath: great spurts of blood coming from the dying man. Then the story of his wounding is told, but given no point: "There was no murder. It was no one's fault but his own." This summary leads into the kind of parodic eulogy Forster had given Gerald in *The Longest Journey*: "Giuseppe had all the virtues of the dead. He was brave and beautiful and strong. All loved him."[11] But the discursive episode is unconnected to the central relationship since Lucy is neither present nor affected by it.

In the published novel, Lucy, who "wanted something big," recalls Charlotte's prissy explanation that big things were unladylike: "It was not that ladies were inferior to men; it was that they were different. Their mission was to inspire others to achievement rather than to achieve themselves. Indirectly, by means of tact and a spotless name, a lady could accomplish much. But if she rushed into the fray herself she would be first censured, then despised, and finally ignored. Poems had been written to illustrate this point" (46). Feeling full of "strange desires" to escape her stereotypical gender role, Lucy longs to move over the earth like men, "not because they are masculine, but because they are alive." She enters the piazza reflecting, "Nothing ever happens to me," and immediately witnesses an altercation between two men: "They sparred at each other, and one of them was hit lightly upon the chest. He frowned; he bent towards Lucy with a look of interest, as if he had an important message for her. He opened his lips to deliver it, and a stream of red came out between them and trickled down his unshaven chin." Feeling responsible for this death, perhaps for having desired "something big," perhaps for being the object of the dying man's attention, she faints and is rescued by George. She tries unsuccessfully to sneak away by sending him to find photographs she dropped on fainting. Both feel that something transformative has occurred: waking with the knowledge that she had been embraced, Lucy "thought that she, as well as the dying man, had crossed some spiritual boundary." And George says, " 'something tremendous has happened; I must face it without getting muddled ... It has happened,' he repeated, 'and I mean to find out what it is' " (48–51). It takes most of the rest of the book for them to realize there is no going back. When George finally declares his love for Lucy, he revealingly says, "I have cared for you since that man died" (195).

That Lucy ultimately ends her engagement to the pompous and silly Cecil and marries the appropriate George represents a victory for passion over conventionality, freedom over bondage, Italy over England. But as the manuscript called "The Lucy Novels" reveals, it almost did not happen; in the early version a falling tree kills George when Lucy cancels their elopement. Oliver Stallybrass, Forster's editor, says that "One can only speculate on the reasons that caused Forster, in *A Room with a View*, to reprieve George as well as his father; perhaps *The Longest Journey* had sated for the moment his vicarious death-wish. That his clemency later troubled his artist's conscience is suggested in the Introduction to *A Room with a View*."[12] Forster's harsh reviewers may also have affected him: he responded to Bertrand Russell's praise of *Longest Journey* with, "You are gentle, too, to the corpses. They, and other things, displease me a good deal."[13] Forster is referring to his workmanship generally, but specifically to his "throwaway" deaths. The dying Italian's transformation from inorganic datum to sacrificial victim, anticipating the far more elaborated Septimus Smith in Woolf's *Mrs. Dalloway*, allows not only for George's survival, but for the triumph of eros. In *A View without a Room* (1958), his "prophetic retrospect" on *A Room with a View*, Forster, expressing no regret over the book's published ending, says that George and Lucy have had fifty years of happy marriage – plus three children, all of whom survive.

Howards End combines the sudden deaths of *Angels* and *Longest Journey* with the happy ending of *A Room with a View*; but, becoming more overt about his interests, Forster makes his central relationship between women rather than husband and wife. The death of Mrs. Wilcox, like Mrs. Moore's in *Passage to India*, is treated brusquely, even crudely; the shocks are all the greater because, unlike Charles Herriton in *Where Angels Fear to Tread*, both are major characters. As Joyce's Bloom suggests, propinquity and relationship largely determine how death affects us (*Ulysses* 84). The sudden disappearance of major characters renders their deaths less rather than more definite, and creates a huge gap in their texts: they are gone, and we experience neither the dying nor mourning that nineteenth-century fiction would have provided. The lack of warning or preparation reverses the usual order of events, denies traditional causality and climax, and focuses attention on survivors, including the deceased themselves, rather than the dead or dying: first the telegram, then the explanatory letter that fails to explain. In *Howards End* we are abruptly told, "The funeral was over" (87); only afterwards do we learn – obliquely, through the reactions of the local poor, grave-diggers, and then the family – that it was Mrs. Wilcox's. "She had gone," the narrator says as if describing Forster's technique, "and as if to make her going the more bitter, had gone with a touch of mystery that was all unlike her ... Without fully explaining, she had died" (90). Victorian death is explained, or else is self-explanatory; modern death is more rather than less mysterious. Mrs. Wilcox remains a continuing powerful presence, the focus for everything that follows.

When asked about "the significance of Mrs. Wilcox's influence on the other characters after her death," Forster replied: "I was interested in the imaginative effect of someone alive, but in a different way from other characters – living in other lives."[14] For Mrs. Wilcox, who is referred to as "this shadowy woman" (85) while she is still alive and about whom it is said "How easily she slipped out of life!" (93), death seems to alter little. Like Mrs. Moore in *A Passage to India*, she finds life's common distinctions meaningless: "Mrs. Wilcox's voice ... suggested that pictures, concerts, and people are all of small and equal value" (70); and she remains hovering – "that unquiet yet kindly ghost" (243) – to help sort out the muddle her death causes: "Mrs. Wilcox strayed in and out, ever a welcome ghost; surveying the scene, thought Margaret, without one hint of bitterness" (166). She is not a Christian ghost, like Hamlet's father's "perturbèd spirit" (1.5.191), whose presence signals something profoundly wrong. She is, rather, an evocation belonging to spiritualist tradition: benign, willing to serve those left behind.

Yet her husband and son block her dying wish: to leave Howards End to Margaret because of a felt spiritual affinity between them, their shared commitment to Forster's epigraph, "Only connect ... " It must be fulfilled despite them, for in Forster the living interfere with the dead at their peril. As Garland says of the ancient Greeks, of whom Forster was a great admirer: "One who failed to show proper respect towards the dead was not so much likely to invite reprisals directly at their hands ... as to lay himself open to the vengeance of the gods."[15] In *Howards End*, the sorting out requires another death, that of Leonard Bast, as well as the birth of his son by Margaret's sister, Helen. Vengeance then falls where it should: on Charles, imprisoned by the law "made in his image" (334), and Henry, "broken" by the scandal.

Having been ruined by a combination of Wilcox smug indifference to those they consider socially inferior and Schlegel well-intentioned but clumsy interference, Leonard internalizes his failure as a "sense of sinfulness" (318). Abandoning all hope of this world – "Death alone still charmed him, with her lap of poppies, on which all men shall sleep" (319) – he desperately seeks Margaret in order to confess, in the mistaken belief that he seduced Helen rather than vice versa. Forster's analogizing of sleep and death manifests Leonard's true purpose: "He did not suppose that confession would bring him happiness. It was rather that he yearned to get clear of the tangle. So does the suicide yearn" (319). Leonard's death, the "supreme adventure," may be consummatory and clarifying for him since it fulfills and ends his quest to confess and die: "He was terrified but happy" (324). But it shocks both the novel's characters and readers, to all of whom it is news that Leonard "was in the last stages of heart disease" (326–7).

Forster writes Leonard's death as medieval allegory: having sought learning, Leonard is crushed by books that "fell over him in a shower"; having sought love, he is hurt by the Schlegel sword that Charles wields, "not where it descended, but in the heart" (324). Leonard's death, like Gerald's, is not tragic since the characters about whom we care survive; and it contrasts strikingly with Mrs. Wilcox's, since Forster compares Leonard to a suicide whose crime lies "in its disregard for the feelings of those [left] behind" (319). More catalyst than catastrophe, Leonard's death enables Forster to maneuver the novel to its satisfying resolution.

The moral chasm between Margaret and Henry may be measured by their contrasting attitudes toward her pregnant sister and his dead wife. When Margaret joins with Helen against male dominance and standards, "A new feeling came over her; she was fighting for women against men. She did not care about rights, but if men came into Howards End, it should be over her body" (290). In her loyalty to her dead friend and predecessor as the first Mrs. Wilcox, Margaret attains identity with her – so that there is an inevitability (despite Henry Wilcox's hollowness and Forster's wrenching his plot to recreate the heterosexual relationship) about Margaret's marrying her widower, living in her place and with her name, even to being mistaken for her (202). As Margaret says, however, Henry is "a man who insults his wife when she's alive and cants with her memory when she's dead" (308). Though she wonders if "perhaps it is superstitious to speculate on the feelings of the dead" (258), Margaret always acts with her predecessor lovingly in mind. She seems to realize instinctively that spirits have changed dramatically since *Hamlet*'s time, when their presence boded ill. Maeterlinck writes, "When our dead speak to us it is the best in ourselves that is speaking to us, having borrowed their voice."[16] Helen had earlier said that she loves death because it validates life (238–9); Margaret later tells her, "I feel that you and I and Henry are only fragments of [Mrs. Wilcox's] mind. She knows everything. She is everything" (313). Margaret, who embodies Forster's moral perspective, finally gains her bequest without trying for it, without even knowing about it. She learns about it on the last page, by which time the Wilcox men are enfeebled and broken by their betraying the living and dead.

Margaret, who always refers to Henry's first wife as Mrs. Wilcox, is herself blessed, *as* Mrs. Wilcox, for the vision of the world she offers and sustains: "They were building up a new life, obscure, yet gilded with tranquillity" (336). The dead woman, who did not revolt from traditional gendered power relations, has her will fulfilled by the living women, her "daughters," who do. Explicitly pre-suffrage, Mrs. Wilcox is like someone from another world at the luncheon-party Margaret gives for her: "Mrs. Wilcox, whose life had been spent in the service of husband and sons, had little to say to strangers who had never shared it, and whose age was half her own. Clever talk alarmed her, and withered her delicate imaginings" (74). She maintains that Howards End stands more by bricks and mortar than by discussion and ideas, says "that it is wiser to leave action and discussion to men," and is thankful not to have the vote (77–8). Forster kills her off so that he can replace her conservative social opinions by her unconscious, ghostly intuition that England's modern heirs are liberal and liberated women, and the children of the lower middle class.

The men, on the other hand, are punished by Forster's equivalent of the gods: Charles is in prison for manslaughter in Leonard's death; Henry, his masculine authority collapsed, is exhausted and debilitated by events and hayfever, and there is a touch of something new about him, "more like a woman" (329). The ending provides something "uncanny in [Margaret's moral] triumph" (341), as well as resolution and continuity in the birth of Helen and Leonard's son, a rare Forster baby who survives. London's "red rust" creeps closer on the horizon, swallowing the green world: "Life's going to be melted down, all over the world" (339). Yet as the mower's "whirring blades" encompass "with narrowing circles the sacred centre of the field," the abundant hay crop is a source of "infectious joy" and excitement (343), and the novel's ending enacts a fertility rite that reconciles the living and dead. As the vacuous Dolly summarizes, "It does seem curious that Mrs. Wilcox should have left Margaret Howards End, and yet she get it, after all" (342). Claude Summers compares the end to that of *The Longest Journey*: Forster here "achieves the equally impossible feat of having sorority beget progeny."[17]

Maurice (written 1913–14, but published 1971, the year after Forster's death) is the Forster novel that says most about homoerotic love and least about death, the only one whose title is not a metaphorical reference to death (though *Where Angels Fear to Tread* was a publisher's title that replaced Forster's uncommercial "Monteriano"). *Maurice* was begun the year after Alfred Douglas' lawsuit against Arthur Ransome's *Oscar Wilde: A Critical Study*, which would have reminded Forster of the impossibility of publishing it. *Maurice*'s strengths and weaknesses both result from the major impetus behind its creation: sexual and literary frustration.[18] After what Forster called his "awakening" from Christianity at Cambridge, his second great self-discovery, his homosexuality, was both troubling and exhilarating. Although he had begun to recognize it earlier, his fully conscious acceptance originated, in 1907, with a touch: "on my backside – gently and just above the buttocks ... It was as much psychological as physical. It seemed to go straight through the small of my back into my ideas, without involving my thoughts." It was as if, Forster adds, "at that precise moment I had conceived." In a way he had, for he "immediately began to write *Maurice*."[19]

With *Maurice* (and the posthumous short story collection, *The Life to Come*), Forster turned from what he felt he should write to what truly possessed him, and from death to life. In his diary he wrote: "Weariness of the only subject that I both can and may treat – the love of men for women & vice versa."[20] *Maurice* came to him wholly outlined, as a cure for frustration. "It was the only occasion that he would write a novel in this manner, without lengthy planning and premeditation."[21] Although it could not be published "until my death or England's,"[22] or at least until "the Wolfenden Report [recommending that homosexuality be decriminalized] becomes law,"[23] his writing it would be liberating for him even if his country continued to wallow in phobias. *Maurice* was made deliberately anachronistic: originally set during the period of its composition, it remained there through numerous revisions over the next several decades. The novel defines this time on the eve of war as "the last moment of the greenwood" ("Terminal Note" 254), Forster's version of rural Greece.

For all its attempt to deny death, *Maurice* too demonstrates the power wielded by an unexorcised dead parent. Maurice feels great pressure to grow up "like his father," who had died as he had lived: without passion or struggle. At his crisis, when he sees the emptiness of Clive's proffered platonic relationship and diagnoses his own condition as lust, Maurice foresees only despair: "He did not know what lay ahead. He was entering into a state that would only end with impotence or death" (150–1). At this moment of blindness, to both past and future, he receives a visitation to which he is also blind:

> he could not see the vast curve of his life, still less the ghost of his father sitting opposite. Mr Hall senior had neither fought nor thought; there had never been any occasion; he had supported society and moved without a crisis from illicit to licit love. Now, looking across at his son, he is touched with envy, the only pain that survives in the world of shades. For he sees the flesh educating the spirit, as his has never been educated, and developing the sluggish heart and the slack mind against their will. (151–2)

Forster's notion that envy is "the only pain that survives in the world of shade," derives from Homer's representation of Achilles, whom Odysseus greets in *The Odyssey* as "royal / among the dead men's shades." Achilles responds scornfully, with regret for choosing glory over long life in *The Iliad* and envy of those still living: "Better, I say, to break sod as a farm hand / for some poor country man, on iron rations, / than lord it over all the exhausted dead."[24] The envious shade of Mr. Hall foresees a future that Maurice, but not

Forster, will experience: one that honors rather than shames the life of the body.

Maurice's ability ultimately to move beyond the timid love of his father's generation and his own early homosexuality (a platonic relationship with the rich, fatuous Clive) leads to his cross-class "marriage" to Alec Scudder, a relationship that initially offends his own social sensibilities: "The feeling that can impel a gentleman towards a person of lower class stands self-condemned" (151). Though Forster is far less explicit than Lawrence, his gamekeeper serves Maurice's liberation as Mellors serves Connie Chatterley's.[25] That service is to provide escape from the modern industrial wasteland, and from marriage based on property and power, through full and reciprocated sexual love. "They must live outside class," Maurice thinks, "without relations or money; they must work and stick to each other till death" (239).

Alec is based on Syed Ross Masood, to whom *A Passage to India* is dedicated "out of gratitude as well as out of love," with whom Forster had a long, intimate relationship. Memorializing him in 1937, Forster hinted strongly at its terms:

> I cannot speak of our affection here – it is not the time or the place ... There never was anyone like him and there never will be anyone like him. He cannot be judged as ordinary men are judged. My own debt to him is incalculable. He *woke me up* out of my suburban and academic life, showed me *new horizons* and a *new civilisation* and helped me towards the understanding of a *continent*. (*Two Cheers* 292; my emphases).

Forster's language here sounds metaphoric and erotic, but because "it is not the time or the place," he develops it literally, in terms of his coming to understand India.

With the revised *A Room with a View* and *Howards End*, Forster moved away from gloomy endings, even while acknowledging the provisional nature of any other kind: "The only permanence that is not a theory but a fact is death. And perhaps I surfeited myself with that in *The Longest Journey*. At all events the disinclination to kill increases."[26] Like Adela Quested in *A Passage to India* (206), Maurice at his lowest ebb contemplates suicide (an action no one in Forster's novels actually commits – death perhaps being so pervasive that it requires no assistance). But just as Mrs. Moore's death seems to release Adela from a destructive course of action, so a surrogate is offered for Maurice: he "would have shot himself but for an unexpected event. This event was the illness and death of his grandfather, which induced a new state of mind" (136), one that allows eros to triumph over thanatos.

Forster maintains that *Maurice*'s ending was part of his initial conception: "A happy ending was imperative. I shouldn't have bothered to write otherwise. I was determined that in fiction anyway two men should fall in love and remain in it for the ever and ever that fiction allows." He was determined, that is, that they would achieve, lastingly and openly, what was closed to him. He adds, "I dedicated it 'To a Happier Year' and not altogether vainly. Happiness is its keynote" – yet the ending made it impossible to publish: "If it had ended unhappily, with a lad dangling from a noose or with a suicide pact, all would be well ... But the lovers get away unpunished and consequently recommend crime" ("Terminal Note" 250). Assailed for excessive death in his earlier novels, Forster refuses death in *Maurice*, where it would conventionally be expected to act as terminus: he transgresses both moral and fictive conventions to affirm homoerotic love.

Death in *A Passage to India* occurs via a telegram that both announces Mrs. Moore's passing and deflects attention from its occurrence. In fact, the telegram arrives second-hand, indirectly: Fielding says of Ronny, her son, "Fate has treated him pretty roughly to-day. He has had a cable to the effect that his mother's dead, poor old soul" (246). Only subsequently are we told directly, "Dead she was" (256), and that she died and was buried at sea – though we are informed immediately about her ghost's actions. Death may also speak through its denial: when the Rajah's health is inquired after, the medicine man, concealing his death "lest the glory of the festival were dimmed," says, "It always improves" (298). The norm in Forster is the oddly angled and retrospective death, which denies death its full validation, and thereby creates a sense of continuing presence, even as absence is intensely felt, during the remainder of the novel. As Godbole says, "the difference between presence and absence is great ... Yet absence implies presence, absence is not non-existence" (178), a paradox that Forster literalizes in Mrs. Wilcox's and Mrs. Moore's continuing vital presences.

Like Woolf's Mrs. Ramsay, they attain in their deaths a peculiar limbo status: neither wholly addressed nor accommodated and mourned, they seem to belong equally to future and past. Though beyond mortality, they remain in and of this world, part of the context in which crises in the lives of others occur. In the Middle Ages, according to Ariès, the dead were "always present among the living ... but their presence is perceptible only to those who are about to die" (*Hour* 7). Modern revenants appear mainly to visionary or artistic characters – Mrs. Wilcox to Margaret Schlegel, Mrs. Dedalus to Stephen in *Ulysses*, Mrs. Ramsay to Lily in *To the Lighthouse* – and provide access to what Blavatsky calls "Cosmic Ideation" in a way that *A Passage to India*'s misnamed "bridge party" (38–48), that connects nothing with nothing, cannot. Forster's concern to "connect" echoes Blavatsky's theosophical notion of Spirit manifesting itself in Matter, Subject in Object: "It is the 'bridge' by which the 'Ideas' existing in the 'Divine Thought' are impressed on Cosmic Substance as the 'Laws of Nature.'"[27] This notion implies that mystery rather than muddle lies at the heart of Forster's India, and his larger universe.

Going Eliot's Apeneck Sweeney one better, Forster reduces life's cyclical pattern to an alternation between death and marriage, with little copulation and less birth. Unable to write contentedly of heterosexuality, he subverts the form he felt constrained to adopt: the novel of manners. Mrs. Moore, twice a widow, comes to India to help arrange the marriage of Ronny and Adela. But while Adela, after her engagement, thinks that "marriage makes most things right enough" (98), Mrs. Moore finds that the novel's traditional concerns no longer sustain her and the role that initially defined her. Despairing of meaningful distinctions, of material connections, "She felt increasingly (vision or nightmare?) that, though people are important, the relations between them are not, and that in particular too much fuss has been made over marriage; centuries of carnal embracement [and a century of the Victorian domestic novel], yet man is no nearer to understanding man" (135). Forster's gendered "man ... to ... man" seems purposeful.

Mrs. Moore's first experience of India, meeting Aziz in the mosque, contains a warning about death; and during the climax of her visit, the expedition to the Marabar Caves, death, "the undying worm itself" (208), had spoken to her, reducing everything to "'bou-oum,' or 'ou-boum,' – utterly dull. Hope, politeness, the blowing of a nose, the squeak of a boot, all produce 'boum'" (147). The lesson of the Caves assails bourgeois Western religion, with its insistent hierarchical distinctions: "Pathos, piety, courage – they exist, but are identical, and so is filth. Everything exists, nothing has value" (149). The Caves "robbed infinity and eternity of their vastness, the only quality that accommodates them to mankind." They thus subvert "poor little talkative Christianity" as well, for "she knew that all its divine words from 'Let there be Light' to 'It is finished' only amounted to 'boum'" (150). The impact is devastating: the echo in the cave "began in some indescribable way to undermine her hold on life" (149), and she soon sinks "in apathy and cynicism" (158), emergence from which seems impossible this side the grave.

Thus, the train returning from the Caves becomes a hearse carrying corpses rather than live passengers; and Mrs. Moore, who now wishes only to retire "into a cave of my own" (200), despairs of all human connection and distinction, marriage most specifically: "Why has anything to be done, I cannot see. Why all this marriage, marriage? . . . The human race would have become a single person centuries ago if marriage was any use. And all this rubbish about love, love in a church, love in a cave, as if there is the least difference, and I held up from my business over such trifles!" (201–2). Forster mirrors the novel's traditional "comic" plot when her "business," which seemed to be marriage, turns out to be death, into which she enters and over which she presides. Like Mrs. Ramsay, she first helps to muddle things by sponsoring an inappropriate marriage, one certain to be loveless; her doing so produces her despondency. Her demise helps to prevent the marriage, for, as the conventional and brusque Ronny thinks, "What does happen to one's mother when she dies? Presumably she goes to heaven, anyhow she clears out . . . And Adela – she would have to depart too" (257–8). A marriage of a different sort is offered in its place: Fielding tells Adela that marriage "is too absurd in any case . . . I suspect that it mostly happens haphazard [*sic*], though afterwards various noble reasons are invented. About marriage I am cynical" (262). Yet Mrs. Moore's spirit presides over the presumably more appropriate one between Fielding and her daughter.

Mrs. Moore's transfiguration embodies the novel's arc from Islam and Christianity to Hinduism. The debilitating cave echo that Adela awakened "flourished, raging up and down like a nerve in the faculty of her hearing" (194). It subsides as she listens to Mrs. Moore proclaim Aziz's innocence, and then Christianity's meaninglessness: "Was he in the cave and were you in the cave and on and on . . . and Unto us a Son is born, unto us a Child is given . . . and am I good and is he bad and are we saved? . . . and ending everything the echo" (204–5). Adela's echo "come[s] back again badly" (212) after Mrs. Moore's departure when, preparing for the trial, "Adela, after years of intellectualism, had resumed her morning kneel to Christianity. There seemed no harm in it, it was the shortest and easiest cut to the unseen, and she could tack her troubles on to it. Just as the Hindu clerks asked Lakshmi [goddess of prosperity] for an increase in pay, so did she implore Jehovah for a favourable verdict" (211). The harm lies in its being an act of bad faith, one that ends only when, upon envisioning the ghost of Mrs. Moore (about whose death she is ignorant [240]), she withdraws her charge against Aziz (230); then her echo stops (239). Ronny, on the other hand, remains bound by puerile Christianity:

> Ronny's religion was of the sterilized Public School brand, which never goes bad, even in the tropics. Wherever he entered, mosque, cave, or temple, he retained the spiritual outlook of the Fifth Form, and condemned as "weakening" any attempt to understand them . . . In due time he and his half-brother and sister would put up a tablet to her in the Northamptonshire church where she had worshipped, recording the dates of her birth and death and the fact that she had been buried at sea. This would be sufficient. (257–8)

Ronny's "sufficient" epitaph for his mother reveals nothing about her life, but much about his.

Hinduism, in which the image of the god is believed to be the god, is incarnated at the trial as a "splendidly formed," nearly naked figure who, pulling the punkah, "seemed to control the proceedings," and not just the mortal ones: "he seemed apart from human destinies, a male fate, a winnower of souls." Yet his divine form "was of the city, its garbage had nourished him, he would end on its rubbish heaps" (217). Adela feels his aloofness rebuking "the narrowness of her sufferings," as well as her religion and culture: "Her particular brand of opinions, and the suburban Jehovah who sanctified them – by what right did they claim so much importance in the world, and assume the title of civilization?" (218). At the moment of thinking this, Adela turns, as if to question Mrs. Moore, who had given voice to her conscience (220). Her absence exacerbates the muddle: confusion erupts at the trial when both sides invoke her; but then her name, transmogrified into "Esmiss Esmoor," becomes a mantra or magic charm for the assembled crowd. Momentarily wiser than he knows, Ronny says, "They get just like that over their religion" (225). After Adela's recanting ends the trial, "no one remained on the scene of the fantasy but the beautiful naked god. Unaware that anything unusual had occurred, he continued to pull the cord of his punkah" (231), an indifferent deity who had presided over the workings of justice.

A second muddle occurs when Aziz refuses to believe Fielding who tells him Mrs. Moore is dead – so that (as happens later with the Rajah) it struck Fielding "that people are not really dead until they are felt to be dead. As long as there is some misunderstanding about them, they possess a sort of immortality" (255). Aziz insists that he will consult Mrs. Moore about suing Adela for compensation (253), and in a sense he does: "Fielding was not ashamed to practise a little necromancy. Whenever the question of compensation came up, he introduced the dead woman's name" – until "Aziz yielded suddenly" (261), as Mrs. Moore presumably would have wanted. Forster's revealing verb is consistent with his feminization of Aziz throughout – including his gracious acceptance of subordinate status, his empathy for Mrs. Moore, his status as single parent and mourning spouse – his sympathy generally for the "feminine."

Despite Ronny's desire to get rid of her and despite her death, Mrs. Moore does not "clear out." After her death, her "ghost followed the ship up the Red Sea, but failed to enter the Mediterranean" (256). Having been reincarnated at the trial "into Esmiss Esmoor, a Hindu goddess" (225), she is summoned by Godbole to preside over the Hindu celebration of God's birth: "He had, with increasing vividness, again seen Mrs. Moore ... He was a Brahman, she Christian, but ... it made no difference whether she was a trick of his memory or a telepathic appeal. It was his duty, as it was his desire, to place himself in the position of the God and to love her, and to place himself in her position and to say to the God, 'Come, come, come, come'" (290–1).

A third muddle results from Aziz's thinking that Fielding has married Adela, who had in fact introduced him to Mrs. Moore's daughter (302). At first, Aziz blusters to cover over his mistake; he lets it go only when, encountering in Ralph Moore the goodness and wisdom he encountered in his mother, he calls him "an Oriental." Aziz realizes with a shudder that he had said those words "to Mrs. Moore in the mosque in the beginning of the cycle ... And here he was starting again" (311–12). But the reconciliation is followed by parting: "All the stupid misunderstandings had been cleared up, but socially they had no meeting-place" (319).

What Mrs. Moore cannot do, as their failed kiss at the end demonstrates, is remove the wedge placed between Fielding and Aziz by Adela's charge of rape by the colonized "other," a charge embedded in history. The logic of colonialism, which had constructed Indian men as effeminate and passive, transformed them into rapists after the Mutiny of 1857 in order to justify continuing oppression. The charge also appears in Forster's manuscript, which depicts both an illicit romance between Aziz and Adela and Aziz assaulting Adela in the cave.[28] Perhaps such rupture is inevitable in *any* colonizer/colonized relationship, and Adela's sexual outburst merely represents and foregrounds that failure. Her outcry, which occurs when she realizes she does not love Ronny, also deflects attention from the novel's most deeply felt relationship, that between the men. Ending their "brotherhood," Forster can largely suppress the fact that at least as crucial here as colonial difference is unconfronted sexual identity, and then cover over that suppression with the "surprise" conventional marriage of Fielding to Stella Moore. She is, we are told, "beautiful," and the marriage both passionate and blessed (302, 318), but unlike her brother Ralph, who is also introduced in the last section, she is unrealized as a character, a perfunctory and abstract device.

"Death closes all," says Tennyson's Ulysses, but not in Forster. His dead characters do not survive in any traditional Christian sense, though they are sometimes spoken of in such terms; but their sudden departures, which are emphasized by their being announced before (or instead of) the dying, create a gap, a rent in the fabric of the living. (Only once does a Forster novel depict the dying process, Aunt Juley's in *Howards End*, but she survives.) The resulting vacuum seems to suck in others to replace those lost or gone before (Rickie for Gerald in *Longest Journey*, then Stephen for Rickie; Margaret for Mrs. Wilcox in *Howards End*). Or else sudden absence promotes an equally traumatic reaction (unlikely marriages in *Longest Journey* and *Room with a View*; baby snatching and death in *Where Angels Fear to Tread*). Worst of all, it may perpetuate postures of bad faith. Mr. Wilcox betrays his wife's dying legacy – he fails generally to consider her, alive or dead – which does not ultimately thwart her, but does break him. Hypocritically, Harriet, Lilia's mean-spirited sister-in-law in *Where Angels Fear to Tread*, thinks they should mourn Lilia: "She had been detestable to Lilia while she lived, but she always felt that the dead deserve attention and sympathy" (109). Equally nasty but more consistent, Ronny in *A Passage to India* decides, after learning of his mother's death, "to persist in unkindness towards her," rather than repent his ill-treatment of her while she lived (257).

Margaret Schlegel speaks what sound like Forster's thoughts concerning "the senselessness of Death. One death may explain itself, but it throws no light upon another: the groping inquiry must begin anew" (276). What makes death seem senseless is our tendency to generalize about it, our often having to experience it *en masse*: meaning lies in uniqueness. The most powerful refrain in *Howards End* – in Forster generally – is that hope survives "even on this side of the grave" (103; also 104, 206, 330; *Passage* 303), as the pattern of Margaret's life argues. Despite the accusations that he enacts death obsessively and capriciously, Forster fully rewards with such happiness as the world provides those characters who act in good faith toward the dead – and also toward the living, the two being corollaries for him. George and Lucy are well married at the end of *A Room with a View*, and still happy fifty years later. Margaret and Helen and Helen's child come to possess Howards End, and a piece of the future. Maurice thinks of Alec's ship sailing off as "heroic, she was carrying away death" (238), because Alec remains with him. Aziz's loyalty to his wife, dead in childbirth, as well as to Mrs. Moore is validated by his moral victory; while Fielding, who had been cynical about marriage but also loyal to both Aziz and Mrs. Moore, finds, Forster's narrator maintains, that his union with Stella "had been blessed" (318). Forster's distinctions concerning how death deals with his characters, and his characters with death, are meaningful and important.

What should we make, then, of Forster's linkage of death and sex, thanatos and eros? Richard Martin writes, "An examination of Forster's fiction limited to the attitude revealed towards personal relations discloses the disintegration of Forster's optimism and the development of a pessimism generated by frustration."[29] But the heterosexuality that Forster felt compelled to treat is most disastrously expressed – in the form of destructive marriages, a death in childbirth, the demise of two infants – in his first two novels. Instead of the deadly marriages that seemed imminent, successful ones occur in both *A Room with a View* and *A Passage to India*, while even

Margaret, against the odds, makes something positive of hers; and in *The Longest Journey*, *Howards End*, and the retrospective on *A Room with a View* children survive being born.

Nonetheless, Forster's heterosexual relationships, which generally distract and deflect, are stratagems for representing interests of greatest moment: not Lilia and her baby in *Where Angels Fear to Tread*, but the violent scene in which Gino (ravaged by his son's death) nearly kills Philip and then, with "almost alarming intimacy" (174), tenderly nurses him back to health; not the Rickie–Agnes relationship in *The Longest Journey*, but Rickie's intense identification with two mythologized males: the dead Gerald for whom he marries Agnes and the live Stephen for whom he gives his life; not even the more or less successful marriages in *Howards End* and *A Passage to India*, but the relationships between sisters in the former and men in the latter. Only *A Room with a View* is written totally against the grain, and it changed radically during revision. In general and usually without their knowing it (or being allowed to know it), Forster's exemplary figures strive to couple with images of themselves rather than with their opposites. But except in the posthumous *Maurice*, that consummation remained unavailable to them, so Forster had to dispose of them in other ways. In so doing, he laid himself open to various charges – brutality, pessimism, sexism – none of which is more than superficially true.

Deeply conflicted about his own sexuality, Lawrence wrote to Forster with some sympathy: "What do you want for yourself? You used to want the fulfilment of the natural animal in you – which is after all only an immediate need. So you made an immediate need seem the Ultimate Necessity – so you belied and betrayed yourself."[30] *Maurice*, the novel Forster wrote next, though not his best, may have been his most important: certainly his writing it neither belied nor betrayed himself. Had it been published when written, and accepted on its own terms, he might have sustained the impetus to continue writing fiction, and to treat what mattered most to him: the subject of "bodies, since bodies are the instruments through which we register and enjoy the world" (*Two Cheers* 74). Shortly before his death, he wrote in his diary: "how *annoyed* I am with Society for wasting my time by making homosexuality criminal. The subterfuges, the self-consciousness that might have been avoided."[31]

Had Forster published his homosexual writings, reached a larger and more discriminating audience than himself, and heeded his more intelligent critics (whom Forster always heard), he would doubtless have advanced beyond *Maurice*. In 1960, however, Forster wrote that he had become less optimistic about public acceptance of homosexuality: he "had supposed that knowledge would bring understanding. We had not realized that what the public really loathes in homosexuality is not the thing itself but having to think about it" ("Terminal Note" 255). Moments before Leonard Bast's death in *Howards End*, Forster's narrator says, "Death destroys a man, but the idea of death saves him" (324). With Forster's sexual orientation the reverse was true: his homosexuality helped to make him the fine writer he was, but given the climate of his time the idea of his homosexuality destroyed the extraordinary novelist he might have been.

CHAPTER 10

Virginia Woolf

Though omnipresent, death during the modern period, like sex for the Victorians, was often treated with prudery and reticence. Recalling the deaths of her mother and half-sister, Stella Duckworth, Woolf wrote, "We never spoke of either of them; I can remember the awkwardness with which Thoby avoided saying 'Stella' when a ship called Stella sank" (*Moments of Being* 107). Death was too important to be confronted directly: as Forster's characters usually "die in relative clauses,"[1] so Woolf's deaths, if not averted through sleep or trance, are consigned to parentheses, to another country, or to a scapegoat double.[2] Such technique signals her refusal to adhere to nineteenth-century conventions.

The Victorian pattern was established early on for Woolf: women gave until they dropped from exhaustion, men demanded or simply presumed and took. Her vividest memories were of women serving and dying, and of men using and abusing both them and her. "My mother," she writes, "believed that all men required an infinity of care," a belief her father shared: "His health was her fetish; she died of overwork easily at forty-nine; he found it very difficult to die of cancer at seventy-two" (*Moments of Being* 143, 114). After his wife's death, Stephen claimed his step-daughter as his "slave" (125), a duty Stella accepted unquestioningly. Possessive, hurt, and jealous, he opposed the idea of Stella's marrying (106), treated her engagement as a betrayal, failed to mourn her when she died, and swiftly sought a replacement: "We remembered how he had tasked Stella's strength, embittered her few months of joy, and now when he should be penitent, he showed less grief than anyone. On the contrary none was more vigorous, and there were signs at once ... that he was quite prepared to take Vanessa for his next victim" (55–6). Woolf confronted his utter selfishness most directly in her searing autobiographical writings, the posthumously published

Moments of Being; and most clinically when, as Colonel Pargiter in *The Years* (1937), he visits his mistress while his wife is dying (6–9).

Victorian moral and familial conventions survived in a household that Leslie Stephen, though a rationalist and an agnostic, was determined would remain bound by them. Stephen family life was "a complete model of Victorian society": "the patriarchal machinery" in which men achieved intellectually and socially while women, enslaved and silent, nurtured their needs (*Moments of Being* 127, 132–5).[3] Woolf writes that "Father himself was a typical Victorian: George and Gerald [her older half-brothers] were unspeakably conventional" (127) – perhaps, if Freud's first formulation of the incest theory is correct, primarily in making first Vanessa and then Virginia victims of sexual abuse. From the age of "six or seven, perhaps," through the period of her mother's death, and again as her father lay dying, Woolf was molested by first one half-brother and then the other (67–9).[4] As DeSalvo summarizes, "Virginia Stephen was raised in a household in which incest, sexual violence, and abusive behavior were a common, rather than a singular or rare occurrence."[5]

But Vanessa, and then Virginia, finally rebelled; they formed "a very close conspiracy" against playing "angel in the house" (*Moments of Being* 123–5). They were not good slaves: they withheld from their father the flattery and consolation he required for being a failure (125); they ultimately refused the Duckworths' various demands; and while they suppressed their own desires for a time they did not altogether deny them. Leslie Stephen responded to female rebellion with "self-pity, anger and despair" (124), scenes, which "were never indulged in before men," that could have been no more brutal if he had used a whip instead of words (125). Though gripped by the past, the sisters were driven into a future that looked very different. Retrospectively, Woolf writes, she and Vanessa recognized that two ages were confronting each other: "the Victorian age; and the Edwardian age. We were not his [Leslie Stephen's] children, but his grandchildren" (126). They continued to carry, however, a heavy load from a past they could never entirely escape or express. As Martin and Rose put it in *The Years*: "'What awful lives children live!' ... 'Yes ... And they can't tell anybody'" (159).

Woolf's life was replete with death and its aftershocks. Spilka maintains that "she was engaged from childhood on in a conflict as devastating in its toll on feelings and relations as the First World

War. She suffered personally from as many casualties in family ranks as did any combatant from the loss of comrades; and the disruptions in her family life were as great as those affected by the war."[6] Her texts, which assert and acknowledge the fleeting nature of human relationships and achievement, read as laments for unceasing loss. Jane Marcus calls *A Room of One's Own* (1929) "an elegy for all the lives of women left out of history"[7] – those unacknowledged, unhonored, and unmourned. The Stephen family was full of them, and Woolf, who could not grieve within it, determined to acknowledge, honor, and mourn them in fictions she termed "elegy" (*Diaries* 3: 27 June 1925, 34), and that were, in Hillis Miller's phrase, "the place of death made visible."[8]

The heroine's death from typhoid fever in Woolf's first novel, *The Voyage Out* (1915), was modeled on that of her brother, Thoby Stephen, in 1906 (Thoby is again elegized in *Jacob's Room* and *The Waves*). She sought to fictionalize Thoby's emotionally uncomplicated death by relating it to distant innocent happiness. Yet, as Spilka writes, what she found in recalling her parents' marriage was as troubling as subsequent events:

> the passionate love which her undemonstrative mother withheld from Leslie Stephen, and which she reserved in Virginia's fantasy for her patient ghostly lover [her dead first husband], became the model for the passion Virginia too withheld from all living men, gave only fleetingly to living women, and similarly reserved for her own beloved ghosts. Thus her lifelong inability to love . . . seems to have been peculiarly intertwined with her lifelong inability to grieve.[9]

Spilka's conclusion is dubious (she loved many), but *The Voyage Out* serves his argument by climaxing in death rather than marriage, while depicting a wholly satisfied lover: "An immense feeling of peace came over Terence . . . he listened again . . . she had ceased to breathe. So much the better – this was death . . . It was happiness, it was perfect happiness. They had now what they had always wanted to have, the union which had been impossible while they lived" (353). Woolf replicates the language her mother used in speaking of Herbert Duckworth, her first husband, the figure Woolf had seen on her mother's deathbed (*Moments of Being* 32, 89). Resurfacing in *To the Lighthouse*, Duckworth is even more tenuous, an imagined explanation for Mrs. Ramsay's sadness: "Had he blown his brains out, they asked, had he died the week before they were married – some other, earlier lover, of whom rumours reached one?" (46). The "happy" memory of earlier love is predicated on irretrievable loss, on marriage become death, on the bedside meeting of eros and thanatos.

All her writings after *The Voyage Out*, like her life, were framed by war, which, as Nigel Nicolson writes, she considered "absurd and obscene," the "inevitable outcome of male chauvinism"[10] that she learned to hate from growing up its victim. She denounced the war and its causes, "the most violent and filthy passions" (*Letters* 2: 15 November 1915, 71), as if explaining the consequences of her family life: "I become steadily more feminist ... and wonder how this preposterous masculine fiction keeps going a day longer – without some vigorous young woman pulling us together and marching through it ... I feel as if I were reading about some curious tribe in Central Africa" (*Letters* 2: 23 January 1916, 76). Fearing zeppelin raids on London and the threat of conscription, refusing to have anything to do with the war she called "a nightmare" except to help conscientious objectors (*Letters* 2: 3–16 June 1916, 97–100), she had a serious breakdown six months into it.

Both a paean to pre-war England and an elegy on its demise, *Jacob's Room* (1922) avoids "strict representation" (*Letters* 2: 23 November 1922, 588) in order to "convey character without realism" (*Letters* 2: 20 October 1922, 571). In the midst of war, she wrote of wanting to break with inherited fictional modes, of attempting "to invent a completely new form" (*Letters* 2: 26 July 1917, 167). In *Jacob's Room* ordinary life is impacted by the sounds of gunfire, thoughts of "sons fighting for their country," and battlefield imagery: "the army covers the cornfield, moves up the hillside, stops, reels slightly this way and that, and falls flat, save that ... one or two pieces still agitate up and down like fragments of broken match-stick" (155–6, 175). But the war and Jacob's battlefield death are largely elided, assumed rather than accommodated, read into what he leaves behind. Without becoming present, they are over, gone: and the room that was replete with Jacob's presence is suddenly, at the end, replete with his absence.

Susan Smith argues that death is culturally gendered as well as engendered: women's deaths (as in childbirth or from domestic servitude) were deemed natural, and needed no explanation; men's were violent, as in Forster, and were treated as surprising accidents.[11] Woolf reverses this distinction in these two novels: Jacob's death in the war receives no explanation, is simply past. Rachel's disturbing death from fever in *The Voyage Out* commands full consideration, though it is ultimately denied: "this was death. It was nothing" (353). Woolf's only other fictional deathbed scene is also that of a woman: the Victorian mother, Rose Pargiter, in *The Years*.

In Woolf's fiction, death is a given, both pervasive and elided; the elegiac mode, lyrical rather than narrative, accords with her notion that, since life does not narrate, neither should fiction.[12] She finds surpassing value only in the moment – "this, here, now" (*Mrs. Dalloway* 12) – and all it contains, its very brevity intensifying the desire, as Mrs. Ramsay expresses it, to make "Life stand still here" (*Lighthouse* 240). Woolf's finest elegies, *Mrs. Dalloway* (1925) and *To the Lighthouse* (1927), inhabit the space created by World War One and the sense of futility that massive, man-made death inspired in her generation of writers. Human existence seemed to become insubstantial, hollowed out.

Haunted by death from first to last, *Mrs. Dalloway* is set in June 1923 when, Clarissa Dalloway belatedly thinks, "The War was over ... thank Heaven – over," though its full horror remains unconfronted. The sorting out is, in fact, central to her novel, as Clarissa acknowledges: "The War was over, except for some one like Mrs. Foxcroft at the Embassy last night eating her heart out because that nice boy was killed and now the old Manor House must go to a cousin; or Lady Bexborough who opened a bazaar, they said, with the telegram in her hand, John, her favourite, killed" (5). As in *A Passage to India* and *To the Lighthouse*, such handling of death accentuates by indirection; because deaths have become too numerous to detail and ritualize, their oblique occurrences are all the more shocking. Though she hated the war, Woolf felt despondent on Armistice Day because nothing fundamental had changed. The atmosphere seems that "of the death bed," she writes, and the rejoicing "has been very sordid and depressing ... I felt more and more melancholy and hopeless of the human race" (*Letters* 2: 11–13 November 1918, 290–3). Apparently she felt the inevitability of future wars.

Action in *Mrs. Dalloway*, which was originally entitled "The Hours," is marked by the chiming of Big Ben, of time running down or out, as at the end of Marlowe's *Dr. Faustus*. Woolf conceived the central plot, Clarissa Dalloway's day that culminates with her party, as ending with her death. "In the first version," she writes, "Mrs. Dalloway was originally to kill herself or perhaps merely to die at the end of the party,"[13] and traces of the initial conception remain embedded in the text despite revision. A second plot, created to counterpoint and contextualize the first, depicts Septimus Smith, the shell-shocked war veteran ("one of the first to volunteer" [130]) whose frenzied invocation of his dead attempts to deal with the war's unfinished business. He is, however, driven to suicide by patriarchal medical practitioners, "men who never weighed less than eleven stone six, who sent their wives to Court, men who made ten thousand a year and talked of proportion . . . judges they were; who . . . saw nothing clear, yet ruled, yet inflicted" (224–5).

Septimus Smith is Clarissa Dalloway's *Doppelgänger*,[14] her "young sacrificial double";[15] or they may be regarded "as different facets of one single person."[16] Elaine Showalter suggests that he "owes something of his name, his appearance, and his war experience" to Siegfried Sassoon, who visited Woolf while she was writing *Mrs. Dalloway*, and whose war poems she had reviewed.[17] Marcus sees Septimus' belated war death as an act of homage to Clarissa "as symbolic Mother Country . . . and as a figure of the Home Front."[18] Septimus is haunted by "legions of men prostrate behind him" (106), and especially by his friend Evans – "killed, just before the Armistice" (130) – whose death he carries within him like a guilty conscience because he both survived and then failed to mourn him. Smith envisions himself as "this last relic . . . this outcast . . . who lay like a drowned sailor, on the shore of the world" (140). He experiences the anguish and despair of the accidental survivor: "He had committed an appalling crime and been condemned to death by human nature" (145).

Those who survive when those around them do not often experience the remainder of their lives posthumously, as if they *had* died. Hence Septimus' obsession with having ceased to feel, to survive affectively (130–3), renders his suicide anticlimactic, merely the disposal of a body whose inhabitant, embodying the insanity society refuses to confront in itself, can never wholly return from the war. In this he resembles Conrad's Marlow in *Heart of Darkness* who, having nearly been buried in the Congo and then passed "through some inconceivable world that had no hope in it and no desire," returns like an alien creature to "the sepulchral city" (285), where he encounters only the death he bears. The contrast is with Dante, for whom Hell is minatory and salutary: he learns its lessons and returns to a world where change can still save him. For modernist revenants hell is commonly here and now, and there is, as Sartre dramatizes it, no exit.

Clarissa would seem Smith's antithesis, totally alien to him and his impending doom. In her diary, Woolf implies that the mundaneness and affirmation of Clarissa's life mean that she and Septimus occupy different worlds: "In this book I have almost too many ideas. I want to give life & death, sanity & insanity" (*Diaries* 2: 19 June 1923, 248). Clarissa finds an extraordinary richness in the moment, for "What she liked was simply life" (183). In fact, the linkage between Clarissa and Septimus, as Woolf acknowledged, is the novel's greatest structural problem – and at its heart.

John Lehmann suggests that Woolf's solution is mechanical: the character of Dr. Bradshaw (who is both Smith's doctor and Clarissa's guest) links the plots, "so putting into sharp contrast the world of success and power and the tragic world of the helpless, the innocent, the visionary."[19] Bradshaw plays a more active role than this, however, for his peremptory attitude feeds Septimus' paranoia and helps to precipitate his suicide, and Bradshaw's mention of Septimus infects Clarissa and her party: "Oh! thought Clarissa, in the middle of my party, here's death, she thought ... What business had the Bradshaws to talk of death at her party? A young man had killed himself. And they talked of it at her party – the Bradshaws talked of death" (279–80). Though such talk is not wholly inappropriate (Hillis Miller sees the party as helping to perpetuate "a moribund society"[20]), Clarissa views Bradshaw as "obscurely evil ... capable of some indescribable outrage," perhaps even responsible for Septimus' death; for Bradshaw sees it as his business to deaden spontaneity by imposing "a sense of proportion" (146, 149, 150) that conforms soldiers and eccentric women to military and social decorum.

For Woolf, Bradshaw embodied the patriarchy that prescribes warfare as the solution to cultural malaise, and then, asserting the healer's authority, usurps its victims' claims to their own souls. In the years before the war, and again later, Woolf came under male medical authority, like that whose "two unnecessary blunders" she saw as having killed her mother and half-sister in the 1890s (*Moments of Being* 117). In 1920 Freud wrote that the "terrible war which has just ended" had eliminated the tendency to consider "traumatic neurosis," whether from shell-shock, accidents, or hysteria, to be psychosomatic;[21] but Woolf's doctors seem never to have developed this enlightened view. Early on Woolf wrote what remained true to the end: "My life is a constant fight against doctors follies, it seems to me" (*Letters* 1: 26 November 1904, 159).

Quentin Bell describes Woolf's first enforced incarceration, in "a kind of polite madhouse for female lunatics": "Here her letters, her reading, her visitors would all be severely rationed, she would be kept in bed in a darkened room, wholesome foods would be pressed upon her and she would be excluded from all the social enjoyments of London. Faced by the possibility of madness she accepted her fate; but she accepted it in a sullen and rebellious spirit."[22] Her stay, arranged by the appropriately named Dr. Savage, resulted from "some great conspiracy ... going on behind my back ... I really don't think I can stand much more of this" (*Letters* 1: 28 July 1910, 430–1).[23] Unlike Freud with his hesitations and doubts, Woolf's doctors arrogantly deployed reductive labeling (psychotic, manic-depressive, mad) and modern technology to silence and "cure" patients. Drawing upon Foucault's analysis of the psychiatric "discourse of power," Poole, Trombley, and Showalter convincingly argue that "reductive and doctrinaire views" justified forcing supposedly hysterical women and psychologically disabled men back to "normal" behavior. Woolf, who wrote that "I don't expect any doctor to listen to reason" (*Letters* 1: November 1904, 152), was subjected, among other treatments, to confinement, enforced rest periods, and forced feeding (which once caused her to gain 50 percent of her previous weight). Drawing upon her own experience, Woolf has Dr. Bradshaw imperiously tell Rezia Smith that her husband must be institutionalized: "He had threatened to kill himself. There was no alternative. It was a question of law." There, he tells Septimus, "we will teach you to rest" (*Mrs. Dalloway* 146–7).

Another party guest, Peter Walsh, also links Clarissa with Septimus. Her former suitor newly returned from India, Peter thinks often of love and death (which were always complementary for Woolf), the distant past and what might have been, his fear of time running out. Earlier in the day, when Peter passes Septimus in Regent's Park, Septimus believes he is the figure who haunts him, his friend Evans, who was killed in the war. In turn, Peter imagines Septimus and his wife Rezia to be unhappy lovers, and he thinks confusedly of life and death when he hears the ambulance, "one of the triumphs of civilisation" (229), carrying off Septimus' body. While fearfully contemplating Clarissa's mortality and his own –

"No! No! he cried. She is not dead! I am not old, he cried" (75) – Peter encounters both memorialized and still-living war relics: "the statue of the Duke of Cambridge" and a troop of young soldiers laying a wreath on the cenotaph commemorating the war.

The Duke of Cambridge, who commanded the British army during the last half of the nineteenth century, helped create the modern war machine; appropriately, his statue stands outside Whitehall's War Office. Young troops, "in uniform, carrying guns, marched with their eyes ahead of them, marched, their arms stiff, and on their faces an expression like the letters of a legend written round the base of a statue praising duty, gratitude, fidelity, love of England" (76), the "big words" that no longer cover over modernist death's unpalatable messiness. Unaware of the obscenity of such anachronistic rhetoric (what the novel elsewhere calls "sentiments in alphabetical order of the highest nobility" [167]), they are destined to reenact it: "as if one will worked legs and arms uniformly, and life, with its varieties, its irreticences, had been laid under a pavement of monuments and wreaths and drugged into a stiff yet staring corpse by discipline" (77). Woolf adumbrates the process by which young males, having put on the uniform of "manhood," prepare to be unmanned and then transmuted into artifices of mortality. Their future may be read in their already deadened features as they march past those who have preceded them: "all the exalted statues, Nelson, Gordon, Havelock, the black, the spectacular images of great soldiers stood looking ahead of them ... [those who had] achieved at length a marble stare" (77). As Forster writes: "She was convinced that society is man-made, that the chief occupations of men are the shedding of blood, the making of money, the giving of orders, and the wearing of uniforms, and that none of these occupations is admirable" (*Two Cheers* 255).

In their reactions to life and death, Clarissa and Septimus are integrally related; they are, as Woolf insists, "entirely dependent upon each other" (*Letters* 3: 14 June 1925, 189). Sitting on the windowsill about to leap out, Septimus replicates Woolf's desperation during her first enforced incarceration: "I shall soon have to jump out of a window ... My God! What a mercy to be done with it!" (*Letters* 1: 28 July 1910, 431). Unlikely as it seems, he also shares Clarissa's sense of vitality and life's plenitude. His final thought is, "he would wait till the very last moment. He did not want to die. Life was good" (226). And Clarissa shares Septimus' view that death offers escape from futile existence.[24] Woolf herself apparently felt this doubleness when she came to her own suicide.[25]

Clarissa also, like Septimus, seems to lack affect: "she could not dispel a virginity preserved through childbirth which clung to her like a sheet" (46). Virginity, a withholding of oneself from intimacy, may imply purity and integrity, but though she has borne a child, Clarissa is represented as sexually cool toward men: "through some contraction of [her] cold spirit she had failed" her husband; she "was as cold as an icicle," "was rather a prig," "lacked something" (46, 121–2, 268, 287). Yet the hostility toward Clarissa's sexuality is often that of Peter, still bitter over having been rejected. In reconsidering her refusal of Peter, Clarissa rejects him again: "she had been right ... not to marry him." He would have denied her all freedom and independence: "with Peter everything had to be shared; everything gone into. And it was intolerable ... she had to break with him or they would have been destroyed, both of them ruined, she was convinced." Peter, instead of looking within himself, had denounced Clarissa: "Cold, heartless, a prude, he called her" (10).

Like Woolf in her affair with Vita Sackville-West,[26] Clarissa cannot "resist sometimes yielding to the charm of a woman" (46), for whom "she did undoubtedly then feel what men felt. Only for a moment; but it was enough" (47). Her intensest love (51) is for Sally Seton, the New Woman who smokes cigars, may have had a French ancestor who died with Marie Antoinette (a code figure for lesbian love[27]), is an impassioned free spirit who runs naked through the house, seems able to "say anything, do anything" (48), and who means "to reform the world" (49). Clarissa and Sally, who "spoke of marriage always as a catastrophe" (50), meet as doomed lovers, a tension Clarissa expresses in Othello's words: "feeling as she crossed the hall 'if it were now to die, 'twere now to be most happy.' That was her feeling – Othello's feeling, and she felt it, she was convinced, as strongly as Shakespeare meant Othello to feel it, all because she was coming down to dinner in a white frock to meet Sally Seton!" (51; the *Othello* lines recur on 281). Clarissa's intense happiness, like Othello's, cannot survive the moment: his because, fearing intimacy, he kills Desdemona; hers because, like Forster's homosexuality, "this falling in love with women" (48) is forbidden. When in "the most exquisite moment of her whole life ... Sally stopped [and] kissed her on the lips" (52), Peter, the representative of heterosexuality, breaks in on their intimacy: "It was shocking; it was horrible!" (53). Clarissa rejects him as instinctively, and for the same reasons, as Woolf rejected war.

Clarissa's worldview is dual from the beginning, for interspersed with "what she loved; life; London; this moment of June" (5) are fear, peril, loss: she always felt "it was very, very dangerous to live even one day" (11). Her tenuous hold on mortality results from both the world's sickness and her own, since she was ill with influenza before the novel opens (an allusion to the 1918–19 pandemic that Woolf herself suffered from in February 1918 and December 1919[28]). Like Woolf, Clarissa also still mourns her sister: "To see your own sister killed by a falling tree . . . before your very eyes, a girl too on the verge of life . . . Clarissa always said, was enough to turn one bitter" (117–18). Her loss resonates with the war's – "thousands of poor chaps, with all their lives before them" (174) – and turns her against orthodox religion, which again replicates Woolf's experience. After being incarcerated in an asylum run by a religious obsessive named Jean Thomas, Woolf dismissed as "really unendurable [the] self conceit of Christians" (*Letters* 1: 25 December 1910, 442). Thomas appears in *Mrs. Dalloway* as the appropriately named Miss Kilman, "the most unattractive character in the whole of Virginia's *œuvre*."[29] Already inclined toward ethical humanism, "this atheist's religion of doing good for the sake of goodness" (118), Clarissa welcomes the "birth of a new religion" (33) that Septimus' sacrifice seems to offer.

Mortality's perils are embedded in Clarissa's name, which derives from Samuel Richardson's doomed heroine in *Clarissa*, a novel on Woolf's mind at this time (*Diaries* 2: 3 August 1924, 309). For both Clarissas, thanatos' appeal supersedes and displaces that of eros, though in eros' language and imagery. While responding excitedly, light-heartedly, to Peter's visit and the life of "gaiety" she might have led if she had married him, Clarissa has a sudden vision of her deathbed: "It was all over for her. The sheet was stretched and the bed narrow. She had gone up into the tower alone and left them blackberrying in the sun . . . I am alone for ever, she thought" (70). This passage echoes Clarissa's other Shakespearean refrain, "Fear no more the heat of the sun" (13, 44, 59), from *Cymbeline*, a play, like *Othello*, about male jealousy and female virtue. The elegy Imogen's brothers sing over her apparently lifeless body expresses death's inevitability, but tropes itself as rest and reward:

> Fear no more the heat o' the sun,
> Nor the furious winter's rages;
> Thou thy worldly task hast done,
> Home art gone, and ta'en thy wages.
> Golden lads and girls all must,
> As chimney sweepers, come to dust. (4.2.261–6)

In *Cymbeline* the husband, appropriately named Posthumus, only thinks he has killed his wife; Imogen soon awakens and is ultimately reconciled with her penitent husband.

In both the manuscript and final versions of *Mrs. Dalloway*, Clarissa leaves her party after hearing of Septimus Smith's death, though in the former she apparently dies and so never returns: "Eight said Big Ben, nine, ten, eleven; and then with a sort of finality, though presumably the strokes were accurately spaced, the last no more emphatic than the first twelve ... But Clarissa was gone" ("Mrs. Dalloway" ms. 99). In the published text an echo of Septimus' death replaces Clarissa's. She hears the clock striking, and thinks: "The young man had killed himself; but she did not pity him; with the clock striking the hour, one, two, three, she did not pity him" (283), which repeats the tolling of Septimus' death: "The clock was striking – one, two, three" (227). Gilbert and Gubar call *Mrs. Dalloway*, like *The Waste Land*, a meditation "on the figure of a dead 'good soldier.'"[30] It is, in fact, such a meditation twice over, for Septimus is to Clarissa as Evans is to Septimus. Clarissa spends her brief time alone contemplating death generally – and then, specifically, Septimus' and her own. At first death seems a way of overcoming isolation, destroying barriers: "Death was defiance. Death was an attempt to communicate; people feeling the impossibility of reaching the centre which, mystically, evaded them; closeness drew apart; rapture faded, one was alone. There was an embrace in death." She recalls "the terror" she had felt "only this morning" – and her sense of how easily "she must have perished. But that young man had killed himself" (280–2). Knowledge of the novel's first draft deepens this passage, for Clarissa came closer to dying than she knows.

Quentin Bell, in his aunt's biography that he "constructed backward" from her suicide,[31] writes of Clarissa: "To some extent she may be identified with Kitty Maxse, and Kitty's sudden death in October 1922 – she fell from the top of a flight of stairs and Virginia believed that she had committed suicide – almost certainly helped to transform the stories into a book and to give that book its final character."[32] This comment helps explicate Peter's sudden "terror ... ecstasy ... extraordinary excitement" as Clarissa returns from her encounter with death (296). The moment was presaged when she anticipated the party: "She stiffened a little; so she would stand at the top of her stairs" (25). At the end, she is poised, only slightly less perilously, on the threshold of "the little room" in which "her body went through" death. The verbal and rhythmic parallels of the last lines in the two versions – "But Clarissa was gone." / "For there she was." – are more than fortuitous. She remains, as often throughout the book but now permanently, hovering between life and death, equally susceptible to both, as if their distinctions were obliterated and she forever held in this transitional, but final and therefore frozen, moment.

Clarissa's death, since it occurs literally in the draft but only metaphorically in the final version, exists in suspended animation: past without having been present, implicit but never explicit, vicarious because when she hears of Septimus' death "her body went through it first" (280). Her existence, like his, has a posthumous quality, so she shares his survivor's guilt. Alex Zwerdling notes that, "Septimus and Clarissa think the same thoughts in almost the same words without having met. Clarissa accurately imagines his state of mind at the moment of his suicide."[33] His experiences are hers: "Somehow it was her disaster – her disgrace. It was her punishment to see sink and disappear here a man, there a woman, in this profound darkness, and she forced to stand here in her evening dress" (282). Yet in the moment's richness, she feels the rightness and necessity of death's part in the natural process:

> she had never been so happy. Nothing could be slow enough; nothing last too long. No pleasure could equal, she thought ... this having done with the triumphs of youth, lost herself in the process of living, to find it, with a shock of delight, as the sun rose, as the day sank ... She felt somehow very like him – the young man who had killed himself. She felt glad that he had done it; thrown it away. The clock was striking ... But she must go back ... And she came in from the little room. (282–4)

The party's business, it turns out, is both death and resurrection. Sally Seton, who is recalled in Clarissa's phrase about never having "been so happy," returns "after all these years!" to announce that she has "five enormous boys" (260–1); Clarissa's Aunt Helena Parry, whom all had thought dead, indomitably appears although the war had "dropped a bomb at her very door" (271). Clarissa, vicariously experiencing Septimus' sacrifice, recognizes that her party "was an offering; to combine, to create . . . An offering for the sake of offering, perhaps. Anyhow, it was her gift" (184–5).

Thus, she both mourns Septimus' death and returns "from the little room" (or tomb) that was to contain hers, and her. Gilbert and Gubar write, "Septimus is a scapegoat whose self-immolation somehow *works* . . . Woolf portrays a country where women are not just triumphant survivors but also potential redeemers and potent inheritors."[34] Having felt death's appeal, Clarissa returns from its brink: "He made her feel the beauty, made her feel the fun. But she must go back. She must assemble" (284). Clarissa's vision and action seem to fulfill the promise of Septimus' spiritualism. Like Yeats, he had received messages from his ghosts "about war; about Shakespeare; about great discoveries; how there is no death." Such a "discovery," as modern spiritualists know, radically transforms the meaning of suicide. Just before impaling himself, he became excited "and waved his hands and cried out that he knew the truth! He knew everything! That man, his friend who was killed, Evans, had come, he said. He was singing behind the screen. She [his wife] wrote it down just as he spoke it" (212). Clarissa's communing with her spirits, transcending death, and creating harmony from disparate presences, further explain the "extraordinary excitement" her survival and return generate.

Winifred Holtby calls Woolf's next elegy, *To the Lighthouse*, a "ghost story,"[35] in which she evokes, mourns, and reburies her dead. Woolf had the first of her breakdowns after the deaths of her mother (May 1895) and her father (February 1904),[36] and their shades returned repeatedly to haunt almost everything she wrote. Had her father lived, she writes, "His life would have entirely ended mine . . . No writing, no books; – inconceivable. I used to think of him & mother daily." Still, she thought of this book as an act of exorcism. She confided to her diary that "writing The Lighthouse, laid them [the ghosts of her parents] in my mind . . . I was obsessed by them both, unhealthily; & writing of them was a necessary act" (*Diaries* 3: 28 November 1928, 208). Her sister, Vanessa Bell, thought she had "done them" perfectly: "you have given a portrait of mother which is more like her to me than anything I could ever have conceived of as possible. It is almost painful to have her so raised from the dead . . . You have given father too I think as clearly . . . the only thing about him which ever gave a true idea."[37] Shortly before she began *To the Lighthouse* (which was initially called "Old Man" [*Diaries* 2: 17 October 1924, 317]), Woolf offered an imagistic explanation (something like Faulkner's "muddy drawers" in *The Sound and the Fury*) for the book's originating impulse: "This is going to be fairly short: to have father's character done complete in it; & mothers [*sic*]; & St Ives; & childhood; & all the usual things I try to put in – life, death, &c. But the centre is father's character, sitting in a boat, reciting We perished, each alone, while he crushes a dying mackerel" (*Diaries* 3: 14 May 1925, 18–19). The episode in the book is not quite like this (perhaps it would have been too crude), but the boat contains dying mackerel (caught by Macalister's boy), and the self-indulgent phrase from Cowper's "The Castaway" – "We perished, each alone" – recurs a half-dozen times as one of Ramsay's posturing refrains.

Woolf's focus quickly shifted, however: "The dominating impression is to be of Mrs. R's character"[38] because, according to Beth Daugherty, her obsession with her mother was more pressing. Julia Stephen both sacrificed herself to male demands and collaborated with social pressures to have her daughters do the same: "Mrs. Ramsay feels the pressure to play the Angel in the House as inherent and her drive to sacrifice self as natural. She cannot possibly see how she participates in her own destruction, because the myths preventing such insight ... are so firmly entrenched and intertwined."[39] Spilka finds at the heart of Woolf's fiction "the same nexus of ungrieved grief, and of troubled parental relations" as in *Ulysses*,[40] but *To the Lighthouse* evokes and allays Julia Stephen's "perturbèd spirit" (*Hamlet* 1.5.191). Woolf needed first to represent her mother and then to destroy her as Angel in the House if she were to free both her mother and herself from that role. Echoing Othello's last speech, as he prepares to kill his wife's murderer, Woolf wrote of the "villain of my story": "I turned upon that Angel and caught her by the throat. I did my best to kill her ... I acted in self defence. If I had not killed her, she would have killed me – as a writer."[41] Having succeeded with *To the Lighthouse*, Woolf could finally write: "I ceased to be obsessed by my mother. I no longer hear her voice; I do not see her" (*Moments of Being* 81).

To the Lighthouse's first section is set earlier than *Mrs. Dalloway*, several years before World War One, as if Woolf sought to account for Clarissa's and Septimus' fragile world. Peace and catastrophe are already clashing for Mrs. Ramsay, for the ocean waves, that "for the most part beat a measured and soothing tattoo," at times become "a ghostly roll of drums [that] remorselessly beat the measure of life, made one think of the destruction of the island and its engulfment in the sea, and warned her whose day had slipped past in one quick doing after another that it was all ephemeral ... and made her look up with an impulse of terror" (27–8). Opposing transience and ephemerality, Mrs. Ramsay would keep her children (she has eight, the same number as in the Stephen household) exactly as they are, "never to see them grow up into long-legged monsters. Nothing made up for the loss" (89). Similarly, she works unsuccessfully at matchmaking: but Lily and William Bankes do not marry; Paul and Minta do, but "the marriage had turned out rather badly" (258).

Section One's crowning achievement is the dinner that Mrs. Ramsay both arranges for and arranges. It begins in a dead mood, almost posthumously: Mrs. Ramsay, who has "a sense of being past everything, through everything, out of everything" (125), recalls when she was an apparition: "it was still going on, Mrs. Ramsay mused, gliding like a ghost among the chairs and tables of that drawing-room on the banks of the Thames where she had been so very, very cold twenty years ago; but now she went among them like a ghost" (132). She saves the present occasion by summoning her powers to resist oblivion, bring everything miraculously together (148), transform this domestic scene, with its color, pattern, order, composition, beauty, into a painting or sculpture, something solid and enduring: "It partook, she felt ... of eternity ... there is a coherence in things, a stability; something, she meant, is immune from change ... Of such moments, she thought, the thing is made that endures" (158). Yet like the ball Prue throws up in the air and catches "brilliantly high up in her left hand," the moment of stasis *is* the moment of change – and if from perfection, then toward disintegration: "as if solidity had vanished altogether" (111). Mrs. Ramsay's departure from the dinner echoes Clarissa's return at the end of *Mrs. Dalloway*: "With her foot on the threshold she waited a moment longer in a scene which was vanishing even as she looked, and then, as she moved and took Minta's arm and left the room, it changed, it shaped itself differently; it had become, she knew ... already the past" (167–8). Her creation's harmony disintegrates as she views it, for her medium, like that of Hemingway's bullfighter, is impermanent: achievement survives performance only in the memory of witnesses, and in Woolf's text.

Death in *To the Lighthouse* occurs in neither of the two long sections in which human consciousness is the locus of meaning and where it would, therefore, have to be confronted, but parenthetically, in "Time Passes," the short middle section that links the Victorian era, presided over by Mrs. Ramsay as Angel in the House, to the modern in which, as Mr. Bankes says, "we must wait for the future to show" (189).[42] A dark night of the soul, "Time Passes" consumes ten years and, like the war it contains, seems to render human action trivial and useless. Disrupting the natural vision "of divine bounty," the war is "out of harmony with this jocundity and this serenity." It is imaged in "the silent apparition of an ashen-coloured ship," a "dead" U-boat that had "come, gone," bringing death rather than life out of the ocean and leaving "a purplish stain upon the bland surface of the sea as if something had boiled and bled, invisibly, beneath" (201).

For all Mr. Ramsay insists his children face facts, Mrs. Ramsay could momentarily deny death for her daughter, Cam, by covering the skull that hangs in the nursery (172). But her shawl loosens, swinging "to and fro," immediately Mrs. Ramsay's death is announced (196); war's "repeated shocks ... further loosened the shawl and cracked the tea-cups" (200). In consequence, the family does not come, nature usurps the house, and death begins to claim the children Mrs. Ramsay can no longer protect. Prue and Andrew die conventionally gendered deaths shortly after she does: Prue, like Stella, "in some illness connected with childbirth" only a few months after marrying (199); Andrew in the war: "[A shell exploded. Twenty or thirty young men were blown up in France, among them Andrew Ramsay, whose death, mercifully, was instantaneous.]" (201). Both references to Andrew's death in the third section are also parenthetical (232, 289). No one, it seems, remains to answer the key question in "Time Passes": "What power could now prevent the fertility, the insensibility of nature?" (207).

Yet within "Time Passes" and the war, Augustus Carmichael, named for the age whose great epic poet sings of men at arms and of love well lost for empire and who lies awake reading Virgil, "brought out a volume of poems ... which had an unexpected success. The war, people said, had revived their interest in poetry" (202). This passage occurs just after Andrew's death is announced, and evokes their earlier, barely acknowledged relationship: Mrs. Ramsay recalls "how devoted he was to Andrew, and would call him into his room, and Andrew said, 'show him things'" (145). After Andrew's death, "somebody had said . . . Mr. Carmichael had 'lost all interest in life'" (289). Like much of the war poetry, then, Carmichael's is implicitly homoerotic. Unable to sustain an epic vision of heroic transcendence, modern poets like Wilfred Owen produced anthems "for doomed youth": a lyric poetry predicated on forbidden love in the face of senseless death.

"Time Passes," with its "squandering of living energy and an orgy of annihilation,"[43] is structurally central to the novel and the life/death process it depicts. Noting the "dashing fluency" with which she had written "Time Passes," Woolf contrasts it "with the excruciating hard wrung battles I had with Mrs. Dalloway (save the end)" (*Diaries* 3: 30 April 1926, 76). Completing the earlier novel became easier after she created Septimus Smith (who replaced H.Z. Prentice in the early Dalloway stories[44]), for his death serves a climactic function and insures Clarissa's survival. Mrs. Ramsay lacks a surrogate and so dies for herself.

Yet in a sense, Mrs. Ramsay's death also never happens. Parenthetical and retrospective, it is past before being present: "[Mr. Ramsay, stumbling along a passage one dark morning, stretched his arms out, but Mrs. Ramsay having died rather suddenly the night before, his arms, though stretched out, remained empty.]" (194).[45] Lily saw the Ramsays' relationship as unidirectional: Mrs. Ramsay "pitied men always as if they lacked something – women never, as if they had something" (*Lighthouse* 129). The force of sterility drains that of energy: never having existed except as wife, mother, and angel, Mrs. Ramsay does not so much die as become subtracted, piece by piece: "Mrs. Ramsay had given," Lily thinks. "Giving, giving, giving, she had died" (223). Like Forster's Mrs. Wilcox and Mrs. Moore, Mrs. Ramsay is never represented as a dead body, as if literally nothing were left. The absence of any depiction of Mrs. Ramsay's death weakens its status as fact – "Some said he was dead; some said she was dead. Which was it?" (210) – and the lack of mourning ritual leaves her among the unburied. In *The Waves*, after the death of Percival (another reworking of Thoby's death), the writer Bernard says, "We have no ceremonies" with which to mourn the dead, "only private dirges and no conclusions, only violent sensations, each separate. Nothing that has been said meets our case" (284). Lacking deathbed and funeral, Mrs. Ramsay, "Ghost, air, nothingness" (266), fails to have the story of her dying, like that of her life, enacted or told.

But perhaps such failure was better than the alternative, what Woolf remembers of her mother's death:

> the atmosphere of those ... days before the funeral was so melodramatic, histrionic and unreal that any hallucination was possible. We lived through them in hush, in artificial light. Rooms were shut. People were creeping in and out. People were coming to the door all the time. We were all sitting in the drawing room round father's chair sobbing ... we seemed to sit all together cooped up, sad, solemn, unreal, under a haze of heavy emotion ... I see us now, all dressed in unbroken black ... Father used to sit sunk in gloom ... The tragedy of her death was not that it made one, now and then and very intensely, unhappy. It was that it made her unreal; and us solemn, and self-conscious. We were made to act parts that we did not feel; to fumble for words that we did not know. It obscured, it dulled. It made one hypocritical and immeshed in the conventions of sorrow.
>
> *Moments of Being* 92–5)

If "the conventions of sorrow" proper to Victorian dying produce unreality, their modernist absence may produce the opposite: Mrs. Ramsay's powerful presence in Section Three of *To the Lighthouse.*

Shifting our optical focus, we may read "Time Passes" as liminal rather than terminal, the transitional passage linking two polar states of being as depicted in a van Gennep schema. Though isolatable, solid, and replete with death, it is also, like all else in this elegy, in flux, unenduring, always fading or becoming something else. For beyond the death of the deserted house is its resurrection and rebirth as Mrs. McNab and Mrs. Bast, artists of the domestic scene, reverse the corruption and rot by reimposing human order: "some rusty laborious birth seemed to be taking place ... they contemplated now the magnificent conquest" (210). "Time Passes" may be read as the process a surviving spouse or death-stricken culture must undergo before a condition of (temporary) equilibrium can be restored. Writing of early Indonesian practice, Huntington and Metcalf note that "Of all relatives, the widow is the most disfigured by death. Like the dead man, she must undergo a liminal phase during which her identity is readjusted. To a lesser extent, the entire community goes through a period of redefinition ... A widower is subjected to an identical restriction."[46] Mr. Ramsay, like Western civilization during and after the war, the "long night" of

"Time Passes," barely manages to "survive the flood, the profusion of darkness," and, his "identity ... readjusted," he emerges as "Messages of peace breathed from the sea to the shore" (189, 206, 213).

Though Mrs. Ramsay's demise is announced in "Time Passes" and, along with the war with which it is conflated, seems to trigger the "gigantic chaos" of nature run riot, she participates as fully, if differently, in the action of the third section as in the first. Section Three opens interrogatively with Lily wondering, "What does it mean then, what can it all mean?", an echo of Mrs. Ramsay's thought at the dinner: "What did it all mean?" (159). Lily's immediate answer, which denies meaning, feeling, and expression, is two-fold: Mrs. Ramsay's death has left an unfillable void, "Nothing, nothing – nothing that she could express at all" (217). She feels, however, a superiority in being alive: "oh, the dead! [Lily] murmured, one pitied them, one brushed them aside, one had even a little contempt for them. They are at our mercy" (260). Lily also feels justified in having resisted Mrs. Ramsay's attempts to impose Victorian roles on her. Yet she thinks of Mrs. Ramsay's efforts to hold back time as successful, and she survives in the mind, Lily thinks, "affecting one almost like a work of art" (240).

Recalling an episode in which Mr. Ramsay brutalized Prue, Lily remembers Mrs. Ramsay "making it up to her; assuring her that everything was well; promising her that one of these days that same happiness would be hers" (298). Then Prue "had let the flowers fall from her basket, Lily thought ... She let her flowers fall from her basket, scattered and tumbled them on to the grass" (298–9). Woolf's intertext here is Shakespeare's *Winter's Tale*, in which Leontes destroys his family in a jealous rage, but is allowed to earn redemption through time, atonement, and empathy. In the sheep-shearing scene of renewal, Perdita invokes the daughter of Ceres, who was stolen away by Pluto (Dis) while she was gathering flowers: "O Proserpina, / For the flow'rs now that, frighted, thou lett'st fall / From Dis's wagon!" (4.4.116–18). Like Ceres and Hermione, Mrs. Ramsay has lost her daughter, but also gets her back in a way: not the daughter who died in childbirth but the spiritual one who has become an artist. Lily's vision climaxes in "an odd-shaped triangular shadow," both an "ordinary experience ... and yet at the same time, It's a miracle, it's an ecstasy" – and then, reprising *Mrs. Dalloway*'s last line, "There she sat" (299–300).

For all his authoritativeness, Mr. Ramsay fails to assert himself in

Section One: he is hated and feared by his children, his wife will not say she loves him, and his philosophical thinking cannot reach R, the letter of his name, a fictional metaphor but a literal disaster for the editor of the *Dictionary of National Biography*. In Section One Mr. Ramsay paid homage to his wife because of his need for "sympathy, and whiskey, and some one to tell the story of his suffering to at once" (57). Like Leslie Stephen, who described himself as " 'skin-less', over-sensitive and nervously irritable,"[47] he demands solace for his sense of failure, "to be assured of his genius," "to have his barrenness made fertile," to be "restored, renewed" (58–60; *Moments of Being* 125). Like Leontes, he flounders before his dead during much of Section Three. The surviving spouse and his death-stricken culture, disoriented by profound and inexplicable loss, fail to see their own responsibility. Still bullying, he forces his need for sympathy upon Lily, who rebuffs him; and he attempts to expiate the past by dragging his children on the journey to the lighthouse over which, in proclaiming it impossible ten years before, he quarreled with his wife.

Browbeaten and victimized, James and Cam, like Vanessa and Virginia, establish their silent "compact; to resist tyranny to the death." But they are compelled to do his bidding, to "take part in these rites he went through for his own pleasure in memory of dead people, which they hated, so that they lagged after him, and all the pleasure of the day was spoilt" (246). Though we rarely enter Mr. Ramsay's mind or see with his eyes, his wife's death and his insistence on the journey concentrate attention on him, and suggest his ability finally to mourn and express sympathy. The transformation climaxes when he praises James: "At last he said, triumphantly: 'Well done!' James had steered them like a born sailor" (306). The children's hatred yields instantly to adoration: "What do you want? they both wanted to ask. They both wanted to say, Ask us anything and we will give it you" (307–8). Lily similarly comes into her own when, feeling suddenly vitalized, she thinks, "I'm happy like this" – peculiarly, uniquely, alive, and not as Mrs. Ramsay might have wished to define her, and so "For a moment Lily, standing there ... triumphed over Mrs. Ramsay" (260). Consequently, she simultaneously completes her painting and experiences the ecstatic sense that her empathy has somehow sustained Ramsay's journey: " 'He must have reached it,' said Lily Briscoe aloud, feeling suddenly completely tired out ... Whatever she had wanted to give him, when he left her that morning, she had given him at last" (308–9), but on her own terms.

Mrs. Ramsay's death, then, *has* made a difference. Her living presence had kept Lily and Mr. Ramsay, who seemed to matter less when she was alive, fixed in postures of bad faith. Her absence inspires such fiercely felt anger that it is experienced as a powerful presence: she returns, transfigured into the goddess who presides silently in the memory of the five figures of Section Three, and masterminds the novel's reconciliations and achievements.[48] Finally, Mr. Ramsay and Lily find release in reaching through death to another in need: Lily empathizes with him as she completes her painting; he reaches out to his children as the boat nears the shore. Mrs. Ramsay's reenvisioned return inspires, unifies, and validates this elegy's liberating conclusion.

Outside the novel, however, the ineffectually mourned and inadequately understood World War One largely defined the period that quickly became the run-up to the second. Fussell maintains that the "whole texture of British daily life" in the 1920s and 1930s "could be said to commemorate the war still," and that World War Two and its literature self-consciously repeated events during and after the first. He writes, "The way the data and usages of the Second War behave as if 'thinking in terms of' the First is enough almost to make one believe in a single continuing Great War running through the whole middle of the twentieth century."[49] In the 1930s, a time of intensifying violence and crises, the forces of madness regained the upper hand. Poole writes that "the evolution of Virginia's fear was part and parcel of the psychological and mental history of an entire nation in 1939–41,"[50] for, like Forster, she "hated violence," which she associated with "masculine assertiveness ... 'the beastly masculine.'"[51] She was not, however, consistently pacifistic since she hated fascism, the ultimate political assertion of patriarchy, even more. She could not share Clive Bell's view that "a Nazi Europe would be ... heaven on earth compared to Europe at war."[52]

Pervasive throughout Woolf's life and writings, war was again foregrounded, for her and her culture, in her last years. Marcus reads *The Waves* (1931) as haunted by World War One and prophetic of the second;[53] *Three Guineas* (1938) passionately denounces war and men's responsibility for it; her last novel, *Between the Acts* (published posthumously in 1941, the year Woolf drowned herself), envisions human evil poised to destroy civilization "on a

June day in 1939" (75). In her first diary entry after the outbreak of World War Two, Woolf wrote:

> All meaning has run out of everything ... Emptiness. Inefficiency ... Lord this is the worst of all my life's experiences ... its an empty meaningless world now ... At a pinch eno' adrenalin is secreted to keep one calm. But my brain stops. I took up my watch this morning & then put it down. Lost ... No doubt one can conquer this. But my mind seems to curl up & become undecided ... This war has begun in cold blood. One merely feels that the killing machine has to be set in action ... It seems entirely meaningless – a perfunctory slaughter ... Of course all creative power is cut off. (*Diaries* 5: 6 September 1939, 234–5)

"She could not," Forster writes, "assimilate this latest threat to our civilisation" (*Two Cheers* 253). At the outbreak of World War One, she had mockingly written, "All the people expected an invasion" (*Letters* 2: 12 August 1914); now anticipating it herself, and believing that taking one's life could be both rational and moral if the alternatives were worse, she entered into a suicide pact with her husband (*Moments of Being* 100).

Another catastrophic war (this time with defeat likely); dread of a further, perhaps final, breakdown and of again coming under medical authority ("oh the torture they put one to waiting for results, and then not knowing what they mean" [*Letters* 6: 14 January 1938, 207]); fear of failing creative powers – her suicide seems logical and inevitable. When it came to it, however, she went alone, seeking to spare her husband, to whom she addressed her suicide note: "I feel certain I am going mad again. I feel we can't go through another of those terrible times. And I shan't recover this time. I begin to hear voices, and I can't concentrate. So I am doing what seems the best thing to do."[54] Maintaining that the "language, the idiom, the conceptual limits" of this text are those of Leonard Woolf, who always had unquestioning faith in medical authority, Poole calls it "the most generous fraud, and the most magnificent deception, in modern literature."[55] Her epitaph, "Against you I will fling myself, unvanquished and unyielding, O Death!,"[56] acknowledges her most impassioned embrace: one she resisted as long as she could.

CHAPTER 11

Late modernism: Graham Greene

Greene defined his early fiction against high modernism's apolitical and irreligious stance, Bloomsbury's elitism, Woolf's rejection of storytelling.[1] He resurrects the dying god on the cross that modernists like Ford and Forster had ignored and others, like Lawrence and Joyce, had sought, once and for all, to kill. Greene did not, however, subscribe to nineteenth-century pieties: his obsession with deathbed repentance was more medieval than Victorian. Catholic conversion offered Greene a way out of modernist incertitude (as well as into a marriage), but he remained skeptical about heaven and the afterlife, rejected papal infallibility and the condemnation of suicide, and opposed dictators and supported liberation theology and left-wing politics.

Against critics who assert otherwise, Greene insisted he was "not a Catholic writer ['detestable term!'], but a writer who happens to be Catholic" (*Ways of Escape* 77). Yet Greene's fictive obsessions echo his religious ones; and more than the modernists, he looked through them to historical and political events: the Depression, World War Two, the rise of dictators, the Cold War. Peripheral to rather than engaged in such events, Greene's protagonists are judged by Catholic rather than worldly criteria: are they damned? are they saints? Greene maintained that "the greatest saints have been men with more than a normal capacity for evil, and the most vicious men have sometimes narrowly evaded sanctity" (*Essays* 174, 180, 173). Vitality existed for Greene only at the moral spectrum's extremes.

Greene's self-fashioning derived from "voluptuous gloom," the sense of life's tenuous, posthumous, status that prevailed whether he looked ahead or back. His early years, he writes, "cry for rescue [from the unconscious] like the survivors of a shipwreck" (*Sort of Life* 19); the autobiography he made of them is a *memento mori* whose self-reflexive dedication reads: "For the Survivors." His first grand adventure was discovering he could read, which he equated with encountering mortality. He saw the future "around on bookshelves everywhere waiting for the child to choose . . . happiness and misery, eventually one particular form of death, for surely we choose our death much as we choose our job." He kept his fearful secret as long as he could: "I was safe so long as I could not read." When he finally acknowledged it, the books he fixed upon – Captain Gilson's *The Pirate Aeroplane*, Anthony Hope's *Sophy of Kravonia*, Rider Haggard's *King Solomon's Mines*, Marjorie Bowen's *The Viper of Milan* – offered adolescent adventure and escape, and two formative lessons: the fascination and ubiquity of evil and "the sense of doom that lies over success." What Greene found in these books (as later in Catholicism) reinforced his temperamental morbidity, and under their influence his first writings are "marked with enormous brutality and a despairing romanticism" (*Essays* 14, 18, 17).

Early memories include stories of children being murdered or left to die; a nearby inn where "travellers had been done to death"; a man cutting his throat; fear of drowning, of creatures lurking in dark corridors, of his house catching fire at night. The first airplane he saw nose-dived and crashed, so that "watching planes cross the sky, I half expect to see them fall to earth, as though it were my gaze which had caused that first crash" (57). Perhaps in consequence, he had dreams of disasters as they occurred, including that of a shipwreck the night the *Titanic* sank. Having discovered Jung and Freud when he was a teenager undergoing analysis, he delved into dreams and unconscious motivation. Mrs. Richmond, the spiritualist wife of his analyst, thought he was "a natural medium."[2]

A Sort of Life climaxes with Greene's attempts at a sort of suicide: his playing Russian roulette "to escape in one way or another" his "agonizing crises of boredom" (58, 129–30). The game provided an erotic kick ("a flick of the whip to keep me going"), but eventually he abandoned it for the same reason he began it: "I found myself tempting the end to come . . . I hadn't the courage for suicide, but it became a habit with me to visit troubled places, not to seek material for novels but to regain the sense of insecurity which I had *enjoyed* in the three blitzes on London" (*Ways of Escape* 146; my emphasis). He sought what he recoiled against: "the fear of ambush served me just as effectively as the revolver from the corner cupboard in the lifelong war against boredom" (*Sort of Life* 133). Greene's childhood misery impelled a boyhood weakling to prove his manhood "in life as well as art, [in] situations of extreme physical danger that test personal courage."[3] Ultimately his treks proved fruitful: ending not in death, but in texts, artifices of his mortality.

Pathologically morbid, Greene shared Camus' view of suicide, which became as central in Greene's writings as in his life. In addition to Scobie in *The Heart of the Matter*, his suicides include Rose in his play, *The Living Room*, and implicitly Sarah in *The End of the Affair* and the whiskey priest in *The Power and the Glory*, since both desperately seek death. The theme of suicide is crucial to *The Man Within*; *Brighton Rock* turns on a fake suicide pact; the protagonist in *Doctor Fischer of Geneva* contemplates suicide. Greene's unconventional Catholicism allowed him to deny that Bobby Sands and Jan Palach were suicides: presumably because, though they destroyed themselves, they were, like Socrates, politically motivated rather than despairing. In the year he converted to Catholicism (1926), Greene wrote of his eldest brother, the black sheep Herbert: "His is a case where I can't help feeling that suicide far from being sinful would be meritorious. It's fearfully depressing and hopeless for my people ... I think in his case the sin is in not shooting himself."[4] He would have forgiven his brother for committing suicide even had he acted out of despair.

Greene shared a spiritual orientation with Eliot; what Eliot says of Baudelaire applies to Greene:

> He could not escape suffering and could not transcend it, so he *attracted* pain to himself. But what he could do, with that immense passive strength and sensibilities which no pain could impair, was to study his suffering ... in his way of suffering is already a kind of presence of the supernatural and of the superhuman ... His *ennui* [is] a true form of *acedia*, arising from the unsuccessful struggle towards the spiritual life.[5]

Eliot insists that Baudelaire's "morbidity of temperament" is not "an unfortunate ailment which can be discounted"; nor can we "detach the sound from the unsound in his work. Without the morbidity none of his work would be possible or significant" (422).

Greene encapsulates his whiskey priest's mothlike flight in the phrase, "The desire of life, which moves in cycles, was returning – any sort of life" (*Power* 159). The desire Greene's characters feel for "any sort of life" provides the title and thesis of the autobiography he began "as a form of therapy,"[6] an attempt to sublimate self-destructive urges that remained fruitful all his life. In the aptly named second volume of his autobiography, *Ways of Escape* (1980), he writes, "sometimes I wonder how all those who do not write, compose or paint can manage to escape the madness, the melancholia, the panic fear which is inherent in the human situation" (285). Again, texts serve as death's surrogate.

His autobiographical titles inscribe a series of meanings on the life Greene sought to recuperate. The notion of "a sort of life" suggests a theory of the genre: "An autobiography is only 'a sort of life' – it may contain less errors of fact than a biography, but it is of necessity even more selective: it begins later and it ends prematurely. If one cannot close a book of memories on the deathbed, any conclusion must be arbitrary," for Greene found meaning only in contemplating death. Second, autobiography's ability "to reduce a chaos of experience to some sort of order" depends on omitting, among other things, imaginary characters, with whom "I have spent almost as much time ... as with real men and women" (*Sort of Life* 11–12), the omission, that is, of those Greene brought to life as opposed to those he saw disappear. But his novels "too were after all 'a sort of life'" (*Ways of Escape* 9). Third, the rhythm of failure and escape that pervades his life and writings results from suicidal ennui, a sense of being "neither / Living nor dead."[7] Greene's bleak and shadowy autobiography, its vision of human nature as "not black and white but black and grey" (*Essays* 18), derives less from its specific deaths (an unsurprising number for a large family during a world war), than from a death obsessiveness in which thanatophobia and thanatophilia vie for precedence and ultimately become inextricable.

The term "elegy" that Woolf (whose novels Scobie's wife Louise reads in *Heart of the Matter*) applies to her fictions of loss and grief is equally felicitous for Greene's narratives: every achievement seems posthumous, a life-denying account from beyond the death he and his characters seek. Like Woolf, Greene experienced a harrowing childhood dominated by a sense of betrayal that led to breakdowns, to suicide attempts, and to his coming under medical authority. The differences are gendered: he was abused not sexually within the family but by bullies at school; he attempted suicide not with pills but by playing Russian roulette; and his medical treatment was largely self-determined, within his control. Unlike Woolf's doctors, Greene's analyst, Kenneth Richmond, an untrained and uncredentialed Jungian and spiritualist, was non-directive, a listener, indifferent to social decorum and respectability, non-judgmental even about Greene's homosexual inclinations. Quoting Freud's claim that "much is won if we succeed in transforming hysterical misery into common unhappiness" (*Sort of Life* 102), Greene suggests that his psychoanalysis was a kind of success: that his "common unhappiness" enabled him to live "a sort of life." Sixty-three years later he wrote that his time with the Richmonds was "one of the happiest periods of my life."[8] One can only wonder how Woolf would have fared had she received such treatment.

Greene's conversion from atheism, a hallmark of modernism after the death of God, had an erotic basis: Vivien Dayrell-Browning, with whom he had fallen in love, would not go to bed with him unless they were married, and she would not marry him unless he became a Catholic.[9] To his surprise, he became serious about his new faith because it addressed his need for "something fine & hard & certain, however uncomfortable, to catch hold of in the general flux."[10] He usually spoke of conversion as an intellectual act: "I had not been converted to a religious faith. I had been convinced by specific arguments in the probability of its creed" (*Ways of Escape* 56). Like his fictional converts, Greene found consolation "of a kind" in Catholicism, because its death-orientation proved congenial to his "morbidity of temperament,"[11] especially its Jansenist strain, with its doctrine of moral predeterminism, denial of free will, belittlement of human nature and action – and, doubtless, its having been condemned as heretical.[12] "One began to believe in heaven," Greene writes, "because one believed in hell, but for a long while it was only hell one could picture with a certain intimacy" (*Lawless Roads* 5). Even Catholicism has become problematic, un-Dantesque, after the modern apocalypse and transformation of death: paradise is meaningless wish-fulfillment, but hell accords with earthly existence.

Greene's conflating of sanctity and evil echoes Eliot's anti-Dantean essay on Baudelaire (1930), which Greene quotes approvingly (in an essay called "Henry James: The Religious Aspect" [*Essays* 50]):

> So far as we are human, what we do must be either evil or good; so far as we do evil or good, we are human; and it is better ... to do evil than to do nothing: at least, we exist. It is true to say that the glory of man is his capacity for salvation; it is also true to say that his glory is his capacity for damnation. The worst that can be said of most of our malefactors ... is that they are not men enough to be damned.[13]

Dante's afterworld rigorously links sin and punishment, merit and reward; Eliot's dehumanized malefactors, too emasculated to achieve damnation, remain in limbo.

This post-romantic, post-Nietzschean extolling of evil over inaction, sin over moral neutrality, has anti-democratic and fascistic implications. An "indifferent" is likely to be a "mass man," one lacking a sense of individuality. Gilbert and Gubar argue that World War One "virtually completed the Industrial Revolution's construction of anonymous dehumanized man, that impotent cipher who is frequently thought to be the twentieth century's most characteristic citizen ... the war, the dark satanic mill of death, soon taught him just what he and his aspirations were worth."[14] Eliot's position, which Greene endorsed despite his left-wing politics and Catholic conversion, seems particularly decadent and outrageous in this century of genocide and extermination camps. Orwell writes dismissively, "Graham Greene would probably subscribe to the statement of Maritain, made apropos of Léon Bloy, that 'there is but one sadness – not to be a saint.'"[15] Greene's spiritual focus offends collectivists and socialists committed to improving the human condition. Despite their very different moral worth, Greene accords equal empathy to those characters who share his obsession with sin: Pinkie and Rose in *Brighton Rock*, the lieutenant and whiskey priest in *The Power and the Glory*, Scobie in *The Heart of the Matter*, Bendrix and Sarah in *The End of the Affair*.

Such perverse discrimination presumes what Bataille calls "the underlying affinity between sanctity and transgression ... Even in the eyes of believers, the libertine is nearer to the saint than the man without desire."[16] Eliot and Greene imply that "even" should be "especially." In Greene's fallen world, "Goodness has only once found a perfect incarnation in a human body and never will again" (*Essays* 17); hence, evil alone partakes of transcendence. His exemplars of grace recall those in Browning's "Bishop Blougram's Apology," which Greene called "an epigraph for all the novels I have written" (*Sort of Life* 117):

> Our interest's on the dangerous edge of things.
> The honest thief, the tender murderer,
> The superstitious atheist, demirep
> That loves and saves her soul in new French books –
> We watch while these in equilibrium keep
> The giddy line midway.[17]

Though "sin," Greene says, "has always stuck in my throat"[18] and hell is a concept he only intermittently accepted, faith leads Greene's reluctant adherents, occupants of a merciless cosmos, to attempt a giddy balancing act "on the dangerous edge of things." In the end, Greene suggests, salvation awaits although (or because) they elect damnation.

Discussing the "new literature of crime" with which Greene identified much of his writing, Foucault says,

> crime is glorified, because it is one of the fine arts, because it can be the work only of exceptional natures, because it reveals the monstrousness of the strong and powerful, because villainy is yet another mode of privilege: from the adventure story to de Quincey, or from the *Castle of Otranto* to Baudelaire, there is a whole aesthetic rewriting of crime ... it is the discovery of the beauty and greatness of crime; in fact, it is the affirmation that greatness too has a right to crime and that it even becomes the exclusive privilege of those who are really great.[19]

The hard-boiled detective novel of the 1920s and 1930s popularized the modernist shift to death as initiatory, effaced, and affectless. Lacking moral or emotional dimension, murder inaugurates intellectual action, the puzzling out of "who dunnit," rather than rituals of loss and mourning.

Yet Greene, fascinated by Browning's "tender murderer," the notion of evil resulting, Oedipus-like, from good motives, rarely enacts Foucault's Sadean notion of "the beauty and greatness of crime." He comes closest in *Brighton Rock*, where the evil Pinkie finds pleasure only in criminality: inflicting pain is "the finest of all sensations" (102–3). But Pinkie is hounded to death by Ida, the spoil-sport who subverts the genre by insisting on right and wrong. *Brighton Rock*'s first line – "Hale knew they meant to murder him before he had been in Brighton three hours" – establishes the novel's furious tone of apparently conclusive yet repeated violence. Attention is drawn to a particular criminal action, but Hale's murder becomes one in a series that began before the book opens and promises to continue beyond its end. Thus, the opening initiates the novel's double rhythm and perspective: the moment's uniqueness counterpoints endlessly, fruitlessly, recurring action. Greene's grammatical ambiguity underscores this sense of dis-ease in the moment: did Hale, before he had been in Brighton three hours, know he was an intended murder victim? Or was he to be murdered within three hours of his arriving there? Both, it turns out, are true. The murderous Pinkie shares many of Greene's morbid obsessions: fear of drowning, pathological loathing of praise (146), reversal of the damned and saved (190), a view of life as fatally ailing: "the horror of the world lay like infection in his throat" (207). An inverted idealist, Pinkie finds neither solace nor fulfillment in action: always the next murder looms. Time is frozen; the moment of violent discharge repeats and entraps.

Having elided dying or represented it as the "dirty death," modernists like Joyce, Forster, and Lawrence sought to enact bodily fulfillment rather than depletion: the bed as site of eros rather than death. Greene's morbidity compelled him to link the two: to conflate copulation with sordid dying. Both Pinkie's criminality and his sense of guilt result from his having witnessed, because of their impoverished circumstances, the primal scene of his parents' lovemaking. He recalls it on his wedding night: "His father panted like a man at the end of a race and his mother made a horrifying sound of pleasurable pain. He was filled with hatred, disgust, loneliness; he was completely abandoned: he had no share in their thoughts – for the space of a few minutes he was dead, he was like a soul in purgatory watching the shameless act of a beloved person" (189). Never does Greene's fiction represent lovemaking positively.

Pinkie is both product and embodiment of the Depression-era modern city, whose rust spreads over the meadows at the end of *Howards End*, and to where Paul Morel in *Sons and Lovers* and Stephen Dedalus in *Portrait of the Artist* head at the end of their novels. Rupert's loathing of London in *Women in Love*, Joyce's depiction of Dublin as "a dunghill," and Stephen's failure in Paris, as recalled in *Ulysses*, presage Greene's 1930s urban environment as a place of violence and social death. Growing up in a sordid Brighton slum ironically named Paradise Piece, Pinkie, an anti-Wordsworthian innocent known as the Boy, "trailed the clouds of his own glory after him: hell lay about him in his infancy. He was ready for more deaths" (69). Greene implies that social conditions, not original sin, produce evil.

Pinkie abhors not only non-sacramental marriage but all sex, which for him is debasement, pornography, damnation. Baudelaire says, "the sole and supreme pleasure in Love lies in the absolute knowledge of doing *evil*,"[20] but Pinkie is denied even such perverse pleasure: he views sex as physically and morally repellent, which accords perfectly with Greene's Jansenism. On his wedding night,

Pinkie says of his registry office marriage, "'It's a mortal sin,' getting what savour there was out of innocence, trying to taste God in the mouth ... It seemed to him more like death than when Hale and Spicer had died ... It was as if he was damned already ... This was hell" (183–4) – nor, like Marlowe's Mephostophilis, is he out of it. Pinkie consequently surrenders the myth of escaping from the moment: "The Boy said with bitter and unhappy relish: 'It'll be no good going to confession ever again – as long as we're both alive.'" In *Paradise Lost* Milton sees "man's first disobedience" as bringing "death into the world, and all our woe" (1: 1–3). But Pinkie literalizes the Fall as sexual intercourse: "they felt as if they were shut out from an Eden of ignorance. On this side there was nothing to look forward to but experience" (169, 173). Pinkie rewrites Milton's radical optimism – "The world was all before them, where to choose" (12: 646) – into a despairing vision of damning existence.

Yet Pinkie longs for an ultimate Catholic ritual and reprieve, the sort Jeremy Taylor condemned: "One confession when he was safe to wipe out everything" (110). He marries in order to silence a witness: "his temporal safety in return for two immortalities of pain" (171).[21] But this action, intended to break the novel's destructive pattern, instead raises its stakes by precluding salvation: "He had a sense now that the murders of Hale and Spicer were trivial acts, a boy's game, and he had put away childish things. Murder had only led to this – this corruption. He was filled with awe at his own powers" (169). Pinkie's perverse position, an extension of Scobie's belief that blasphemous communion is far worse than adultery, results from Catholicism's concern for the soul's salvation no matter its material cost, a view that *Brighton Rock*, and its author, find congenial.

Ida, who pursues Pinkie like an avenging fury, is his (and Greene's) antithesis: she believes in human justice ("an eye for an eye"), in right and wrong, rather than Good and Evil, in human nature and nurture. "Death shocked her, life was so important ... Let Papists treat death with flippancy: life wasn't so important perhaps to them as what came after; but to her death was the end of everything ... She took life with a deadly seriousness: she was prepared to cause any amount of unhappiness to anyone in order to defend the only thing she believed in ... There was something dangerous and remorseless in her optimism." Greene views Ida's goodhearted vitality as superficial, sensuous, and dangerous. Like the Richmonds she believes "in ghosts, ouija boards, tables that rapped and little inept voices speaking plaintively of flowers" (36). But her optimism, which presumes the possibility (shocking for Greene) of living life happily and well, denies transcendence and the power to transform the moment.

Brighton Rock's narrator mocks Ida's life-affirming nature. Instead of having her appealing qualities serve as an antidote to criminality, Greene satirizes her as a whore with a heart of gold, large-bosomed but childless, "her big breasts ready for any secrets. She carried her air of compassion and comprehension about her like a rank cheap perfume" (236). Our sympathies are urged not toward her but her quarry, the loathsome Pinkie, whom she pursues to his death. Greene's interest in "the human factor," then, means a commitment not to mortal life but to its containing and suspending death, which seems always both past and obsessively present. Greene's fiction consequently depicts a curious if powerful pattern of reenactment, of time constantly reconstituting itself, a process at odds with linearity of plot.

Unlike the modernists, Greene employs traditional novel structure when he has Pinkie's climactic death, which occurs while he is trying to kill his wife, complete action already in process prior to the novel's beginning. Yet the pattern repeats until it catches Rose who, echoing Milton's Satan, had chosen the evil Pinkie as her good. In the last line Rose, proudly pregnant with Pinkie's child, goes to hear Pinkie's recorded "loving message" (222). What awaits her, however, is "the worst horror of all" (250), one that will presumably destroy her and the life she bears: "God damn you, you little bitch, why can't you go back home for ever and let me be?" (179).

For Pinkie, the moment is all: the moment of damnation when he commits mortal sin, the moment of redemption forever precluded by his unsanctified marriage. Greene would have us believe that Pinkie's murderous aggression, pathological revulsion against sex, and obsession with damnation distinguish him from his creator, who says: "I tried, as a sort of intellectual exercise, to present the reader with a creature whom he could accept as worthy of hell. But in the end," Greene adds, "I introduced the possibility that he might have been saved 'between the stirrup and the ground.' I wanted to instill in the reader's mind a fundamental doubt of hell." Greene himself leaps from skepticism to certainty: "I don't think that Pinkie was guilty of mortal sin because his actions were not committed in defiance of God but arose out of the conditions to which he had been born."[22] Greene's defense of Pinkie is oddly materialist, given his theological absolutism, implying that childhood hardship excuses subsequent choices and actions. He sounds more like a social worker, or an Ida, than a Jansenist, except in focusing on the man–God relationship, as expressed in deathbed repentance even for a life of unmitigated evil, and the belief that victims are a matter of indifference.

Evil was always profound, ascetic, spiritual for Greene (as for Baudelaire and Eliot), perhaps because it crystallizes the central mystery of Godhood. Hardy had written, "I have been looking for God 50 years, and I think that if he had existed I should have discovered him."[23] As if responding to Hardy, Greene says, "If God exists – I'm not convinced He does – He is omniscient; if He is omniscient, I can't bring myself to imagine that a creature conceived by Him can be so evil as to merit eternal punishment. His grace must intervene at some point."[24] What Greene cannot imagine may, of course, represent only imagination's failure.

Set in Mexico during what Greene calls "the fiercest persecution of religion anywhere since the reign of Elizabeth," *The Power and the Glory* is Greene's most programmatic novel, "the only novel I have written to a thesis." Its story was first written as *Another Mexico*, an account of Greene's visit to examine the consequences of the Revolution, which "was phony from the start" (*Ways of Escape* 84–8). The novel begins with a posthumous retrospective on mortality, the life not quite over: "A few buzzards looked down from the roof with shabby indifference: he wasn't carrion yet" (9). Elsewhere Greene maintains that "in its journey towards death" (*Essays* 13), all life abides in the teleological orientation, the unidirectional temporality, of that ephemeral "yet." Such a view of life might be expected to dictate the form of the fiction. In discussing the structure of his books, however, Greene says that "The idea of A to Z has always scared me ... and I have always broken the continuity of a story with the memories of my chief character" (*Ways of Escape* 51). He speaks also of learning structure by "continual rereadings of that remarkable novel, *The Good Soldier*" (143), and insists that "It is the 'human factor' that interests me, not apologetics."[25] Yet his characters devoted to this world are trivialized, stereotyped.

Most fascinated by those who do God's work despite themselves, or even against themselves, Greene insists that any intense commitment serves the cause. "For me, the sinner and the saint can meet; there is no discontinuity, no rupture. I believe in reversibility."[26] Catholicism, Greene suggests, will out: those it claims, regardless of how they live, cannot escape its hold. Like Pinkie, who as a kid "swore I'd be a priest" (166), *Power and the Glory*'s whiskey priest retains belief in the redemptive confession. Sarah in *End of the Affair*, baptized as a child without her knowledge, "returns" to a faith she never knew. *The Power and the Glory*'s lieutenant epitomizes this pattern: "the idealistic police officer ... stifled life from the best possible motives," unlike "the drunken priest who continued to pass life on" (*Ways of Escape* 89). An ascetic who inhabits a room "as comfortless as a prison or a monastic cell" (*Power* 32), the lieutenant resembles "a priest in his intent observant walk – a theologian going back over the errors of the past to destroy them again" (32). His appearance – "perhaps the scar on his jaw was the relic of an escape" (26) – both images and foreshadows the priest (each uncannily doubles the other) "who carried about with him still the scars of time" (57). Like Pinkie, lieutenant and priest both believe that the deaths they cause are as nothing to the ends they pursue.

The narrator calls the lieutenant a mystic, but "what he had experienced was vacancy – a complete certainty in the existence of a dying, cooling world, of human beings who had evolved from animals for no purpose at all. He knew" (33). As with Bendrix in *End of the Affair*, however, the lieutenant's hatred of Catholicism comes to serve Greene's God rather than secularize the world: he feeds a famished people's need for martyrs and provides the persecution that nourishes faith. The lieutenant also unwittingly helps to define "the dangerous moment" that crystallizes the novel's overarching design. The book's never-completed/ever-repeated action exists in a temporal limbo, a present haunted by revenants. It begins after the end: "The last [priest] was shot weeks ago," the lieutenant says when he first appears (28); and occurs during a frozen, recurring moment: "We've shot him half a dozen times." He adds, "They all look alike to me" (29, 30). And it ends before the beginning: the arrival, on the novel's final page, of the *next* "last priest."

For all his sense of mission, the lieutenant, like Ida seeking revenge against Pinkie, confounds the pleasure of decisive action with the desired end: for both, "The hunt was what mattered" (*Brighton Rock* 153). Its completion induces misreadings of time as linear rather than cyclical: the lieutenant "felt moody, as though now that *the last priest* was under lock and key there was nothing left to think about. The spring of action seemed to be broken. He looked back on the weeks of hunting as a happy time which was *over now for ever*. He felt without a purpose, as if life had drained out of the world" (*Power* 279; my emphasis). Since "the last priest" is also always the next one, neither complacency about the past nor despondency about the future is appropriate. "Success is always temporary, success is only a delayed failure" (*Sort of Life* 219), and it leaves the lieutenant exhausted – worn out, purposeless – and *again* unprepared for the reprise, the inevitable replay. Despite never losing, he cannot ever win, each repetition underscoring God's supposedly greater staying-power.

Like the lieutenant but also like a priest conducting the mass, the nameless, generic whiskey priest replicates the actions of those preceding and following him. Locked in a dance of death with the lieutenant, he wonders, as Greene did in childhood, whether he *wants* to escape, and if so to what. At one point he discovers that "He was travelling in the actual track of the police" (*Power* 112), but he continues on. His wanderings, like the unwinding of autobiography, move backward in time. He journeys first to his old parish, "the scene of his despair" (83); there, in a loveless act, he had fathered a child whom he now loves so desperately that he prays for damnation because he persuades himself that this absurd bargain will spare her suffering. He continues back to where "he had been born and where his parents were buried" (116); and finally he seeks to reclaim the innocent time that predated the persecution (226). Driven from his old parish and unable to enter the village of his birth, "He felt like a man without a passport who is turned away from every harbour" (138). But his journey "into a region of abandonment ... a kind of limbo" (199) is one of return, like Pinkie's, to the capture and death implicit in his and the novel's beginning.

The priest's hegira to martyrdom seems at first a mocking echo of a Mexican mother's reading the life of a saint, "young Juan," to her children. The hagiography rings increasingly false as the priest sinks further into despair: from his moral neutrality in limbo to a Mephistophelian belief that, like Pinkie, "he carried Hell about with him ... Evil ran like malaria in his veins" (*Power* 237). At the moment of reversal, Greene provides the inevitable epiphany: the priest "knew now that at the end there was only one thing that counted – to be a saint" (284). And, we are told, the miracle occurs: the mother's cynical teenage son, whose soul is the priest's and lieutenant's battlefield and prize, is transformed. Having earlier salivated over the lieutenant's gun (77), symbolic of secular, masculine authority, the boy, in an act of homage to the priest, now spits on "the revolver butt" (299). He then dreams "that the priest whom they had shot that morning was back in the house dressed in the clothes his father had lent him and laid out stiffly for burial" (300), a dream that summons, at the novel's end as at its opening, the *next* last nameless priest.

The structure of *The Power and the Glory* suggests, in Greene's phrase, that "A story has no beginning or end." But this line, which begins *The End of the Affair*, contradicts both its novel's title and Greene's teleology, again creating tension between linear and cyclical patterns. Bendrix, the writer who narrates Greene's most self-reflexive and self-subverting novel, posits arbitrariness and absence of design in order to withhold coherence and meaning from the story he simultaneously tells and fails to tell. He insists that meaning resides only in the moment, in his illicit relationship with Sarah, another man's wife. Yet in what Greene represents as his sinful overvaluing of the physical and the immediate (in erotic and then theological terms), Bendrix perversely destroys what he "wrongfully" loves, causing precisely what he would prevent: "Deliberately I would put the caustic soda of the word 'affair,' with its suggestion of a beginning and an end, upon my tongue" (67).

Bendrix had at first intended "just to pick her brain" (58); later, looking forward to spending a night with Sarah, it was "as a writer looks forward to the last word of his book" (8). Like Othello with Desdemona, he never envisages Sarah as independent and alive: for him the affair is death-oriented, pervaded by its end, from its inception. The novel's opening, then, is willful self-deception, what Bendrix wants to believe rather than what he experiences and then represents in his writing. Self-deprecation is as fundamental to Bendrix's character as to Greene's. Despite Sarah's devotion to him, Bendrix says, "I could feel no trust; in the act of love I could be arrogant, but alone I had only to look in the mirror to see doubt . . . why me?" (56). The last thing he writes before reproducing Sarah's diary is: "It is a strange thing to discover and to believe you are loved, when you know that nothing is there for anybody but a parent or a God to love" (107).

Self-loathing allows Bendrix to believe in neither the affair nor his novel, and he spoils both as he had spoiled their night together: "All the time I knew I was forcing the pace. I was pushing, pushing the only thing I loved out of my life ... If love had to die, I wanted it to die quickly ... My novel lagged, but my love hurried like inspiration to the end" (39–40). Unable to serve his fiction, love has no function except as ultimate threat. Like Pinkie, Bendrix finds it far deadlier than violence or murder: "The act of sex may be nothing, but when you reach my age you learn that at any time it may prove to be everything" (199). Bendrix alludes not to the possibility of love enduring but to eternal damnation.

The period's major military and political events contextualize the book's action. Sarah and Bendrix meet during the time of the Spanish Civil War; the book ends shortly after World War Two. Sarah's husband Henry is involved in the war effort; Bendrix is not. The moment on which the book turns and re-turns is the "miracle" of Bendrix's resurrection. He and Sarah have just made love, which Bendrix calls "the little death" (55), during a V-1 attack: "It made no difference. Death never mattered at those times; in the early days I even used to pray for it: the shattering annihilation that would prevent forever the getting up, the putting on of clothes" (83). The rocket that falls in Greene's novel kills Bendrix; but he is then, we are meant to believe, resurrected, his prayer perversely answered since he will never again take off his clothes with Sarah: "I woke after five seconds or five minutes in a changed world ... as though I had been on a long journey. I had no memory at all of Sarah and I was completely free from anxiety, jealousy, insecurity, hate; my mind was a blank sheet on which somebody had just been on the point of writing a message of happiness. I felt sure that when my memory came back the writing would continue, and that I should be happy" (85).

In this bleak account Bendrix's sudden lightness of tone is startling, every word unintentionally ironic: the "changed world," the link between peace and forgetting Sarah, of being written by a greater author, of being happily determined. Returning from his "longest journey," his near-death experience of a happy beyond, he sees a door suspended above him and finds himself "bruised from the shoulders to the knees as if by its shadow" (85). Sarah's diary later reveals that the door "actually" crushed Bendrix, and that he revived after she promised God she would end the affair if he were accorded a "second-fate." Greene's treatment of Bendrix's "miraculous" posthumous life gives it enormous weight and significance; yet, since Bendrix subverts from the first both his relationship with Sarah and the book that was its origin and justification, it is irrelevant: with or without God, the affair was always doomed.

When Bendrix covertly obtains Sarah's diary, he reads what he could neither live nor write: a successful version of their affair. "In writing that I could believe as I couldn't believe her voice," he sees the truth of her love for him, and he offers that revelation as epigraph to the diary entries he reproduces: "For it was the last couple of pages I read first, and I read them again at the end to make sure" (107).

> Did I ever love Maurice as much before I loved You? Or was it really You I loved all the time? . . . Was it me he loved, or You? For he hated in me the things You hate. He was on Your side all the time without knowing it. You willed our separation, but he willed it too. He worked for it with his anger and his jealousy, and he worked for it with his love. For he gave me so much love and I gave him so much love that soon there wasn't anything left when we'd finished but You. (150–1)

Greene defines God negatively, as absence of life, the death left over when everything we ordinarily value is gone. Of his "second-fate," Bendrix thinks bitterly, "here it is: the empty life, odourless, antiseptic, the life of a prison. And I accused her as though her prayers had really worked the change – what did I do to you that you had to condemn me to life?" (180). Greene invariably represents God's adherents as vacuous, depleted, devoid of vitality and decency, unhappy, like Lazarus, at having to live, and die, again.

Sarah's diary convinces Bendrix of what he had never accepted: the enduring nature of her love for him. It also underscores what seems to contradict that love: the end of their relationship. A third truth it reveals, that he is responsible for the affair's end, is one he has always tried not to know: "My love and fear acted like conscience. If we had believed in sin, our behaviour would hardly have differed" (66). Both the diary and novel express Greene's Jansenism, that the writer who would play God plays by God's rules and serves God's ends: "I am beginning to doubt whether anything I can do will ever alter the course of events" (78). Bendrix's moral myopia deflects from his self-awareness, yet even he ultimately discerns an overarching, if malevolent, pattern. Sarah's death, it turns out, was doubly "the end of the affair": not only its terminus, but also its purpose and achievement. Thus, Greene suggests, the failures of art and life synchronize with their transcendent success. Greene's Catholicism inscribes a text and structure on those it claims, even as desire, weakness, corruption, ennui, all that define and focus "the dangerous moment," would subvert it.

The End of the Affair, like autobiography and other retrospective narration, is written back to front, which is how, an omniscient perspective would suggest, we live our lives: teleology imposes itself retrospectively. Bendrix's perverse jealousy and will to destroy love are read initially, by him and by us, as character flaws. Subsequently, they are seen as Bendrix's instruments for unwittingly serving God. Bendrix's deepest emotions – jealousy, frustration, and rage – do not begin with Sarah's loss and the end of the affair, any more than Greene's morbidity began with his conversion to Catholicism. Central to narrative and story from the outset are Bendrix's antipathy toward the ultimate Rival. Bendrix's initial hostility toward Sarah, as well as his growing obsession with her and his loss of her as he is displaced, may be explicated by Girard's notion that desire depends on rivalry, is mimetic: "Rivalry does not arise because of the fortuitous convergence of two desires on a single object; rather, *the subject desires the object because the rival desires it.* In desiring an object the rival alerts the subject to the desirability of the object." What results, Girard adds, is that the imitator, the disciple, "feels both rejected and humiliated, judged unworthy by his model of participating in the superior existence the model himself enjoys."[27] Bendrix is fixated on Sarah's material being both before and after her death. After she dies, he speaks derisively of her as a set of relics, her bones "like a saint's" (178). Even while seeing his action as absurd, Bendrix opposes the priest's offer of a Catholic burial for Sarah, insisting that she be cremated because the priest represents the Rival and because he means to prevent her resurrection. Yet Bendrix arrives late and misses the cremation he had arranged: "I hadn't, after all, 'seen the last' of Sarah" (196). In fact, he immediately prays to Sarah to save him from an awkward situation with a woman he has picked up, and her mother appears as if sent: Sarah's first posthumous miracle on her way to sanctification.

Despite himself, Bendrix is an old-fashioned Catholic in his obsession with the body. Although, as Morley writes, not until 1968 in England were over half of those who died cremated, "The complete revolution in the method of disposing of the dead that cremation constituted, and the decline in formalized mourning, were obviously closely connected; both, as obviously, were connected with the decay of institutionalized religion."[28] In *Brighton Rock*, Greene has Hale cremated in a parody of religious ritual that sounds like Waugh's *Loved One*: "no cemetery, wax flowers, impoverished jam-pots of wilting and wild flowers," a voice intoning "we believe that this our brother is already at one with the One ... He has attained unity. We do not know what that One is with whom (or with which) he is now at one." The clergyman then "touched a little buzzer, the New Art doors opened, the flames flapped, and the coffin slid smoothly down into the fiery sea" (35–6). Sarah's cremation in *The End of the Affair* is similar: "It was so inhuman. Like a conveyor belt." The priest, who "talked about the Great All," made it sound like "the Great Auk" (202). Even Bendrix is unsatisfied with his "victory" over the church, recognizing its hollowness as his own rather than Catholicism's.

When Sarah's mother, who had secretly baptized her in revenge against the husband who forbade her Catholicism, says Sarah "could have been a saint," Bendrix uses patriarchal language as he contemptuously recoils from the "horrible coincidence": "You can't mark a two-year-old child for life with a bit of water and a prayer. If I began to believe that, I could believe in the body and the blood. You didn't *own* her all those years; I *owned* her. You won in the end, you don't need to remind me of that, but ... I was with her, not you. It was I who *penetrated* her, not you" (205–6; my emphasis). Finally, no longer able to deny Sarah's transcendence, he mocks it: "if this God exists, I thought, and if even you ... can change like this, we could all be saints by leaping as you leapt, by shutting the eyes and leaping once and for all; if *you* are a saint, it's not so difficult to be a saint" (238).

Greene's views, however, are not nearly so conventionally Catholic as this sounds. For not only is the end of the affair independent of Bendrix's "resurrection" – since it is implicit in Bendrix's fearfulness, jealousy, and self-loathing – so too is Sarah's conversion: both are there from the start in order to be replicated. Though Sarah was ignorant of her baptism, Bendrix calls her "a born Catholic" because "she was unhaunted by guilt." Each moment, like the confessional, freed her from "the mortmain of the past." That the *substance* of her "Catholicism" is secular, agnostic, and manifested in orgasmic "abandonment" in an adulterous affair seems gratuitous at first – though it is ultimately central. Greene was indifferent to commonplace believers and religious practitioners; *only* in "sinners" like Sarah does he locate grace. He even goes so far as to imply that she was a believer (as she was a Catholic) all along: "although," Bendrix adds, "she believed in God as little as I did – or so I thought then and wonder now" (59). The ambiguity – is Bendrix referring primarily to Sarah or to himself, or equally to both? – accords with Greene's sense that achievement and desire are always at odds.

Greene shares Bendrix's view that "the present is never here, it is always last year or next week" (60). Time, however conceived, is the enemy, the uncongenial element we inhabit briefly and badly. Like *Brighton Rock*'s Pinkie, the whiskey priest in *Power and the Glory*, who feels the appeal in death's "simplicity" (175), concentrates all life into the ultimate "dangerous moment" of temporal cessation: "Nobody really knew how long a second of pain could be. It might last a whole purgatory – or for ever" (180). Bendrix, who claims never to "lose the consciousness of time," also wonders "whether eternity might not after all exist as the endless prolongation of the moment of death" (*End of the Affair* 60, 83). What fills Bendrix's days simultaneously depletes them: "My book wasn't going well (what a waste of time the act of writing seemed, but I knew no other way of using time)" (230). Killing, whether it be time or Sarah or his own best instincts, is what Bendrix does best, yet Greene would have us believe in the life of love he shares with Henry at the end. The notion of killing time is exactly how Greene came to speak of his most ambiguous experience: his Catholic conversion (*Sort of Life* 118).

Greene's view that actions in the world do not matter subverts moral distinctions; yet his fictional exemplars, even if motivated by "inordinate pride" (*Ways of Escape* 126), behave as if they still obtained. The whiskey priest risks death to hear a dying murderer's confession; Scobie commits suicide in hope of sparing others pain; Sarah ends the affair because of her promise to God. Such quietism, though foolish and futile, is surely preferable to the activism of Pinkie, the murderer in *Power and the Glory*, and the renegade Marxist priest in *Honorary Consul* (1973). But it contradicts Eliot's defense of evil as superior to passivity and Greene's assertion, in an essay praising Mauriac, that "We are saved or damned by our thoughts, not by our actions" (*Essays* 119). Greene's fiction is wiser than his theology.

An obsession with one's own salvation or damnation would seem to be the ultimate denial of love, yet Greene argues the opposite.

The priest, Scobie, and Sarah all persuade themselves that, while salvation alone matters, they are sacrificing themselves for those they claim to love. The objects of such love are unconsoled by the sacrifice: it is not what they desire or need. The withdrawals cause immediate, measurable harm to the survivors, while the value of self-willed death is highly dubious, even for Greene. We are meant to look past the priest's fornication and cowardice, Scobie's and Sarah's adultery, even Pinkie's murders, in order to discern the spiritual worth of these characters. But acting out of Faustian pride and despair, each accepts, wills, or prays for damnation. Greene, implying that their turning from traditional morality proves their sanctity, reverses the moral condemnation of despair: "It is, one is told, the unforgivable sin, but it is a sin the corrupt or evil man never practices. He always has hope. He never reaches the freezing point of knowing absolute failure. Only the man of good will carries always in his heart this capacity for damnation" (*Heart of the Matter* 61). In *Sickness unto Death*, Kierkegaard characterized despair as "unaware of being despair." But Scobie, obsessively aware, consciously aligns himself with Pinkie and Rose of *Brighton Rock*, with life-denying forces generally.

What redeems Greene's writing is not his monolithic vision but its cracks: skepticism about the next world as well as this one, the untranscendent specificity of his fictional explorations, the doubt within his faith. Greene's habit of belief developed without certitude, its tensions not only unresolved but always increasing: "I eventually came to accept the existence of God not as an absolute truth but as a provisional one."[29] "With the approach of death," he adds, "I care less and less about religious truth. One hasn't long to wait for revelation or darkness" (*Sort of Life* 168). Yet Greene's waiting was active and productive. In a telling metaphor he claims that a writing career "has its own curious form of hell," but "It is for the act of creation one lives." He viewed his writings and travels, self-exhaustion in the pursuit of self-recuperation, as "ways of escape" (*Ways of Escape* 241, 93, 9–10) from otherwise intolerable existence; but the process validates what he would escape or deny, as he acknowledges in a credo-like statement: "The storyteller's task is 'to act as the devil's advocate, to elicit sympathy and a measure of understanding for those who lie outside the boundaries of state approval,' "[30] himself not least of these. In fulfilling this task the elegist in mourning for himself makes his most moving appeal.

CHAPTER 12

Late modernism: Lawrence Durrell

Durrell's art is death defying, a Faustian refusal to condone or accept the finite, an overreaching of self in search of permanence, or at least survival. Echoing Greene, Durrell writes, "either I start a novel or I commit suicide."[1] His novels, "inquests with open verdicts" ("Postface," *Nunquam* 259), are a problematic and equivocal record of the failure inherent in both suicide and writing, and the self-reflexive awareness that death is always both imminent and inspiriting. Durrell's fictions are trials, essays; conflicting modes of apprehension; seemingly random and jumbled collections of notes, diaries, journals, apothegms, epigrams, allusive quotations both appropriated and imagined, anecdotes, songs, syllogisms: endless language play often for play's sake. Balthazar calls *Justine*, the novel on whose manuscript he comments, a palimpsest whose multiple layers appear simultaneously.[2]

The narrator of *The Black Book* (1938), Durrell's first significant novel, calls it "the log of that universal death, the English death, which I have escaped" (83). An Anglo-Irishman born in Himalayan India, Durrell went to school in England in 1923 and lived there, alienated, until 1935: "that mean, shabby little island up there wrung my guts out of me and tried to destroy anything singular and unique in me" (*Durrell–Miller Letters*, 28 January 1937, 51). The novel fictionalizes a dreary year spent on "thin rations" in a London residential hotel in what he considered the smug, dying England of the Depression decade and the run-up to World War Two, the decade treated in *Brighton Rock*.

Originally subtitled "A Chronicle of the English Death," *The Black Book*, which self-reflexively calls itself a "strange procession of symbols across the consciousness" (154), initiates themes and motifs elaborated in Durrell's later writings. The young narrator, Lawrence Lucifer, seeks to assert his will to write, to love, to defy death, but he never explains whether his failure results from his being inherently depressive or from living through the Depression. We know he escapes England because the book begins and ends in Corfu, where it was written. Yet his two worlds are complementary, as if escape were only return, finding, like Conrad's Kurtz, in "primitive" experience only what he brings to it. The book opens retrospectively, "in the winter of our discontent," with "a gale blowing up from the Levant," bringing "the nascent fust of the tombs; the stale explosions of ancient life breathed coldly on up like leper's breath" (1–2). Deathly and deadly, the storm seems world-destroying: "we lay there in bed, dark as any dungeon, and mourned the loss of the Mediterranean. Lost, all lost" (1). Yet rather than explain what is lost or why, Lucifer depicts devitalization as inspirational: "This is the day I have chosen to begin this writing, because today we are dead among the dead; and this is an agon for the dead, a chronicle for the living . . . There is a correspondence between the present, this numbness, inertia, and that past reality of a death, whose meaning is symbolic, mythical, but real also in its symptoms . . . The correspondence of deadness with deadness is complete" (2). Lucifer has become the effigy of the death he writes of escaping, sharing "that correspondence of death with the season, and with all those other seasons which oppress me when I begin to write of them. No mummies, chunks of tissue latched to bone; no pillars of salt, no cadavers, have ever been half so dead as we are today" (3). And so he recounts "the English death," which explains everything and nothing.

Until the end, which is also the beginning, Lucifer represents himself as trapped in a stultifying malaise, victimized by an alter ego named Herbert "Death" Gregory, who insists that "My disease is egocentric, and therefore mortal" (161), and who mourns, when his wife dies, his own death: "Are there only the dead *left* to bury the dead?" he asks rhetorically (201). Satiated with the death in which he has wallowed, Lucifer seeks an erotic escape from morbid self-absorption, but finds love that "which we dare not offer to the world" (141). He attempts, then, to make order of chaos, art out of failure: "If there is any passion in this writing, anywhere, it is because I am creating a death I almost shared" (210). Lucifer implies what he soon explicates, and what Durrell, like a secular Greene, often reiterates: that the embracing and rendering of death may be the only self-validating gesture. At the end, "Greece lies dead among the oak leaves, the bare mulch, the merdes, outside the window"; the narrator, in bed with the woman he has anatomized more than loved, concludes irresolutely, "This is how it ends" (222–3). Escape and entrapment become indistinguishable.

The Black Book established a pattern for Durrell: loss, survival, mourning. Early in World War Two he fled Corfu ahead of the Nazi invasion, and worked for the British Council and Foreign Office in Cairo and Alexandria. After his resettlement, he wrote *Prospero's Cell*, an ostensibly spontaneous artist's journal from 10 April 1937 to 1 January 1941. Yet, written in Alexandria during the War (*Letters* May 1944, 169), it was achieved only with time and distance. In "Epilogue in Alexandria," the coda to *Prospero's Cell*, Durrell writes that his present location is the "last landmark on the edge of Africa. The battleships in their arrowed blackness turn slowly in the harbour. The loss of Greece [to the Nazis] has been an amputation. All Epictetus could not console one against it" (131). *Prospero's Cell*'s retrospective recounting makes it an elegiac fiction like Durrell's novels.

Durrell became unhappily cognizant of his new surroundings while recalling Corfu. His "Note" to *Justine*, to *The Alexandria Quartet*'s virtual heroine, reads, "Only the city is real." Yet that reality was initially enervating: a "smashed up broken down shabby Neapolitan town, with its Levantine mounds of houses peeling in the sun. A sea flat dirty brown and waveless rubbing the port . . . if one could write a single line of anything that had a human smell to it here, one would be a genius" (*Letters* May 1944, 168). He wrote the first part of his "Book of the Dead," as he called the *Quartet* for ten years (*Letters* March 1937, 65; 9 July 1947, 212), on Cyprus as the war between the Greeks and Turks was beginning; *that* crisis was recorded in *Bitter Lemons* (1957), which was written in England. Then the last three books of the *Quartet* were written in Provence. Like Lawrence, Forster, and Greene, Durrell, who called himself "one of the world's expatriates" (*Letters* 27 January 1937, 50), constantly sought a congenial environment: "I am, and I remain, an expatriate. That vague sense of exile has never quite left me. But at the same time it has meant that I can feel at ease anywhere, given a minimum of sunshine. The expatriate carries his country with him, inside him: everywhere belongs to him, because he belongs to nowhere."[3] He seeks always to depict the last, lost world, which, though displaced, remains a powerful ghostly presence until it is written through. As he writes in *A Key to Modern British Poetry* (1952), "Art describes the kind of reality which is already dead for the artist" (39).

In this book of criticism, based on lectures he delivered while the *Quartet* was gestating, Durrell seeks to do what literature, "only one facet of the prism which we call culture," necessarily does: incorporate such understanding as "other departments of human thought" like psychology, anthropology, and science can provide. Modern writers like Joyce, Proust, Eliot, and Rilke, he writes, deployed contemporary rethinking about the universe, time, language, and character. Just as ancient Greeks viewed mathematics, music, poetry, and sculpture as interconnected, so today the arts and sciences are "interlocking and mutually fertilizing" (*Key* 1, xii). Durrell analyzes (not always successfully) the ideas of Darwin, Frazer, Einstein, Freud, and Groddeck as fundamental to the cultural revolution of modernism and, eventually, to his own fictional enterprise. He examines Freud's theories of repression and dreams for what they reveal about inner reality and otherwise unexpressed desires (51–2). Quoting Freud's "idea of regarding every sexual act as a process in which four persons are involved" as epigraph to *Justine*, Durrell explores androgyny as a key to human identity, creating a quadrangle of lovers – Melissa, Justine, Nessim, and Darley – of whom Darley says, "The four of us were unrecognized complementaries of one another, inextricably bound together" (*AQ* 165).

Durrell also sought to apply Einsteinian relativity and space–time continuum to relationships as a means of persuading people "to become their own contemporaries" (*Key* x). Asserting that "the Relativity proposition was directly responsible for abstract painting, atonal music, and formless (or at any rate cyclic forms in) literature" (*AQ* 306), Pursewarden endorses Einsteinian perspectivism: "Our view of reality is conditioned by our position in space and time – not by our personalities as we like to think. Thus every interpretation of reality is based upon a unique position. Two paces east or west and the whole picture is changed" (210). Similarly, Darley decides that "death is a relative question" (176), and Justine says, "the dead think of us as dead" (164). Like many others, however, Durrell confounded relativity and quantum mechanics: for example, when he speaks of the joining of "subject and object," the denial of causality and finite understanding, and the principle of indeterminacy (*Key* 27–30). It is Heisenberg, not Einstein, who might have voiced Pursewarden's thought that "observation throws down a field about the observed person or object" (*AQ* 520), or asked Darley's question: "If two or more explanations of a single human action are as good as each other then what does action mean but an illusion?" (791). Durrell later confessed to certain mistakes, as in having "confused Bergsonian time with Einsteinian time."[4]

Throughout his career Durrell deployed death as incident, theme, motif, setting, even character. Echoing Lawrence Lucifer, he writes of his war-time situation, the context for both the *Quartet* and *The Avignon Quintet*, "we are all in Limbo and deader than the really dead or the practically dying" (*Letters*, April 1944, 164), which the *Quartet* echoes: "we are dead and live this life as a sort of limbo" (76). Like *The Black Book*'s characters, his inhabitants of Alexandria, with its "atmosphere of sex and death" (*Letters* May 1944, 168), are dead and kicking from the first, for death is initiatory rather than terminal. Durrell accepts death as radically reconceptualized by Freud and Einstein: "It is one of the paradoxes of the new space-time," Durrell writes, that if time is conceived as synchronic "*we can just as easily situate death in the present as in the future*" (*Key* 36). Hence, his characters are "playing-card characters of the living" (*AQ* 661), shades partaking of the city's "obsessive rhythms of death" (567). When Darley returns to Alexandria in *Clea*, it is "like a summons back to the Underworld" (657), to the wasteland of martial conflict that is both external and internal. "The dead are everywhere," he says (833), and during the war, the barber is told, "you are shaving the dead while they are still alive" (663).

Death is modernist in the *Quartet*: characters disappear but remain hovering presences, or return in altered form. The paradigmatic figure is Capodistria, known as Da Capo, whose musical name means play it again from the beginning. His supposed death, hanging "in the still air like a bad smell, like a bad joke" (176), climaxes *Justine*. Subsequently, flowers are placed annually on the elaborate grave on which he "had certainly spared no expense ... On the slab was engraved the ironic text: 'Not Lost But Gone Before'" (807). Toward the *Quartet*'s end several characters gather at the gravesite to resurrect the past by reading an apparently posthumous letter of Capodistria's in which he ambiguously describes black magic experiments: "I have chosen the Dark Path towards my own light." Balthazar portentously suggests that "We get too certain of ourselves travelling backwards and forwards along the tramlines of empirical fact" (812–13); yet the truth *seems* to be simply that Capodistria is alive.

Scobie, the *Quartet*'s most vital "minor" character, is a homosexual policeman who is unaccountably made head of the Secret Service. He has, as he puts it, "tendencies," when there is a full moon and the fleet is in, to "slip on female duds and my 'Dolly Varden'" hat (231). Both joyously alive and death-obsessed from the first, "Scobie is getting on for seventy and still afraid to die; his one fear is that he will awake one morning and find himself lying dead" (101). After much foreshadowing and imaging, Scobie's death, from being fatally kicked by sailors he accosts while dressed in his "tendency" clothes, seems unequivocal. In *Justine*'s Workpoints, which are and are not part of the novel, Balthazar describes Scobie's farcical funeral in loving detail:

> His pockets were full of love-letters to his aide Hassan, and the whole vice squad turned out to sob at his grave. All these black gorillas crying like babies. A very Alexandrian demonstration of affection. Of course the grave was too small for the coffin. The grave-diggers had knocked off for lunch, so a scratch team of policemen was brought into action. Usual muddle. The coffin fell over on its side and the old man nearly rolled out. Shrieks. The padre was furious. The British Consul nearly dead of shame. But all Alexandria was there and a good time was had by all. (199–200)

This funeral, full of pomp and confusion, elicits a not unfitting epitaph: "You would have thought he was a saint" (332). Instead of fading, Scobie attains a two-fold immortality, first through rhetorical recreation: nearly everyone does an imitation indistinguishable from the original. Second, he exemplifies Foucault's notion that a "convicted criminal could become after his death a sort of saint, his memory honoured and his grave respected,"[5] for Scobie is sanctified, as El Scob, a reincarnation of El Yacoub, a long forgotten local holy man. And his bathtub, formerly a still that produced lethal whiskey, is now "invoked to confer fertility upon the childless – and with success, too, if one could judge by the great number of the offerings" (715).

Scobie's representation is rich with intertexts. His name derives from Greene's suicidal policeman in *The Heart of the Matter*, which is also set during World War Two. Forster wrote his *Alexandria*, to which Durrell acknowledges his debt in Notes to *Justine* (203), when stationed there during World War One;[6] and Aziz who, though not overtly homosexual, reserves his love for his dead wife, an old woman, and a man, is a character source for Durrell's Scobie. Scobie's sanctification echoes that of Mrs. Moore, whose "eternal goodness" had transformed her into "Esmiss Esmoor, a Hindu goddess" (*Passage to India* 312, 225). He also reincarnates Eliot's Tiresias (233), a figure of transsexual and regenerative power. Durrell does what Forster could not: write approvingly of homosexuality and still have his work published. Balthazar, a more fully developed homosexual character than Scobie, thanks God, or rather the Demiurge "who wrongly believed himself to be God" (39), for sparing him "an undue interest in love. At least the invert escapes this fearful struggle to give oneself to another. Lying with one's own kind enjoying an experience, one can still keep free the part of one's mind which dwells in Plato, or gardening, or the differential calculus" (82). Balthazar shows the fallacy of his thinking when he attempts suicide because of a disastrous infatuation for a handsome Greek actor who is "small-spirited, dirty, venal and empty" (704). But as Forster does Aziz, Durrell treats Balthazar, who learns through his suffering, with consistent sympathy.

Durrell also shares Greene's and Waugh's antipathy to cremation. Parodying the scene in Greene's *The End of the Affair* when Bendrix successfully opposes the church's offer of burial, Durrell has Clea write of *his* priest, "What a beast that man is. He behaved as though her body had become Church property" (823). Yet Durrell represents cremation as equally ghastly, lacking in ritual; the hideous crematorium was "like a hastily improvised furnace in a concentration camp" (822). Lacking religious orientation, Durrell seems to find all the alternatives devoid of meaning.

Most important of those who are "Not Lost But Gone Before" is Pursewarden, the *Quartet*'s main speaker for artistic vision despite his being a suicide of apparently little significance in *Justine*, an action, Darley thinks, that Pursewarden had "taken so easily, with so little premeditation" (180). Pursewarden's death is equivocal because much of the *Quartet* offers inadequate explanations of its motivation; because large chunks of his posthumous papers appear in full and many characters quote him verbatim; because he embodies the central themes of artistic reshaping, erotic love, and "resurrection from the dead" (707); and because Durrell elevates him above mortality by reenacting the ancient notion that the king, "as God the star, wandering on earth, is immortal and may therefore not ...

die a natural death" (803). An increasingly forceful presence, Pursewarden insists that the artist "seeks his real friends among the dead and the unborn" (439), in whose realm he resides even while alive. Just before his suicide, he demonstrates the interchangeability of eros and thanatos when he makes love to Melissa, who tells him, "Your life is dead, closed up" (531); sympathizing with *her* plight (she too is dying), he leaves her £500 that he earned, appropriately, for writing an epitaph.

In a reversal reminiscent of Wilde's eponymous hero of *Dorian Gray*, Pursewarden finds life draining from him as his art becomes successful: "He has realized that people are walking the street with a Reputation now and not a man. They see him no longer – and all his work was done in order to draw attention to the lonely, suffering figure he felt himself to be. His name has covered him like a tombstone. And now comes the terrifying thought perhaps there *is* no one left to see?" (97). His death, according to one view, is a form of self-assertion, a fulfillment of Shelley's notion that poets are the unacknowledged legislators of the world: Pursewarden was "fond of saying 'People will realize one day that it is only the artist who can make things really *happen*; that is why society should be founded upon him.' A *deus ex machina*! In his dying he had used [people] like ... a public convenience, as if to demonstrate the truth of his own aphorism!" (566). Yet his death's mystery allows survivors to re-create him for their own purposes.

Seeing writing as a form of death and herself as a character in someone else's fiction, Clea says that Pursewarden's "art overleaps the barrier ... what we actually saw in him was only the human disguise that the artist wore ... Pursewarden carried the secret of his everyday life over into the grave with him, leaving us only his books to marvel at and his epitaph to puzzle over: 'Here lies an intruder from the East' ... The death of an artist is quite unassailable. One can only smile and bow" (383). In this fiction of proliferating perspectives, later versions of Pursewarden's death tell different stories: for example, everyone "seemed to be afflicted by the air of gravid depression which sudden death always confers upon the uncomfortably living" (539). Pursewarden, then, is a minor character who dies a seemingly unequivocal death early in *Justine*, yet whose words and voice, and the endless talk about him, articulate the *Quartet*'s values and concerns. Darley ultimately says of him: "He seems to change shape so quickly at every turn of the road that one is forced to revise each idea about him almost as soon as it is formulated" (744). He is even recalled as an influential writer in Durrell's later novel, *Tunc* (242).

In *Clea*'s Workpoints, Durrell writes, "Death is a metaphor; nobody dies to himself" (881), at least not in this text in which one character dies for another, a third apparently dies but returns after another is buried for him, one is resurrected as a saint, others as characters we thought were someone else; or they seem to grow new parts – a hand, a nose, hair, a smile – to replace those worn out by mortality, Durrell anticipating medical technology's interchangeable organs. *Tunc*'s narrator speaks of "Chemical reincarnations by the terms of which we all become spare parts of one another" (53); elsewhere Durrell writes:

> Time is the measure of our death-consciousness. There are other organisms, we know, which measure time by a heat-unit. They must have a different idea of death. Then there are those so-called simple cells which multiply by binary fission – they simply divide into two. You might say one dies into two, leaving no corpse behind it as a human being does. Does the caterpillar die to become a moth or would you call it being born? We do not know. In some cases birth and death would seem to be almost interchangeable terms. (*Key* 4)

Durrell's cue for this representation of death is *Beyond the Pleasure Principle*, in which Freud writes of "how little agreement there is among biologists on the subject of natural death." Freud cites one scientist who "does not regard the appearance of a 'dead body' – a dead portion of the living substance – as the criterion of death, but defines death as 'the termination of individual development'. In this sense protozoa too are mortal; in their case death always coincides with reproduction, but is to some extent obscured by it, since the whole substance of the parent animal may be transmitted directly into the young offspring" (45, 47). Hence, birth and death and reproduction become indistinguishable from each other.

In the *Quartet* love and art arise from, and are fertilized by, life's carnage. Its synchronic first three books all anticipate the war about to begin. *Clea* opens with Darley's return to "a city now swallowed by a war" (658) in which "death heightens every tension and permits us fewer of the half-truths by which we normally live" (665). Darley describes Alexandria transformed by an air raid: "I had no idea . . . that the city could be so beautiful in the mere saturnalia of a war ... We were staring at the burning embers of Augustine's

Carthage ... we are observing the fall of city man" (668). The destruction seems worse for ignoring those below: "I had not realized the impersonality of war before. There was no room for human beings or thought of them under this vast umbrella of coloured death. Each drawn breath had become only a temporary refuge" (669).

Like Sarah and Bendrix in *End of the Affair*, Clea and Darley seek a comforting touch: "Shivering, we turned to one another, feeling suddenly orphaned in this benighted world between light and darkness" (669), and then make love amid bombardment, "with the deliberate affirmation which can come only from the foreknowledge and presence of death" (727). Later they swim idyllically in a lake containing corpses of seven Greek sailors, mummified in a continuation of ancient Egyptian practice: the corpses "had been roped in sacks and leadweighted at the feet, so that they now stood upright ... in the traditional funeral dress of mariners" (834). This underwater necropolis, with its inhabitants whom they view as familiars (846), recalls the "whole universe" of death that Lawrence's Gerald Crich discovers when he tries to save Diana, his drowning sister (*Women in Love* 184). It becomes the scene of Clea's crucifixion in an underwater spear-gun accident: "her right hand had been pierced and nailed to the wreck by the steel arrow." Darley, who imagines the horrific accident to be "some incomprehensible dream, fabricated perhaps in the dead minds of the seven brooding figures," cuts her free and then, after pronouncing her dead, pumps her back to life in what he calls "this pitiful simulacrum of the sexual act – life saving, life-giving ... It must have hurt," he thinks, "as the first few breaths hurt a newly born child. The body of Clea was protesting at this forcible rebirth" (848–52). She subsequently receives a steel hand, that proves "almost more competent even than an ordinary flesh-and-blood member," with which she paints "pictures of truly troubling originality and authority" (874). After successfully surviving her death, she becomes, like Lily Briscoe, an artist at last.

In the futuristic *Revolt of Aphrodite*, which comprises *Tunc* and *Nunquam*, Durrell takes the notion of artificial revitalization to its logical extreme when he has Iolanthe – prostitute, world-famous actress, but now dead – replicated as a robot indistinguishable from the original. The process recalls the ancient Egyptian faith in the power of invocation: "To speak the names of the dead is to make them live again," for when the narrator begins to recreate Iolanthe, his beautiful dead lover, "I repeated her name to myself in the Greek way, reclaiming the original image of her" (*Nunquam* 180). This invention, the ultimate death-defying act in Durrell's writings, is a great success at first: "she was so damn real that it was difficult not to think of her as a 'person'" (222). But the pressures of the world and love again prove too great: the machine Iolanthe, like the original, "commits suicide."

The invented love goddess is a triumph of the appropriately named international cartel, Merlin – "cartelization" serving post-modern texts as industrial technology does modern ones.[7] The novel's narrator and chief inventor of Iolanthe is Felix Charlock, whose name suggests one burned by playing with supernatural powers. He spends the first half of *Nunquam* undergoing the "pain of regained identity" (2), a sense of self he had lost in *Tunc*. Having succumbed in the earlier book to the malign temptations of Merlin and the beautiful Benedicta, he entered into a relationship with her that he calls "the whole deathscapade of lovemaking ... afterwards she lay like the ghost of rigor mortis itself" (*Tunc* 137, 142). Then, ineffectually fighting Merlin's autocracy, he causes the death of his son rather than that of his intended target: the Faustian Julian, the firm's head, who maintains that "I have always behaved as much like an immortal as I could" (*Nunquam* 160). Julian ordered the new Io built out of love and fear, seeking not to imitate nature but to transcend and improve it. "I wasn't hoping for reality," he says, "so much as for the perfect illusion which is probably more real than reality itself is for most people" (124). He desires a simulacrum of love, but it proves life-defying and fatal, a parody of Darley's with Clea, a playing at Abelard and Eloise. Incapable of eating and defecating, the robot Iolanthe is also as incapable of sex as Julian, who was castrated by his father, Merlin, for having sexually enslaved Benedicta, his sister. In the novel's most bizarre episode, Benedicta showed "herself worthy" of Julian by turning killer, like everyone else in the family, pushing her first husband into quicksand and then watching "with a holy concentration" as he slowly died (24–30).

Like all of Durrell's artists, Felix is both haunted by the past and determined to escape it by shaping the future. He seeks through invention to weld memory and desire, but the creative act invariably defines itself self-reflexively, against its author (like the invention that kills his son), rather than as successful control. Early in

Nunquam, he says, "While I am writing one book ... I write another about it, then a third about *it*, and so on ... Like those monkeys in the Indian frescoes (so human, so engaging, like some English critics) who can dance only with their index fingers up each other's behinds" (6). Of the second Iolanthe, created in the image of the first but supposedly uncontaminated by her death, we are told: "She was, so to speak, free" (223). Her construction, in fact, would be an act of hubris except that, as Felix says gloomily, "The gods are all dead, or gone on holiday" (186). Awakened into life, what Felix calls "the land of the living, the land of the dying" (220), she can do little but repeat prior failures while clutching at illusions of freedom. So she arouses jealousy in Benedicta, now Felix's wife (193); "falls in love" with Julian; scolds him "for defections of behavior toward an all too real (though now dead) Iolanthe!" (233); tries to resume "her" acting career; flees her captors/creators; again becomes both prostitute and murderer; and finally leaps from St. Paul's Whispering Gallery, with the obsessed Julian clutching her. She can no more live Io's life successfully than could her human original.

The novel's ending, anticipating that of many postmodernist novels, is pseudo-apocalyptic carnivalesque despite, or perhaps because of, the robot's demise. Felix is not only supposedly cured and free (always dubious concepts in Durrell), but also reunited, and at one for the first time, with the transformed Benedicta, herself finally released from Julian's dominance. Felix even winds up in charge of Merlin, including its "special little funerary monument" that houses the firm's contracts on microfilm (209). Seeking to leap into freedom and mutual trust, Felix intends to destroy the past's records, and to dance and keep on dancing with Benedicta "even though Rome burn." The result is that all will change, or perhaps not. As he is told: "Either everything will disintegrate, the firm will begin to dissolve; or else nothing, Mr. Felix, absolutely nothing." He responds: "So it will be either/or once again; it will be now or never" (258). The problem, however, lies in Durrell's vagueness, his tendency to use material circumstances as backdrop, or fictional pyrotechnics, rather than as matter of greatest moment, a tendency he indulges most fully in his last major work, *The Avignon Quintet*.[8]

Blanford, the *Quintet*'s clandestine protagonist/novelist, seeks "to reassess the meaning and value of all these episodes on paper ... Scribbling all this gives me something to do, I am resetting the broken bones of the past ... I am in touch with them all through their diaries and manuscripts and letters" (*Monsieur* 13). Abandoning the modernist elision of authorial presence, the *Quintet* explicitly evokes a master's hand at work both in and above the texts: not only Blanford but "someone like old D – the devil at large?" (292). Such intrusiveness need not be bound by conventional mortal or fictive constraints, though Blanford supposes that "he was simply another vainglorious fool of a writer with insufficient courage to tell the whole truth about life" (291).

In *Livia*, which follows *Monsieur*, Blanford calls the series "a quincunx of novels" (11), a form bearing mystical meaning derived from the pattern of trees in "an ancient Greek temple grove" (158). Durrell's source is Thomas Browne's "The Garden of Cyrus" (1658), a treatise on the quincunx's spiritual significance. What Browne calls "the sacred letter X"[9] may be rotated to produce a circle, the geometrical sign of perfection; as a form of the Greek cross, it has come to symbolize Christ. But with a dot (or tree) at its center, the quincunx also images the Greek *theta*, which, as the first letter of thanatopsis, represents death. Browne found the quincunx, which has long been regarded as having spiritual properties, everywhere in the ancient and natural worlds, a fact to which he attached great significance. The quincunx's form and traditional associations emblematically express Durrell's view, which he shared with Lawrence, of Christianity as death-obsessed,[10] but Durrell's is an attenuated version, lacking Browne's and Lawrence's historic and spiritual resonance.

Contemporary Marxist critics Fredric Jameson and Terry Eagleton view postmodernism as pastiche, devoid of parody's satiric motive or political content, a "cynical belated revenge wreaked by bourgeois culture" on the revolutionary *avant-garde*. In the next chapter, I will examine texts that challenge Eagleton's notion that postmodernism is "depthless, styleless, dehistoricized, decathected" and "remorselessly empt[ied] of its political content."[11] Here, however, I would agree that Jameson and Eagleton accurately characterize much postmodern architecture, Andy Warhol's paintings, deconstructive criticism, and recent fiction like *The Avignon Quintet*.

Monsieur opens with a self-conscious narrative about a train journey, initiated by death, in which the narrator, perhaps unintentionally, numbers himself among the deceased: "The *late* traveller was myself, Bruce, and the journey was none of my choosing. The telegram which had summoned me . . . told me of the suicide of my oldest and best friend, Piers de Nogaret" (4; my emphasis). Blanford later places this episode under erasure: "The suicide – was that right?" (26). In *Monsieur*'s last episode, Blanford dines with his old friend, the Duchess of Tu, or rather with her ghost: "for it was some time since the name Duchess had appeared on the death-map of the stars" (305). The Escher-like structure becomes even more prominent if we pursue the question of when Tu's death occurs. At the end of *Monsieur* she has been dead for "some time," yet at the beginning of *Livia* Blanford says that she has just died. If so, then *Livia* must be earlier, in fictional time, than the end of *Monsieur*; but *Monsieur* is mentioned as an extant novel early in *Livia* (8). Further, Blanford gets an orthopedic brace at the beginning of *Livia* that he does not have at the end of *Monsieur* and which, it appears, he obtains later in time. Though Blanford says that only Sutcliffe is a creature of his imagination, Tu's death, like Sutcliffe's, becomes a fiction within a fiction, or a series of fictions, indulged in for the sake of gameplaying. Unlike death in the *Quartet*, which matters because of the felt reality of characters like Capodistria, Scobie, and Pursewarden, and about which incertitude concerns knowledge and perspective, Tu's life and death, neither of which is represented, are interchangeable and meaningless, merely words on the page.

Blanford receives "a telegram signed by Sutcliffe" but sent by Tu (who is "already dead") about *Monsieur*'s manuscript: "Refuse to be rushed off the planet in this clumsy and ignominious fashion. Kindly arrange to have me die by less theatrical means. Rob." Blanford stares mockingly in the mirror, contemplating the self, his own and those he has struggled to create and destroy, "the most fragile of illusions," and he thinks: "It is still a moot point whether Socrates, in fact, existed as something more than a character in a novel by Plato. And what of me? he thought. Am I possibly an invention of someone like old D [Durrell?] – the devil at large?" (*Monsieur* 289–92). Although Socrates exists and dies for us only within the Dialogues, Plato never represents him contemplating his author's death, as Blanford contemplates Durrell's.

When Vonnegut meets his alter ego, Kilgore Trout, in *Breakfast of Champions* or Fowles his characters toward the end of *French Lieutenant's Woman*, the author challenges the independent status of his creations; but their fictional reality, like our own mortality, has been both firmly established and contingent. The craft consists in making the characters and their plights sufficiently mimetic to survive authorial intrusiveness. "Reality," the Wildean Pursewarden says, "was always trying to copy the imagination of man, from which it derived" (*AQ* 286). Creator and creature, character and text, substance and shade – all seek to invent worlds in order to live in them, for as Pursewarden proclaims, "There are only as many realities as you care to imagine" (315). The ontological indeterminacy of the *Quintet*'s fictive levels, however, suggests not only that everything about its characters is unknowable, but that nothing about them matters: there are no worlds in which to live, and no one to live in them.

Toward the end of *Quinx*, the *Quintet*'s final book, Durrell evokes richly allusive historical events and meaning that might have contextualized his fiction. His surviving characters gather after World War Two at the Pont du Gard, the ancient Roman aqueduct outside of Avignon associated with the Knights Templar and their treasure. Although the richest and most powerful military force in Europe, the Templars were destroyed in the early fourteenth century by an alliance between King Philip of France and Pope Clement V. Historians have never satisfactorily shown why or how this destruction occurred, but explanations have been advanced concerning religious heterodoxy and sexual deviance. The *Quintet* conceives of Hitler, who was interested in the occult, as seeking the long-lost treasure, whether gold or Grail, in order to establish a new knightly order, and thus insure victory and world domination. What is unearthed, however, in an echo of the *Quartet*'s end, is only and always the possibility of beginning anew, as "Blanford thought that if ever he wrote the scene he would say: 'It was at this precise moment that reality prime rushed to the aid of fiction and the totally unpredictable began to take place!'" (*Quinx* 201). But unfortunately it does not: the history is inert backdrop, only another fictive layer.

One postmodernist tendency, as Jameson and Eagleton imply, is to extrapolate from the notion that history is relative, in Einstein's sense, to its being unknowable, or merely a series of retrospective reconstructions. But having many stories to tell is not the same as having none; nor does revisionist history make reality solipsistic or life and death synonymous. Forster's Mrs. Moore and Woolf's Mrs. Ramsay seem "alive" after their deaths, but their survival is largely a matter of speaking, and of seeing, and of our awareness that the vitally alive remain a force in the world after their material demise.

Durrell knows this in the *Quartet*, where his fictionally dead characters continue as presences, so that, as in mourning, "after" and "before" become both definitive and elusive. Writers like Beckett, Robbe-Grillet, Fuentes, Nabokov, Barth, Barthelme, and Coover, especially in their later fiction, often reject this modernist premise, refusing to vitalize characters, flattening out affect, undermining fictional worlds even as they are being posited. The *Quintet* takes this tendency to an extreme by transforming relativistic incertitude into quantum mechanics' indeterminacy and chaos theory's non-linear dynamics, but abstractly, in a vacuum.

Forster may not explain Mrs. Wilcox's death or Woolf Mrs. Ramsay's, but their lives are fully realized and explored, and the relationship between their lives and deaths and continuing presence is central to their texts. For Greene, Bendrix's return from death in *The End of the Affair* is a miracle; for Durrell's *Quartet* death is a mystery that cannot be fully explained but that can be inexhaustibly explored because it matters greatly. The *Quintet* seems the dead end of a moribund tradition because it reduces life and death to a fictional trope, a textual question about the fictive level on which characters exist. The thinness of its conception is all the clearer when juxtaposed with postmodernist texts that return to history.

CHAPTER 13

Postmodernism: history, chaos, and death

Despite the charge that postmodernism is affectless, depthless, and ahistorical, many post-World War Two novelists directly engaged the war and the Holocaust, or used these events as a springboard into history, "that which hurts" (in Jameson's memorable phrase). Robert Darnton writes that history "refuses to confine itself to the past and flows into the present, pushing and moving things that seem to be fixed in a narrow frame of time."[1] He suggests that to enter what Henry James called "a palpable imaginable *visitable* past"[2] is to enter the land of the dead and have what we "know" destabilized:

> Exposure to the past unsettles the sense of the knowable. One is always running up against mysteries – not simply ignorance . . . but the unfathomable strangeness of life among the dead. Historians return from that world like missionaries who once set out to conquer foreign cultures and then come back converted, won over to the otherness of others. When we resume our daily rounds we sometimes harangue the public with our tales . . . Like the ancient mariner, we have talked with the dead, but we find it hard to make ourselves heard among the living.[3]

What seems metaphoric in Darnton's description is literalized by postmodernist writers: victims of war, genocide, slavery, and the Holocaust appear as they might have lived or to exact revenge for lives denied them. Their posthumous discourses both articulate a transcendence of death and give voice to death itself.

Postmodernist revenants differ from their predecessors. Braz Cubas, Lawrence's man who died, and Faulkner's Addie Bundren speak from beyond their deaths "to th' yet unknowing world" (in Horatio's phrase), offering a perspective that would be otherwise unavailable. Mrs. Ramsay imagines herself a revenant in someone's drawing-room and then, like Forster's Mrs. Wilcox and Mrs. Moore, becomes a posthumous presence in Part III of *To the Light-*

house. Conrad's Jim, Ford's Dowell, Faulkner's Uncle Ike become shades prematurely, without literally dying. Such boundary violations traditionally required "realistic" explanation, or else seem uncanny because unconstrained by rational understanding.

But boundary violations are central to postmodernism: the *donées* that need and receive no explanation. Enacting modernism's rhetorical strategies, postmodernist fictions flaunt their scaffolding and seams rather than hiding them; make author and character interchangeable; and freely juxtapose irreconcilable realities inhabited by the living and dead, new characters and intertextual ones, the fictive and historical – without, as was once common practice, privileging the first term in each of these pairings. Linda Hutcheon writes, "There is no dialectic in the postmodern"[4] – mutually exclusive worlds and conditions exist side by side without qualifying each other. In the writings of Fuentes, Pynchon, Grass, Coover, Reed, Doctorow, Thomas, and Rushdie, dead, borrowed, and historical personages, no more circumscribed than other characters, participate in all levels of action. Postmodernist writers themselves commonly intrude into their characters' worlds and fates. In *The Exaggerations of Peter Prince*, Steve Katz's narrator says that his character "knew he was going to die, no doubt about it, and he tossed my way such an immense glare of hate that if I wasn't sure of what was happening I might have turned away in shame" (257). Brian McHale comments on Prince's awareness of his doubly unstable existence: "a character's knowledge of his own fictionality often functions as a kind of master-trope for determinism – cultural, historical, psychological determinism, but especially the inevitability of death."[5] Postmodernist texts undermine categorical barriers between levels of fictional realities.

Juxtaposing the endings of Lawrence's "Woman Who Rode Away" (1925) and Pynchon's *Gravity's Rainbow* (1973) illustrates the modernist/postmodernist transformation. Lawrence's final moment focuses on the sacrificial woman who, understanding now "what the men were waiting for" (581), remains forever poised to receive the knife that always/never strikes. *Gravity's Rainbow*, the great postmodernist conspiracy/apocalypse text, finally reveals that, the screen "a dim page spread before us, white and silent," we have "always been at the movies (haven't we?)." The ending interrogates all that has gone before, rewriting its ontological status, denying it without undoing it. The final image is a rocket, "a bright angel of death," which is launched within and without the novel's film. It is poised to annihilate everyone – "Now everybody –" including the film's and the book's characters, Pynchon's readers, and the Cold War world beyond (887). Narrative failure in modernist texts like *Heart of Darkness*, *The Good Soldier*, *Portrait of the Artist*, and "The Woman Who Rode Away" results from the incompatibility between the characters' fears, memories, or desires and the fictive reality that contains them; the status of the material world beyond subjectivity is essentially unchallenged. *Gravity's Rainbow*'s inconclusive conclusion, however, spills beyond its fictional confines in order to threaten not only all its represented worlds, but ours as well.

Fictionalizing the breakdown of national boundaries and wartime alliances after World War Two, as well as the establishment of German zones, Pynchon juxtaposes historic and imagined events, "the new Uncertainty" of personal and political identity, without privileging either: "Ghosts used to be either likenesses of the dead or wraiths of the living. But here in the Zone categories have been blurred badly ... some still live, some have died, but many, many have forgotten which they are ... images of the Uncertainty" (353). Seeking to reconstitute Slothrop's identity, unknown forces had sent him "into the Zone to be present at his own assembly – perhaps, heavily paranoid voices have whispered, *his time's assembly*," but the plan "went wrong. He is being broken down instead, and scattered" (860–1). *Gravity's Rainbow* identifies layers of conspiracy (international cartels, technological forces, secret societies, alien intruders) beneath the official history of World War Two that help to explain the paranoia of Cold War history and fiction.

The current revolution in scientific thought, chaos theory and its corollary, complexity (the latest attempt to discover the universe's principles of order[6]), follows from relativity and quantum mechanics as postmodernist fiction does from high and late modernism. Though seeming to extend the randomness and unpredictability of quantum mechanics, chaos/complexity theory may ultimately link Einstein and Heisenberg, physics and metaphysics, a dubious past and an unpredictable future. David Lodge sees randomness as one of postmodernism's five strategies (along with contradiction, discontinuity, excess, and short circuit[7]), but this strategy requires great care in planning even (or especially) if *apparent* randomness is to result. Similarly, chaos theory turns out to oppose randomness, for it depends on principles of ordering like "sensitive dependence on initial conditions" and scaling or self-similarity: "symmetry across scale . . . recursion, pattern inside of pattern."[8] Slight variations in initial conditions suggest why history, human existence, can easily go wrong. In *Great Expectations*, a Proustian-sounding Pip says of his first visit to Miss Havisham's: "That was a memorable day to me, for it made great changes in me. But it is the same with any life. Imagine one selected day struck out of it, and think how different its course would have been . . . think for a moment of the long chain of iron or gold, of thorns or flowers, that would never have bound you, but for the formation of the first link on one memorable day" (72). Dickens anticipates Poincaré's turn-of-the-century warning that "small differences in the initial conditions produce very great ones in the final phenomena. A small error in the former will produce an enormous error in the latter. Prediction becomes impossible,"[9] a pronouncement scientists largely ignored until computers proved it true. Like chaologists, postmodernists like Pynchon, Spark, Roth, Morrison, and Swift keep circling back to initial conditions, imagine them different, pursue the consequences, and find the new versions radically different.

In "Connoisseur of Chaos," Wallace Stevens presciently anticipates a second tenet of chaos theory:

> A. A violent order is disorder; and
> B. A great disorder is an order. These
> Two things are one.

Scaling in postmodernist fiction elaborates the infinite regress graphically and punningly represented by Escher's woodcut *Fish and Scales*, "in which each scale of two large fish is itself a tiny fish exactly duplicating the larger fish of which it constitutes a part [or] the picture which used to appear on Quaker Oats packages, showing a Quaker holding a Quaker Oats package on which there is a picture of a Quaker holding a Quaker Oats package, and so on."[10] Recursion simultaneously repeats and parodies, validates and subverts, whatever is taken as primary reality. All ten embedded novels in Calvino's *If on a Winter's Night* echo the primary story that contains them; Barth's *Letters* is a collective sequel to all his earlier novels, revivifying their major characters in a new fictional world.[11] Enacting chaos theory, postmodernist fiction constitutes order within disorder in ways that replicate and subvert realistic and modernist expectations.

Characters in these fictions need never die, or their deaths need not be final. Such representation can trivialize death (as well as history and fiction), as in Durrell's *Quintet*, or reconfigure it as a powerful refusal to release a fictional or even an historic character to death until opportunity is afforded to confront the past. Crossing "the ultimate ontological boundary," many postmodernist texts enact "the venerable *topos* of the 'world to come'": Flann O'Brien's *The Third Policeman*, Pynchon's *Gravity's Rainbow*, Stanley Elkin's *The Living End*, Alasdair Gray's *Lanark*.[12] To paraphrase *The Communist Manifesto*, history and death are specters haunting postmodernist fiction; the imagined, dead, or unborn inhabit texts that reconceive their lives. Civilization's carnage – man's assault on planet, species, and self – has become so prevalent as to render life often impossible, and history surreal; fiction has had to devise strategies for keeping pace. Slavery, colonial exploitation, genocide, mass slaughter and warfare, the threat of annihilation, and the social institutions that sustain them, not only refused to disappear after the modernist attempt to elide them, but moved to the forefront of twentieth-century life and came to define what Langer, in his study of death in modern literature, calls *The Age of Atrocity*.

For decades before and after World War Two, our century's cumulative man-made deaths and increasing technological control of life and death were the central facts of existence. The Cold War's technology of killing seemed likely to climax in nuclear cataclysm, so modernism's metaphoric apocalypse is enacted in fictions of macrocosmic devastation like Shute's *On the Beach* (1957), Vonnegut's *Cat's Cradle* (1963), Angela Carter's *Heroes and Villains* (1969) and *The Passion of New Eve* (1977), and Bernard Malamud's *God's Grace* (1982). Fuentes' *Terra nostra* (1975) represents the end of the world as a monstrous Parisian carnival. In *Dying, in Other Words* (1981) Maggie Gee writes her own death into the text, and then her world's nuclear destruction. Postmodernist fictive meditations on history, which Hegel calls the record of "what man does with death," reenact the continuing presence of our horrific past. Foregrounding "history as nightmare," such fiction, seeking not to despair of making sense of human senselessness, destabilizes its ontological status in the hope of breaking with inherited destructive patterns of self and society, and shifting into new ways of beginning.

Alternative historical possibilities, like those James explores in "The Jolly Corner," are played out, for example, in Philip Roth's

"Kafka," in which the writer survives, flees to New Jersey to escape the Holocaust, and inhabits rather than creates a fictional world.[13] Muriel Spark's *The Hothouse by the East River* (1973) is set in 1970s New York, a death-world "of the mentally vivisected still to be reassembled" (12). Its dead and resurrected inhabitants include English World War Two victims who, killed by a direct V-2 hit (150), experience the unfinished business of lives cut short by sudden death. During the war "people were normal" (58), but now the past throws an unnatural penumbra: Elsa's shadow always falls wrong, she "gets light or something from elsewhere" (18); fact and imagination become indistinguishable; the dead return to haunt each other. Increasingly upset by these unreal beings he has summoned from the grave, Paul, who mistakenly believes that he alone did not die, thinks, "One should live first, then die, not die then live; everything to its own time . . . they will have to go back to the dead, they must all go back" (113, 142). Failing to understand how their "mortality problem" relates to New York's urban problems (130–1), and unable to sort out identities and events from the past, they find their world disintegrating once they realize that they died during the war. After a frenzied night on the town, including visiting their adult/unborn children to ask if they exist, Paul and Elsa return home to discover their apartment building half demolished, and a billboard announcing the new construction to be erected there: now perhaps "they can have some peace" (167). Unable to live lives history denied them, and that Spark tries to give them, they finally accept the death they can no longer evade.

In Valerio Camillo's Theater of Memory in Fuentes' *Terra nostra*, "History repeats itself only because we are unaware of the alternate possibilities for each historic event: what that event could have been but was not. Knowing, we can insure that history does not repeat itself; that the alternate possibility is the one that occurs for the first time" (646). This is the vision and hope many postmodernist novels enact. Holocaust novels like Vonnegut's *Slaughterhouse-Five*, Federman's *Take It Or Leave It*, and Styron's *Sophie's Choice* confront the challenge of Adorno: "To write poetry after Auschwitz is barbaric." Postmodernist fiction seeks to shatter traditional historiographical patterning so as to escape or at least not repeat it. Like chaos theory, it reconstitutes order within disorder in ways violative of realistic or modernist expectations that have proven disastrous. Encounters with other worlds (alien, dreamlike, posthumous, post-apocalyptic) are no longer metaphorical, the experience of reading, but desperate strategies envisioned within postmodernist texts. Thus, the ontological shift at the end of *Gravity's Rainbow*, which attempts to escape the past by aestheticizing it, rewriting what precedes as a film, recurs in *The White Hotel*: Lisa, who experiences her death at Babi Yar, awakens in "The Promised Land," the place of "Anagnorisis," where, after "the nightmarish journey" from their "previous life," she and her mother suckle each other (301–2, 306, 315–16). Whether "The Promised Land" represents the afterlife, Israel, or Lisa's dying fantasy, the excruciating pains in her breasts and ovaries, prescient of Babi Yar rather than traces of suppressed erotic desire, disappear there.

Despite Thomas' disingenuous "Author's Note" claiming that he did "not intend to put into question the scientific validity of psychoanalysis" (xi), *The White Hotel* is a postmodernist rejection of Freud's *Beyond the Pleasure Principle*, for Lisa's suffering results not from female hysteria (as seems the case for most of the book), but from material history. Mary Robertson argues that the book's structure implies a judgment: Babi Yar renders the book's psychoanalytical sleuthing morally frivolous, if not responsible for history's nightmare. Freud, who returns as a sick old man in the mythic "Promised Land," is condemned for failing "to put himself in dialogue with real history."[14] Some critics consider this visionary section Thomas' betrayal of history, a too-easy recuperation of the Holocaust. Yet where classical historical fiction generally adheres to accepted fact, avoids cultural anachronism, and accepts realistic conventions, postmodernist texts like *The White Hotel* willfully interrogate, even annihilate, the traditional boundaries of historical fiction by flaunting anachronisms, juxtaposing lived and fantasized events, reconceiving the historical record. They do so not like David Irving, who denies that the Holocaust occurred,[15] or even like such revisionist historians as Hayden White, who view the past as knowable only in the stories invented about it, but in order to tease out history's implications or alternatives, to change initial circumstances, to consider what went wrong.

Graham Swift's *Waterland* also reconceives history in terms of individual lives, though it accepts White's conception of knowing it through recounting. *Waterland* begins with the narrator, a history teacher, introducing his father, "a superstitious man [with] a knack for telling stories," who insists that everyone "has a heart" and was "once a tiny baby sucking his mother's milk" (1). The first story told, that of Freddie Parr's body discovered floating down the Ouse, leads to all the others. In confronting this death, Tom Crick is led back through Dresden, Flanders, the French reign of terror, and forward to the nuclear holocaust: seeking, in Thomas' terms, to render history's Armageddons meaningful through the "thousands of white hotels" in Babi Yar. Yet this corpse produced by history refuses to accommodate itself to either of the Cricks' attempts, through artificial respiration or storytelling, to resuscitate it, "to refute reality ... the law of nature, that a dead thing does not live again" (27).

Like his father, Crick translates history into stories, like that of Louis XVI's first-born son, whose death history ignores. Crick is fired after thirty-two years of unraveling "the mysteries of the past" because, as the headmaster (whose supposedly solider subject is physics) puts it: "We're cutting back on history" (4, 18, 21). But the actual reason, Crick tells his class, is "that old Cricky, your history teacher, had already in one sense, and of his own accord, ceased to teach history," at least as traditionally conceived, as master narrative. Instead, telling stories of himself, "old Cricky was trying to put himself into history; old Cricky was trying to show you that he himself was only a piece of the stuff he taught" (4–5). So the public and private rationales are really the same: the firing attempts to repudiate and constrict history, to keep it from becoming interchangeable with its narrator.

"Cutting history" results, too, from the indifference of students who, living amid the Cold War and "the apparently unhaltable build-up of nuclear arms," find it irrelevant to "the here and now." Valuing only the material present, the aptly named Price challenges his teacher: "The only important thing about history, I think, sir, is that it's got to the point where it's probably about to end" (6). But telling stories, we are told, is a way of surmounting and outwitting reality, as well as creating it, a way of making sense of corpses.

It is also analogous to fenland labor that seems to produce nothing permanent, for "however much you resist them, the waters will return ... the land sinks; silt collects ... something in nature wants to go back ... the bare and empty Fens yield so readily [only] to the imaginary – and the supernatural" (14–15). Yet dredging must be performed if civilization is not to drown. Like reclamation and the Fens, history too "goes backwards as it goes forwards. It loops. It takes detours ... the great, so-called forward movements of civilisation, whether moral or technological, have invariably brought with them an accompanying regression" (117–18). Neither revolutionary nor progressive, "history is a thin garment, easily punctured by a knife blade called Now" (31), out of whose wounds emerges a series of repeated, intensifying apocalypses (174, 258–9, 291), as well as uncountable corpses, each with its own story.

Waterland also juxtaposes history with Freud's explanation of female problems as well as with fenland rhythms. Mary's hysteria, unlike Lisa's in *The White Hotel*, results not from her being victimized by history, but from a botched abortion and her subsequent inability to bear children. Yet Mary's erotic relationship with Tom inaugurates a series of events that resembles history's chaotic unfolding: her pregnancy, Dick's jealous killing of Freddie, her becoming infertile and then stealing a child out of desperation to be a mother, Dick's fatal swim at the end, Tom's loss of his job and the cutting of history.

Waterland treats historic telling, and historic events like the French Revolution, as subject to detection: we learn why Louis XVI was guillotined and why Dick killed Freddie. As in chaos theory, underlying patterns emerge from what seems random and unpredictable. The question is posed as to what exactly the Revolution was and whether it lies "in some impenetrable amalgam of countless individual circumstances too complex to be analysed ... the more you try to dissect events, the more you lose hold of what you took for granted in the first place – the more it seems it never actually occurred, but occurs, somehow, only in the imagination." But the failure to accommodate historic events causes them to repeat, with changed costume, slightly altered rhetoric, and mounting body count:

> Why was it that this revolution in the name of liberty and equality ended with ... a reincarnation of the old Sun King? ... Why is it that every so often history demands a bloodbath, a holocaust, an Armageddon? And why is it that every time the time before has taught us nothing? ... How it repeats itself, how it goes back on itself, no matter how we try to straighten it out ... How it goes in circles and brings us back to the same place.
>
> (121–3)

The alternative to historic understanding is to view the past as a dead thing, and "to liken the study of history to an inquest. Suppose we have on our hands a corpse – viz., the past. A corpse not always readily identifiable but now and then taking a specific and quite personal form. For example, the headless trunk of Louis XVI" (93), or Freddie Parr's body. What seems required, and most difficult, is to negotiate a viable place for the individual between history and imagination, as the haunting presence of the narrator's ancestor, Sarah Atkinson, attempts.

Waterland's structural loops, replicating those of history, subvert the binary opposition between fact and fiction, historic and imagined storytelling, as it seeks, like the French Revolution, a "return to a new beginning" (119): the hope expressed repeatedly in postmodernist texts. Whether "domestic tragedy, historical epic, or just straight farce" (108), Philip Roth's *The Counterlife* (1986) literalizes this hope. It begins with Nathan Zuckerman's inappropriate eulogy for his brother Henry, who died from surgery he underwent to restore his potency. But Henry arises in the second chapter and flees to Israel, even as his wife Carol complains that "he couldn't have gone any further from me if he *had* died in surgery" (80). Like Lawrence's man who died, Henry "appears to have totally repudiated his life, all of us, and all he's been through, and anybody who does that, I thought, *must* be taken seriously. Not only do such people qualify as true converts but ... they become criminals of a kind" (109) – because no longer susceptible to ordinary social or fictive constraints.

Seeking to align himself with history in Israel, Henry feels likely to satisfy "the vital need" he "had been fumbling toward during his recuperation ... It might even be the resuscitated potency that he was really escaping" (131–2). Henry tells Nathan, who tracks him down: "beyond the Freudian lock you put on every single person's life, there is ... a world defined by *action*, by *power*, where how you wanted to please Momma and Poppa *simply doesn't matter*! ... Here they're making history! There's a world outside the Oedipal swamp" (140). As in *The White Hotel*, the self-obsessed individual can seem counter-historical, bourgeois, selfish. Postmodernist "character" is less portraiture than it is in "realistic" bourgeois novels or Freud's "character" sketches, genres in which death is final.

Roth has come far from *Portnoy's Complaint* (1969), in which Israel exists only to render impotent his sexual adept. In *The Ghost Writer* (1979), Nathan Zuckerman conceives of using history to make peace with his family: meeting a woman he imagines to be Anne Frank, who has survived the war, he fantasizes marrying her to prove he is not anti-Semitic despite his uncompromising depiction of US Jews. In *The Counterlife*, in which self becomes a product of history rather than of psychoanalysis, Roth maintains that only by entering history can anyone, but especially a Jew, enter identity: "Jews are to history what Eskimos are to snow." Nathan, who now wishes to transcend the self, sees Zionism as "a highly conscious desire ... to reverse the very form of Jewish existence. The construction of a counterlife that is one's own anti-myth was at its very core. It was a species of fabulous utopianism, a manifesto for human transformation as extreme – and, at the outset, as implausible – as any ever conceived ... The power of the will to remake reality" (147–8). The orientation becomes outer-directed, an engagement with material reality.

Between Jimmy the Jewish terrorist and the security agent who subdues him, Roth enacts a schematic dialogue of opposites that recalls the whiskey priest and lieutenant in *The Power and the Glory*. Wanting to make "a plaything of history," to *un*do it, Jimmy tries to destroy Jerusalem's Museum and Remembrance Hall of the Holocaust in order, he maintains, to insure the future by wiping out the past. He proclaims: "Now what we have to suffer is *the loss of our suffering*! ... We have reminded them enough, we have reminded *ourselves* enough – *we must forget*!" (165–7). The security agent, who speaks of Jews as both history's victims and Israel's successful defenders in 1967, sees dualism as crucial: product of memory and desire, Israel both tracks history's teleology and determines to rupture it (179–80). That Jimmy is bent on destroying the past indicates how strongly it retains its grip.

For Nathan, as for Jimmy, "the worm in the dream is always the past, that impediment to all renewal" (310). The past that for James was simply "visitable" has become "unevadable ... had gained control and was about to vandalize our future unless I did something to stop it" (309). In the novel's second half, Nathan acquires Henry's disease, also elects to have the potency-restoring operation, and shares his fate: "No dying, no decay – just death. All very thoughtful. Quite a performance" (218). But Nathan, who had written his own eulogy, also replicates Henry's paradigm of return, and in so doing spares Henry from having to write "a kind of counterbook to each of Nathan's" (205). The possibility of new life, whether the product of biology or imagination, opens out beyond text and present. In Roth's early novels, individuals strive to escape from history into selfhood; in later ones, counterlife and counterstory becoming indistinguishable, they fall in and out of fiction and history. The question for postmodernists is whether the two can be reconciled and made viable.

Toni Morrison's *Beloved* poses the same question in parallel historic terms. Haunted by slavery's legacy, a US-made holocaust, *Beloved* evokes and multiplies the Jewish experience with its epigraph, "Sixty Million and more." Like Roth, Morrison fictionalizes historic wrestling with past and future in order to reconceive her dead who will not stay dead, to reconfigure their stories. Though "Remembering seemed unwise" (274), *Beloved* is told as obsessive "rememory." The infant Beloved, a rare victim of matrilineal sacrifice, was slaughtered by Sethe, desperate to prevent her daughter from reenacting her own fate. Like Styron's Sophie forced by the Nazis to choose which of her children to send to the ovens, Sethe's action results from history's positioning her to become a moral being *only* by becoming complicit in genocide. Returning as the adult she would and should have been, Beloved, history's victim and survivor, lays claim to the voice and self that have been silenced and denied: "I am Beloved and she is mine" (214). Yet having lost her unique potential for being, she can speak "only what others had thought; anyone fits her footprints" (274–5). Echoing Lisa in *The White Hotel* ("it's the future that counts, not the past" [317–18]), the wise and loving Paul D., aware of the shackles they seem still to wear and determined to step free of history's ruins, tells Sethe: "me and you, we got more yesterday than anybody. We need some kind of tomorrow," some way to put their stories next to each other (273). And Morrison offers a way to do so within and despite history's death-dealing.

Echoing Morrison's epigraph, Leslie Silko's *Almanac of the Dead* (1991) claims 60 million Native American deaths from contact with Europeans in the sixteenth century, the continent's first holocaust (723). Seeing contemporary urban violence as the past's revenge, a Mexican revolutionary reflects that "the white man didn't seem to understand he had no future here because he had no past, no spirits of ancestors here" (313). Ghosts of Native Americans return to inspire violence and slaughter, for as "Marx had understood ... within 'history' reside relentless forces, powerful, spirits, vengeful, relentlessly seeking justice" (316). The only alternative to apocalypse is cooperation: "Now it was up to the poorest tribal people and survivors of European genocide to show the remaining humans how all could share and live together on earth, ravished as she was" (749). The US's unfaced and unaccommodated past, as the media inform us daily, stalks its cities.

The postmodernist fiction considered in this chapter is far from affectless or ahistorical. It desperately confronts and reconceives the past in the hope of being able to go forward. As often happens, ontological and fictive realities have begun to accommodate themselves to each other; historic and fictional death are revising themselves along postmodernist lines. If not at its end (as both the character Price in *Waterland* [6] and Francis Fukuyama's *The End of History* proclaim), history is less likely to climax in the apocalypse implicit in modernist texts and explicit in many postmodernist ones. The rapid political and cultural transformations of the 1980s and early 1990s, especially the Soviet Union's demise, have denaturalized what long seemed the inevitable "fact" of global destruction, only to resuscitate savage ethnic and national conflicts. Fiction will surely perform *that* turn before long.

Simultaneously, the triumphalist sense of what has been "secured" by medical technology has been assailed by widespread famine, the environmental crisis, the virulent return of old diseases like malaria and tuberculosis, and the AIDS pandemic that may eventually claim lives on the scale of the flu epidemic of 1918–19, which, with medical science advances, was supposed to be the last of its kind. Lawrence Henderson, a Harvard biochemist and medical historian, says that medical practice was always a dubious resource: not until the second decade of this century were patients more likely to be helped than harmed by doctors; some argue that, where dying is concerned, we are returning to earlier conditions. Edward Lambert, Director of Cardiology at Buffalo's Children's Hospital, maintains that the twentieth century's dramatic medical advances have all been accompanied by physician-produced diseases, "diseases of medical progress," and that most twentieth-century medical disasters were avoidable.[16] Indeed, the history of medicine enacts a rhythm of alternating triumph and defeat, as Frank Ryan's *The Forgotten Plague* (1993) demonstrates in discussing tuberculosis, which claimed an estimated billion lives in the last 200 years, including writers such as Keats, Emily Brontë, Chekhov, Kafka, and Lawrence. Ryan documents the heroic and seemingly successful quest for a tuberculosis cure – as well as its devastating comeback, in conjunction with AIDS, in recent years.

The return of plague, and the remarkable literature it is spawning, has painfully furthered the process, begun by Gorer and Kübler-Ross, of bringing dying out of the closet and into the public domain. AIDS narratives proclaim the pain, outrage, and tragedy of individuals whose experiences, contradicting medical technology's promise of a better life, have been marginalized by a society conflicted over whether to deny death, or sex, or the relationship between them. Susan Sontag's *AIDS and Its Metaphors* (1989) explores the cultural and linguistic implications of this, "one of the most meaning laden of diseases," and one of many "byproducts of advanced society" that have dystopian, global implications.[17] Randy Shilts' *And the Band Played On* (1985), a history of AIDS in the US, exhaustively details this "drama of national failure, played out against a backdrop of needless death" (xxii). The early years were marked by denial, by both medical personnel and afflicted individuals, as well as infighting by politicians, the scientific community (which labeled it a "homosexual disease" despite the dying women and children[18]), and gays who resisted changing their lifestyle. When researchers in the mid-1980s announced the discovery of the AIDS virus, US health officials boasted they would have a vaccine within two years. No one ventures such claims today. The more researchers learn about AIDS the more questions arise, and the likelier it seems that modern medical technology, through inoculation or the transfusion of blood, blood products, and tissue products, is more the problem than the solution.[19]

Recent personal accounts, both written and televised, ritualize the last transition by depicting how lovers with AIDS, performing a postmodern *ars moriendi*, nurse each other and, in some cases, assist in committing suicide. Paul Monette's *Borrowed Time* (1988), one of the first and most powerful AIDS narratives, enacts a double coming out: first homosexuality and then dying – in fact, a double dying. Monette depicts the exhilarating life and excruciating final months of Roger Horwitz, his lover, with whom he experienced all of Kübler-Ross' stages from denial to acceptance, when Roger's living will meant "that we couldn't take him to intensive care and put a tube down his throat." Then Monette, like Shilts, discovered he would have to reenact the process for himself. Monette's title suggests that those diagnosed as HIV positive, while they may live healthy lives for years, are in a sense already dead, yet the "extra" life afforded AIDS sufferers provides opportunity for what he calls "the new and ghastly rituals of separation," and then for writing about them (340–1). History is neither metaphor nor pastiche in such lives or texts, elegies of love and loss that foreground and literalize the modernist trope of authorial death. Unlike traditional elegists, Monette finds nothing to celebrate: the figure mourned is the beloved, not a poet who has departed to leave space for one emerging; the death mourned is followed not by springtime renewal but anticipation of the elegist's own; and Monette's obsessive detailing of material decay recalls modernist "dirty dying." Yet the love they have shared and that Monette enacts in nurturing and then depicting Horwitz's bodily failings echoes the Victorian "beautiful death," though with neither denial nor aestheticization: only the stark confrontation with life and love that represents AIDS' only positive achievement.

The culture of creating life and confronting death has entered a new phase: a society unable to agree on when life begins or ends nonetheless set out to engage in artificial and transplanted organs, laboratory fertilization, genetic research, and the deployment of "life support" systems. For much of this century the ultimate ontological narrative, that of dying, was suppressed to our society's disadvantage; in fewer than three generations we have gone from prolonging living to prolonging dying. The great danger lies in technology's becoming master rather than slave: doctors, having found it easier to turn their machines on than off, often seem helpless before the technology they supposedly control, as if they too were its victims.[20] Life-support systems, a cryogenics or mummification of the living, often perpetuate modernist denial and silencing. The practice, particularly grotesque in a world of continuing mass slaughter, is class- and race-based: vast amounts spent on the last days of white, well-off individuals, while people of color starve.

Yet recent years have witnessed a growing public debate about alternative ways of addressing dying. AIDS and other fatal diseases have sparked a renewed interest in "rational suicide" and euthanasia, ways of taking Camus' "absurd reasoning" unto death.[21] These options are espoused by organizations like "Compassion in Dying" in Oregon and the Hemlock Society; by Derek Humphry's best-selling *Final Exit*, a suicide manual; and by doctors like Jack Kevorkian who help patients perform what he calls "medicide." In a postmodernist projection, "Jean Baudrillard envisages a situation in which suicide may be performed in specialized motels where 'for a substantial sum, one can procure death in the most pleasant conditions (like any other kind of consumer good, with perfect service, everything necessary laid on, even hostesses, who try to revive your wish to go on living, then, with professional conscientiousness, let the gas enter your room).' "[22] Baudrillard's vision differs little from Kevorkian's proposal for legalized suicide centers to assure "a humane and painless death for all those who need and desire it."[23] But pressure to transform the permitted into the mandatory, as Plato feared, can be enormous, and our morally crude culture currently lacks appropriate safeguards for insuring that the self-appointed determiners of life and death are not, in effect, being granted licenses to kill.

A second movement, that of hospices and dying-at-home, has gained momentum since Cecily Saunders founded St. Christopher's Hospice in London in 1967. Her work inspired others to provide "palliative and supportive care to meet the special needs arising out of the physical, emotional, spiritual, social and economic stresses which are experienced during the final states of illness and during dying and bereavement."[24] An initially skeptical doctor found his experience of a hospice "quite different from what I had expected. Instead of a terminal care or 'death house' environment with cachectic, narcotized, bedridden, depressed patients, I found an active community of patients, staff, families, and children of staff and families."[25] Andrea Sankar's *Dying at Home* offers guidance to a once-prevalent practice that is again gaining acceptance; the hospice and home-dying movements, like birthing at home, have gone far toward returning our central cultural rituals to female control.

The alternatives of euthanasia, whether active or passive, and making dying as comfortable as possible seem complementary at first, but the movements are antagonistic; each rejects the other's moral and practical premises. Euthanasia supporters focus on materiality: physical suffering, cost, ending life that lacks a certain quality. Hospices, based in Christianity but opposing D.H. Lawrence's view of its death-orientation, nurture the dying by recognizing death's inevitability and avoiding high-tech gadgetry.[26] These antagonistic alternatives can be reconciled, Dr. Timothy Quill argues, by maximizing dignity and choices for the terminally ill, and by legal reforms that free doctors to help rather than having to worry about peripheral matters like law suits.[27]

Attitudes change slowly and reluctantly. Medical personnel, like most of us, have difficulty facing and accepting death and still tend to see it as preventable, finding it easier to sustain "life" than to question its worth. Nonetheless, signs of change are widespread. The US 1991 Patient Self-Determination Act requires health facilities to inform patients of their rights to refuse and withdraw treatment, and to designate proxy-decision-makers if they are incapacitated. Last testaments are reclaiming spiritual force as living wills, which set out the terms of dying and, often, determine what happens to the material parts that remain. According to the American Hospital Association, nearly three-quarters of the average day's 5,800 American deaths are now timed or negotiated. Such triage has multiple causes: cost, limited personnel and facilities, changing moral standards, the desire to minimize patient and family suffering, greater openness on the part of doctors and a declining belief that death necessarily equals failure. Edward Lambert speaks of a new "healthy humility": "The doctrine of professorial infallibility, the arrogant, authoritarian, autocratic attitude so common among successful academic physicians and surgeons, is disappearing in the western world and is being replaced by a willingness to submit all treatments to critical tests."[28] Long considered taboo or failure, death is again becoming part of life rather than something alien that must be denied, and the dying who had been silenced are reasserting both their centrality in the process and a voice with which to speak it. Medical science is inching toward accepting what F.W. Farrar and Dr. William Osler empirically demonstrated in the nineteenth century: that, though the causes of dying are often traumatic and painful, death itself rarely is (see chapter 4 above). Through such acceptance we may hope to transmute our "dirty little secret" into James's "distinguished thing," and thereby reclaim the power and dignity inherent in successfully performing the ritual of our living and dying.

Notes

INTRODUCTION

1 Hence death is to be contrasted with life, which James called "the most valuable thing" (*Letters* 1: 101).
2 See Cameron, "Surviving Death" 8.
3 See Guthke, *Last Words* 81–9. Ellmann credits both versions, as well as several others, though not as Wilde's last words (*Oscar Wilde* 580–1).
4 Macksey, "Last Words" 505.
5 Shneidman, *Death: Current Perspectives* 3rd ed. 2.
6 Wilson, *After Death Experience* 17.
7 Hoffman, *Mortal No* 3.
8 Yeats, "Death," *Collected Poems* 264.
9 Miller, *Fiction and Repetition* 61.
10 Ong, *Interfaces* 232–3.
11 Kübler-Ross, *On Death and Dying* 2.
12 Kuhn, *Scientific Revolutions* xi.
13 Johnson, *Birth of the Modern.*
14 Adams, *Education* 382.
15 See Fussell, *Great War* 11.
16 Symons, *Symbolist Movement* 5.
17 Keating, *Haunted Study* 285–7.
18 R.W.B. Lewis, *Picaresque Saint* 19. See Elliot, *Book of the Dead* 6–10.

1 FICTIONAL DEATH AND THE MODERNIST ENTERPRISE

1 Hemingway, *Death in the Afternoon* 122.
2 For Scheherazadean narrative as mediating and meditating on death, see Faris, "1001 Words" 829–30.
3 T.S. Eliot, "Burnt Norton," *Complete Poems and Plays* 118.
4 Elliot, *Book of the Dead* 10.
5 Huntington and Metcalf, *Celebrations* 2.
6 See Ariès, *The Hour of Our Death* 5–10. Hereafter cited as *Hour.*
7 Darnton, *Kiss of Lamourette* 273–4. See also McManners, "Death and the French Historians," in Whaley 109, 121.

8 Morris, "Attitudes Toward Death" 300. Morris cites six other historians who employ Ariès' methods or ideas.
9 In Holton, *Thematic Origins* rev. ed. 210.
10 Jürgen Habermas, "Modernity – An Incomplete Project," in Foster, *The Anti-Aesthetic* 9.
11 Both Gleick, *Chaos* 14, and Ian Stewart, *Does God Play Dice?* 12, quote this statement, which Stewart calls "awe-inspiring."
12 Laplace, *On Probabilities* 3.
13 Michelson himself agreed with Kelvin, however (*Light Waves* 23–4).
14 Pais, *'Subtle is the Lord . . . '* 26. Pais overstates: H.A. Lorentz, whom Einstein called "the leading mind" among turn-of-the-century theoretical physicists (*Ideas and Opinions* 73), did, according to Hans Mark, anticipate this transition (private conversation).
15 Holton, *Thematic Origins* rev. ed. 211.
16 Kuhn, *Scientific Revolutions* 6.
17 Hoffmann, *Quantum* 76.
18 Ferris, *Mind's Sky* 98.
19 In Pais, *'Subtle is the Lord . . . '* 460.
20 Holton, *Thematic Origins*, rev. ed. 195, 220.
21 In Seelig, *Albert Einstein* 97.
22 Mark, private conversation.
23 See Holton, *Thematic Origins* 52–3.
24 Einstein, "What I Believe" (1930); in *Ideas and Opinions* 11.
25 Gleick, *Chaos* 7. Many contemporary physicists endorse Einstein's quest. Hawking suggests that "we may now be near the end of the search for the ultimate laws of nature" (*Brief History* 156); see also Weinberg, *Final Theory* and Davies, *Mind of God*. Others argue, however, that if science's limits are being reached it is not because all fundamental questions are answered but because science has so fractured that a comprehensive vision may be unsustainable. See Elvee, *End of Science?* and Lindley, *End of Physics*.
26 See Pais, *'Subtle is the Lord . . . '* 39, and Chernikov, Sagdeev, and Zaslavsky, "Chaos" 27.
27 Einstein, *Theoretical Physics*, in Pais, *'Subtle is the Lord . . . '* 460.
28 In Pais, *'Subtle is the Lord . . . '* 319, 389, 461. For Weinberg, too, scientific theories are based in "the essential objectivity of . . . empirical data" (*First Three Minutes* 9).
29 In Pais, *'Subtle is the Lord . . . '* 414.
30 Holton, *Thematic Origins*, rev. ed. 103–4.
31 Zukav, *Wu Li Masters* 290.
32 Holton, *Thematic Origins* rev. ed. 20, 208–9, 15.
33 See Lindley, *End of Physics*.
34 Popper, *Scientific Discovery* 278. Linda Hutcheon discusses a similar breakdown in postmodern criticism ("Beginning to Theorize Postmodernism" 14).

35 See Popper, *Scientific Discovery* 6–8. In the 1950s, Heisenberg said only a few technicalities remained before the unified field theory would be explained.
36 In Gleick, *Chaos* 6–7. Hawking's assertion is contradicted by chaologists tracking everyday phenomena like the motions of pendulums and clouds, dripping faucets and running water, the demography of bees and fish.
37 Gleick, *Chaos* 7.
38 Sharing Einstein's belief in an objective reality ultimately explicable by a single theory (*Final Theory* 6–7), Weinberg parts company with his predecessor concerning its origins: "The more the universe seems comprehensible, the more it also seems pointless," that is, without divine purpose (*First Three Minutes* 154).
39 Heisenberg quotes Bohr's remark approvingly in *Physics and Beyond.*
40 In Gleick, *Chaos* 314.
41 Ian Stewart, *Does God Play Dice?* 2, 293.
42 Gleick, *Chaos* 36.
43 See Kuhn, *Scientific Revolutions* 4.
44 See Huntington and Metcalf, *Celebrations* 9–11. For the quest by Freud, Frazer, Havelock Ellis, and Malinowski, among others, for "the universal truth about human nature [in] primitive societies," see Torgovnick, *Gone Primitive* 7.
45 Van Gennep, *Rites* 11; see Huntington and Metcalf, *Celebrations* 9–11. Echoing van Gennep, Robert Garland cites "three distinct stages" in Socrates' passing "from here to there" in the *Phaedrus*: dying, dead but uninterred, dead and interred (*Greek Way* 13).
46 Geertz, *Interpretation of Cultures* 35.
47 See Tiger and Fox, *The Imperial Animal.*
48 Huntington and Metcalf, *Celebrations* 43.
49 Geertz, *Interpretation of Cultures* 53.
50 Fromm, *Human Destructiveness* 498. Fromm credits Ernest Jones with first proposing this idea.
51 Fromm, *Human Destructiveness* 498.
52 Fromm, *Human Destructiveness* 516.
53 Girard, *Violence and the Sacred* 197, 145.
54 Fromm, *Human Destructiveness* 37.
55 Durrell, *A Key to Modern British Poetry* 21. Hereafter cited as *Key*. See also Russell, *The Impact of Science on Society.*
56 Friedman and Donley, *Myth and Muse* 2. See also Fleishman, *Ways of Knowing* 136–48; Herring, *Joyce's Uncertainty Principle*; and Shlain, *Art & Physics.*
57 Hayles also discusses his anticipation of chaos theory, *Chaos Bound* 61–90.
58 See Holton, *Thematic Origins*, rev. ed. 102.
59 Bergsonian *durée* was anathema to Einstein (see Hoffman, *Mortal No*

351). Bergson's insistence on the reality of *only* human time led Einstein to say of him "God forgive him" (in Pais, '*Subtle is the Lord . . .*' 510).

60 Ford Madox Ford, *Joseph Conrad* 6. See Schatzberg, Waite, and Johnson's annotated bibliography, *Literature and Science*.

61 See Garrett Stewart, *Death Sentences passim*. See also Schleifer's notion of "the negative materiality of death," especially in the rhetoric of modernism (*Rhetoric and Death* 7–8, 30–1).

62 Fussell, *Great War* 11, 21, 7–8. Bury's *Idea of Progress* examines "progress" from the early eighteenth century; Nisbet's *History of the Idea of Progress* shows how millions died because some eagerly increased misery in order to impose their vision of progress.

63 Bland, *Royal Way* 13.

64 Fussell, *Great War* 22.

65 Oring, "Forest Lawn" 68.

66 "Address upon Receiving the Nobel Prize for Literature" (10 December 1950), in *Portable Faulkner* 723–4.

67 R.W.B. Lewis, *Picaresque Saint* 17. Ziolkowski, who quotes this line of Lewis', adds that "The last years of the nineteenth century also resounded with its knell" (*Modern Novel* 217).

68 Elliot, *Book of the Dead* 6–10.

69 Foucault, *History of Sexuality* 1: 143.

70 Shneidman, *Death: Current Perspectives* 3rd ed. 2.

71 Although reliable demographic evidence is scanty and deceptive (Drake, *Population in Industrialization* 2), Rostow notes that "Infant mortality and the ravages of infectious disease remained powerful forces in the industrializing West [and even worsened for urban dwellers crowded in squalid tenements]; but improvements in food, shelter, clothing, water supply, and sanitation gradually brought down death rates" (*World Economy* 9) – an early version of trickle-down economics. Buer's *Health, Wealth*, William Frazer's *History of English Public Health*, and Haley's *Healthy Body* also examine nineteenth-century mortality and health.

72 Fromm, *Human Destructiveness* 377.

73 In *International Herald Tribune*, 25 January 1990, 4. See Cartwright, *Disease and History*.

74 Beveridge estimates "between 15–25 million – the greatest visitation ever experienced by the human race" (*Influenza* 32). Such estimates vary widely: Craig and Egan propose 41,435,000 as the number of World War One dead (*Extreme Situations* 3).

75 Russell, *Human Society* 208.

76 Foucault, *Discipline and Punish* 11. Belkin's *First, Do No Harm* – whose title derives from the still apt physician's adage: "There are some patients whom we cannot help; there are none whom we cannot harm" – describes how hospital medical committees now decide on extra-

ordinary life-prolonging measures. In *Medicine Betrayed*, Black, *et al.* examine doctors' role in torture and executions. Extreme but hardly unique were Nazi Germany's health care system and scientific community, much of whose resources were dedicated to so-called racial hygiene. See Lifton, *Nazi Doctors*.

77 Brivic, *Joyce between Freud and Jung* 88.

78 McHale, *Postmodernist Fiction* 186–7. See also Langer, *Holocaust and the Literary Imagination*; Lang, *Writing and the Holocaust*; and Young, *Writing and Rewriting the Holocaust*.

79 In Gorer, *Death, Grief and Mourning* 192–9.

80 Kübler-Ross, *On Death and Dying* 6–7, 20–1.

81 Feifel encountered similar resistance in the 1950s (Ariès, *Hour* 589). Peschel discusses "the defenses that people, especially paramedical – or medical – people use" ("Callousness or Caring" 80). See also her collection, "Doctor Writers," *Medicine and Literature* 1–77.

82 First detailed in Kübler-Ross, *On Death and Dying* 34–121.

83 Kastenbaum, "Do We Die in Stages?" 131.

84 Shneidman, *Deaths of Man* 6.

85 Bourke, "Irish Traditional Lament" 288.

86 Choron, "Death as a Motive of Philosophic Thought," in Shneidman, *Essays in Self-Destruction* 59–77; also in Choron, *Death and Western Thought*.

87 Darnton, *Kiss of Lamourette* 269.

88 Shneidman, *Death: Current Perspectives*, 3rd ed., 1, 4.

2 CLIMACTIC DEATH

1 Garland, *Greek Way* 19. Kübler-Ross' chapter called "Hope," considers that condition a positive step toward "of final acceptance" (*On Death and Dying* 140).

2 London *Times*, 29–30 June 1830.

3 Phillips, *Caring for the Dying* 45.

4 Frye, *Anatomy of Criticism* 158–9.

5 Montaigne, *Essays* 35–6.

6 T.S. Eliot, "The Dry Salvages," *Complete Poems and Plays* 134.

7 London *Morning Post*, 1 February 1820.

8 Ariès, *Western Attitudes toward Death* 104. Hereafter cited as *Western Attitudes*.

9 Kübler-Ross, *Death, The Final Stage of Growth* 10.

10 Murray, "Passions of Herman Melville," in Shneidman, *Self-Destruction* 28.

11 Weisman, "Appropriate and Appropriated Death," in Shneidman, *Death: Current Perspectives* 3rd ed. 33–4.

12 Peter Brooks, "Freud's Masterplot" 711, 716.

13 For elaboration of this reading of *Hamlet*, see Friedman, "Hamlet the Unready."
14 T.S. Eliot, "Murder in the Cathedral," *Complete Poems and Plays* 196.
15 Browne, *Hydriotaphia* 284.
16 Frye, *Anatomy of Criticism* 192.
17 Foucault, *History of Sexuality* 1: 142.
18 Watt, *Rise of the Novel* 11.
19 Frye, *Anatomy of Criticism* 163.
20 In Boswell, *Life of Johnson* 169.

3 THE *ARS MORIENDI*

1 See *Birth of Tragedy* 85 and "The Problem of Socrates," *Twilight of the Idols* (*Portable Nietzsche* 473–9) and Rank, *Trauma of Birth* 182.
2 Garland, *Greek Way* 14.
3 Garland, *Greek Way* 17.
4 See Girard, *Violence and the Sacred* 68–88.
5 Freud, "*Uncanny*" 231.
6 Girard, *Violence and the Sacred* 83, 85.
7 Girard, *Violence and the Sacred* 86–7, 102.
8 Garland, *Greek Way* 88.
9 Bede, *Ecclesiastical History* 167–8.
10 See Twombly, "Remembering Death" 195–6.
11 Huntington and Metcalf, *Celebrations* 203.
12 Eissler, *Psychiatrist and the Dying Patient* 150. See Gilbert and Gubar's discussion of Eliot's early unpublished poem, "The Love Song of St. Sebastian" (*No Man's Land* 1: 30–1).
13 Camus, *Myth of Sisyphus* 4.
14 Garland, *Greek Way* 98–9.
15 Marker's *Deadly Compassion* traces the life and death of Ann Humphry, cofounder along with her husband Derek of The Hemlock Society USA and deserted by him when she was diagnosed as having cancer. Marker insists that the euthanasia movement seeks to impose death sentences on those it deems unfit to live.
16 Pliny, *Letters* 1: 249.
17 Tacitus, *Annals* book 16. Durrell's play *Acté* depicts Petronius committing suicide slowly, with great care, in accord with "a lifetime's reputation for measure and elegance" (69).
18 Garland, *Greek Way* 99.
19 Helen Silving, "Suicide and Law," in Shneidman and Farberow 80.
20 Paul W. Pretzel, "Philosophical and Ethical Considerations of Suicide Prevention," in Weir 392.
21 See Fedden, *Suicide* 10.
22 Helen Silving, "Suicide and Law," in Shneidman and Farberow 80.
23 See M.D. Faber, "Shakespeare's Suicides: Some Historic, Dramatic

and Psychological Reflections," in Shneidman, *Self-Destruction* 30–58. Durkheim's groundbreaking study of suicide elucidates many of these categories.

24 M.D. Faber, "Shakespeare's Suicides," in Shneidman, *Self-Destruction* 31–2.

25 Faber, "Shakespeare's Suicides," in Shneidman, *Self-Destruction* 35.

26 Helen Silving, "Suicide and Law," in Shneidman and Farberow 83. McManners traces suicide's increasing acceptance during the French Enlightenment (*Death and the Enlightenment* 409–37).

27 Blackstone, *Commentaries* 1: 189.

28 Blackstone, *Commentaries* 1: 190.

29 See, for example, Stoker's *Dracula* 325, 330.

30 Holdsworth, *History of English Law* 13: 395.

31 Helen Silving, "Suicide and Law," in Shneidman and Farberow 82.

32 Shneidman, *Deaths of Man* 127.

33 Gay, *Freud* 651.

34 Thomas S. Szasz, "The Ethics of Suicide," in Weir 380.

35 Camus, *Myth of Sisyphus* 3.

36 Hoffman, *Mortal No* 112.

37 *Portable Nietzsche* 473–9.

38 Choron, *Suicide* 109.

39 Durkheim, *Suicide* 44.

40 Choron, *Suicide* 20.

41 Panati, *Extraordinary Endings* 347–9. The Hemlock Society USA, which supports euthanasia, chose its name for symbolic reasons only since, its literature maintains, ingesting hemlock is a painful way to die.

42 D.H. Lawrence, *Apocalypse* 85; *Lady Chatterley's Lover* 44 and *Etruscan Places* 52–6 similarly attack Socrates.

43 Hinz and Teunissen, "Savior and Cock" 289.

44 Taylor, *Holy Dying* 133.

45 Huntington and Metcalf, *Celebrations* 203.

46 Gunther, *Death Be Not Proud* 18–21. See Langer's discussion, *Age of Atrocity* 18–21.

47 Bataille, *Erotism* 81.

48 Girard, *Violence and the Sacred* 124–5.

49 Bataille, *Erotism* 234.

50 Millett, *Sexual Politics* 285, 288.

51 Lawrence's setting and timing echo what Wilson describes as having occurred at Newgrange in ancient Ireland. Early Irishmen constructed a "monumental 'house of eternity' for their royal dead. They did this with such careful planning and technical skill that they contrived that just once a year – at dawn on the year's 'deadest' day, the winter-solstice – the sun's light would shine through the structure's special roof-box, dart along its 701 foot tunnel-like passageway, and illuminate for just a few minutes the chamber that once housed the dead, a

happening they knew would continue into perpetuity" (*After Death Experience* 12).

52 Gilbert and Gubar, *No Man's Land* 2: 24–5.

53 Bataille maintains that human sacrifice is recent; victims of early sacrifices were animals. If so, stories of human sacrifice like "The Woman Who Rode Away," "Dry September," and "The Lottery" would seem *less* contemporary, more anachronistic if animals were substituted. Animals, not men, were commonly considered sacred, god-like, and "the killing of an animal may well have aroused a powerful feeling of sacrilege, and performed collectively, would consecrate the victim and confer a sort of godhead on it" (*Erotism* 81). See also Scholtmeijer, *Animal Victims*.

54 Bataille, *Erotism* 22.

55 Girard, *Violence and the Sacred* 49.

56 Huntington and Metcalf, *Celebrations* 208.

57 Girard, *Violence and the Sacred* 95.

58 Girard, *Violence and the Sacred* 94, 100.

59 Girard, *Violence and the Sacred* 124.

60 Foucault, *History of Sexuality* 1: 135.

4 DYING IN BED

1 Bishop, *Joyce's Book of the Dark* 66–7.

2 Ariès, *Hour* 107–9. See also Paxton, *Christianizing Death*.

3 Huntington and Metcalf, *Celebrations* 3. Boose sees *Othello* as essentially "about a *marriage*, memorially the most ritualized and symbolized of all human acts" ("Othello's Handkerchief" 361).

4 Huizinga, *Middle Ages* 144.

5 Darnton, *Kiss of Lamourette* 270. Morris makes a similar distinction between "ideologies of death" and "individual attitudes to death" ("Attitudes Toward Death" 297).

6 Taylor, *Holy Dying* 164–5.

7 Taylor, *Holy Living* 251.

8 In Boswell, *Life of Johnson* 169.

9 See Cockshut, "The Death Scene," *Truth to Life* 41–54; Garrett Stewart, "Transitions," *Death Sentences* 101–38; and Michael Wheeler, "The Deathbed: Consolation and Communication," *Death and the Future Life* 28–47.

10 Gorer, *Death, Grief and Mourning* 195.

11 Wilson, *After Death Experience* 5.

12 Morley, *Death, Heaven* 18.

13 Farrar, *Mercy and Judgment* 159–61.

14 See Osler, *Science and Immortality* and Lewis Thomas, "The Long Habit" 50. In *How We Die* Sherwin Nuland details a far more mixed experience.

15 Michael Wheeler, *Death and the Future Life* 33.
16 Wilson, *After Death Experience* 110.
17 Wilson, *After Death Experience* 109.
18 In Bataille, *Erotism* 11.
19 MacKay discusses thanatological and erotic rhetoric in Dickens and Thackeray ("Controlling Death and Sex," in Barreca 120–39). McManners, *Death Bed of Voltaire* and "Deathbeds" in *Death and the Enlightenment* 234–69; Ariès, *Hour* 14–21; and Michael Wheeler, *Death and the Future Life* 28–47 offer extended discussions of deathbed scenes.
20 See Ariès, *Hour* 310–12 for the "beautiful death" and 568–70 for "the dirty death."
21 Woolf, *The Diaries of Virginia Woolf* 2: 5 May 1924, 300–1; 4: 12 September 1934, 242; and *Moments of Being: Unpublished Autobiographical Writings of Virginia Woolf* 92. Hereafter cited as *Diaries* and *Moments of Being*, respectively.
22 Spilka, *Woolf's Quarrel* 6–8.
23 Ellmann, *James Joyce* 129–30, 136, 144.
24 See, for example, Donne's "Holy Sonnet 7."
25 Gorer, *Death, Grief and Mourning* xv, 195. Gorer's vividest childhood memories concern the death of Edward VII.
26 Gorer, *Death, Grief and Mourning* 5–7.
27 See McManners, "Death and the French Historians," in Whaley 109.
28 In Allain, *The Other Man* 148.
29 Lawrence Henderson, cited in Panati, *Extraordinary Endings* 259.
30 Macksey, "Last Words" 504.
31 Michael Wheeler discusses the tradition of the "comforting angel" at the deathbed (*Death and the Future Life* 31–3).
32 Twain in *Huckleberry Finn* provides a trans-Atlantic difference: laying-out done by men (255).
33 David Wheeler, *Journey to the Other Side* 3.
34 Garland, *Greek Way* 121.
35 Wilson, *After Death Experience* 5.

5 ARTIFICES OF MORTALITY

1 Yeats, *Collected Poems* 222–3.
2 Yeats, *Collected Poems* 217–18.
3 T. Sturge Moore, letter to Yeats, 16 April 1930, in Yeats and Moore, *Their Correspondence* 162.
4 Macksey, "Last Words" 509.
5 Ragon, *Space of Death* 70.
6 Wilson, *After Death Experience* 4.
7 See Boose's brilliant discussion of the subject, "Father and Bride in Shakespeare."

8 Vovelle, *Piété baroque*. See also McManners, *Death and the Enlightenment* 239–43, and Darnton, *Kiss of Lamourette* 280–92.
9 Ruskin, *Modern Painters* 4: 360.
10 Ackroyd, *Dickens* 940.
11 See Millgate, *Testamentary Acts*.
12 Hardy, *Collected Poems* 143.
13 The first living will law was California's Natural Death Act of 1976 (Marker, *Deadly Compassion* 43); the US Supreme Court endorsed the concept in 1990.
14 Shneidman, "The Death Certificate," *Death: Current Perspectives* 2nd ed. 148–53. See also Weisman, *Realization of Death*.
15 Peschel and Peschel, *When a Doctor Hates a Patient* 72.
16 Shneidman, "The Death Certificate," *Death: Current Perspectives* 2nd ed. 154, 151.
17 See Silverman, "Proposed New Death Certificate."
18 Nissel, *People Count* 32.
19 Trilling, *Experience of Literature* 896.
20 Huntington and Metcalf, *Celebrations* 117, 211.
21 E.O. James, *Beginnings of Religion* 133–4.
22 See Huntington and Metcalf, *Celebrations* 17, and Hertz, "Death."
23 Van Gennep, *Rites* 72.
24 Huntington and Metcalf, *Celebrations* 54.
25 Garland, *Greek Way* 46–7, 122, 41.
26 Stone, *Crisis of the Aristocracy* 575.
27 Ragon, *Space of Death* 284.
28 Morley, *Death, Heaven* 37.
29 Morley, *Death, Heaven* 98, 91.
30 Laqueur, "Bodies, Death" 122 and Hutter, "Novelist as Resurrectionist" 4. See Richardson, *Death, Dissection*, especially "Corpse as Commodity" 52–72 and "Trading Assassins" 131–58.
31 Michael Wheeler, *Death and the Future Life* 278.
32 Hutter, "Novelist as Resurrectionist" 2.
33 Hutter, "Novelist as Resurrectionist" 1.
34 As a reporter writing about prisons and executions, Dickens once referred to himself as "CHARLES DICKENS, Resurrectionist, In Search of a Subject" (Ackroyd, *Dickens* 169–70).
35 Sudnow, "Death, Uses of a Corpse, and Social Worth," in Shneidman, *Death: Current Perspectives* 2nd ed. 114. For corroborating evidence of social discrimination, see Ragon, *Space of Death* 291, and Ariès and Duby, *History of Private Life* 5: 262.
36 Sudnow, *Passing On* 116.
37 Stone, *Crisis of the Aristocracy* 579.
38 London *Morning Post*, 1 February 1820.
39 *Sunday Times*, 29/30 June 1830.

40 In Oring, "Forest Lawn" 62.
41 See Remnick, *Lenin's Tomb*.
42 Geertz, *Interpretation of Cultures* 181.
43 Mumford, *City in History* 7.
44 Campbell, "Poetry as Epitaph" 657.
45 Maeterlinck, *Before the Great Silence* 150.
46 Ariès, *Hour* 29–31. Stone also discusses the cemetery's central role in village life during the early modern period (*Family, Sex and Marriage* 54).
47 Morley, *Death, Heaven* 33, 34.
48 Loudon, *On . . . Cemeteries* 2, 37, 67.
49 McHale discusses death as both end and ending of Joyce's fictive texts (*Postmodernist Fiction* 233–5).
50 Ragon, *Space of Death* 110–11.
51 Fussell, *Great War* 6, 70.
52 Oring, "Forest Lawn" 69.
53 Brochure, "Forest Lawn Memorial-Parks and Mortuaries" (1977).
54 Oring, "Forest Lawn" 68.
55 Oring, "Forest Lawn" 62–5.
56 A team of biological anthropologists at Howard University is working to reconstruct the cultural and biological history of those buried in the Negroes Burial Ground. Useful discussions of cemeteries include Panofsky, *Tomb Sculpture*; Morley, *Death, Heaven* 41–51; Stanley French, "The Cemetery as Cultural Institution: The Establishment of Mount Auburn and the 'Rural Cemetery' Movement," in Stannard, *Death in America* 69–91; Jordan, *Texas Graveyards*; Ariès, *Hour* 475–556; Sloane, *Last Great Necessity*; and Ragon, *Space of Death*.
57 Garland, *Greek Way* 10.
58 Maeterlinck, *Before the Great Silence* 123.
59 Morley, *Death, Heaven* 60–1.
60 Miller, *Fiction and Repetition* 59.
61 Hinz and Teunissen, "Savior and Cock" 290–1.
62 Aldington, Introduction, *Apocalypse* xxiii.
63 Moore, *Intelligent Heart* 463.
64 Ragon, *Space of Death* 111, 107.
65 Ragon, *Space of Death* 107–10. See also Descamps, *Les Monuments aux morts*.
66 See James E. Young, *Texture of Memory*. In 1994, Young also mounted a superb exhibition, "The Art of Memory: Holocaust Memorials in History," shown at the New York Jewish Museum and then in Germany.
67 Ehrhart, "The Invasion of Grenada," in Rowe and Berg, *Vietnam War* 257–8. See Gotera's discussion of poetry by Vietnam veterans in *Radical Visions*.

6 FUNERALS AND STORIES

1 Forster, *Aspects of the Novel* 34.
2 Kafka, *Parables and Paradoxes* 93.
3 Ariès discusses "tame death" in *Western Attitudes* 1–25 and *Hour* 5–28
4 Huntington and Metcalf, *Celebrations* 34.
5 Stone, "Death and Its History" 22.
6 Spengler, *Decline of the West* 10.
7 Goody, *Death, Property* 11.
8 Huntington and Metcalf, *Celebrations* 95.
9 See R.S. Oppenheim, *Maori Death Customs.*
10 See Des Pres, *Survivor* (242–3), and Huntington and Metcalf, *Celebrations passim.*
11 G.S. Frazer, *Fear of the Dead* 168, 177–8. For all its impact on modernism, Frazer's work was largely discredited by later anthropologists.
12 Huntington and Metcalf, *Celebrations* 23.
13 Garland offers an exception: "the predominant image of the ordinary Greek dead is of beings which evoke pity rather than fear . . . the dead as perceived by the living were in a very literal sense mere shadows of their former selves" (*Greek Way* 12).
14 See Kübler-Ross, *On Death and Dying* 5 and Becker, *Denial of Death* ix.
15 G.S. Frazer, *Fear of the Dead* 167, 40.
16 G.S. Frazer, *Fear of the Dead* 4–7.
17 Cleanth Brooks, *Toward Yoknapatawpha* 102 and *Yoknapatawpha Country* 35.
18 Hertz, *Death* 77–8; Goody, *Death, Property* 26.
19 Gorer, *Death, Grief and Mourning* 15.
20 Geertz, *Interpretation of Cultures* 162.
21 Freud's *Totem and Taboo* examines taboos concerning naming the dead during mourning.
22 Hertz, *Death* 78–9, 86. Huntington and Metcalf concur, "All roads lead to preserving the social system" (*Celebrations* 28).
23 Garland, *Greek Way* 21.
24 Danforth, *Death Rituals* 37–8.
25 Witoszek, "Funerary Culture?" 206–7.
26 Joseph Henderson, "Ancient Myths and Modern Man," in Jung, *Man and His Symbols* 145.
27 Huntington and Metcalf, *Celebrations* 101, 93. See also van Gennep, *Rites* 146–65 and Hertz, *Death* 78–86.
28 Iles, *Pagan Funeral* 4–8.
29 Garland, *Greek Way* 10.
30 McManamon, *Funeral Oratory.*
31 Freud, *War and Death* 290.
32 *Morning Chronicle*, 31 January 1820.

33 See Sacks, *English Elegy* 1–37; Gilbert and Gubar, *No Man's Land* 2: 311–12.
34 See Heffernan, "'Adonais': Shelley's Consumption of Keats." Ramazani's *Poetry of Mourning* convincingly treats the modern war elegy as anti-elegiac in its refusal of traditional consolation; hence it becomes an elegy for the war elegy.
35 Ariès, *Hour* 168; Stone, *Crisis of the Aristocracy* 572, 577.
36 Laqueur, "Bodies, Death" 110–11.
37 Laqueur, "Bodies, Death" 113–14.
38 Morley, *Death, Heaven* 18, 11, 17, 63.
39 Morley, *Death, Heaven* 23.
40 Morley, *Death, Heaven* 11.
41 London *Times*, 17 November 1852.
42 Morley, *Death, Heaven* 80, 83.
43 London *Times*, 21 September 1852 (my emphases).
44 Morley, *Death, Heaven* 77.
45 See Bland, *Royal Way* 169, 190.
46 Morley, *Death, Heaven* 11. See also Laqueur, "Bodies, Death" 110.
47 Freud, *"Uncanny"* 242.
48 Barbara Tuchman, *Guns of August* 1.
49 Morley, *Death, Heaven* 79.
50 Howe, "Introduction," *Jude the Obscure* xxi–xxii.
51 See Bewell, "History of Death" 190.
52 Detweiler, "Moment of Death" 272.
53 Huntington and Metcalf, *Celebrations* 49.
54 Critics of *The Good Soldier* now question all these "facts." See Reichert's "Poor Florence Indeed!" and Ganzel's "What the Letter Said."
55 Woolf, "Modern Fiction" 154.
56 Frazer, *Fear of the Dead* 167, 40.
57 Ellmann, *James Joyce* 245. Detailing Joyce's extensive use of *The Egyptian Book of the Dead* (or "*Bug of the Deaf*" [*Wake* 134]), a "mythography of postmortality," in *Finnegans Wake*, Bishop (*Joyce's Book of the Dark*) also summarizes previous criticism on the subject (86–125, 405 fn.4).
58 See Florence L. Walzl, "Gabriel and Michael: The Conclusion of 'The Dead,'" in *Dubliners* 423–43.
59 Joyce, *Critical Writings* 172–4.
60 Wilde to Yeats; in Joyce, *Critical Writings* 174.
61 Joyce, *Critical Writings* 224–8.
62 Joyce, *Critical Writings* 193.
63 Joyce, *Critical Writings* 228.
64 Ellmann, "Introduction," *Joyce Letters* xviii.
65 Ellmann, *James Joyce* 244.
66 Ellmann, *James Joyce* 129. Joyce refused a demand from his uncle, John Murray, when his mother was already in a coma (136).
67 Ellmann, *James Joyce* 136.
68 Yeats, *Collected Poems* 338.

7 LIFE AFTER LIFE

1 Gosse, *Omphalos* 347–9.
2 In Pais, *'Subtle is the Lord . . . '* vi.
3 Pais, *'Subtle is the Lord . . . '* 23.
4 In Ragon, *Space of Death* 301.
5 Owen, *Darkened Room* xv–xvi. See also Janet Oppenheim, *The Other World.*
6 See Morley, *Death, Heaven* 104–5.
7 Florence Hardy, *Thomas Hardy* 148.
8 Owen, *Darkened Room* xvii.
9 Blavatsky, *Key to Theosophy* 27.
10 Blavatsky, *Secret Doctrine* 3–4.
11 Ellmann, *Yeats* 58.
12 Linda Henderson discusses this subject in detail in *Fourth Dimension.* See also Ringborn, *Sounding Cosmos.*
13 Gilbert and Gubar, *No Man's Land* 2: 29.
14 Maurice Tuchman, "Hidden Meanings" 18.
15 Blavatsky's spelling in *Secret Doctrine* 6.
16 Cullingford, *Gender and History* 38. Torgovnik speaks similarly of primitivism: "the Aryan folk were the vital 'primitive,'" but the primitive labeling of Jews and Gypsies marked them for death camps (*Gone Primitive* 253–4).
17 Blavatsky, *Key to Theosophy* 26, 39.
18 Garland, *Greek Way* 100–1.
19 Freud, *"Uncanny"* 243, 241.
20 Rank, *Double* 83–4.
21 Rank, *Double* 78–9.
22 Freud, *"Uncanny"* 242; my emphases.
23 Russell, "Do We Survive Death?" in Shneidman, *Death: Current Perspectives* 2nd ed. 409–10. Repudiating the claims of spiritualism, Henry James reluctantly arrived at the same conclusion in "Is There Life After Death?"
24 Owen, *Darkened Room* xv–xvii.
25 Zukav, *Wu Li Masters* 129. The search for "dark matter," however, the current hypothetical explanation of the gravitational force causing the high-speed rotation of spiral galaxies, strongly echoes the ether theory.
26 Zukav, *Wu Li Masters* 134–5.
27 Pagels, *Cosmic Code* 312.
28 Symons, *Symbolist Movement* 5
29 Woolf, "Mr. Bennett and Mrs. Brown" 95; "Modern Fiction" 151, 155.
30 See *Ulysses,* 247–8.
31 In Rank, *Double* 35. See also Hillis Miller, "*Wuthering Heights*: Repe-

tition and the 'Uncanny,'" *Fiction and Repetition* 42–72, and McHale's discussion of uncanny doubling in *Postmodernist Fiction* 223–4.

32 Freud, *"Uncanny"* 238; also *Pleasure Principle, passim.*

33 See Miller, *Fiction and Repetition* 22–41 for another view of compulsive repetition in this novel.

34 Rank, *Double* 77–8.

35 Rank, *Double* 6.

36 Rank, *Double* 12, 17.

37 Freud, *"Uncanny"* 235.

38 Fussell, *Great War* 3–4.

39 Gilbert and Gubar, *No Man's Land* 2: 267–9.

40 Fussell, *Great War* 115.

41 Bland, *Royal Way* 13.

42 See Gernes, "Porter's Version."

43 Pagels, *Cosmic Code* 150, 157. In *Dreams of Reason*, however, Pagels suggests that scientists now "tend to be antiphilosophers," but complexity theory may reunite the two (14).

44 Many recent books treat the religious implications of new cosmological discoveries: Corey, *God and the New Cosmology*; Davies, *God and the New Physics* and *The Mind of God*; Drees, *Beyond the Big Bang*; Jaki, *God and the Cosmologists*; Jastrow, *God and the Astronomers*; Lederman, *The God Particle.* In Margenau and Varghese, *Cosmos, Bios, Theos* sixty scientists speculate on God, the universe's origin, and the relationship between science and religion.

45 Schroeder, *Genesis and the Big Bang* 116.

46 See Penrose, *Emperor's New Mind.*

47 Heisenberg, *Physicist's Conception of Nature* 41.

48 See also Delacour, *Glimpses of the Beyond*; Stevenson, *Reincarnation*; David Wheeler, *The Other Side*; Ritchie, *Return From Tomorrow*; and Moody, *Reflections on Life after Life.*

49 Moody, *Life after Life* 97. Further investigations of near-death experiences include Ring, *Life at Death* and *Heading toward Omega*; Sabom, *Recollections of Death*; Grey, *Return from Death*; Wilson, *After Death Experience* 108–37; and Lundahl, *Near-Death Research.*

50 Wilson, *After Death Experience* 150.

51 See, for example, Noyes and Kletti, "Dying From Falls."

52 Freud, *Pleasure Principle* 13.

53 Sagan, "Amniotic Universe," in *Broca's Brain* 353–68.

54 Rank, *Trauma of Birth* 24.

55 Huntington and Metcalf, *Celebrations* 116.

56 Forster, *Two Cheers for Democracy* 76. Hereafter cited as *Two Cheers.*

57 Freud, *"Uncanny"* 245.

58 Wilson, *After Death Experience* 124–31, 155.

59 See Lundkvist, *Journeys in Dream and Imagination.*

8 SURVIVORS OF APOCALYPSE

1 In Ronald Clark, *Einstein* 370.
2 Thomas Renna, "Einstein on War and Peace," in Dennis Ryan, *Einstein and the Humanities* 144.
3 Elliot, *Book of the Dead* 6.
4 Fussell, *Great War* 74.
5 Craig and Egan, *Extreme Situations* 1.
6 Miller, "*Heart of Darkness* Revisited," in *Joseph Conrad, "Heart of Darkness"* 210–11, 221.
7 Bradbury, "The Denuded Place: War and Form in *Parade's End* and *U.S.A.*," in Klein, *First World War* 193–4.
8 Fussell, *Great War* 270–309. Bertrand Russell also discusses the exhilaration that greeted the war ("Justice in War-Time," in Russell and Perry, *The Ethics of War* 15).
9 Gilbert and Gubar, *No Man's Land* 2: 260.
10 Gilbert and Gubar, *No Man's Land* 2: 318.
11 Gilbert and Gubar, *No Man's Land* 1: 35–6. Peter Hays' *Limping Hero* discusses emasculated modern heroes.
12 Foucault, *Order of Things* 387. See also Bradbury and McFarlane, "The Name and Nature of Modernism," in *Modernism* 19–55.
13 Auerbach, *Mimesis* 487; Kermode, *Sense of an Ending* 40.
14 Fussell, *Great War* 311–12.
15 Gilbert and Gubar, *No Man's Land* 2: 319.
16 I am not, of course, justifying such "sport." As Fromm says, the Colosseum is "one of the greatest monuments to human sadism" (*Human Destructiveness* 317).
17 In *A View to a Death in the Morning*, Matt Cartmill, a biological anthropologist, offers a superb cultural and historical study of the ritual and meaning of hunting.
18 Faulkner, *Lion in the Garden* 255.
19 In Grenier, "Art of Fiction" 175.
20 Hemingway, *Selected Letters*, 18 June 1952, 765. Hereafter cited as *Letters*.
21 Latham, "Farewell to Machismo" 55.
22 Eliade, *Sacred and Profane* 107.
23 Baker, "Introduction," *Hemingway: Selected Letters* xi.
24 Hemingway, "Bullfighting, Sport and Industry" 83.
25 James Michener, Introduction, *Dangerous Summer* 3.
26 Michener, a fellow aficionado, maintains that Hemingway's second bullfight book caused the Spanish to reenshrine him "as the patron saint of the art" (Introduction, *Dangerous Summer* 15).
27 See Spilka, *Hemingway's Quarrel*, *passim*.
28 See D.H. Lawrence, "Man Is a Hunter," *Posthumous Papers* 33.
29 Foucault, *Discipline and Punish* 51–2.

30 Bataille, *Erotism* 82.
31 *Faulkner in the University* 206–7.

9 E.M. FORSTER

1 Previous discussions of Forster and death include Hoffman, *Mortal No* 78–87; Garrett Stewart, "Forster's Epistemology of Dying" and *Death Sentences* 179–213; and Jha, "Death in . . . Forster."
2 Anon., in Gardner, *Critical Heritage* 83.
3 Anon., in Gardner, *Critical Heritage* 309.
4 Heilbrun, *Androgyny* 98.
5 Trilling, *Forster* 134–5.
6 Heilbrun, *Androgyny* 97–101.
7 In Trilling, *Forster* 64.
8 Trilling, *Forster* 17.
9 Robert Martin says that the hopeless love in *Longest Journey* resulted from Forster's beginning to confront his homosexuality ("Edward Carpenter and the Double Structure of *Maurice*," in Kellogg, *Gay Literature* 36–7).
10 Summers, *Forster* 72.
11 Forster, *Lucy Novels* 36–8.
12 Forster, *Lucy Novels* 131.
13 In Furbank, *Forster* 1: 151.
14 Cowley, *"Paris Review" Interviews* 30.
15 Garland, *Greek Way* 8.
16 Maeterlinck, *Before the Great Silence* 89.
17 Summers, *Forster* 136.
18 Most of *Maurice*'s early commentators attacked it as dated, narrow, an artistic failure; some proceeded to revalue all of Forster downward. See Meyers, *Homosexuality and Literature* 99–108; Ozick, "Forster as Homosexual" (she castigates *Maurice* for not depicting explicit homosexual coitus 83); and Steiner, "Greenwood Tree." More positive and thoughtful analyses include Stephen Adams, *Homosexual as Hero* 106–20; Martin, "Edward Carpenter," in Kellogg, *Gay Literature*; Summers, *Forster* 141–80; and John Fletcher, "Forster's Self-Erasure: *Maurice* and the Scene of Masculine Love," in Bristow, *Sexual Sameness* 64–90.
19 Forster, "Terminal Note" to *Maurice* 249–50. Hereafter cited as "Terminal Note."
20 Forster, 16 June 1911; in Furbank, *Forster* 1: 199.
21 Furbank, *Forster* 1: 257.
22 Furbank, *Forster* 1: 259.
23 Forster, "Terminal Note" 250. The Wolfenden Report became law with the passage of the 1967 Sexual Offences Act.
24 Homer, *The Odyssey* 11: 539–40, 544–6.
25 David Lodge made this point first (in "Before the Deluge," in Gardner,

Critical Heritage 474). Those who argue that *Maurice* influenced *Lady Chatterley's Lover* include John Beer, "'The Last Englishman': Lawrence's Appreciation of Forster," in Das and Beer 245–68; King, "Influence of ... *Maurice*"; and Summers, *Forster* 11. Both *Maurice*'s Alec and *Lady Chatterley's Lover*'s Mellors reincarnate Annable, the gamekeeper in Lawrence's first novel, *The White Peacock* (1911), though Forster said he "had not the advantage" of Lawrence's "prickly gamekeepers" ("Terminal Note" 252).

26 Forster, letter, 13 December 1914; in Furbank, Introduction, English edition of *Maurice* 8–9.

27 Blavatsky, *Secret Doctrine* 12.

28 See Sharpe, *Allegories of Empire* 117–27.

29 Martin, *Love That Failed* 41.

30 *Letters of D.H. Lawrence* 2: 28 January 1915, 266.

31 In Elizabeth Heine, Introduction, *Arctic Summer* xxx.

10 VIRGINIA WOOLF

1 Cockshut, *Truth to Life* 76.

2 Spilka, *Woolf's Quarrel* 2.

3 DeSalvo, *Virginia Woolf* 20–35.

4 See Poole, *Unknown Virginia Woolf* 24–32 and DeSalvo, *Virginia Woolf* 1–6.

5 DeSalvo, *Virginia Woolf* 1.

6 Spilka, *Woolf's Quarrel* 46.

7 Marcus, "Britannia Rules *The Waves*," in Karen Lawrence, *Decolonizing Tradition* 143.

8 Miller, *Fiction and Repetition* 201.

9 Spilka, *Woolf's Quarrel* 7.

10 Nicolson, Introduction, *Letters* 2: xvii.

11 Smith, "Woolf and Death."

12 Woolf, "Modern Fiction" 154–5.

13 Woolf, Introduction to Modern Library edition (1928; vi). For these revisions, see Charles Hoffmann, "From Short Story to Novel"; A.J. Lewis, "From 'The Hours' to *Mrs. Dalloway*"; and Brenda Silver, "Textual Criticism as Feminist Practice: Or, Who's Afraid of Virginia Woolf Part II," in Bornstein, *Representing Modernist Texts* 193–222.

14 Suzette A. Henke, "Mrs. Dalloway: The Communion of Saints," in Jane Marcus, *New Feminist Essays* 139.

15 Spilka, *Woolf's Quarrel* 20.

16 Forster, *Two Cheers* 248.

17 Showalter, *Female Malady* 192.

18 Marcus, "Britannia Rules *The Waves*," in Karen Lawrence, *Decolonizing Tradition* 147.

19 Lehmann, "Woolf's *Mrs. Dalloway*" 9.
20 Miller, *Fiction and Repetition* 194.
21 Freud, *Pleasure Principle* 12.
22 Bell, *Virginia Woolf* 1: 164. See Trombley, *"All That Summer"* 249–65.
23 Showalter discusses "the ideology of psychiatric Victorianism," including George Savage, in *Female Malady* 101–93.
24 Lehmann, *Virginia Woolf* 51.
25 See Poole, *Unknown Virginia Woolf* 258–79.
26 See Bell, *Virginia Woolf* 2: 115–20; Poole, *Unknown Virginia Woolf* 51; and Spilka, *Woolf's Quarrel* 111–12.
27 See Castle, "Marie Antoinette Obsession."
28 Bell, *Virginia Woolf* 2: 53, 231, 233.
29 Trombley, *"All That Summer"* 253. See Bell, *Virginia Woolf* 2: 16.
30 Gilbert and Gubar, *No Man's Land* 2: 264, 311.
31 Marcus, "Britannia Rules *The Waves*," in Karen Lawrence, *Decolonizing Tradition* 141.
32 Bell, *Virginia Woolf* 2: 87. Woolf wrote that her creation of Clarissa "was true to my feeling for Kitty" (*Diaries* 3: 18 June 1925, 32).
33 Zwerdling, *Virginia Woolf* 279.
34 Gilbert and Gubar, *No Man's Land* 2: 316–17.
35 Holtby, *Virginia Woolf* 159.
36 Bell, *Virginia Woolf* 1: 44, 89–90.
37 Bell, *Virginia Woolf* 2: 128. Leonard Woolf, though he admired *Lighthouse*, thought Leslie Stephen's portrait unfairly "exaggerated his exactingness and sentimentality" (*Sowing* 182). But he had not been Stephen's victim.
38 Woolf, *To the Lighthouse: The Original Holograph Draft*, 6 August 1925, 2.
39 Daugherty, "'There She Sat'" 289–91.
40 Spilka, *Woolf's Quarrel* 12.
41 Woolf, "Speech Before the London/National Society for Women's Service," in *Pargiters* xxix, xxxi.
42 See Kelley, *"To the Lighthouse"* 103–10.
43 Bataille, *Erotism* 61.
44 See Hoffmann, "From Short Story to Novel" 172.
45 The passage is even eerier in the English edition: "[Mr. Ramsay stumbling along a passage stretched his arms out one dark morning, but, Mrs. Ramsay having died rather suddenly the night before, he stretched his arms out. They remained empty.]" (146–7).
46 Huntington and Metcalf, *Celebrations* 65, 77.
47 In Spater and Parsons, *True Minds* 9.
48 See Sprague, *Virginia Woolf* 9.
49 Fussell, *Great War* 315–26.
50 Poole, *Unknown Virginia Woolf* 278.
51 Bell, *Virginia Woolf* 2: 186–7.
52 In Nicolson, Introduction, *Letters* 6: xv.

53 Marcus, "Britannia Rules *The Waves*," in Karen Lawrence, *Decolonizing Tradition* 154–5.
54 In Bell, *Virginia Woolf* 2: 226.
55 Poole, *Unknown Virginia Woolf* 258. The "kindly formula" of the coroner's report was that she killed herself "while the balance of her mind was disturbed" (Nicolson, Introduction, *Letters* 6: xvii).
56 Woolf, *The Waves* 383. See Nicolson and Trautmann, *Letters* 6: 487.

11 LATE MODERNISM: GRAHAM GREENE

1 See MacArthur, "Last Word."
2 In Sherry, *Graham Greene* 105.
3 Lodge, "Graham Greene" 51.
4 Unpublished letter to Vivien Dayrell-Browning, 10 March 1926, University of Texas, Humanities Research Center.
5 Eliot, "Baudelaire" 423.
6 In Allain, *Other Man* 17.
7 Eliot, *The Waste Land* lines 39–40 in *Complete Poems.*
8 See Sherry, *Graham Greene* 93–9, 107.
9 Claud Cockburn, in Sherry, *Graham Greene* 192–3. Sherry discusses Greene's atheism (255).
10 Letter, 2 November 1925; in Sherry, *Graham Greene* 256.
11 Eliot's phrase, "Baudelaire" 422.
12 Waugh embraced Pelagianism, the orthodox alternative. For a discussion of their differences, see Donald Greene, "Greene and Waugh: 'Catholic Novelists,'" in Meyers, *Graham Greene* 5–37.
13 Eliot, "Baudelaire" 429.
14 Gilbert and Gubar, *No Man's Land* 2: 259.
15 Orwell, *Collected Essays* 440–1.
16 Bataille, *Erotism* 122n.
17 Robert Browning, "Bishop Blougram's Apology" lines 395–400 in *Poems.*
18 In Allain, *Other Man* 148.
19 Foucault, *Discipline and Punish* 68–9.
20 Baudelaire, *Intimate Journals* 31.
21 For Taylor, see *Holy Dying* 164–5, and discussion in chapter 4 above.
22 In Allain, *Other Man* 148.
23 In Florence Emily Hardy, *Thomas Hardy* 224.
24 In Allain, *Other Man* 151.
25 In Allain, *Other Man* 150.
26 In Allain, *Other Man* 153.
27 Girard, *Violence and the Sacred* 145–6.
28 Morley, *Death, Heaven* 91.
29 In Allain, *Other Man* 144.
30 In Allain, *Other Man* 73.

12 LATE MODERNISM: LAWRENCE DURRELL

1 In Alyn, *Lawrence Durrell* 97.
2 Durrell, *The Alexandria Quartet* 215, 338. Hereafter cited as *AQ*.
3 In Alyn, *Lawrence Durrell* 24–5.
4 Kenneth Young, "Dialogue with Durrell" 64.
5 Foucault, *Discipline and Punish* 67.
6 See William Godshalk, "Some Sources of Durrell's *Alexandria Quartet*," in Friedman, *Essays on Durrell* 158–9.
7 McHale, *Postmodernist Fiction* 66–7.
8 *The Avignon Quintet* includes *Monsieur, or The Prince of Darkness* (1975); *Livia or Buried Alive* (1978); *Constance* (1983); *Sebastian or Ruling Passions* (1984); and *Quinx or The Ripper's Tale* (1985).
9 Browne, "Garden of Cyrus" 222.
10 Pursewarden "deeply loved" Lawrence this "side idolatry" (*AQ* 284).
11 Eagleton, *Against the Grain* 132; see also Jameson, *Postmodernism* 6–54.

13 POSTMODERNISM: HISTORY, CHAOS, AND DEATH

1 Darnton, *Kiss of Lamourette* xv.
2 Henry James, Preface, *Aspern Papers* 31.
3 Darnton, *Kiss of Lamourette* xiv. See also Lowenthal, *Foreign Country*, *passim*.
4 Hutcheon, *Poetics of Postmodernism* x.
5 McHale, *Postmodernist Fiction* 123.
6 See Lewin, *Complexity* and Waldrop, *Complexity*.
7 Lodge, *Modes of Modern Writing* 220–45. Briggs and Peat discuss the relationship between scientific thought (especially chaos theory) and the arts of literature, painting, and music (*Turbulent Mirror* 194–200).
8 Gleick, *Chaos* 103.
9 Gleick, *Chaos* 321.
10 McHale, *Postmodernist Fiction* 124.
11 McHale, *Postmodernist Fiction* 125, 58.
12 McHale, *Postmodernist Fiction* 65.
13 Roth, "'I Always Wanted You to Admire My Fasting'; or, Looking at Kafka," *Reading Myself* 247–70.
14 Robertson, "Hystery, Herstory, History" 462–3. Ozsvath and Satz, "Audacity," and Laura Tanner, "Sweet Pain," condemn Thomas for exploiting the Holocaust.
15 See Lipstadt, *Denying the Holocaust*, and Vidal-Naquet, *Assassins of Memory*.
16 Lambert, *Modern Medical Mistakes* 11, 167.
17 Sontag, *AIDS and Its Metaphors* 92–3.
18 See Corea, *Invisible Epidemic*.
19 Diamond, "Mysterious Origin of AIDS" 27–9. See also Arno and

Feiden, *Against the Odds*; Farmer, *Aids and Accusation*; Gould, "Terrifying Normalcy of AIDS"; Grmek, *History of AIDS*.

20 See McLeod, "Death in the Family."

21 See Margaret Pabst Battin, "The Concept of Rational Suicide," in Shneidman *Death: Current Perspectives* 3rd ed. 297–320, and Humphry and Wickett, *Right to Die*.

22 Ragon, *Space of Death* 295.

23 Kevorkian, "Physician-Assisted Suicide Should Be Legal," in Biskup, *Suicide* 67.

24 "Hospice Programs," Report of the AMA Council on Medical Services, in Fruehling, *Sourcebook* 193.

25 Leonard M. Leigner, in "Hospice Programs," Fruehling, *Sourcebook* 193.

26 See Spring, "A Genuinely 'Good Death.'"

27 See Quill, *Death and Dignity*.

28 Lambert, *Modern Medical Mistakes* 157.

Bibliography

Ackroyd, Peter. *Dickens*. New York: HarperCollins, 1990.

Adams, Henry. *The Education of Henry Adams* (1918). New York: Modern, 1946.

Adams, Stephen. *The Homosexual as Hero in Contemporary Fiction*. New York: Barnes, 1980.

Aeschylus. *The Oresteia* (5th century BC). Trans. Robert Fagles. New York: Viking, 1975.

Albee, Edward. *All Over*. New York: Atheneum, 1971.

Allain, Marie-Françoise, ed. *The Other Man: Conversations with Graham Greene* (1981). Trans. Guido Waldman. New York: Simon, 1983.

Alyn, Marc. *Lawrence Durrell: The Big Supposer*. New York: Grove, 1974.

Anon. *The Battle of Maldon* (10th century). Trans. Kevin Crossley-Holland. London: Macmillan, 1965.

Anon. *Beowulf* (8th century). Trans. E. Talbot Donaldson. New York: Norton, 1966.

Anon. *Everyman and Medieval Miracle Plays*. Ed. A.C. Cawley. New York: Dutton, 1959.

Anon. *The Song of Roland* (*c.* 1100). Trans. Frederick Goldin. New York: Norton, 1978.

Ariès, Philippe. *The Hour of Our Death*. Trans. Helen Weaver. New York: Knopf, 1981.

Western Attitudes toward Death: From the Middle Ages to the Present (1974). Trans. Patricia M. Ranum. Baltimore: Johns Hopkins University Press, 1976.

Ariès, Philippe, and Georges Duby, eds. *A History of Private Life* (1985–7). 5 vols. Trans. Arthur Goldhammer. Cambridge, MA: Harvard University Press, 1987–91.

Arno, Peter S., and Karyn L. Feiden. *Against the Odds: The Story of AIDS Drug Development, Politics and Profits*. New York: Harper, 1992,

Arnold, Matthew. *Poems*. Ed. Kenneth Allott. New York: Barnes & Noble, 1965.

Auerbach, Erich. *Mimesis: The Representation of Reality in Western Literature*. Trans. Willard Trask. New York: Doubleday, 1957.

Austen, Jane. *Emma* (1816). Ed. Stephen M. Parrish. New York: Norton, 1972.
Barreca, Regina, ed. *Sex and Death in Victorian Literature.* Bloomington: Indiana University Press, 1990.
Barth, John. *Letters.* New York: Putnam, 1979.
Bataille, Georges. *Erotism: Death and Sensuality* (1957). Trans. Mary Dalwood. San Francisco: City Lights, 1986.
Baudelaire, Charles. *Intimate Journals* (1857; 1930). Trans. Christopher Isherwood. London: Panther, 1969.
Becker, Ernest. *The Denial of Death.* New York: Free Press, 1973.
Beckett, Samuel. *Three Novels: Molloy. Malone Dies. The Unnamable* (1951–3). New York: Grove, 1965.
Bede, The Venerable. *The Ecclesiastical History of the English Nation* (731). New York: Dutton, 1930.
Belkin, Lisa. *First, Do No Harm.* New York: Simon, 1993.
Bell, Quentin. *Virginia Woolf: A Biography.* 2 vols. New York: Harcourt, 1972.
Beveridge, W.I.B. *Influenza: The Last Great Plague: An Unfinished Story of Discovery.* New York: Prodist, 1977.
Bewell, Alan. "The History of Death." *Wordsworth and the Enlightenment: Nature, Man, and Society in the Experimental Poetry.* New Haven: Yale University Press, 1989. 187–234.
Bishop, John. *Joyce's Book of the Dark: "Finnegans Wake."* Madison: University of Wisconsin Press, 1986.
Biskup, Michael. *Suicide: Opposing Viewpoints.* San Diego: Greenhaven, 1992.
Black, Douglas, *et al. Medicine Betrayed: The Participation of Doctors in Human Rights Abuses.* London: Zed, 1992.
Blackstone, William. *Commentaries on the Laws of England.* 4 vols. Oxford: Clarendon Press, 1765–9.
Bland, Olivia. *The Royal Way of Death.* London: Constable, 1986.
Blavatsky, Helena Petrovna. *An Abridgement of The Secret Doctrine* (1888). Eds. Elizabeth Preston and Christmas Humphreys. London: Theosophical, 1966.
Isis Unveiled: A Master-Key to the Mysteries of Ancient and Modern Science and Theology (1877). Los Angeles: Theosophy, 1968.
The Key to Theosophy (1889). Pasadena: Theosophical, 1946.
Boose, Lynda E. "The Father and the Bride in Shakespeare." *PMLA* 97.3 (May 1982): 325–47.
"Othello's Handkerchief: 'The Recognizance and Pledge of Love.'" *English Literary Renaissance* 5.3 (Autumn 1975): 360–74.
Bornstein, George, ed. *Representing Modernist Texts: Editing as Interpretation.* Ann Arbor: University of Michigan Press, 1991.
Boswell, James. *The Life of Samuel Johnson* (1791). New York: Modern, 1952.

Bourke, Angela. "The Irish Traditional Lament and the Grieving Process." *Women's Studies International Forum* 2.4 (1988): 287–91.

Bradbury, Malcolm, and James McFarlane, eds. *Modernism 1890–1930*. Harmondsworth: Penguin, 1976.

Briggs, John, and F. David Peat. *Turbulent Mirror: An Illustrated Guide to Chaos Theory and the Science of Wholeness*. New York: Harper, 1989.

Bristow, Joseph, ed. *Sexual Sameness: Textual Differences in Lesbian and Gay Writing*. London: Routledge, 1992.

Brivic, Sheldon. *Joyce between Freud and Jung*. Port Washington, NY: Kennikat, 1980.

Brontë, Charlotte. *Jane Eyre* (1847). New York: Norton, 1987.

Brontë, Emily. *Wuthering Heights* (1847). New York: Odyssey, 1968.

Brooke-Rose, Christine. *Such*. London: Michael Joseph, 1966.

Brooks, Cleanth. *William Faulkner: Toward Yoknapatawpha and Beyond*. New Haven: Yale University Press, 1978.

William Faulkner: The Yoknapatawpha Country. New Haven: Yale University Press, 1974.

Brooks, Peter. "Freud's Masterplot." *The Critical Tradition: Classic Texts and Contemporary Trends*. Ed. David H. Richter. New York: St. Martin's, 1989. 710–20.

Browne, Thomas. "The Garden of Cyrus; or, The Quincunciall Lozenge" (1658). *The Religio Medici and Other Writings of Sir Thomas Browne*. New York: Dutton, 1925.

"Hydriotaphia, or Urne-Buriall" (1658). *The Prose of Sir Thomas Browne*. Ed. Norman Endicott. New York University Press, 1968.

Browning, Robert. *Poems of Robert Browning*. Ed. Donald Smalley. Boston: Houghton, 1956.

Buer, M.C. *Health, Wealth, and Population in the Early Days of the Industrial Revolution*. London: Routledge, 1926.

Bunyan, John. *The Pilgrim's Progress* (1678). Baltimore: Penguin, 1965.

Bury, J.B. *The Idea of Progress: An Inquiry into its Origin and Growth* (1920). New York: Dover, 1955.

Calvino, Italo. *If on a Winter's Night a Traveller* (1979). Trans. William Weaver. New York: Harcourt, 1981.

Cameron, J.M. "Surviving Death." *New York Review of Books* (31 October 1974): 6–11.

Campbell, Karen Mills. "Poetry as Epitaph." *Journal of Popular Culture* 14.4 (Spring 1981): 657–68.

Camus, Albert. *The Myth of Sisyphus and Other Essays* (1942). New York: Vintage, 1955.

Carter, Angela. *Heroes and Villains*. New York: Simon, 1969.

The Passion of New Eve. London: Gollancz, 1977.

Cartmill, Matt. *A View to a Death in the Morning: Hunting and Nature through History*. Cambridge, MA: Harvard University Press, 1993.

Cartwright, Frederick F. *Disease and History* (1972). New York: NAL, 1974.

Castle, Terry. "Marie Antoinette Obsession." *Representations* 38 (Spring 1992): 1–38.
Cather, Willa. *Death Comes for the Archbishop* (1927). New York: Knopf, 1968.
Cervantes Saavedra, Miguel de. *Don Quixote* (1605, 1615). Trans. J.M. Cohen. Harmondsworth: Penguin, 1950
Chadwick, Edwin. *A Report on the Results of a Special Inquiry into the Practice of Interment in Towns* (1843). Philadelphia: C. Sherman, 1845.
Chaucer, Geoffrey. *The Works of Geoffrey Chaucer.* Ed. F.N. Robinson. Boston: Houghton, 1961.
Chernikov, Alexander A., Roald Z. Sagdeev, and George M. Zaslavsky. "Chaos: How Regular Can It Be?" *Physics Today* (November 1988): 27–35.
Chopin, Kate. *The Awakening* (1899). New York: Norton, 1976.
Choron, Jacques. *Death and Western Thought.* New York: Collier, 1963.
Suicide. New York: Scribners's, 1972.
Clark, Ronald W. *Einstein: The Life and Times.* New York: World, 1971.
Clark, Walter Van Tilburg. *The Ox-Bow Incident* (1940). New York: Readers Club, 1942.
Cockshut, A.O.J. *Truth to Life: The Art of Biography in the Nineteenth Century.* London: Collins, 1974.
Conrad, Joseph. *Chance* (1913). London: Dent, 1949.
Great Short Works of Joseph Conrad. New York: Harper, 1967.
Joseph Conrad, "Heart of Darkness": A Case Study in Contemporary Criticism. Ed. Ross C. Murfin. New York: St. Martin's, 1989.
Lord Jim (1899–1900). New York: Norton, 1968.
A Personal Record (1908–9). London: Thomas Nelson, 1912.
Coover, Robert. *The Universal Baseball Association, Inc. of J. Henry Waugh, Prop.* (1968). New York: Signet, 1969.
Corea, Gena. *The Invisible Epidemic: The Story of Women and AIDS.* New York: Harper, 1992.
Corey, Michael A. *God and the New Cosmology: The Anthropic Design Argument.* Lanham, MD: Rowman, 1992.
Cowley, Malcolm, ed. *Writers at Work: The "Paris Review" Interviews.* New York: Viking, 1967.
Craig, David, and Michael Egan. *Extreme Situations: Literature and Crisis from the Great War to the Atom Bomb.* London: Macmillan, 1979.
Crane, Stephen. *The Red Badge of Courage and Other Writings* (1895). Ed. Richard Chase. Boston: Houghton, 1960.
Crashaw, Richard. "A Hymn to the Name and Honor of the Admirable Sainte Teresa" (1646). *Seventeenth-Century English Poetry.* Ed. R.C. Bald. New York: Harper, 1959.
Cullingford, Elizabeth Butler. *Gender and History in Yeats's Love Poetry.* Cambridge University Press, 1993.
Danforth, Loring M. *The Death Rituals of Rural Greece.* Princeton University Press, 1982.

Darnton, Robert. *The Kiss of Lamourette: Reflections in Cultural History*. New York: Norton, 1990.

Das, G.K., and John Beer, eds. *E.M. Forster: A Human Exploration*. New York University Press, 1979.

Daugherty, Beth Rigel. "'There She Sat': The Power of the Feminist Imagination in *To the Lighthouse*." *Twentieth Century Literature* 37.3 (Fall 1991): 289–308.

Davies, Paul. *God and the New Physics*. New York: Simon, 1984.

The Mind of God: The Scientific Basis for a Rational World. New York: Simon, 1992.

Delacour, Jean-Baptiste. *Glimpses of the Beyond*. New York: Delacorte, 1973.

DeSalvo, Louise. *Virginia Woolf: The Impact of Childhood Sexual Abuse on Her Life and Work*. Boston: Beacon, 1989.

Descamps, Olivier. *Les Monuments aux morts de la guerre 14–18 chefs-d'œuvre d'art public*. Paris: Francis Deswarte, 1978.

Des Pres, Terrence. *The Survivor: An Anatomy of Life in the Death Camps*. New York: Pocket, 1977.

Detweiler, Robert. "The Moment of Death in Modern Fiction." *Contemporary Literature* 13.3 (Summer 1972): 269–94.

Diamond, Jared. "The Mysterious Origin of AIDS." *Natural History* (September 1992): 24–9.

Dickens, Charles. *Bleak House* (1853). London: Collins, 1953.

"A Christmas Carol" (1843). *The Best Short Stories of Charles Dickens*. Ed. Edwin Valentine Mitchell. New York: Scribners's, 1947. 422–84.

Great Expectations (1860–1). New York: Holt, 1962.

The Mystery of Edwin Drood (1870). Ed. Margaret Cardwell. Oxford: Clarendon Press, 1972.

The Old Curiosity Shop (1841). Oxford University Press, 1975.

Our Mutual Friend (1864–5). Oxford University Press, 1978.

A Tale of Two Cities (1859). New York: Watts, 1967.

Donne, John. *Biathanatos* (1608/1647). Eds. Michael Rudick and M. Pabst Battin. New York: Garland, 1982.

Dostoevsky, Fyodor. *The Possessed* (1871–2). Trans. David Magarshack. Harmondsworth: Penguin, 1971.

Drake, Michael, ed. *Population in Industrialization*. London: Methuen, 1969.

Drees, Willem B. *Beyond the Big Bang: Quantum Cosmologies and God*. Peru, IL: Open Court, 1990.

Durkheim, Emil. *Suicide* (1897). Trans. John A. Spaulding and George Simpson. New York: Free Press, 1963.

Durrell, Lawrence. *Acté*. New York: Dutton, 1966.

The Alexandria Quartet (1957–60). London: Faber, 1962.

The Black Book (1938). New York: Pocket, 1962.

Constance. London: Faber, 1983.

A Key to Modern British Poetry. Norman: University of Oklahoma Press, 1952.

Livia or Buried Alive. London: Faber, 1978.
Monsieur, or The Prince of Darkness. New York: Viking, 1975.
Nunquam. New York: Pocket, 1971.
"Prospero's Cell" and "Reflections on a Marine Venus" (1945, 1953). New York: Dutton, 1962.
Quinx or The Ripper's Tale. London: Faber, 1985.
Sebastian Or Ruling Passions. New York: Viking, 1984.
Tunc. London: Faber, 1968.
Durrell, Lawrence, and Henry Miller. *The Durrell–Miller Letters, 1935–80* (1964). Ed. Ian S. MacNiven. New York: New Directions, 1988.
Eagleton, Terry. *Against the Grain: Essays 1975–85*. London: Verso, 1986.
Ehrenreich, Barbara, and Deirdre English. *Witches, Midwives, and Nurses: A History of Women Healers*. New York: Feminist, 1973.
Einstein, Albert. *Ideas and Opinions* (1954). Trans. Sonja Bargmann. New York: Crown, 1962.
On the Method of Theoretical Physics. Oxford University Press, 1933.
Eissler, K.R. *The Psychiatrist and the Dying Patient*. New York: International Universities Press, 1955.
Eliade, Mircea. *Cosmos and History: The Myth of the Eternal Return* (1949). Trans. Willard R. Trask. New York: Harper, 1959.
The Sacred and the Profane: The Nature of Religion (1957). Trans. Willard R. Trask. New York: Harper, 1961.
Eliot, George. *Middlemarch* (1871–2). Ed. Gordon S. Haight. Boston: Houghton, 1956.
Eliot, T.S. "Baudelaire" (1930). *Selected Essays* (1932). London: Faber, 1969. 419–30.
The Complete Poems and Plays 1909–1950. New York: Harcourt, 1962.
Elliot, Gil. *Twentieth Century Book of the Dead*. London: Allen Lane, 1972.
Ellison, Ralph. *Invisible Man* (1952). New York: Vintage, 1990.
Ellmann, Richard. *James Joyce* (1959). Rev. ed. Oxford University Press, 1983.
Oscar Wilde. New York: Knopf, 1988.
Yeats: The Man and the Masks (1948). New York: Norton, 1979.
Elvee, Richard Q., ed. *The End of Science? Attack and Defense*. Lanham, MD: University Press of America, 1992.
Elyot, Thomas. *The Book Named the Governour* (1531). Ed. S.E. Lehmberg. London: Dent; New York: Dutton, 1962.
Faris, Wendy B. "1001 Words: Fiction Against Death." *Georgia Review* 36.4 (Winter 1982): 811–30.
Farmer, Paul. *Aids and Accusation: Haiti and the Geography of Blame*. Berkeley: University of California Press, 1992.
Farrar, Frederic William. *Mercy and Judgment: A Few Last Words on Christian Eschatology with Reference to Dr. Pusey's "What is of Faith?"* New York: Dutton, 1881.
Faulkner, Peter. *Modernism*. London: Methuen, 1977.

ed. *A Modernist Reader: Modernism in England 1910–1930*. London: Batsford, 1986.

Faulkner, R.O., ed. *The Ancient Egyptian Book of the Dead*. London: British Museum, 1985.

Faulkner, William. *Absalom, Absalom!* (1936). New York: Modern, 1951.

As I Lay Dying (1930). New York: Vintage, 1957.

Big Woods: The Hunting Stories of William Faulkner. New York: Random, 1955.

The Collected Stories of William Faulkner. New York: Random, 1950.

A Fable. New York: Random, 1954.

Faulkner in the University: Class Conferences at the University of Virginia, 1957–1958. Eds. Frederick L. Gwynn and Joseph L. Blotner. New York: Vintage, 1959.

Flags in the Dust (1929). New York: Random, 1973.

Go Down, Moses. New York: Modern, 1942.

Light in August (1932). New York: Modern, 1959.

Lion in the Garden: Interviews with William Faulkner, 1926–1962. Eds. James B. Meriwether and Michael Millgate. Lincoln: University of Nebraska Press, 1980.

The Portable Faulkner (1946). Ed. Malcolm Cowley. New York: Viking, 1985.

Soldiers' Pay (1926). New York: Signet, 1968.

The Sound and the Fury (1929). New York: Modern, 1956.

Fedden, Henry Romily. *Suicide: A Social and Historical Study*. London: Davies, 1938.

Federman, Raymond. *Take It or Leave It*. New York: Fictive Collective, 1976.

Feifel, Herman, ed. *The Meaning of Death*. New York: McGraw, 1959.

Ferris, Timothy. *The Mind's Sky: Human Intelligence in a Cosmic Context*. New York: Bantam, 1992.

Fleishman, Avrom. *Fiction and the Ways of Knowing: Essays on British Novels*. Austin: University of Texas Press, 1978.

Ford, Ford Madox. *The Good Soldier* (1916). New York: Vintage, 1955.

Henry for Hugh. Philadelphia: Lippincott, 1934.

Joseph Conrad: A Personal Remembrance. London: Duckworth, 1924.

Parade's End (1924–8). New York: Knopf, 1961.

The Rash Act. London: Cape, 1933.

Ford, Joseph. "How Random is a Coin Toss?" *Physics Today* 36 (April 1983): 40–7.

Forster, E.M. *Alexandria: A History and a Guide* (1922). Garden City: Doubleday, 1961.

Arctic Summer and Other Fiction. Ed. Elizabeth Heine. New York: Holmes, 1981.

Aspects of the Novel (1927). Harmondsworth: Penguin, 1964.

Howards End (1910). New York: Vintage, 1921.

The Longest Journey (1907). New York: Vintage, 1962.

The Lucy Novels: Early Sketches for "A Room with a View." Ed. Oliver Stallybrass. London: Edward Arnold, 1977.

Maurice (1914/1971). New York: Norton, 1981; Harmondsworth: Penguin, 1975.

A Passage to India (1924). New York: Harcourt, 1952.

A Room with a View (1908). London: Abinger, 1977.

Two Cheers for Democracy. New York: Harcourt, 1951.

A View without a Room (1958). New York: Albondocani, 1973.

Where Angels Fear to Tread (1905). New York: Vintage, 1920.

Foster, Hal, ed. *The Anti-aesthetic: Essays on Postmodern Culture*. Port Townsend, WA: Bay Press, 1983.

Foucault, Michel. *Discipline and Punish: The Birth of the Prison* (1975). Trans. Alan Sheridan. New York: Vintage, 1979.

The History of Sexuality (1976). 2 vols. Trans. Robert Hurley. New York: Vintage, 1980.

The Order of Things: An Archaeology of the Human Sciences (1966). New York: Vintage, 1973.

Fowles, John. *The French Lieutenant's Woman* (1969). New York: Signet, 1970.

Frazer, James George. *The Fear of the Dead in Primitive Religion* (1933). New York: Biblo, 1966.

The New Golden Bough (1890). Ed. Theodor H. Gaster. New York: Criterion, 1959.

Frazer, William M. *A History of English Public Health, 1834–1939*. London: Bailliere, 1950.

Freud, Sigmund. *The Standard Edition of the Complete Psychological Works of Sigmund Freud* (*SE*) (1886–1939). 24 vols. Ed. and trans. James Strachey. London: Hogarth and the Institute of Psycho-Analysis, 1964.

Beyond the Pleasure Principle (1920). *SE* 18 (1920–2): 7–64. New York: Norton, 1961.

Civilization and Its Discontents (1929–30). *SE* 21 (1927–31): 64–145. New York: Norton, 1961.

Thoughts for the Times on War and Death (1915). *SE* 14 (1914–16): 273–300. New York: Basic, 1959.

Totem and Taboo: Some Points of Agreement between the Mental Lives of Savages and Neurotics (1912–13). *SE* 13 (1913–14): 1–161. New York: Norton, 1950.

The "Uncanny." SE 17 (1919): 217–52. London: Hogarth, 1955.

Freud, Sigmund, and Albert Einstein. *Why War? SE* 22 (1933) 197–215. Paris: International Institute, 1933.

Friedman, Alan J. and Carol C. Donley. *Einstein as Myth and Muse*. Cambridge University Press, 1985.

Friedman, Alan Warren. "Hamlet the Unready." *Modern Language Quarterly* 37.1 (March 1976): 15–34.

ed. *Critical Essays on Lawrence Durrell*. Boston: Hall, 1987.
Friedman, Bruce Jay. *Steambath*. New York: Knopf, 1971.
Fromm, Erich. *The Anatomy of Human Destructiveness* (1973). Greenwich, CT: Fawcett, 1975.
Fruehling, James A. *Sourcebook on Death and Dying*. Chicago: Marquis, 1982.
Frye, Northrop. *The Anatomy of Criticism* (1957). New York: Atheneum, 1967.
Fuentes, Carlos. *Terra nostra* (1975). Trans. Margaret Sayers Peden. New York: Farrar, 1976.
Fukuyama, Francis. *The End of History and the Last Man*. New York: Free Press, 1992.
Furbank, P.N. *E.M. Forster: A Life*. 2 vols. London: Secker, 1977.
Fussell, Paul. *The Great War and Modern Memory* (1975). Oxford University Press, 1977.
Wartime: Understanding and Behavior in the Second World War. Oxford University Press, 1989.
Ganzel, Dewey. "What the Letter Said: Fact and Inference in *The Good Soldier*." *Journal of Modern Literature* 11.2 (July 1984): 277–90.
Gardner, Philip, ed. *E.M. Forster: The Critical Heritage*. London: Routledge, 1973.
Garland, Robert. *The Greek Way of Death*. Ithaca: Cornell University Press, 1985.
Gay, Peter. *Freud: A Life for Our Time*. New York: Norton, 1988.
Gee, Maggie. *Dying, in Other Words*. Brighton: Harvester, 1981.
Geertz, Clifford. *The Interpretation of Cultures: Selected Essays*. New York: Basic, 1973.
Gernes, Sonia. "Life After Life: Katherine Anne Porter's Version." *Journal of Popular Culture* 14.4 (Spring 1981): 669–75.
Gilbert, Sandra M., and Susan Gubar. *No Man's Land: The Place of the Woman Writer in the Twentieth Century*. 3 vols. New Haven: Yale University Press, 1988–.
Girard, René. *Violence and the Sacred* (1972). Trans. Patrick Gregory. Baltimore: Johns Hopkins University Press, 1981.
Gleick, James. *Chaos: Making a New Science*. New York: Viking, 1987.
Golding, William. *Pincher Martin*. New York: Harcourt, 1956.
Goody, Jack. *Death, Property and the Ancestors: A Study of the Mortuary Customs of the Lodagaa of West Africa*. Stanford University Press, 1962.
Gorer, Geoffrey. *Death, Grief and Mourning in Contemporary Britain*. London: Cresset, 1965.
Gosse, Philip Henry. *Omphalos: An Attempt to Untie the Geological Knot*. London: Van Voorst, 1857.
Gotera, Vince. *Radical Visions: Poetry by Vietnam Veterans*. Athens: University of Georgia Press, 1994.
Gould, Stephen Jay. "The Terrifying Normalcy of AIDS." *The New York Times Magazine* (19 April 1987): 31–3.

Greene, Graham. *Brighton Rock* (1938). New York: Penguin, 1977.
Collected Essays (1969). New York: Viking, 1981.
The End of the Affair (1951). Harmondsworth: Penguin, 1977.
The Heart of the Matter (1948). New York: Viking, 1963.
The Human Factor. London: Bodley Head, 1978.
The Lawless Roads (1939). London: Heinemann, 1955.
The Power and the Glory (1940). New York: Viking, 1962.
A Sort of Life. New York: Simon, 1971.
Ways of Escape. New York: Simon, 1980.

Grenier, Cynthia. "The Art of Fiction: An Interview with William Faulkner – September 1955." *Accent* 16.3 (Summer 1956): 167–77.

Grey, Margot. *Return from Death: An Exploration of the Near-Death Experience*. London: Arkana, 1985.

Grmek, Mirko D. *History of AIDS: Emergence and Origin of a Modern Pandemic*. Trans. Russell C. Maulitz and Jacalyn Duffin. Princeton University Press, 1990.

Gunther, John. *Death Be Not Proud: A Memoir*. New York: Harper, 1949.

Guthke, Karl S. *Last Words: Variations on a Theme in Cultural History*. Princeton University Press, 1992.

Haley, Bruce. *The Healthy Body and Victorian Culture*. Cambridge, MA: Harvard University Press, 1978.

Hardy, Florence Emily. *The Life of Thomas Hardy: 1840–1928* (1928–30). New York: St. Martin's, 1962.

Hardy, Thomas. *The Complete Poems of Thomas Hardy*. Ed. James Gibson. London: Macmillan, 1979.
Jude the Obscure (1895). Ed. Irving Howe. Boston: Houghton, 1965.
The Mayor of Casterbridge (1886). London: Macmillan, 1981.
The Return of the Native (1878). Ed. James Gindin. New York: Norton, 1969.
Tess of the d'Urbervilles (1891). New York: Norton, 1965.

Hawkes, John. *Travesty*. New York: New Directions, 1976.

Hawking, Stephen W. *A Brief History of Time: From the Big Bang to Black Holes*. New York: Bantam, 1988.

Hayles, N. Katherine. *Chaos Bound: Orderly Disorder in Contemporary Literature and Science*. Ithaca: Cornell University Press, 1990.

Hays, Peter. *The Limping Hero: Grotesques in Literature*. New York University Press, 1971.

Heath, Stephen. *The Sexual Fix* (1982). London: Macmillan, 1986.

Heffernan, James A.W. "'Adonais': Shelley's Consumption of Keats." *Studies in Romanticism* 23.3 (Fall 1984): 295–315.

Heilbrun, Carolyn G. *Toward a Recognition of Androgyny* (1964). New York: Norton, 1982.

Heisenberg, Werner. *The Physicist's Conception of Nature* (1955). Trans. Arnold J. Pomerans. New York: Harcourt, 1958.
Physics and Beyond. Trans. Arnold J. Pomerans. New York: Harper, 1971.

Hemingway, Ernest. *Across the River and Into the Trees* (1950). New York: Scribner's, 1978.

"Bullfighting, Sport and Industry." *Fortune* 1 (March 1930): 83–88, 139–50.

The Dangerous Summer (1960). Intro. James A. Michener. New York: Scribner's, 1985.

Death in the Afternoon (1932). New York: Scribner's, 1960.

A Farewell to Arms (1929). New York: Scribner's, 1957.

For Whom the Bell Tolls. New York: Scribner's, 1940.

The Old Man and the Sea. New York: Scribner's, 1952.

Selected Letters 1917–1961. Ed. Carlos Baker. New York: Scribner's, 1981.

The Short Stories of Ernest Hemingway. New York: Scribner's, 1938.

The Sun Also Rises (1926). New York: Scribner's, 1987.

To Have and Have Not. New York: Scribner's, 1937.

Henderson, Linda Dalrymple. *The Fourth Dimension and Non-Euclidean Geometry in Modern Art*. Princeton University Press, 1983.

Herring, Phillip F. *Joyce's Uncertainty Principle*. Princeton University Press, 1987.

Hertz, Robert. *Death and the Right Hand* (1907, 1909). Trans. Rodney and Claudia Needham. New York: Free Press, 1960.

Hinz, Evelyn J., and John J. Teunissen. "Savior and Cock: Allusion and Icon in Lawrence's *The Man Who Died*." *Journal of Modern Literature* 5.2 (April 1976): 279–96.

Hoffman, Frederick J. *The Mortal No: Death and the Modern Imagination*. Princeton University Press, 1964.

Hoffmann, Banesh. *The Strange Story of the Quantum* (1947). New York: Dover, 1959.

Hoffmann, Charles G. "From Short Story to Novel: The Manuscript Revisions of Virginia Woolf's *Mrs. Dalloway*." *Modern Fiction Studies* 14.2 (Summer 1968): 171–86.

Holdsworth, William. *A History of English Law*. 15 vols. London: Methuen, 1908–52.

Holtby, Winifred. *Virginia Woolf*. London: Wishart, 1932.

Holton, Gerald. *Thematic Origins of Scientific Thought: Kepler to Einstein* (1973). Rev. ed. Cambridge, MA: Harvard University Press, 1988.

Homer. *The Odyssey*. Trans. Robert Fitzgerald. Garden City: Anchor/Doubleday, 1975.

Huizinga, Johan. *The Waning of the Middle Ages* (1949). Garden City: Doubleday, 1954.

Humphry, Derek. *Final Exit*. Eugene: Hemlock, 1991.

Humphry, Derek, and Ann Wickett. *The Right to Die: Understanding Euthanasia*. New York: Harper, 1986.

Huntington, Richard, and Peter Metcalf. *Celebrations of Death: The Anthropology of Mortuary Ritual*. Cambridge University Press, 1979.

Hutcheon, Linda. "Beginning to Theorize Postmodernism." *Textual Practice* 1.1 (Spring 1987): 10–31.

A Poetics of Postmodernism: History, Theory, Fiction (1988). New York: Routledge, 1990.

Hutter, Albert D. "The Novelist as Resurrectionist: Dickens and the Dilemma of Death." *Dickens Studies Annual: Essays in Victorian Fiction* (12). Eds. Michael Timko, Fred Kaplan, and Edward Guiliano. New York: AMS, 1983. 1–39.

Iles, Norman. *A Pagan Funeral*. Leeds: Leeds Community Press, 1977.

Jackson, Shirley. "The Lottery." *The Magic of Shirley Jackson*. New York: Farrar, 1969. 137–45.

Jaki, Stanley L. *God and the Cosmologists*. Lanham, MD: Regnery Gateway, 1990.

James, E.O. *The Beginnings of Religion; An Introductory and Scientific Study*. London: Hutchinson, 1950.

James, Henry. *"The Aspern Papers" and "The Turn of the Screw"* (1888, 1898). Intro. Anthony Curtis. Harmondsworth: Penguin, 1987.

The Complete Tales of Henry James. 12 vols. Ed. Leon Edel. London: Hart-Davis, 1964.

"Is There Life After Death?" *In After Days; Thoughts on the Future Life*. Ed. William Dean Howells. New York: Harper, 1910. 199–233.

The Letters of Henry James. 4 vols. Ed. Leon Edel. Cambridge, MA: Belknap Press, 1974.

Jameson, Fredric. *Postmodernism, or, The Cultural Logic of Late Capitalism*. Durham: Duke University Press, 1991.

Jastrow, Robert. *God and the Astronomers: Two Faces of Reality*. New York: Norton, 1992.

Jha, Mohan. "Death in the Novels of E.M. Forster." *Osmania Journal of English Studies: A Journal of English Language and Literature* 17 (1981): 49–59.

Johnson, Paul. *The Birth of the Modern: World Society 1815–1830*. New York: Harper, 1991.

Jones, Ernest. *The Life and Work of Sigmund Freud*. 3 vols. New York: Basic, 1957.

Jordan, Terry. *Texas Graveyards: A Cultural Legacy* (1982). Austin: University of Texas Press, 1984.

Journal of Thanatology. New York: Foundation of Thanatology, 1971– .

Joyce, James. *The Critical Writings* (1959). Eds. Ellsworth Mason and Richard Ellmann. New York: Viking, 1970.

Dubliners (1914). Eds. Robert Scholes and A. Walton Litz. New York: Viking, 1971.

Finnegans Wake (1939). New York: Viking, 1962.

A Portrait of the Artist as a Young Man (1916). Harmondsworth: Penguin, 1985.

Selected Joyce Letters. Ed. Richard Ellmann. New York: Viking, 1975.

Ulysses (1922). New York: Random, 1986.

Jung, Carl G., ed. *Man and His Symbols* (1964). London: Pan, 1978.

Kafka, Franz. *Parables and Paradoxes* (1935). Ed. Nahum N. Glatzer. New York: Schocken, 1974.

Kastenbaum, Robert. *Death: Society and the Human Experience.* 3rd ed. New York: Merrill, 1986.

"Do We Die in Stages?" (1975). In Wilcox and Sutton 124–32.

Is There Life after Death? Englewood Cliffs: Prentice, 1986.

Kastenbaum, Robert, and Ruth Aisenberg. *The Psychology of Death.* New York: Springer, 1973.

Katz, Steve. *The Exaggerations of Peter Prince.* New York: Holt, 1968.

Keating, Peter. *The Haunted Study: A Social History of the English Novel 1875–1914.* London: Secker, 1989.

Kelley, Alice van Buren. *"To the Lighthouse": The Marriage of Life and Art.* Boston: Twayne, 1987.

Kellogg, Stuart, ed. *Essays on Gay Literature.* New York: Harrington Park, 1985.

Kermode, Frank. *The Sense of an Ending: Studies in the Theory of Fiction.* Oxford University Press, 1967.

King, Dixie. "The Influence of Forster's *Maurice* on *Lady Chatterley's Lover.*" *Contemporary Literature* 23 (1982): 65–82.

Klein, Holger, ed. *The First World War in Fiction.* London: Macmillan, 1976.

Kübler-Ross, Elisabeth. *Living with Death and Dying.* New York: Macmillan, 1981.

On Death and Dying. New York: Macmillan, 1969.

ed. *Death, The Final Stage of Growth* (1975). New York: Simon, 1986.

Kuhn, Thomas S. *The Structure of Scientific Revolutions.* University of Chicago Press, 1962.

LaCapra, Dominick. *History and Criticism.* Ithaca: Cornell University Press, 1985.

Lambert, Edward. *Modern Medical Mistakes.* Bloomington: Indiana University Press, 1978.

Lang, Berel, ed. *Writing and the Holocaust.* New York: Holmes, 1988.

Langer, Lawrence L. *The Age of Atrocity: Death in Modern Literature.* Boston: Beacon, 1978.

The Holocaust and the Literary Imagination. New Haven: Yale University Press, 1975.

Laplace, Pierre Simon de. *A Philosophical Essay on Probabilities* (1796). Trans. Frederick Wilson Truscott and Frederick Lincoln Emory. New York: Dover, 1951.

Laqueur, Thomas. "Bodies, Death, and Pauper Funerals." *Representations* 1.1 (February 1983): 109–31.

Latham, Aaron. "A Farewell to Machismo." *New York Times Magazine* (16 October 1977): 54–5.

Lawrence, D.H. *Apocalypse* (1931). New York: Viking, 1966.

The Complete Short Stories of D.H. Lawrence. 3 vols. New York: Viking, 1966.

The Escaped Cock (1928). Ed. Gerald E. Lacy. Los Angeles: Black Sparrow, 1973.

Etruscan Places (1932). London: Heinemann, 1956.

Kangaroo (1923). New York: Viking, 1963.

Lady Chatterley's Lover (1928). New York: Modern, 1983.

The Letters of D.H. Lawrence (1932). 7 vols. Ed. James T. Boulton. Cambridge University Press, 1979–.

The Man Who Died. New York: Vintage, 1953.

The Posthumous Papers of D.H. Lawrence (1936). Ed. Edward D. McDonald. New York: Viking, 1968.

The Rainbow (1916). Ed. John Worthen. Harmondsworth: Penguin, 1987.

Sons and Lovers (1913). Ed. Julian Moynahan. New York: Viking, 1968.

The White Peacock (1911). Cambridge University Press, 1983.

Women in Love (1920). Ed. David Farmer. Cambridge University Press, 1989.

Lawrence, Karen, ed. *Decolonizing Tradition: The Cultural Politics of Modern Literary Canons.* Urbana: University of Illinois Press, 1991.

Lederman, Leon M. *The God Particle: If the Universe Is the Answer, What Is the Question?* Boston: Houghton, 1993.

Lehmann, John. "Virginia Woolf's *Mrs. Dalloway*: A Reconsideration." Unpublished ms. University of Texas Humanities Research Center.

Virginia Woolf and Her World. New York: Harcourt, 1975.

Lessing, Doris. *The Grass Is Singing.* New York: Crowell, 1950.

Lewin, Roger. *Complexity: Life at the Edge of Chaos.* New York: Macmillan, 1993.

Lewis, A.J. "From 'The Hours' to *Mrs. Dalloway.*" *British Museum Quarterly* 28.1–2 (Summer 1964): 15–18.

Lewis, R.W.B. *The Picaresque Saint; Representative Figures in Contemporary Fiction.* Philadelphia: Keystone, 1961.

Lifton, Robert Jay. *The Nazi Doctors: Medical Killing and the Psychology of Genocide.* New York: Basic, 1986.

Lindley, David. *The End of Physics: The Myth of a Unified Theory.* New York: Basic, 1993.

Lipstadt, Deborah. *Denying the Holocaust: The Growing Assault on Truth and Memory.* New York: Free Press, 1993.

Lodge, David. "Graham Greene." *Six Contemporary British Novelists* (1966). Ed. George Stade. New York: Columbia University Press, 1976. 1–56.

The Modes of Modern Writing: Metaphor, Metonymy, and the Typology of Modern Literature. Ithaca: Cornell University Press, 1977.

Loudon, John Claudius. *On the Laying Out, Planting, and Managing of*

Cemeteries and on the Improvement of Churchyards (1843). Surrey: Ivelet, 1981.

Lowenthal, David. *The Past is a Foreign Country* (1985). Cambridge University Press, 1990.

Lowry, Malcolm. *Under the Volcano.* New York: Vintage, 1947.

Lukacs, John. *The End of the Twentieth Century and the End of the Modern Age.* New York: Ticknor, 1993.

Lundahl, Craig R., ed. *A Collection of Near-Death Research Readings.* Chicago: Nelson-Hall, 1982.

Lundkvist, Artur. *Journeys in Dream and Imagination.* Trans. Ann B. Weissmann and Annika Planck. New York: Four Walls, 1992.

MacArthur, John R. "Last Word from Graham Greene." *Progressive* (1991): 25–8.

Machado de Assis, Joaquim Maria. *Epitaph of a Small Winner* (1880). Trans. William L. Grossman. New York: Avon, 1978.

McHale, Brian. *Postmodernist Fiction.* New York: Methuen, 1987.

Macksey, Richard. "Last Words: The *Artes Moriendi* and a Transtextual Genre." *Genre* 16.4 (Winter 1983): 493–516.

McLeod, Don. "Death in the Family." *AARP Bulletin* 32.5 (May 1991): 1, 10–11.

McManamon, John M. *Funeral Oratory and the Cultural Ideals of Italian Humanism.* Chapel Hill: University of North Carolina Press, 1989.

McManners, John. *Death and the Enlightenment: Changing Attitudes to Death among Christians and Unbelievers in Eighteenth-Century France.* Oxford: Clarendon Press, 1981.

Reflections at the Death Bed of Voltaire: The Art of Dying in Eighteenth-Century France. Oxford: Clarendon Press, 1975.

Maeterlinck, Maurice. *Before the Great Silence* (1936). Trans. Bernard Miall. New York: Arno, 1977.

Malamud, Bernard. *God's Grace.* New York: Farrar, 1982.

Malinowski, Bronislaw. *Magic, Science and Religion* (1948). Garden City: Doubleday, 1954.

Malory, Sir Thomas. *Le Morte d'Arthur* (*c.* 1470). New York: Dutton, 1906.

Mann, Thomas. "Death in Venice" (1911). *Death in Venice and Seven Other Stories.* New York: Vintage, 1966. 3–75.

Marcus, Jane, ed. *New Feminist Essays on Virginia Woolf.* Lincoln: University of Nebraska Press, 1981.

Marcus Aurelius. *The Meditations* (2nd century AD). Trans. A.S.L. Farquharson. Oxford University Press, 1989.

Margenau, Henry, and Roy A. Varghese, eds. *Cosmos, Bios, Theos.* Peru, IL: Open Court, 1992.

Marker, Rita. *Deadly Compassion: The Death of Ann Humphry and the Truth about Euthanasia.* New York: Morrow, 1993.

Marlowe, Christopher. *The Plays of Christopher Marlowe.* Ed. Leo Kirschbaum. Cleveland: Meridian, 1962.

Martin, Richard. *The Love That Failed: Ideal and Reality in the Writings of E.M. Forster*. The Hague: Mouton, 1974.

Martin du Gard, Roger. *Jean Barois* (1913). Trans. Stuart Gilbert. New York: Viking, 1949.

Melville, Herman. *Moby-Dick* (1851). New York: Holt, 1964.

Meyers, Jeffrey. *Homosexuality and Literature 1890–1930*. London: Athlone, 1977.

ed. *Graham Greene: A Revaluation*. London: Macmillan, 1990.

Michelson, Albert A. *Light Waves and Their Uses*. University of Chicago Press, 1903.

Miller, J. Hillis. *Fiction and Repetition: Seven English Novels*. Cambridge, MA: Harvard University Press, 1982.

Millett, Kate. *Sexual Politics* (1970). London: Virago, 1983.

Millgate, Michael. *Testamentary Acts*. Oxford University Press, 1992.

Milton, John. *Complete Poems and Major Prose*. Ed. Merritt Y. Hughes. New York: Odyssey, 1957.

Mitford, Jessica. *The American Way of Death*. New York: Simon, 1963.

Monette, Paul. *Borrowed Time: An Aids Memoir*. San Diego: Harcourt, 1988.

Montaigne, Michel de. *Essays* (1580). Trans. J.M. Cohen. Baltimore: Penguin, 1963.

Moody, Raymond. *Life after Life*. New York: Bantam, 1975.

Reflections on Life after Life (1977). New York: Bantam, 1978.

Moore, Harry T. *The Intelligent Heart: The Life of D.H. Lawrence* (1954). New York: Grove, 1962.

Morley, John. *Death, Heaven and the Victorians*. University of Pittsburgh Press, 1971.

Morris, Ian. "Attitudes Toward Death in Ancient Greece." *Classical Antiquity* 8.2 (October 1989): 296–320.

Morrison, Toni. *Beloved*. New York: Knopf, 1987.

Mosaic 15.1 (1982). Special issue on "Death and Dying."

Mumford, Lewis. *The City in History: Its Origins, Its Transformations, and Its Prospects*. New York: Harcourt, 1961.

Neale, Robert. *The Art of Dying*. New York: Harper, 1973.

Nietzsche, Friedrich. *"The Birth of Tragedy" and "The Genealogy of Morals"* (1872, 1887). Trans. Francis Golffing. New York: Doubleday, 1956.

The Portable Nietzsche. Trans. Walter Kaufmann. New York: Viking, 1969.

Nisbet, Robert. *History of the Idea of Progress*. New York: Basic, 1980.

Nissel, Muriel. *People Count: A History of the General Register Office*. London: HMSO, 1987.

Noyes, Russell, and Roy Kletti. "The Experience of Dying From Falls." *Omega* 3 (1972): 45–52.

Nuland, Sherwin B. *How We Die: Reflections on Life's Final Chapter*. New York: Knopf, 1994.

O'Brien, Flann. *At Swim-Two-Birds* (1939). Harmondsworth: Penguin, 1975.

The Third Policeman (1940/1967). New York: Plume, 1976.

O'Donnell, Patrick. *John Hawkes*. Boston: Twayne, 1982.

Ong, Walter J. *Interfaces of the Word: Studies in the Evolution of Consciousness and Culture*. Ithaca: Cornell University Press, 1977.

Oppenheim, Janet. *The Other World: Spiritualism and Psychical Research in England, 1850–1914*. Cambridge University Press, 1985.

Oppenheim, R.S. *Maori Death Customs*. Wellington: Reed, 1973.

Oring, Elliott. "Forest Lawn and the Iconography of American Death." *Southwest Folklore* 6.1 (1986): 62–72.

Orwell, George. *The Collected Essays, Journalism and Letters of George Orwell*. Eds. Sonia Orwell and Ian Angus. New York: Harcourt, 1968.

Osler, William. *Science and Immortality*. Boston: Houghton, 1904.

Owen, Alex. *The Darkened Room: Women, Power and Spiritualism in Late Victorian England*. London: Virago, 1989.

Ozick, Cynthia. "Forster as Homosexual." *Commentary* 52 (December 1971): 81–5.

Ozsvath, Zsuzsanna, and Martha Satz. "The Audacity of Expressing the Inexpressible: The Relation between Moral and Aesthetic Considerations in Holocaust Literature." *Judaism* 31.2 (1985): 197–210.

Pagels, Heinz R. *The Cosmic Code: Quantum Physics as the Language of Nature* (1982). New York: Bantam, 1984.

The Dreams of Reason: The Computer and the Rise of the Sciences of Complexity. New York: Simon, 1988.

Pais, Abraham. *'Subtle is the Lord ... ': The Science and the Life of Albert Einstein* (1982). Oxford University Press, 1983.

Panati, Charles. *Panati's Extraordinary Endings of Practically Everything and Everybody*. New York: Harper, 1989.

Panofsky, Erwin. *Tomb Sculpture; Four Lectures on its Changing Aspects from Ancient Egypt to Bernini*. Princeton University Press, 1958.

Paxton, Frederick S. *Christianizing Death: The Creation of a Ritual Process in Early Medieval Europe*. Ithaca: Cornell University Press, 1991.

Penrose, Roger. *The Emperor's New Mind: Concerning Computers, Minds, and the Laws of Physics*. Oxford University Press, 1989.

Peschel, Enid Rhodes. "Callousness or Caring: Portraits of Doctors by Somerset Maugham and Richard Selzer." *Mosaic* 15.1 (Winter 1982): 77–88.

Peschel, Richard E., and Enid Rhodes Peschel. *When a Doctor Hates a Patient, and Other Chapters in a Young Physician's Life*. Berkeley: University of California Press, 1986.

Phillips, John Hunter. *Caring for the Dying Patient and his Family*. New York: Health Sciences, 1973.

Plato. *A Plato Reader*. Ed. Ronald B. Levinson; trans. Benjamin Jowett. Boston: Houghton, 1967.

Pliny the Younger. *Letters* (*c.* 95–110 AD). 2 vols. Trans. William Melmoth (1746); rev. W.M.L. Hutchinson. London: Heinemann, 1923.

Poe, Edgar Allan. "William Wilson" (1839). *Collected Works of Edgar Allan Poe.* 3 vols. Cambridge, MA: Belknap, 1978. 2: 422–48.

Poole, Roger. *The Unknown Virginia Woolf.* Cambridge University Press, 1978.

Popper, Karl R. *The Logic of Scientific Discovery.* New York: Basic, 1959.

Porter, Katherine Anne. *Pale Horse, Pale Rider* (1939). New York: NAL, 1967.

Proust, Marcel. *Remembrance of Things Past* (1913–27). 3 vols. Trans. C.K. Scott Moncrieff and Terence Kilmartin. New York: Random, 1982.

Pynchon, Thomas. *The Crying of Lot 49* (1966). New York: Bantam, 1967.

Gravity's Rainbow (1973). New York: Bantam, 1974.

V (1963). London: Pan, 1975.

Quill, Timothy E. *Death and Dignity: Making Choices and Taking Charge.* New York: Norton, 1993.

Ragon, Michel. *The Space of Death: A Study of Funerary Architecture, Decoration, and Urbanism* (1981). Trans. Alan Sheridan. Charlottesville: University of Virginia Press, 1983.

Ramazani, Jahan. *Poetry of Mourning.* University of Chicago Press, 1994.

Rank, Otto. *The Double: A Psychoanalytic Study* (1914). Trans. Harry Tucker, Jr. Chapel Hill: University of North Carolina Press, 1971.

The Trauma of Birth (1923). New York: Brunner, 1952.

Reichert, John. "Poor Florence Indeed! or: *The Good Soldier* Retold." *Studies in the Novel* 14.2 (Summer 1982): 161–79.

Remnick, David. *Lenin's Tomb: The Last Days of the Soviet Empire.* New York: Random, 1993.

Richardson, Ruth. *Death, Dissection and the Destitute.* London: Routledge, 1987.

Richardson, Samuel. *Clarissa* (1747–8). 4 vols. New York: Everyman, 1968.

Rilke, Rainer Maria. *The Notebooks of Malte Laurids Brigge* (1910). Trans. M.D. Herter Norton. New York: Norton, 1964.

Ring, Kenneth. *Heading toward Omega: In Search of the Meaning of the Near-Death Experience.* New York: Morrow, 1984.

Life at Death: A Scientific Investigation of the Near-Death Experience. New York: Coward, 1980.

Ringborn, Sixten. *The Sounding Cosmos: A Study in the Spiritualism of Kandinsky and the Genesis of Abstract Painting.* Finland: Abo, 1970.

Ritchie, George. *Return From Tomorrow.* Lincoln, VA: Chosen, 1977.

Robertson, Mary F. "Hystery, Herstory, History: 'Imagining the Real' in Thomas's *The White Hotel.*" *Contemporary Literature* 25.4 (1984): 452–77.

Rostow, W.W. *The World Economy: History and Prospect.* Austin: University of Texas Press, 1978.

Roth, Philip. *The Counterlife.* New York: Farrar, 1986.

The Ghost Writer. New York: Farrar, 1979.
Portnoy's Complaint. New York: Random, 1969.
Reading Myself and Others. New York: Farrar, 1975.
Rowe, John Carlos, and Rick Berg, eds. *The Vietnam War and American Culture.* New York: Columbia University Press, 1991.
Rushdie, Salman. *The Satanic Verses* (1988). New York: Viking, 1989.
Ruskin, John. *Modern Painters* (1843–60). 5 vols. London: Dent, 1906.
Russell, Bertrand. *Human Society in Ethics and Politics* (1954). London: Allen, 1971.
The Impact of Science on Society. New York: Simon, 1953.
Russell, Bertrand, and Ralph Barton Perry. *The Ethics of War.* New York: Garland, 1972.
Ryan, Dennis P., ed. *Einstein and the Humanities.* New York: Greenwood, 1987.
Ryan, Frank. *The Forgotten Plague: How the Battle Against Tuberculosis Was Won – and Lost.* Boston: Little, 1993.
Sabom, Michael B. *Recollections of Death: A Medical Investigation.* New York: Harper, 1982.
Sacks, Peter M. *The English Elegy: Studies in the Genre from Spenser to Yeats.* Baltimore: Johns Hopkins University Press, 1985.
Sagan, Carl. *Broca's Brain: Reflections on the Romance of Science* (1980). New York: Ballantine, 1983.
Sankar, Andrea. *Dying at Home: A Family Guide for Caregiving.* Baltimore: Johns Hopkins University Press, 1991.
Sartre, Jean-Paul. *"No Exit" and Three Other Plays* (1944). New York: Vintage, 1949.
Schatzberg, Walter, Ronald A. Waite, and Jonathan K. Johnson, eds. *The Relations of Literature and Science: An Annotated Bibliography of Scholarship, 1880–1980.* New York: MLA, 1987.
Schleifer, Ronald. *Rhetoric and Death: The Language of Modernism and Postmodern Discourse Theory.* Champaign: University of Illinois Press, 1990.
Scholtmeijer, Marian. *Animal Victims in Modern Fiction: From Sanctity to Sacrifice.* University of Toronto Press, 1993.
Schroeder, Gerald L. *Genesis and the Big Bang: The Discovery of Harmony Between Modern Science and the Bible.* New York: Bantam, 1990.
Seelig, Carl. *Albert Einstein, A Documentary Biography.* Trans. Mervyn Savill. London: Staples, 1956.
Seneca. *Moral Epistles* (1st century AD). Trans. R.M. Gummere. Cambridge, MA: Harvard University Press, 1920.
Shakespeare, William. *The Complete Works of William Shakespeare.* 4th ed. Ed. David Bevington. New York: HarperCollins, 1992.
Sharpe, Jenny. *Allegories of Empire: The Figure of Woman in the Colonial Text.* Minneapolis: University of Minnesota Press, 1993.
Shelley, Percy Bysshe. *The Complete Poetical Works of Percy Bysshe Shelley.* Ed. Neville Rogers. Oxford: Clarendon Press, 1972.

Sherry, Norman. *The Life of Graham Greene Volume I: 1904–1939*. New York: Viking, 1989.

Shilts, Randy. *And the Band Played On: Politics, People and the AIDS Epidemic*. New York: St. Martin's, 1985.

Shlain, Leonard. *Art and Physics: Parallel Visions in Space, Time and Light*. New York: Morrow, 1991.

Shneidman, Edwin S. *Deaths of Man* (1973). Baltimore: Penguin, 1974.

ed. *Death: Current Perspectives* (1976, 1980). 3rd ed. Palo Alto: Mayfield, 1984.

Essays in Self-Destruction. New York: Science House, 1967.

Shneidman, Edwin S., and Norman L. Farberow, eds. *Clues to Suicide*. New York: McGraw, 1957.

Showalter, Elaine. *The Female Malady: Women, Madness and English Culture 1830–1980*. New York: Pantheon, 1985.

Shute, Nevil. *On the Beach*. New York: NAL, 1958.

Silko, Leslie Marmon. *Almanac of the Dead*. New York: Simon, 1991.

Silverman, Suzann. "Proposed New Death Certificate Is Only as Good a Data Source as Physician Who Fills It Out." *The Journal of the American Medical Association* 261.16 (28 April 1989): 2299–300.

Sloane, David Charles. *The Last Great Necessity: Cemeteries in American History*. Baltimore: Johns Hopkins University Press, 1991.

Smith, Susan Bennett. "Virginia Woolf and Death: A Feminist Cultural History, 1880–1930." Unpublished diss. Stanford University, 1992.

Sontag, Susan. *AIDS and Its Metaphors*. New York: Farrar, 1989.

Sophocles. *Oedipus at Colonus* (*c.* 407 BC). Trans. Robert Fitzgerald. New York: Harcourt, 1941.

Oedipus the King (*c.* 430 BC). Trans. T.H. Banks. Harmondsworth: Penguin, 1947.

Spark, Muriel. *The Hothouse by the East River*. London: Macmillan, 1973.

Spater, George, and Ian Parsons. *A Marriage of True Minds: An Intimate Portrait of Leonard and Virginia Woolf* (1977). New York: Harcourt, 1979.

Spengler, Oswald. *The Decline of the West* (1918–22). Trans. Charles Francis Atkinson. New York: Knopf, 1962.

Spilka, Mark. *Hemingway's Quarrel with Androgyny*. Lincoln: University of Nebraska Press, 1990.

Virginia Woolf's Quarrel with Grieving. Lincoln: University of Nebraska Press, 1980.

Sprague, Claire, ed. *Virginia Woolf: A Collection of Critical Essays*. Englewood Cliffs: Prentice, 1971.

Spring, Beth. "A Genuinely 'Good Death.'" *Christianity Today* 32.10 (15 July 1988): 27–32.

Stannard, David E., ed. *Death in America*. Philadelphia: University of Pennsylvania Press, 1975.

Steiner, George. "Under the Greenwood Tree." *The New Yorker* 47 (9 October 1971): 158–69.
Stevenson, Ian. *Twenty Cases Suggestive of Reincarnation.* Charlottesville: University of Virginia Press, 1974.
Stewart, Garrett. *Death Sentences: Styles of Dying in British Fiction.* Cambridge, MA: Harvard University Press, 1984.
"Forster's Epistemology of Dying." *The Missouri Review* 2 (Spring 1979): 103–21.
Stewart, Ian. *Does God Play Dice? The Mathematics of Chaos.* Oxford: Blackwell, 1989.
Stoker, Bram. *The Annotated Dracula* (1897). New York: Potter, 1975.
Stone, Lawrence. "Death and Its History." *The New York Review of Books* (12 October 1978): 22–32.
The Crisis of the Aristocracy 1558–1641. Oxford: Clarendon Press, 1965.
The Family, Sex and Marriage in England 1500–1800. London: Weidenfeld, 1977.
Stoppard, Tom. *Rosencrantz and Guildenstern Are Dead.* New York: Grove, 1967.
Styron, William. *Sophie's Choice.* New York: Random, 1979.
Sudnow, David. *Passing On: The Social Organization of Dying.* Englewood Cliffs: Prentice, 1967.
Summers, Claude J. *E.M. Forster.* New York: Ungar, 1983.
Swift, Graham. *Waterland* (1983). New York: Poseidon, 1991.
Symons, Arthur. *The Symbolist Movement in Literature* (1899). Rev. 1908, 1919. New York: Dutton, 1958.
Tacitus, Cornelius. *The Annals of Tacitus* (*c.* 70 AD). Ed. F.R.D. Goodyear. Cambridge University Press, 1972.
Tanner, Laura E. "Sweet Pain and Charred Bodies: Figuring Violence in *The White Hotel.*" *Boundary 2* 18.2 (Summer 1991): 130–49.
Taylor, Jeremy. *Holy Living* (1680). Oxford: Clarendon Press, 1989.
Holy Dying (1651). New York: Arno, 1977.
Tennyson, Alfred, Lord. *In Memoriam.* Eds. Susan Shatto and Marion Shaw. Oxford: Clarendon Press, 1982.
Tennyson's Poetry. Ed. Robert W. Hill, Jr. New York: Norton, 1971.
Thomas, D.M. *The White Hotel* (1981). New York: Pocket, 1982.
Thomas, Dylan. *The Doctor and the Devils* (1953). New York: Time, 1964.
Thomas, Lewis. "The Long Habit." *The Lives of a Cell: Notes of a Biology Watcher.* New York: Viking, 1974. 47–52.
Tiger, Lionel, and Robin Fox. *The Imperial Animal.* New York: Holt, 1971.
Tolstoy, Leo. *"The Death of Ivan Ilych" and Other Stories* (1886). Trans. Aylmer Maude. New York: NAL, 1960.
Torgovnick, Marianna. *Gone Primitive: Savage Intellects, Modern Lives.* University of Chicago Press, 1990.
Trilling, Lionel. *E.M. Forster* (1943). New York: New Directions, 1964.

The Experience of Literature: A Reader with Commentaries. New York: Holt, 1967.

Trombley, Stephen. *"All That Summer She was Mad": Virginia Woolf and Her Doctors*. London: Junction, 1981.

Tuchman, Barbara. *The Guns of August*. New York: Macmillan, 1962.

Tuchman, Maurice. "Hidden Meanings in Abstract Art." *The Spiritual in Art: Abstract Painting 1890–1985*. New York: Abbeville, 1986. 17–61.

Twain, Mark. *The Adventures of Huckleberry Finn* (1884–85). Ed. Walter Blair and Victor Fischer. Berkeley: University of California Press, 1985.

Tom Sawyer (1876). New York: Heritage, 1937.

Twombly, Robert G. "Remembering Death and Dismembering the Self; 1418, 1440 and After." *Journal of Literature and Theology* 2.2 (September 1988): 189–210.

Updike, John. *Roger's Version*. New York: Knopf, 1986.

Van Gennep, Arnold. *The Rites of Passage* (1909). Trans. Monika B. Vizedom and Gabrielle L. Caffee. University of Chicago Press, 1960.

Vico, Giambattista. *The New Science* (1744). Trans. Thomas Goddard Bergin and Max Harold Fisch. Ithaca: Cornell University Press, 1970.

Vidal-Naquet, Pierre. *Assassins of Memory: Essays on the Denial of the Holocaust*. Trans. Jeffrey Mehlman. New York: Columbia University Press, 1993.

Villiers de l'Isle Adam, Auguste. *Axel* (1890). Trans. June Guicharnaud. Englewood Cliffs: Prentice, 1970.

Vonnegut, Kurt. *Breakfast of Champions*. New York: Delacorte, 1973.

Cat's Cradle. New York: Delta, 1963.

Slaughterhouse-Five or The Children's Crusade: A Duty-Dance with Death (1966). New York: Dell, 1969.

Vovelle, Michel. *Piété baroque et déchristianisation en Provence au XVIII siècle: Les Attitudes devant la mort d'après les clauses des testaments*. Paris: Plon, 1973.

Waldrop, M. Mitchell. *Complexity: The Emerging Science at the Edge of Order and Chaos*. New York: Simon, 1993.

Watt, Ian. *The Rise of the Novel* (1957). Berkeley: University of California Press, 1974.

Waugh, Evelyn. *Brideshead Revisited* (1944). New York: Dell, 1964.

The Loved One (1948). Boston: Little, 1977.

Weinberg, Steven. *Dreams of a Final Theory: The Search for the Fundamental Laws of Nature*. New York: Pantheon, 1993.

The First Three Minutes: A Modern View of the Origin of the Universe. New York: Basic, 1977.

Weir, Robert F., ed. *Ethical Issues in Death and Dying*. New York: Columbia University Press, 1977.

Weisman, Avery D. *On Dying and Denying: A Psychiatric Study of Terminality*. New York: Behavioral, 1972.

The Realization of Death: A Guide for the Psychological Autopsy. New York: Aronson, 1974.

Whaley, Joachim, ed. *Mirrors of Mortality: Studies in the Social History of Death* (1981). New York: St. Martin's, 1982.

Wharton, Edith. *Ethan Frome* (1911). New York: Scribners's, 1939.

Wheeler, David R. *Journey to the Other Side*. New York: Tempo, 1976.

Wheeler, Michael. *Death and the Future Life in Victorian Literature and Theology*. Cambridge University Press, 1990.

White, Hayden. "The Value of Narrativity in the Representation of Reality." *On Narrative*. Ed. W.J.T. Mitchell. University of Chicago Press, 1981. 1–23.

Wilcox, Sandra Galdieri, and Marilyn Sutton, eds. *Understanding Death and Dying: An Interdisciplinary Approach*. 3rd ed. Palo Alto: Mayfield, 1985.

Wilde, Oscar. *The Picture of Dorian Gray* (1891). Oxford University Press, 1974.

Williams, Tennessee. *A Streetcar Named Desire* (1947). New York: New Directions, 1980.

Wilson, Ian. *The After Death Experience: The Physics of the Non-Physical*. New York: Morrow, 1987.

Witoszek, Nina. "Ireland: A Funerary Culture?" *Studies* 16 (Summer 1987): 206–15.

Woolf, Leonard. *Sowing: An Autobiography of the Years 1880–1904*. London: Hogarth, 1960.

Woolf, Virginia. *Between the Acts* (1941). New York: Harcourt, 1969.

The Diaries of Virginia Woolf. 5 vols. Ed. Anne Olivier Bell. New York: Harcourt, 1977–84.

"Jacob's Room" and "The Waves" (1922; 1931). New York: Harcourt, 1959.

The Letters of Virginia Woolf. 6 vols. Eds. Nigel Nicolson and Joanne Trautmann. New York: Harcourt, 1975–80.

"Modern Fiction" (1919). *The Common Reader: First Series*. New York: Harcourt, 1925, 1953. 150–8.

Moments of Being: Unpublished Autobiographical Writings of Virginia Woolf, ed. Jeanne Schulkind. New York: Harcourt, 1976.

"Mr. Bennett and Mrs. Brown" (1924). *The Captain's Death Bed and Other Essays*. New York: Harcourt, 1950. 94–119.

Mrs. Dalloway (1925). New York: Harcourt, 1953.

"Mrs. Dalloway." Add Mss. 51044–46, unpublished. The British Library.

The Pargiters: The Novel-Essay Portion of "The Years." Ed. Michael A. Leaska. New York Public Library, 1977.

A Room of One's Own (1929). Harmondsworth: Penguin, 1963.

To the Lighthouse (1927). New York: Harcourt, 1955; Harmondsworth: Penguin, 1969.

To the Lighthouse: The Original Holograph Draft. Ed. Susan Dick. University of Toronto Press, 1982.

Yeats, W.B. *The Collected Poems of W.B. Yeats* (1933). London: Macmillan, 1977.

Yeats, W.B., and T. Sturge Moore. *Their Correspondence: 1901–1937*. Ed. Ursula Bridge. Oxford University Press, 1953.

Young, James E. *The Texture of Memory: Holocaust Memorials and Meaning*. New Haven: Yale University Press, 1993.

Writing and Rewriting the Holocaust: Narrative and the Consequences of Interpretation. Bloomington: Indiana University Press, 1988.

Young, Kenneth. "A Dialogue with Durrell." *Encounter* 13.6 (December 1959): 61–8.

Ziolkowski, Theodore. *Dimensions of the Modern Novel: German Texts and European Contexts*. Princeton University Press, 1969.

Zukav, Gary. *The Dancing Wu Li Masters: An Overview of the New Physics*. New York: Bantam, 1979.

Zwerdling, Alex. *Virginia Woolf and the Real World*. Berkeley: University of California Press, 1986.

Index